Introduction to Career Counseling for the 21st Century

ROBERT L. GIBSON
Indiana University

MARIANNE H. MITCHELL
Indiana University

PEARSON

Merrill
Prentice Hall

Upper Saddle River, New Jersey
Columbus, Ohio

Library of Congress Cataloging-in-Publication Data

Introduction to career counseling for the 21st century / Robert L. Gibson,
Marianne H. Mitchell.
    p. cm.
  Includes bibliographical references and index.
  ISBN 0-13-380213-2
  1. Vocational guidance.   2. Career development.   3. Counselors.   I. Gibson, Robert L.
  II. Mitchell, Marianne H.

    HF5381.I597 2006
    331.702—dc22

                                      2005000343

Vice President and Executive Publisher: Jeffery W. Johnston
Publisher: Kevin M. Davis
Editorial Assistant: Sarah Kenoyer
Production Editor: Mary Harlan
Production Coordinator: Shelley L. Creager, *The GTS Companies*
Design Coordinator: Diane C. Lorenzo
Cover Design: Jason Moore
Cover Image: SuperStock
Production Manager: Laura Messerly
Director of Marketing: Ann Castel Davis
Marketing Manager: Autumn Purdy
Marketing Coordinator: Brian Mounts

This book was set in Korinna BT by *The GTS Companies*/York, PA Campus. It was printed and
bound by R.R. Donnelley & Sons Company. The cover was printed by The Lehigh Press, Inc.

Pearson Education Ltd.
Pearson Education Singapore, Pte. Ltd.
Pearson Education Canada, Ltd.
Pearson Education—Japan

Pearson Education Australia Pty, Limited
Pearson Education North Asia Ltd
Pearson Educación de Mexico, S.A. de C.V.
Pearson Education Malaysia Pte. Ltd.

10 9 8 7 6 5 4 3 2 1
ISBN: 0-13-380213-2

To our families, friends, and teachers who have supported and encouraged our career decisions across our life spans.

PREFACE

This book is designed for use in counselor preparation programs and the various specialties in which career counseling courses are required or available as electives. This text presents readers with a current and broad general discussion of characteristics of the world of work and their implications for providing professional career assistance.

The objectives of this book are to provide the reader with a general understanding of (a) the historical relationship between career counseling and the professional field of counseling; (b) the recent and current impacts of the trend toward globalization; (c) the dynamic influences of the new technology on how, where, and why people work; (d) assessment techniques used to help clients better understand their career options; (e) current and emerging theories that provide insights into how and why clients make the decisions they do; (f) the role counselors can play in facilitating career development across the life span; (g) a recognition of the characteristics and career needs of differing populations; and (h) legal and ethical guidelines.

It is important for counselors to recognize that we no longer function in yesterday's career world. The traditional career world of yesterday is gone. Never in history has the world of work been so dramatically altered in such a short period of time. The differences between the career settings of 80 years ago and today's constantly changing workplace are all the evidence one needs. It must also be kept in mind that, in today's society, almost everyone anticipates working. Further, the choice of a career is one of the most influential decisions impacting one's life. The importance of making good choices in today's complex job marketplace and the assistance of career counselors cannot be underestimated.

Recognizing the importance for career helpers to be on top of their game, we have made every effort to provide the most up-to-date information available at the time of this publication. We have also sought to make this text as practical as possible by including many anecdotes and descriptions from actual settings and practicing career counselors. These examples span the globe, as well they should if we are to think globally. Further, we have attempted to recognize the importance of making career assistance available to *all* populations across their life spans, including to underserved individuals.

We sincerely hope our readers find this publication to be readable, enjoyable, and informative. Your comments, reactions, and suggestions are most welcome.

ACKNOWLEDGMENTS

We would like to acknowledge all those who have contributed directly and indirectly to the development of this publication. We would especially like to thank those friends and distinguished colleagues who gave generously of their time to read a chapter and write introductory comments for it: Kenneth B. Hoyt, Peter McNaught, Garry R. Walz, Duane Brown, Sue Whiston, Stanley B. Baker, Edwin L. Herr, Charles R. Ridley, and Theodore P. Remley, Jr.

We also sincerely thank the contributors of anecdotes and descriptions of functioning programs that lend reality to this publication. These include Janelle Dickson, guidance officer, Queensland, Australia; Glen Zagami, guidance officer/certified professional counsellor, Nambour District, Education Queensland, Australia; Lesego Mokgwathise, Gaborone, Botswana, who interviewed and wrote descriptions for information provided by Christopher Tidmane in the Careers and Counseling Center at the University of Botswana (Parastatal) and Lily Chipazi, in the curriculum development and evaluation unit in the Botswana Ministry of Education; Christine Frigault, Mount Saint Vincent University, Halifax, Nova Scotia; Janice Graham-Migel, Nova Scotia, Canada; C. Isaac Tam, Hong Kong University of Science & Technology, Hong Kong; Marisabel Abu-Jaber, who interviewed and wrote a description for information provided by Abdel-Rahim Abdel-Jaber, Vocational Training Corporation in Amman, Jordan; Bob Holmes, Stow, Scotland; Ralph D. Mobley and Marge Dussich, Georgia Institute of Technology, Atlanta, Georgia; Katie T. Anderson, Ivy Tech State College, Bloomington, Indiana; Cantrell Miller, West Virginia University Institute of Technology, Montgomery, West Virginia; Sandi Yoho, Eastern Elementary School, Bloomfield, Indiana; Charles Hablitzel and Tom Przybylski, Perrysburg Junior High School, Ohio; Charles McClain and Linda Stalnaker, East Fairmont High School, Fairmont, West Virginia; and Patrick Donahue, Indiana University, Bloomington, Indiana. We also appreciate information provided to us by Mansfield W. Brock, Jr., Bermuda, and Sherry K. Basile.

We thank our many good friends and colleagues in the field, whose suggestions and comments have contributed to the viewpoints and practices presented, including our close friends and associates in the Department of Counseling and Educational Psychology at Indiana University.

Special appreciation goes to the responsive staff of Merrill/Prentice Hall, particularly our understanding and encouraging editor Kevin M. Davis; Mary Harlan, production editor; and Shelley L. Creager, production coordinator.

We would also like to acknowledge the valuable comments of our reviewers: Jesse Brinson, University of Nevada–Las Vegas; Patti Buxton, University of Central Oklahoma; Marijane Fall, University of Southern Maine; David Kleist, Idaho State University; and Ann Marie C. Lenhardt, Canisius College.

We are grateful to the many considerate authors and publishers who granted us permission to quote from their publications.

Robert L. Gibson
Marianne H. Mitchell

DISCOVER THE COMPANION WEBSITE ACCOMPANYING THIS BOOK

THE PRENTICE HALL COMPANION WEBSITE: A VIRTUAL LEARNING ENVIRONMENT

Technology is a constantly growing and changing aspect of our field that is creating a need for content and resources. To address this emerging need, Prentice Hall has developed an online learning environment for students and professors alike—Companion Websites—to support our textbooks.

In creating a Companion Website, our goal is to build on and enhance what the textbook already offers. For this reason, the content for each user-friendly website is organized by topic and provides the professor and student with a variety of meaningful resources. Common features of a Companion Website include:

FOR THE PROFESSOR

Every Companion Website integrates **Syllabus Manager**™, an online syllabus creation and management utility.

- **Syllabus Manager**™ provides you, the instructor, with an easy, step-by-step process to create and revise syllabi, with direct links into Companion Website and other online content without having to learn HTML.
- Students may logon to your syllabus during any study session. All they need to know is the web address for the Companion Website and the password you've assigned to your syllabus.
- After you have created a syllabus using **Syllabus Manager**™, students may enter the syllabus for their course section from any point in the Companion Website.
- Clicking on a date, the student is shown the list of activities for the assignment. The activities for each assignment are linked directly to actual content, saving time for students.
- Adding assignments consists of clicking on the desired due date, then filling in the details of the assignment—name of the assignment, instructions, and whether it is a one-time or repeating assignment.
- In addition, links to other activities can be created easily. If the activity is online, a URL can be entered in the space provided, and it will be linked automatically in the final syllabus.
- Your completed syllabus is hosted on our servers, allowing convenient updates from any computer on the Internet. Changes you make to your syllabus are immediately available to your students at their next logon.

FOR THE STUDENT

- **Counseling Topics**—17 core counseling topics represent the diversity and scope of today's counseling field.

- **Annotated Bibliography**—includes seminal foundational works and key current works.
- **Web Destinations**—lists significant and up-to-date practitioner and client sites.
- **Professional Development**—provides helpful information regarding professional organizations and codes of ethics.
- **Electronic Bluebook**—send homework or essays directly to your instructor's email with this paperless form.
- **Message Board**—serves as a virtual bulletin board to post—or respond to—questions or comments to/from a national audience.
- **Chat**—real-time chat with anyone who is using the text anywhere in the country—ideal for discussion and study groups, class projects, etc.

To take advantage of these and other resources, please visit the *Introduction to Career Counseling for the 21st Century* Companion Website at

www.prenhall.com/gibson

RESEARCH NAVIGATOR:
RESEARCH MADE SIMPLE!

www.ResearchNavigator.com

Merrill Education is pleased to introduce Research Navigator—a one-stop research solution for students that simplifies and streamlines the entire research process. At www.researchnavigator.com, students will find extensive resources to enhance their understanding of the research process so they can effectively complete research assignments. In addition, Research Navigator has three exclusive databases of credible and reliable source content to help students focus their research efforts and begin the research process.

HOW WILL RESEARCH NAVIGATOR ENHANCE YOUR COURSE?

- Extensive content helps students understand the research process, including writing, Internet research, and citing sources.
- Step-by-step tutorial guides students through the entire research process from selecting a topic to revising a rough draft.
- Research Writing in the Disciplines section details the differences in research across disciplines.
- Three exclusive databases—EBSCO's ContentSelect Academic Journal Database, *The New York Times* Search by Subject Archive, and "Best of the Web" Link Library—allow students to easily find journal articles and sources.

WHAT'S THE COST?

A subscription to Research Navigator is $7.50 but is **free** when ordered in conjunction with this textbook. To obtain free passcodes for your students, simply contact your local Merrill/Prentice Hall sales representative, and your representative will send you the Evaluating Online Resource Guide, which contains the code to access Research Navigator as well as tips on how to use Research Navigator and how to evaluate research. To preview the value of this website to your students, please go to www.educatorlearningcenter.com and use the Login Name "Research" and the password "Demo."

BRIEF CONTENTS

CONTENTS

Chapter 1
Introduction

Chapter 2
Economic Globalization and the World of Work

Chapter 5
Assessment for Career Planning 90

Chapter 6
Career Counseling Across the Life Span: School Populations 120

Chapter 7
Career Counseling Across the Life Span: The Adult Years   158

Chapter 8
Career Counseling for Diverse Populations   174

Chapter 9
Guidelines: Legal, Ethical, and Program Management 190

NOTE: Every effort has been made to provide accurate and current Internet information in this book. However, the Internet and information posted on it are constantly changing, so it is inevitable that some of the Internet addresses listed in this textbook will change.

Chapter 1

Introduction

For most persons, *career* is the totality of work—paid and unpaid—over the life span. It extends from pre-kindergarten through most of the retirement years and includes counseling as a priority.

Kenneth B. Hoyt, PhD
University Distinguished Professor
Kansas State University

OBJECTIVES

To provide readers with an understanding of:

1. The historical relationship between the career world and the development of the counseling profession
2. Significant individuals and events in the historical development of the counseling profession

1

INTRODUCTION

At the dawn of human beings inhabiting the earth, career decision-making was not a concern among those inhabitants. The single occupation that all people pursued was survival. It is possible that the phrase *the quick and the dead* might have been coined for the male species, who was both a hunter and the hunted. Later, as families merged into tribes or clans, individuals who excelled at some phases of survival were identified as the best hunter, the best warrior, and so on. A few specialties began to emerge, such as an individual who was most knowledgeable regarding herbs and other medicinal plants as well as the treatment of injuries and illnesses of the times.

As these tribal societies later merged into what we now call *nation-states,* and civilizations advanced their abilities to care for their citizens, distinct career specialties—some requiring special training—emerged. Many of these specialties were passed from father to son and/or through apprenticeship training. Specialized training institutions, such as schools of medicine, began to emerge. Thus, career decisions were made for most people. Perhaps the earliest use of the label *client* in a helping relationship was noted during the era of the Roman Empire. In ancient Rome, the term was used to designate one who was the recipient in a helping relationship. The client was usually down on his luck—perhaps even a former slave—who received support, both financially and psychologically, from one who was well off and was recognized as the client's patron or benefactor.

In the early tribal societies, the chieftains and elders were sought out by youth for advice and guidance. We can assume that, on occasion, this guidance may have related to the type of work the youth should dedicate their life to. We also recognize that, in some of the early civilizations, philosophers and priests or other representatives of the gods assumed the functions of advising and offering counsel to the younger people. In the early Grecian societies, for example, there was an emphasis on developing and strengthening individuals through education so that all could fulfill roles that reflected their greatest potential for both themselves and their society. Each person was believed to have forces that could be stimulated and guided toward these goals. Later, in the ancient Hebrew and Christian societies, the right of individuals to self-determination was assumed.

In the Middle Ages, the duty of advising and directing youth toward careers became the job of a parish priest. Evidence shows that sporadic efforts were made at placing youth in appropriate vocations during the rise of European kingdoms and the subsequent expansion of colonial empires. During this time, as in the earlier centuries, farming and related careers were still the most popular occupations. Even merchants (also a popular career) usually had farms, especially in the towns and villages. Because travel by horseback was the common means of transportation, the village blacksmith was an important career specialist. In fact, in some villages, the blacksmith's valuable services in keeping the local "transportation system" moving earned him more income than the village doctor.

Although there is no evidence of the existence of professional counselors during the Stone, Roman Empire and Middle Ages, we have tried to envision what they might have looked like to their clients. We hope you enjoy Figure 1-1.

Books aimed at helping youths choose an occupation began to appear in the 17th century (Zytowski, 1972). A number of picture books depicting different occupations also appeared. One of the more popular publications was Powell's *Tom of All Trades: Or the Plain Path Way to Preferment,* published in 1631 in London. "Powell gives much information on the professions and how to gain access to them, even suggesting

FIGURE I-I
Famous career counselors of yesterday.

FIGURE 1-1 (*Continued*)

sources of financial aid and the preferred schools in which to prepare" (Zytowski, 1972, p. 447).

In the 18th century Jean-Jacques Rousseau (1712–1778) suggested that the growing individual can learn best when able to develop according to his or her natural impulses. He advocated permissiveness in learning and learning through doing. At approximately the same time, the famous Swiss educator Johann Pestalozzi (1746–1827) expressed the belief that society could be reformed only to the extent that an individual in that society was helped to develop.

In the United States, the post-Civil War period witnessed an expansion of and an increased interest in career options. This era marked the beginning of the movement from farm labor to the increasing opportunities in manufacturing and industrial settings. Westward expansion also opened up new opportunities, as did the growth in educational options and opportunities.

At the turn of the 20th century (1900) the United States of America was a country of great pride, energy, and optimism. It was established as a world military power following the defeat of the Spanish in the Spanish-American War (1898) and was also rapidly gaining recognition as a world industrial giant. As we entered the 20th century we could point to such hallmarks of Yankee ingenuity as the electric light bulb, the telephone, and the automobile to mention just a few of America's century of progress. Newspapers editorialized their pity for those born into the new century because "there was nothing left to invent or discover" and Congress debated whether to close the U.S. Patent Office. Yet, despite this sense of optimism and well-being, the majority of our population (60%) still toiled on farms, only 1 family out of 7 enjoyed indoor plumbing, and just 1 out of 13 families could communicate by telephone. While the country was linked by railroads, automobiles (6,000 of them) were considered play toys of the rich. New nonskid horse-shoes were bigger sellers than nonskid tires and the Wright Brothers would not initiate their "frequent flyer" program until 4 years into the new century (1904).

As in every century, people's work was influenced by the way they lived and vice versa, and the then new century of the 1900s began to see dramatic changes as the workforce migrated from the farms and rural areas of the South to the factories and industrial cities of the North. Many, perhaps the majority, were disappointed when the anticipated opportunities were not found and unemployment was high, especially among the youthful migrants who had limited skills and experience. Those who found employment worked long hours in harsh and demanding work settings. Among the significant outcomes were (a) the organization of unions by workers seeking better working conditions and higher wages and (b) organized efforts to deal with youth un-employment and its undesirable spin-offs (youth gangs and criminal activities). Of particular significance to the latter was the organization of vocational bureaus in many of America's larger cities to help unemployed youth find some vocational direction by identifying their possible skills and interests, becoming cognizant of appropriate vo-cational preparation programs, and being aware of job opportunities.

The first leader in this movement was Frank Parsons, who established the Boston Vocational Bureau in 1908. The long-term significance of this event is the general recognition of Frank Parsons as the father of the counseling and guidance movement in America and of vocational guidance—now labeled career counseling—as the foun-dation service of the guidance movement (now the counseling profession) in America.

THE WORLD OF WORK: PERSPECTIVES FROM THE 20TH CENTURY

A series of events throughout the 20th century, including frequent recognition by the U.S. Congress, emphasized the recognition of the career guidance services rendered by professional counselors. Congressional acts like the Smith-Hughes Act of 1917 and the George-Dean Act of 1936 (supporting vocational-education programs) and the Wagner-Peyser Act of 1933 (establishing the U.S. Employment Service) were indi-cators of congressional recognition of the potential of the counseling profession in the career area. All of these congressional actions contributed, at least indirectly, to the growth of the career guidance movement.

During World War I, the United States Armed Services developed the Army Alpha test for assessing individual potential and developed programs to facilitate the place-ment of military personnel in appropriate Army career settings. In recognition of the link between the counseling profession and career assistance at the conclusion of World War II, the U.S. Armed Services developed separation counseling programs to assist veterans in their career searches.

Following World War II, U.S. congressional actions also continued to recognize the potential contributions of career guidance and counseling. The George-Barden Act of

1946 provided funding to states to stimulate vocational guidance programs and also allocated monies to established counselor preparation programs.

> Schwebel identified two social conditions that characterized the post-World War II period that led to the rise of the professional practice of counseling, especially career counseling: "(1) the personal and career problems of adjustment faced by vast numbers of veterans, including those handicapped during the war; (2) the influx of new types of students to higher education as a result of the G. I. Bill of Rights, an influx comparable to the compositional changes in the secondary school earlier in the century." (as cited by Pope, 2000, p. 199)

In 1958 the U.S. Congress passed the National Defense Education Act (NDEA), which was not only a landmark in American education but certainly was the most significant Congressional legislation up to that time impacting the counseling profession. This act recognized the career counseling and guidance contributions that the profession could make and provided significant funding to support programs to train counselors to identify students who were talented in the science and mathematics fields and to facilitate their placement in appropriate training programs. The accomplishments of this act were magnificent tributes to the counseling profession. The U.S. Department of Health, Education, and Welfare noted in 1964 that, in a short period of time, the following had been achieved:

- Grants of approximately $30 million were made to states, thereby helping to bring the number of full time high school counselors from 12,000 (one for every 960 students) in 1958 to 30,000 (one for every 510 students) in 1964.
- Through the end of the 1964–1965 academic year, they supported 480 institutes, attended by more than 15,700 secondary school counselors and teachers preparing to become counselors, designed to improve counseling capabilities.
- From 1959 to 1964, they made it possible for 109 million scholastic aptitude and achievement tests to be given to public secondary school students and over 3 million to private secondary school students.
- They helped 600,000 students obtain or continue their college education with federal loans.
- They trained 42,000 skilled technicians to meet critical manpower needs.
- They granted 8,500 graduate fellowships—a first step toward meeting the need for many more college teachers.

> In 1973, the National Commission on the Reform of Secondary Education published its report, with 32 recommendations for the improvement of secondary education. Although the majority of these held implications for the functioning of the secondary school counselor, the following were of particular importance:
>
> - recommendation 6, dealing with bias in counseling
> - recommendation 9, focusing on career education
> - recommendation 10, emphasizing suitable job placement as a part of career education

- recommendation 12, recommending alternative routes to high school completion (Gibson & Mitchell, 2003, p. 12)[1]

In the 1970s the concept of career education being integrated into all courses offered in the schools' curricula was emphasized as the United States Department of Education, under the leadership of Sidney Marland and Kenneth B. Hoyt, made career education a national priority. Dr. Kenneth B. Hoyt has recently (2005) authored a publication entitled *Career Education: History and Future* published by the National Career Development Association (NCDA).

In 1976 the Vocational Education Act was amended to make provisions for the establishment of the National Occupational Information Coordinating Committee (NOICC). This agency was to provide for the dissemination of up-to-date labor market and other career information to federal government and state agencies. These agencies, in turn, would provide information needed for career counseling and other forms of career assistance and decision making.

It is interesting to note that, during the 1970s and 1980s, career development also began to grow in business and industry as such companies as Glaxo Pharmaceuticals, Pacific Bell, and IBM built career service centers. In 1986 a significant report, *Keeping the Options Open,* was published by the College Entrance Examination Board. This report focused entirely on school counseling and guidance programs and emphasized their roles in providing career assistance.

In 1994 Congress continued to recognize the role of counselors in providing career assistance with the passage of the School to Work Opportunities Act, which provided a framework for creating school-to-work opportunity systems in all states with career counseling being a high priority. Pope (2000) noted:

> In the late 1980s and early 1990s, career counseling was extending in various new directions: an upward extension (e.g., outplacement of senior executives); a downward extension (e.g., providing services for poor people, helping homeless people to prepare resumes); an outward extension (e.g., providing services to schools and agencies through federal legislation); and an inward development (e.g., developing career specialties).
>
> The upward extension included the populations of senior managers and executives who had rarely used these services before, but through economic imperatives (i.e., they were losing their jobs and had nowhere else to turn), now found themselves looking for work at times in their lives when they should have been planning for a financially successful retirement from the companies that they had spent their entire lives building.
>
> The downward extension included the poor and homeless socioeconomic classes who were being required to go to work because of new governmental policies. (p. 205)

In conclusion, it is appropriate to note that the role of the counseling profession in providing significant career assistance has been recognized and underscored by

[1] *Gibson, Robert L, & Mitchell, Marianne H., Introduction to Counseling and Guidance, 6/e, © 2003. Reprinted by permission of Pearson Education, Inc., Upper Saddle River, NJ.*

congressional actions; reports of significant educational bodies; and private, educationally oriented agencies.

THE WORLD OF WORK: TRADITIONAL EXPECTATIONS FROM THE PAST

To recognize the significance and extent of changes taking place in the world of work, we need to examine some of the traditional expectancies that guided workers for many generations in America. Career counselors must also recognize that many of these expectancies, though no longer valid, still exist in the minds of their clients. These included the following:

1. *America is the land of opportunity.* The concept of America as a land of near unlimited opportunity was the magnet that drew hundreds of thousands of immigrants to this country during the 20th century. Thousands of youth growing up in America believed—realistically or not—that unlimited career opportunities were out there for the motivated, resourceful, and hardworking. Of course this concept was not without some foundation in fact, as the impact of the industrial revolution, the industrial demands of the world wars, and the expansion into the world markets did create over much of the 20th century increased demands and opportunities for employment.

2. *One should enter a career at least as good, but preferably better, than one's parents.* The concept of continuous betterment by one's children in the world of work is an old and treasured expectancy. With rare exceptions, it was expected that one's offspring would enter the world of work a notch up the career ladder. In the last third of the 20th century, this belief became the proverbial carrot on a stick for many programs designed to advance minorities—and others living in poverty—up the economic ladder.

3. *One prepares for and enters into a career choice for life.* In previous generations, even centuries, our ancestors could, upon choosing their career, enter into it for better or for worse—for life. This not infrequently would also result in individuals settling into a locale that would become their hometown.

4. *With honest and hard work, one will advance in one's career.* The Puritan ethic and early frontier life in this country was based on the belief that work is good (the mark of a good person) and therefore, all people must work. However, it is not enough to just get by in one's work: One is expected to work hard. The Puritans viewed success in one's work as evidence of God's favor. That success was measured in terms of money and property. Thus, it became an assumption that, in this land of opportunity, if one worked hard one would get ahead and advance in salary and other evidences, such as property, or personal wealth.

5. *Many careers are more suitable and are primarily limited to men and some—a much smaller number—are more suitable and primarily limited to women.* For centuries in this and most other civilized countries as well, such professional careers as medicine and law were virtually closed to women. Others such as elementary school teaching and nursing, though not restricted in the same sense, were dominated by women. During this time, the number of career options openly available to

women was severely restricted, thus limiting the careers they might consider. In those relatively rare job settings where men and women performed the same jobs, it was to be expected that the male worker would be paid a higher wage.

6. *The vast majority of available jobs are in the business and industrial sectors.* From the closing years of the 19th century through most of the 20th century, the growth of American industries expanded the production and marketing job force and a related shrinkage in agricultural workers was evident. For a time, these careers appeared to open up highways of opportunity and success in the world of work. Although shifts in recent generations to a service-oriented economy have occurred, some workers may still view the smoke stack as a symbol of opportunity.

7. *The level of education one achieves is related to the level of career opportunities available.* For generations the level of educational attainment has correlated with the socio-economic level of career to which one might aspire. Graphs and charts showing the relationships between educational level and lifetime earning power were common in schools and counseling offices in the last half of the 20th century, and they became selling points in efforts to fight school dropouts and spur college enrollments. The type of education, educational requirements for careers, and opportunities for employment were often lost sight of and more education is still highly valued—as it should be! The career world is now suggesting that the kind of education is at least as important as the extent of education. Also, the previous assumption that education can encompass kindergarten through high school, college, and graduate school; spanning the ages of five years through young adulthood; is now giving way to the suggestion of educational and career development across the life span.

Another less noticeable, but still traditional, expectancy was that one's working life-time would span the period roughly from young adulthood to retirement, usually around age 65. Most workers anticipated an 8-hour work day, 5 days per week. Two to three weeks of paid vacation time was normal in many job settings. In those situations where both the husband and wife worked, the husband's career was expected to take precedence and the wife was still expected to assume most of the housekeeping duties.

As we proceed into the 21st century and a new millennium, we are already anticipating leaving behind many of the traditional guidelines that provided workers with direction in the 1900s. Major changes currently affecting the workplace, and others predicted for the near future, will provide new guidelines that counselors must help their career clients to recognize. Some of these are briefly identified in the section that follows.

CURRENT INFLUENCES ON WORKERS AND THEIR WORKPLACES

GLOBALIZATION OF THE MARKET PLACE

In the 1990s the world witnessed rapid international expansion of businesses and industries. International mergers and partnerships became common as companies strived to remain competitive and, of course, increase profits. American workers witnessed their jobs moving to south and central America–even to Asia—and while on rare occasions they were given the opportunity to move with their job, few Americans wanted to leave home and country (unlike workers in many European and other industrialized countries). Without question, this trend will continue to accelerate well into the 21st century, however, there is little evidence that American workers anticipate or are prepared to become international travelers.

Also, are career counselors prepared and can they assist workers in accepting and adjusting to the opportunities and demands of international work settings? This adjustment may be as demanding on some counselors as on the workers themselves! More discussion of globalization will be presented in Chapter 2.

A MOBILE AND ROOTLESS WORKFORCE

In addition to the international movement of employers and some workers, as noted in the previous paragraphs, there is also an increase in movement within the United States itself as businesses constantly move in search of localities convenient to the natural resources needed for their products, more accessible transportation, land to expand, more desirable environmental settings, needed labor force, and consumer market places.

As a result, increasing numbers of American workers are finding it difficult to settle down, buy a home, and raise a family in the traditional sense. The American dream of home and hometown is violated when the only constant is the moving van. Career counselors will face the difficult task of helping their clients adjust to the adventure of their new mobility and the realization that this is no longer their parents' work world.

A MULTIPLE-CAREER WORKFORCE

Not only will many workers be rootless as far as employment settings and hometowns are concerned, they will also be rootless in their career world. Although predictions vary, it is probable that those entering the workplace in the new century will experience three to seven distinctly different careers over their working lifetime. These frequent career changes will require, in many instances, educational retooling in order to find and enter new and available career opportunities. Thus, the tradition of one life, one career becomes a memoir of our ancestors.

A WORKFORCE OF "TEMPS"

During the past century the American worker became accustomed to—and expected—employment stability and security, pension and health career benefits, paid vacation time, and promotion opportunities. However, another significant trend increasingly evident in the onset of the new century is the trend toward the employment of *temps*—employees labeled as temporary. To the employer, there are many benefits to hiring temps, not the least of which is that no benefits payments (such as retirement and medical insurance) are required, and other benefits such as promotions are at the discretion of the employer. Thus, the worker has no job security and no benefits—a distinct departure from one's expectations based on the historical practices of the past.

Career counselors may have a difficult time assisting clients to cope with this transition from "tenured to temporary." Counseling groups may be helpful in aiding clusters of clients to adequately adjust to this unwelcome trend in the workplace.

A MORE DIVERSE WORKFORCE

One of the more positive trends emerging from the 20th century and projected into the early generations of the 21st century is the increasing diversity in the workplace, cutting across all careers and all levels of work. The percentage of minorities in leadership and other executive positions in the work force has steadily increased in recent generations, as has the percentage of minorities gainfully employed. As increasing numbers of women elect to stay in the work force full time, the percentage of women working is inching closer and closer to the percentage of men working full time.

One outgrowth of this increased percentage of women in the workforce has been the rapid and continuing increase in dual career couples. While there have always been dual career couples, the phenomena of dual career couples being the norm is just beginning to be recognized—as are a new set of dynamics affecting family life, such as dividing housekeeping and home management tasks, choosing whose career takes precedence, and child rearing responsibilities. A serious and comparatively recent concern of the dual career couple has been a rapid increase in the number of latchkey children. Countless studies have pointed out the undesirable outcomes of children who are unattended after school hours. Although there are isolated programs initiated by school systems, communities, and churches, there is no universal effort at this time to counter the growing number of these children.

In addition, women and minorities are finding not only increased accessibility into all careers, but also that movement up career ladders to supervisory, managerial, and executive positions has become possible. Although much remains to increase opportunities in these latter categories, all indicators point to continued progress in this direction in the 21st century.

A final note regarding diversity is a recognition of the increased retention of older workers as congressional action and dramatic advances in personal health practice has resulted in a steady increase in the number of retirement age workers staying in the workforce. This graying of the workforce has, some believe, slowed down the promotion pipeline as many of these senior workers continue to occupy high-level positions.

THE EMERGENCE OF ELECTRONIC COMMERCE

As we enter the new millennium a dramatic increase is being noted in online shopping, which enables consumers to purchase products ranging from stocks and automobiles to psychic readings (and then some). The emergence of electronic cottage industries is another facet for this trend and also adds another dimension to how people will work and live in the generations ahead. Further, much of the educational retooling needed, as individuals move from career to career, will be delivered—through computerized programs—into the home rather than through traditional, at school, courses.

CAREER COUNSELING IN THE 21ST CENTURY

As we enter the dramatically changing world of work in the new millennium and the decades ahead, career counseling and guidance can no longer be the three-step process of assessment, selection, and preparation for the client's lifetime single career choice (with perhaps some incidental adjustments to the world of work thrown in). Today, we may be witnessing a phenomena of change so rapid that it is carrying humankind into technically advanced societies from yesterday to tomorrow. These technological advances are dramatically affecting all aspects of every individual's life. The rate of change has become so rapid and so extraordinary in nature that many individuals are not prepared to cope with the consequences. The present has, in effect, collided with the future and its influences on our behavior may well be seen, in retrospect, as one of the great forces shaping the beginning of the new century.

Thus, while recognizing the prodigious and inevitable changes that affect society in general and the world of work in particular, we must also recognize and accept the reality that counseling programs and their career services must adapt and change as well. Because the world of work is critically important, the field of counseling with its expertise in the career area will, in the immediate generations ahead, have unparalleled opportunities and great challenges along with impressive responsibilities to meet these challenges. Further emphasizing the importance of the contributions the counseling profession may make in the new millennium, the Bureau of Labor Statistics has predicted that social and human services assistance will be one of the fastest growing job markets during the years 2000–2012.

Therefore, whereas career counseling and guidance in recent generations was focused primarily on the needs of youth and their selection, preparation for, and entry into the world of work, the coming generations will clearly see the expansion of career-related needs to populations across the life span. The counseling profession will have both challenges and opportunities for assisting *all* populations in preparing for and adjusting to the ever-changing characteristics of the world of work in the 21st century. We must keep in mind that the career-based uniqueness of our profession enables us to assist individuals and populations with career needs in ways other professions cannot.

When responding to these challenges, counselors and career counseling services must become more evident in community mental health agencies and must make the adult public aware of the nature and availability of such services. Also, in the business and industrial sector, it is becoming increasingly important to stimulate the presence of counseling services and career assistance. Career counselors must also become computer competent and technologically knowledgeable to function competently in the new millennium.

From a career standpoint, we are now living in an age in which the rapidity of technological development can affect what we do and how we do it almost overnight.

Counselors are now more frequently reminded that such changes can result in increasing numbers of adults who, either by choice or necessity, will be making career decisions throughout their working life span.

As will be noted in Chapter 3, the international world of work will, in the near future, be both accessible and assessable through computerized systems and electronic linkages. Counselors must obtain the necessary computer skills and understanding to be up-to-date and to function effectively in this regard.

Career counselors must also recognize that the various information highways and electronic communications systems are the simplistic beginnings of the technology that will affect our function in the future. In addition, we believe counselors should anticipate involvement in the following:

- Counselors should take the initiative to alert and encourage the appropriate local educational establishments to develop training programs commensurate with the retraining needs of the local workforce.
- Counselors should be cognizant of—even conduct research in—the changing dynamics and pressures of family life resulting from changes in how and where people work.
- Counselors should take a lead in the development of sound community programs for latchkey children.
- Counselors should anticipate assisting clients with their career decision making across the workers' life span.

Counselors must continue to increase their sensitivity to our various ethnic/cultural populations: The percentage of Blacks, Hispanics, and Asians especially will continue to increase as a percentage of the workforce in the decades ahead. Currently, minorities are over-represented in lower paying jobs and under-represented in higher paying jobs. Career counselors especially have both a challenge and opportunity to provide minority populations with meaningful assistance in developing their potential and achieving equity in the workplace.

Counselors must ensure that they are free of career stereotypes of minorities, that they do not use biased assessment instruments, and that they are always culturally sensitive and aware. As the career professionals, counselors must keep abreast and ahead of change; anticipating, recognizing, and being knowledgeable about such changes and their probable consequences upon workers and their families. Linkages must be forged with appropriate governmental and other forecasting agencies, professional associations, and state and local trend predicting sources.

Counselors must continuously be involved in the professionalization and updating of their career knowledge and skills if they are to keep pace with the ongoing changes anticipated in the world of work. Career opportunities may no longer be tied directly to the level of educational preparation. Although post-high school education will continue to broaden career opportunities, this education may be more relevant to many projected job markets, if secured through vocational-technical programs.

SUMMARY

In the early centuries of life on earth, career skills could usually be summed up as survival skills. However, as civilizations advanced and became more complicated, the process of identifying and relating to an occupation became more complex. By the time the world entered the 20th century, it became more clear that individuals, industries, and even governments could benefit from some form of career assistance that promoted a liaison between individuals and jobs. Out of this recognition, the career guidance movement began and progressed throughout the 20th century, forming a basic linkage between the counseling movement and the world of work. In the generations following World War I through the remainder of the 20th century, the profession was witness to the expansion of services and the counselor's role and function changed to accommodate a wide range of clients and societal needs. However, through these periods of role expansion, career counselors continued to be recognized as the primary profession for providing professional assistance in the career area. This recognition was underlined by a series of congressional actions and the expansion of career counseling services into business and industry.

When examining career counseling in the 21st century, we take note of the world of work as it existed in much of the previous century. While dramatic and rapid changes took place, especially in the last quarter of the century, many of the traditional expectancies regarding the world of work continued to influence career planning. Recognizing that people often make assumptions regarding the future based on the past, counselors must be prepared to help their career clients realistically examine the world of work and its opportunities as it will exist, not as it did exist. Also, as counselors, we must remember that the human species is the most adaptable of all living species and throughout the history of humankind has demonstrated the capacity to accept and adjust to change, to cope with and overcome adversity, and to meet and overcome the many anticipated challenges to themselves and their societies.

As the American worker and the American workforce enters the 21st century, they are confronted by new and significant changes. These changes include the impact of globalization, a multiple career workforce, a rootless and often more temporary workforce, the reemergence of cottage industries, and a more diverse workforce. Career counseling must also respond to these changes.

DISCUSSION QUESTIONS

1. Discuss the different careers you have considered or experienced thus far. What factors influenced you to consider or enter the field of counseling?

2. If you possessed the skill, training, and opportunity to enter any career, what would your choice be? Why?

3. Review current newspapers and popular publications for reports or articles that would imply a useful role the counseling profession can play in response to human needs in today's society.

4. If you had to select and prepare for a completely different career, what would your choice be? Why?

5. Hazard a guess! What will life and work be like in the United States in 2050?

CLASS ACTIVITIES

1. Divide the class into groups of seven to eight students. Each group should develop an outline of a current equivalent to the 1958 NDEA with its emphasis on counseling. Each project should present (a) a rationale, (b) objectives of the Act, (c) procedures for achieving the objectives, and (d) anticipated outcomes. (Note: Consideration might be given to forwarding the "best" (class consensus) of the proposals to the state's congressional representatives.)

2. Read a newspaper "advice" column and bring the article to class. Comment on the suggested advice.

3. Go to the library (or the Internet) and find the earliest article you can on the subject of counseling or guidance. Report your article, its date, author, publication, and content to the class.

4. Review current articles in professional journals in the field of counseling and careers. Are there any particular themes or concerns that stand out? Discuss your findings in class.

5. Identify a career of interest other than counseling. Then identify the changes that have taken place in that career in the 20th century. Report your findings to the class.

READINGS OF INTEREST

America 1900–2000: Who we were; who we are: How an epic century changed a nation. [Special section]. (2001, August 6). *U.S. News and World Report.*

Carter, R. T. (Ed.). (2003). *The Counseling Psychologist* in the new millennium: Building a bridge from the past to the future. *The Counseling Psychologist, 31*(1), 5–15.

Ginter, E. J. (2002). *Journal of Counseling & Development (JCD)* and counseling's interwoven nature: Achieving a more complete understanding of the present through "historization" (Musing of an exiting editor—An editorial postscript). *Journal of Counseling & Development, 80*(2), 219.

History of psychology. (1997). [Special section]. *American Psychologist, 52*(7).

History of psychology circa 1900. (2000). [Special section]. *American Psychologist, 55*(9), 1014–1024.

Hoyt, K. B. (2005). *Career education: History and future.* Tulsa, OK: National Career Development Association.

Malone, T. W. (2004). *The future of work.* Cambridge, MA.: Harvard Business School Press.

Parsons, F. (2001). Frank Parsons's continuing legacy to career development interventions. [Special section]. *The Career Development Quarterly, 50*(1), 56–88.

Pope, M. (2000). A brief history of career counseling in the United States. *Career Development Quarterly, 48*(3), 194–211.

Special millennium issue. (2001). [Special issue]. *The Career Development Quarterly, 49*(3).

Chapter 2

Economic Globalization and the World of Work

We are, all of us, "citizens of the world." This has always been poetically true. Today, the rhetoric is reality. But what kind of citizen in what kind of world? This chapter explores the problems and challenges that lie ahead.

Peter McNaught
President Emeritus
Craigie College
Scotland

OBJECTIVES

To provide readers with an understanding of:

1. Globalization and its potential impact on the American workplace and worker in the 21st century
2. Implications for career counseling in the era of globalization

INTRODUCTION

Career counseling in the 21st century will undoubtedly witness many dramatic changes in the workplace and career opportunities. These changes will, of course, influence the work of the counselor. Some changes already evident are the effects of globalization. Economic globalization is sometimes defined as a process of rapid economic integration among countries. It embraces the increased international integration of products and markets and the free flow of capital. We have moved from local markets being prominent in the 19th century, to national markets being prominent in the 20th century, and to global markets being prominent in the 21st century.

This drive toward globalization has been accelerated by large, international corporations seeking (a) new markets, (b) new and cheaper sources of raw materials and labor, and (c) the adoption of new technologies. To many corporations, these global opportunities appear to promise faster growth and new markets, which lead to bigger profits. As a result, corporations are thinking and planning on an international level never before experienced in American business and industry. This has been facilitated by the growing ease of economical international communications and the diminishing national control over their imports and exports. Also, popular market trends—even fads—in one country can quickly spread to world marketplaces.

THE GLOBAL WORKFORCE

As we progress through this new century and its globalization, we have become increasingly aware of the global workforce and its impact on workers in the United States. As the 20th century concluded, concern was being expressed over products produced by sweat shop labor in certain Asian, African, and South American countries (and even in the United States). The supply of cheap labor in countries like Mexico was attracting American industries to move away from state-side locations and higher paid state-side workforces. The movement of other industries to natural resources found in other countries was also a trend predicted to increase in the years immediately ahead. Although, in some rare instances state-side workers were invited to move with the industry, the majority of workers did not express a desire to make an international move. Even though rapid advancements in the transportation and communication fields will further stimulate economic transactions on a worldwide basis and will broaden the boundaries for many products and services, it remains unlikely that many American workers will seek employment outside the United States. Also, as American corporations react to significant increases in global competition, they have been forced to cut costs of their products rather than raise prices, resulting in additional job losses in this country, and in some instances, the transfer of jobs abroad to locations where lower labor costs can be secured. This loss of jobs as the result of globalization was, at the turn of the century, most noticeable in the manufacturing sector. As the global economy expands, new markets will continue to open and we can anticipate the continued integration of American manufacturing into global markets (as many fast food chains such as McDonalds and Burger King have already done).

Although controversial, another influence on workforces in industrialized countries will be the degree to which immigration expands a nation's work force. For example, in the United States, immigration accounted for fully half of the increases in the workforce in the United States in the 1990s and has resulted in Hispanics becoming the most populous minority in the United States (*Statistical Abstracts of the United States,* 1996). Although immigration quotas can and do change almost annually, it can be anticipated that immigration will continue to be a source for expansion (with debate) of the workforce in industrialized countries, including the United States, in the decade ahead. Due to the attraction of the United States to foreigners, millions would immigrate if they could, but, of course, the actual number of immigrants admitted annually will depend on U.S. immigration policy and the degree to which it is enforced.

As globalization creates "the global workplace," it is clear that well educated workers will be in demand in countries around the globe. It is also clear that the emerging knowledge and technology explosion, while presenting opportunities for many, will fundamentally change the face of the workplaces and workforces of the past, thus creating insecurity and uncertainty for many as they enter the *new* world of work. For the most part, established industrial countries will invest in each other's industrial expansions rather than investing in underdeveloped countries where cheap labor is available in significant numbers. In some countries, very low wages equate to very poor productivity, which results in the unit cost of goods they produce being quite high. Because many of these underdeveloped countries do not have even a minimally educated workforce, the resultant cost of producing a unit of goods can be very high. The use and abuse of child labor is a concern focused especially on many underdeveloped countries, particularly those that offer minimal educational opportunities for children.

Also of concern has been the loss of some low-skill jobs in developing countries, which is quite commonly associated with globalization and blamed on (a) the increased use of technology to enable globally-oriented companies to compete (and also to not have to depend on large labor forces); and (b) liberalization of international trade, which often results in the replacement of locally produced products with those from abroad. While cost reduction, greater efficiency, and higher incomes for some have been achieved, this has been at the expense of growing uncertainty, unemployment among the lesser skilled and educated, and social inequalities.

Globalization has also reduced the ability of governments to effectively intervene in their economic developments or their economic crises. Unemployment is particularly difficult to control to the degree that a country's employers are involved in or competing on a global playing field that may require a reduction in labor costs in order to remain competitive (Streeten, 2001).

Globalization has also stimulated world societies, departing from the traditional industrial age and moving into the information age. This latter era is based on tremendous advances in the area of telecommunications and information processing (Anderson, 2001). "The information process brings both technological and cultural change. It speeds up the development of devices for storing, processing, and communicating information and it also causes shifts in ways of thinking about information itself" (Anderson, 2001, p.124).

Another international influence on the U.S. economy, and hence the American workplace and worker, will be the continued economic development in both Asia and Latin America. While we have witnessed the phenomenal growth of the Japanese economy in recent decades, as well as the emergence of industrial growth in countries like South Korea, Taiwan, and Malaysia, the remarkable economic growth being experienced by China and the expansion of the Indian economy is introducing new players into the global marketplace. These Asian countries and our Latin American neighbors differ from the underdeveloped countries in that they have a goodly supply of hard working, adequately educated workers who can produce at least medium-technology manufactured goods in great quantities for import into the United States and other countries. While these products may be of benefit to American consumers, they may put the jobs of American workers who produce the same or similar goods at risk.

A significant change in the character of the international workforce is the trend toward the employment of "temporaries," which has already risen in countries of the European Common Market, while at the same time there has been a decline in full-time employment. Unemployment continues to be a world concern as well. The International Labor Office (Geneva, Switzerland, 1998) estimated that the number of unemployed throughout the world had risen to 150 million by 1998. In addition, approximately one fourth of the world's labor force are underemployed or earning less than a living wage. Further, in most developed countries, the unemployment rate has changed little in recent decades.

Unemployment, especially among the young, has led to a universal drive to improve the education of youth in the decades ahead so that they may be more employable and more capable of contributing to the productivity of their country in the high-tech, supersonic years of this new millennium.

> Economic globalization, so often vilified as the enemy of well-paying manufacturing jobs in this country, is, in fact, its strongest ally. The much bemoaned exodus of U.S. manufacturing jobs offshore represents the export of low productivity jobs that America should be happy to exchange for high productivity and better-paying jobs. (Judy & D'Amico, 1997, p. 26)

It is evident that career counselors in the 21st century must be alert to not only the rapid internal changes affecting the work place in the United States, but also the impacts of the global economy and the global workforce. Counselors should be aware of global networking for facilitating job searches and career opportunities around the world. Counselors must also be familiar with sources of information that will ensure their awareness of international economic trends and their impacts on the world of work. Counselors must also increase their multicultural sensitivity in order to effectively communicate with nationalities and cultures throughout the world. An outcome of these many globalization characteristics will be changes in the preparation of American youth to enter the job market. Certainly, one emphasis will be on education—the more the better—and on education that is relevant to the needs of the labor market. School counselors will be expected to guide their student clientele accordingly.

THE AMERICAN WORKPLACE AND THE AMERICAN WORKER OF THE PAST

While dramatic and rapid changes are anticipated in the 21st century workplace, most of the previous century has been characterized by one lifelong employer and one lifelong workplace, with full-time lifelong workers whose jobs and benefits had some degree of protection by both ethical and legal guidelines. In the previous century, it was presumed that:

- People of good character worked hard.
- Employers were duty-bound to exercise paternal regard for their employees (whose duty, in return, was to work hard).
- Management knew best how to create efficient operations that benefitted all parties.
- Hard work was the instrument of success for workers who wanted to improve their lot.

However, in the closing decades of the recent century, these characteristics had begun to disintegrate because of economic globalization; the uncompromising demands from stockholders and investors to increase corporate profits at almost any cost; and a rush of technological, transportation, and communications advances. As a result, American workers in this century may have less control of their destinies and will rarely work and live lifelong in one community and for one employer during their working life span. Further, many of the benefits they had previously taken for granted, especially medical and retirement, are in jeopardy. Many workers feel less secure in their jobs and careers and these feelings are reinforced as collective bargaining has weakened in some areas. Frequent career changes, not just job changes, will be the predicted norm for the worker of the 21st century. In addition, many career changes will require additional education and training. Hence, challenges will confront not only the individual but also our traditional systems and institutions of education. It is also worth noting the following:

- Although many American jobs are moving abroad, American workers are not (in a few instances, they do have the option).
- Frequently, candidates for international transfers are management and supervisory personnel.
- The speed and ease of present-day communications and transportation have lessened the need for long-term assignment of more personnel abroad.

Career counselors should be alert to unexpected changes, affecting careers and the workplace, that may occur as the result of several factors:

- national and international scandals affecting major international conglomerates and corporations
- governmental and political upheavals in major industrialized countries
- threats to lives and security on a large scale, such as posed by wars or international terrorism
- major natural disasters such as floods, fires, and earthquakes that devastate a significant section of a country's economy
- deadly diseases in a contagious mode
- dramatic advances in technology and/or new discoveries that dramatically alter economic demands, needs, and patterns of employment
- consumer demands and trends

GLOBALIZATION AND ITS IMPACT ON THE AMERICAN WORKFORCE

As noted, globalization has stimulated international trade and vice versa. This has resulted in a continuous search for new markets, sources of raw material, and sources of cheap labor. While some American industries have moved abroad seeking low skilled workers who will work for significantly lower wages, some industries are simultaneously encouraging the immigration of highly skilled workers to the United States (even though American industries have shown a preference for filling the higher skilled, higher paying jobs from the American workforce).

The rapid economic growth of very populous countries, such as China, India, Malaysia, Indonesia, and South American countries, is resulting in the production of exportable goods, that can be produced by relatively low skilled workers. This enables these foreign-produced products to undersell similar goods produced in the United States, not only around the world, but frequently in the United States as well. This poses a threat to the comparatively higher wages of the low skilled workers in U.S. industries seeking to compete with those produced in the countries previously indicated.

Also, the increasing rapidity of international transportation, travel, and communications, plus a comparative decline in their costs, has further opened the doors for worker movement around the world.

IMPLICATIONS OF GLOBALIZATION FOR CAREER COUNSELORS

Perhaps the most obvious implication of globalization for career counselors is that they must help their clients to recognize and understand the realities of globalization. It is not enough for the career counselors themselves to be aware of globalization, they must strive to make others aware as well. Other implications and requirements include:

- Career counselors must be aware of significant international happenings that will have influences on careers in the United States (such as wars, depressions, epidemics, scientific discoveries, and political upheavals).
- Career counselors need to be aware of the various World Wide Web sites that provide career opportunities and other career information.
- New careers will emerge much more rapidly than in the past, and some traditional careers will quickly become obsolete.
- Demands for increases in immigration quotas for the United States will grow. Our immigration policies will affect our workforce and our career world. Career counselors must keep a close watch on these developments.
- Career counselors must emphasize to their clients the important relationships between education, careers, career opportunities, and stability.

In his publication, *The End of the Nation State: The Rise of Regional Economies,* Kenichi Ohmae (1995) indicates that there has been a fundamental change to the environment within which the corporations of the triad (Japan, Europe, and the United States) have managed work and workers. At the heart of this continuity is a series of related developments in information technology. These developments have had three broad effects: (a) At the macroeconomic level, it has become possible for capital to be shifted instantaneously anywhere in the world; (b) at the company level, what managers can know in real time about their markets, products, and organizational processes has changed (managers can be more responsive to customer needs); and (c) at the market level, people (customers) around the world can quickly learn how other people are living and what products and services are available to them, as well as the relative values such offerings provide (Ohmae, 1995).

It would be appropriate to conclude this section on globalization by noting the growing international perspectives of our profession. The American Counseling Association has held several international conferences (the last being in Edinburgh, Scotland in 1992). Hundreds of counselors attended and came from a wide, international geographic area. Many counselors have, in recent years, established contact with fellow counselors in other countries. An increasing number of counselors from a variety of countries are attending national professional meetings of counselors in this country, and American counselors have increased their attendance at professional meetings of counselors in foreign countries. In this era of the rapid development of international communications through such means as e-mail (electronic mail) and the Internet, counselors around the world can easily and conveniently communicate with their fellow professionals in other countries. In this period of knowledge explosion in all our professions, this commodity will stimulate international communication among counselors. While our counselor preparation programs have in the last decade witnessed a significant increase in international students, we can also anticipate more American counselor trainees seeking foreign experiences.

The flow and convergence of forces currently and in the predicted near future lead to a world that may *in reality* be called one world, a world that will eventually lead to a global civilization and a global workforce. (Anderson, 2001).

CAREER COUNSELING: A GLOBAL PERSPECTIVE

As the profession of counseling has spread around the world, the basic foundation of career counseling has been perhaps the service most readily adapted and practiced in most countries. Whiston and Brecheisen (2002) noted career studies in a number of international settings. These studies indicated not only the interest and progress in career counseling around the world, but also active research to improve career assistance practices. It might also be useful to mention that the career development facilitator (CDF) for the credentialing of paraprofessionals in the United States has evolved into a credential called the Global Career Development Facilitator. This credential is now available in Japan, Canada, New Zealand, and the United States.

The sections that follow, written by counselors in the described settings, discuss career counseling activities in various global settings. Please note: we did not Americanize the spelling; rather, we presented the materials as submitted.

CASE STUDIES

Career Counseling in Australia

Written by: Janelle Dickson
Guidance Officer
Queensland, Australia

Working as a Guidance Officer for Education Queensland (Australia) in a remote District entails being part of a team in the provision of a wide range of services to clients whose ages range from Preschool (4 years) to completion of Year 12 (17 years). The Longreach District covers a vast area of Central Western Queensland with distances between towns of at least 100 kilometres. Students are located in rural and remote locations with schools ranging in population from 10 to 300. Of these, a small percentage of students are indigenous. Some students are so remote that access to education is provided through the School of Distance Education. For me, one of the most exciting aspects of the role of a Guidance Officer is the provision of Career Education and Counseling.

Much formal Career Counseling begins with students in their transition from Primary School (after Year 7) to Secondary School. This is the first opportunity provided for students to select from a range of subjects. In most schools there is a set core of subjects (including Mathematics, English, Science and Studies of Society and the Environment) and up to four additional subjects are offered. Students work through computer-based programs such as Career Builder, which begins with self-awareness and exploration and moves through a series of decision-making levels regarding career options. This then guides individual consultations with students as to subject selection. This process of individual consultation and review forms part of each transition: Year 7 to Year 8; Year 10 to Year 11; and Year 12 to Tertiary. Being part of small communities offers both opportunities and challenges to exploring future options for students.

Young people in rural and remote towns are often strongly connected to and are integrated into a community of support. Incidental "mentoring" is a part of their everyday life through interactions with staff and school personnel who encourage and assist students through life's challenges and who offer a level of personal support that is unique to remote locations. The adults in the wider community are also willing to share knowledge and expertise in relation to their chosen profession and readily open the doors of their workplace to support a student visit. A Guidance Officer very often works with teachers in the schools to develop the Career Program in an integrated approach through subjects such as Studies of Society and the Environment or Business Studies.

One of the programs that are developed to assist students investigate future options is called Student and Industry Links (SAIL). Students over age 14 are given provision through Education Queensland policy to experience working in a real life environment for up to 30 days (or unlimited hours for students who have disabilities). As many of the communities are small and opportunities are limited, the challenge that this provides is overcome by the option of taking students to a major center (up to 1,000 kilometres away) for a block of time. Remote communities accept, almost as inevitable, that their young people will need to leave home and move away to pursue their careers.

The percentage of school leavers who choose to pursue undergraduate studies at universities for this area is estimated at 30% of the cohort. Most commonly pursued avenues of studies include teaching, nursing, accounting, and engineering. The majority of young rural students prefer to undertake traineeships or apprenticeships that will keep them connected to their communities. With local industries such as shearing sheep, contract mustering, and kangaroo harvesting, it is not difficult for students who have no further academic interests to find seasonal employment. Those who want to further their studies to a tertiary level must choose between Distance Education and full-time or part-time study on campus. The latter choice necessitates leaving their communities, and is a fact of life that causes some young people considerable anxiety. It is with

situations such as this that the role of Career Counselor differentiates from Career Educator.

In a counseling session, one young person was describing the realities of the choices about future options from her perspective. She wanted to go away to train in a profession. If she were to do this, in her mind, coming back to her community would never be the same. Her experiences have shown her there's a difference in the treatment by the locals toward the person who has left and comes back. In going away to study there was a risk of losing her sense of place and belonging, which is a real dilemma for many rural young people. As well as this, the cost of accessing tertiary education is a consideration.

The Queensland government provides support to students who wish to enroll in an undergraduate degree by providing them with the option of deferring higher education fees until they are in full-time employment. These fees are then deducted through the Taxation Department. However, students from rural and remote communities need to be able to live away from home to attend universities or colleges. The government provides financial assistance through Centrelink (social services), so long as the eligibility criteria are met. For those students who come from middle-class families with both parents working, such financial support is usually not accessible. The parents are required to meet the costs of living away from home. For some families, this is not an option. A few dedicated individuals will choose to work and save until they can afford to live independently. Others are willing to choose another starting point, realizing that there are multiple pathways to a destination and many people available to assist them to achieve their goals.

The role of Career Education and Counseling is an important aspect of supporting young people into growth and maturity. A Guidance Officer working in small communities needs to be multiskilled. However, it is important to realize that we work as part of a team with schools, communities, and other service providers. "It takes a village to raise a child" is a saying of no less importance as the child reaches adulthood. There is nothing more exciting than being part of the launch team of a young person, helping that person toward their preferred future.

Outline of Career Services in the State of Queensland, Australia

Written by: Glen Zagami
Guidance Officer/Certified Professional Counsellor
Nambour District, Education Queensland, Australia

Employing Organisation

Education Queensland (EQ); also known as the Queensland Department of Education; is the department responsible for administering state government (public) primary, secondary, and special schools and colleges throughout the state of Queensland.

Population Served

Education Queensland employs over 400 Guidance Officers (GPs) to support students from preschool (aged under 6 years) to year 12 (the final year of secondary schooling), including mature age students. Guidance Officers may work in a single school or across a number of schools, comprising primary (including preschools), secondary, and special schools. I currently work in a large urban primary school of approximately 900 students and a rural preschool to year 10 school (P–10) that has approximately 220 students.

Major Activities of the Organisation

Education Queensland provides educational programs for students 5 to approximately 17 years of age, including students with disabilities. Mature age (adult) students also attend secondary schools to complete years 11 and 12. Guidance services in the field of careers include:

- career education programs for classes
- individual career counselling
- group career guidance and advice
- subject and course selection
- assistance with university entrance and postschool student options

The majority of this work occurs in the secondary school setting (years 8 to 12), with students 13 to 17 years of age.

Frequently Discussed Career Issues

Frequently discussed career issues in the secondary school setting include:

- selection of school subjects
- awareness raising in relation to the world of work
- clarification of vocational interests and options
- career planning
- postschool study options
- school-based apprenticeships and traineeships

Preferred Careers for School Leavers

Student preferences are influenced by the age of the student concerned and the level or amount of secondary (high) schooling completed. Students who leave school after completing year 10 (the minimum school-leaving age is 15 years) usually move into paid employment, study at a college of Technical and Further Education (TAFE), or commence an apprenticeship or traineeship.

Students completing year 12 (the final year of formal schooling) have more options available from which to choose. In addition to those pathways listed above, many students elect to undertake university studies at a degree level at some stage after completing year 12 or after completing other postschool qualifications such as a TAFE course. Some of the more popular university courses in 2002 included business/law/commerce, science and engineering, health sciences, and psychology. Note that the popularity of various university courses varies from year to year.

Additional Information

Readers are also invited to visit the Education Queensland (EQ) Web site to discover more about career guidance and education, including details on the role of Guidance Officers and a range of career-related handouts and resources utilised by Guidance Officers working in schools. The web site address is http://education.qld.gov.au.

On the home page, under the category *Parents & Students*, select *Guidance, Counselling, and Careers*, then *Resources*. The section entitled *Handouts and Information Guides* may be of particular interest to readers.

Career Counseling in Botswana

Prepared by: Lesego Mokgwathise

Information submitted by: Christopher Tidmane
Careers and Counseling Center
University of Botswana (Parastatal), Gaborone, Botswana

Type of Organization that Employs Careers Counsellors

The employing organization is the University of Botswana, which is the only university currently in the country (University Career and Counseling Center).

Population

The university holds about 13,000 students. The main population that the center serves is the university community, including students, staff members and the dependants of staff members. They also attend to members of the community at large but first priority is given to the university community. There is an overwhelming number of out-of-university people needing help, especially after Form 5 (which is a completing year for senior secondary schools) results. This is an indication that students do not utilize services in their schools while they are in school.

Major Activities of the Organization

There are four areas covered:

- career decision-making services
- career exploration
- job search
- employment services

These services are offered, in most cases, on a one-to-one, face-to-face basis. They also conduct group guidance for the students and those members of the larger community who come in groups. They run seminars and organize career fairs especially for the university community. They attend career fairs as resource persons, organized and run by different schools in the country. They make visits to senior secondary schools to advise students on careers. These visits are organized and initiated by the center. Some schools make arrangements to visit the center, so they bring their students to the center to learn more about career guidance. For example, one particular school that has done this on a regular basis is Selibe Pikwe Secondary, which is one of the senior schools in the northern part of the country, about a six-hour drive from their town, Selibe Pikwe, to the center in Gaborone (where the university is located).

Most Frequently Discussed Career Issues of Clients

- *Career decision-making.* One major issue that keeps coming out is career decision-making. Clients come undecided on what they want to do; they do not know what career to pursue and they are concerned whether there will be employment for them when they finish school.
- *Program selection.* Clients are also concerned about program selection (what programs are viable and what programs are marketable).

- *Change of program.* Clients come wanting to change their program of study, sometimes right in the middle of the program. First second, and even third year students have done this. But changing programs is not easy, especially when one is already halfway through.
- *Indecisiveness.* Sometimes students come and say "I do not know what it is that I can do. I am blank." This is very common with school leavers e.g., (Form 5). The problem here is not so much what they are interested in, but what careers are viable in the job market.

Career Counseling in Botswana

Prepared by: Lesego Mokgwathise

Information submitted by: Lily Chipazi
Botswana Ministry of Education
Curriculum Development and Evaluation Unit, Gaborone, Botswana

Type of Organization

The Ministry of Education, under the Government of Botswana, employs career counselors.

Population

Career counselors serve all schools in Botswana. The Guidance and Counseling Department in the unit is responsible for implementation of the Guidance and Counseling Program under which they have:

- career services
- psychological services
- materials development
- youth empowerment
- youth forums

Major Activities of the Organization

- *Career fairs.* Career counselors provide workshops for schools on how to run career fairs, in clusters and at national levels.

- *Job shadowing.* Counselors carry out job shadowing activities where students are given an opportunity to shadow a profession of their choice, such as teaching or nursing.
- *Take a child to work.* This is where a professional takes a child, of any age, to work with them. The purpose is to encourage and expose members of the community to work, and various types of jobs, especially at a very early age. This can be done with a primary school child, a secondary school student, or an out-of-school youth. The earlier the better, as this enables them to make informed career decisions.
- *Career counseling.* Career counseling is offered to Form 5 students and out-of-school youth, mainly those waiting for tertiary education or trying to get employment. This service is offered by taking walk-ins,

especially those waiting for placement and those coming in as referrals from any source. Some of these come as groups. When this happens they are addressed together as a group.

The Most Frequently Discussed Career Issues

The most frequently discussed career issues include:

- *Issues of results dictating what careers to follow instead of the individual's interest.* The individuals come in wanting to know what careers they can follow because they got a certain pass in Form 5.
- *Parent influence.*   For example, the parent has failed to pursue a certain career so they feel their child must learn that particular career.

Most Preferred Careers

Engineering (because of prestige and money) is most preferred, even by those who do not qualify for the simplest jobs. Medical Sciences is also a field that attracts many.

Additional Information

Career fairs are sponsored by the units who cater to the resource persons who are usually invited to come and talk about their companies. They run career guidance workshops for teachers in the country and hold about eight sessions per year. Normally, they enlighten school representatives who then go back to their schools and teach the rest of the staff in their schools. Some of these workshops are initiated by schools who invite the unit to come and teach them. These private workshops, of which there are many, are not counted in the eight total major workshops.

Career Counseling in Canada

Written by: Christine Frigault
Coordinator, Career Planning Centre
Department of Student Affairs, Mount Saint Vincent University, Halifax, Nova Scotia

About Mount Saint Vincent University

Mount Saint Vincent University (MSVU) is primarily an undergraduate institution dedicated to providing innovative education for women. As a result, females make up the majority of our student population (70–80%). Total enrollment is approximately 4,400 students. MSVU offers programs in the liberal arts and sciences, as well as professional programs such as child and youth study, family studies and gerontology, applied human nutrition, education, public relations, business administration, tourism and hospitality management, and information technology.

About the Career Planning Centre

The Career Planning Centre is a division of the Department of Student Affairs. The Centre employs one full time Coordinator/Career Counselor, one part time Career Counselor, one secretary, and three to four part time student staff and volunteers during the academic year. We are committed to the career development of students and recent graduates as well as to providing quality services to employers who wish to recruit students for full-time, part-time, or summer employment.

The Career Planning Centre is dedicated to promoting the knowledge of a proactive career development process through individual and group career counseling services and programs. Services we offer to students include the following:

Career Planning

- individual career counseling
- interest testing (Strong Interest Inventory)
- career resource library
- workshops

Job Searching

- resume and cover letter critiquing
- mock interviews
- online job postings
- career fairs (offered in partnership with other local universities)
- on-campus recruiting (employer information sessions, on-campus interviews)
- employment programs

Student Involvement

- mentoring program (matching students with alumnae mentors)
- Peer Helpers Volunteer Program (allowing students to gain volunteer experience in areas such as health education, library assistance, and career planning)

Although MSVU is unique as a university dedicated to the education of women, the services offered by the Career Planning Centre may be generalized to what is offered at other Canadian universities of similar size.

Most Prevalent Career Concerns of Our Students

Concerns of students visiting the Career Planning Centre vary depending on the student's program, age, and year of study (among other factors). One of the most common concerns of students enrolled in liberal arts programs, regardless of their year of study, is "What can I do with a degree in . . . ?" Many have friends enrolled in professional programs where the degree often points to a clear career path, and they may feel confused about how their general liberal arts program relates to careers. Career counselors assist students by taking them through the self-assessment

process: helping them identify their interests, values, and skills and how these relate to their program of study and potential career paths. Some students take the Strong Interest Inventory to assist with this process. We also encourage students to research possible careers that may interest them by visiting our career resource library, reviewing career planning web sites that we provide to them, volunteering in areas that interest them, and talking to people who perform the careers.

One of the programs we have that assists with career exploration is the mentoring program, which is offered in partnership with the Mount Saint Vincent Alumnae Association. This program matches students with alumnae mentors who are performing a career the student has indicated an interest in. Students meet their mentor at an organized luncheon and then have the opportunity to make further contact with their mentor by e-mail, phone, or in person (job shadowing). Many students have found this program to be helpful in clarifying their career interests.

Another common concern that many of our students have is how to go about finding a job after graduation. Each year we organize career fairs and on-campus employer information sessions, which provide students with the opportunity to meet employers and begin the job search process. We also offer workshops on job searching and resume and interview preparation. Although we advise students to begin this process early, some inevitably wait until graduation is only a few weeks away and many come to us for individual appointments on the above topics. We counsel students in the use of networking, cold-calling, and information interviewing as part of their job search. We also offer the opportunity for students to participate in a videotaped mock interview to assess and improve their interview skills.

Because MSVU is an institution dedicated to the education of women, we attract a significant number of mature female students, many who have left their previous employment and are attending university for the first time or returning after many years. Career counselors assist mature students with similar career planning issues as traditional students and also help them balance the additional issues of family, school, and work.

Most Popular Career Choices of our Students

It is difficult to generalize the most popular career choices of our students. However, given that we offer professional programs in areas such as education, many of our undergraduate liberal arts, science, and child and youth study students are interested in pursuing teaching. Due to the fact that competition for places in this program is difficult, students often have to consider other options, which counselors may help them identify. Other social service occupations are often alternatives these students are interested in (*such as* counseling, social work, and occupational therapy).

Students who are enrolled in our professional programs usually have an idea of what career they are interested in. For example, students in our applied human nutrition program are usually interested in dietetics. Because we offer cooperative education in some of our professional programs (e.g., business administration, information technology, tourism and hospitality management, public relations), students enrolled in these programs often gain a clearer picture of what career they wish to pursue within their professions. Common choices within these programs include accounting, marketing, computer programming, tourism, and communications.

Typical Day for the Coordinator of the Career Planning Centre

9:00–9:30	Respond to e-mail and voice mail messages from students, employers, and other staff members
9:30–10:30	Meet with student assistants for biweekly supervision meeting. Discuss activities undertaken in the past two weeks, upcoming promotions (career fairs, employer visits to campus, workshops) and new resources for the career resource library that need to be filed
10:30–11:30	Career counseling appointment—45-year-old mature student who recently returned to university and is unsure of her career options
11:30–12:30	Career counseling appointment—18-year-old first year liberal arts student who is receiving pressure from his parents to switch to a more "practical" program of study
12:30–1:00	Write notes from two previous appointments
1:00–2:00	Lunch
2:00–3:00	Career counseling appointment—23-year-old fourth year business student who plans to attend the upcoming career fair and would like help with her resume
3:00–4:00	Conduct workshop on finding a job after graduation
4:00–5:00	Write notes from afternoon appointment, respond to e-mail and voice mail messages, prepare agenda for career fair planning meeting to take place tomorrow

Career Counselling in Canada—Middle School

Written by: Janice Graham-Migel
Guidance Counsellor, Ridgecliff Middle School
35 Beech Tree Run, Beechville, Nova Scotia, B3T 2E5
Contact: jgraham@staff.endnet.ns.ca

Setting

The setting is a middle school in the Halifax Regional School Board with a student population of approximately 600 students in Grades 6 to 9 (ages 11 to 16).

Program

Career Counselling is a component of the school's Comprehensive Guidance and Counselling Program (CGCP). The CGCP was piloted for the

Nova Scotia Department of Education in 1996 at Beechville-Lakeside-Timberlea School (Grades Primary to 9) and then moved to the newly-built Ridgecliff Middle School (Grades 6 to 9) in 1999.

Activities

When the Comprehensive Guidance and Counselling Program was implemented at Beechville-Lakeside-Timberlea School, the Career component of the program included a Career Awareness Day. Guest speakers described careers and emphasized its importance at all grades from Primary to 9.

Although students are made aware of careers at all grade levels, Career Education is integrated into the curriculum at the Grade 9 level. Each November, Grade 9 students participate in "Take Our Kids to Work Day" (job shadowing), The Economics of Staying in School (E.S.I.S.) Program, and a Job Fair.

Reference

Graham-Migel, J. (2002). Comprehensive Guidance and Counselling Programs: The Beechville-Lakeside-Timberlea Experience. *Canadian Journal of Counselling*, 36:1, 6–13.

Career Counseling in Hong Kong

Written by: C. Isaac Tam, PhD
Senior Student Counselor
Student Counseling and Career Service, Student Affairs Office
Hong Kong University of Science and Technology
Clear Water Bay, Kowloon, Hong Kong

The Hong Kong University of Science and Technology (HKUST) opened in 1991 as a technological university dedicated to the advancement of learning and scholarship, with special emphasis on research, postgraduate education, and close collaboration with business and industry. It is the newest public university in Hong Kong and is built on a designated 60-hectare site for 7,000 undergraduate and graduate students. The Schools of Science, Engineering, and Business and Management provide undergraduate and graduate education, while the School of Humanities and Social Science offers general education for undergraduates and graduate education. The teaching staff establishment includes 520 full-time positions filled by worldwide recruitment of established academics and promising younger scholars with doctoral degrees.

Most undergraduate students enter the university at the age of 18 or 19, after 13 years of elementary and secondary education. Upon completion of 100 to 105 credits in 3 academic years, they will be awarded honors degrees in one of 41 programs. Nearly all undergraduates are local residents, while about one third of postgraduates are nonlocal. There are 82 postgraduate programs leading to master's and doctoral degrees.

Career counseling is provided by the integrated Student Counseling and Career Services in the Student Affairs office. Led by a senior student counselor who has a doctoral degree in clinical psychology, the core of the team has three full-time workers (two student counselors, one student affairs officer) with master's degrees in counseling, human resource management/training, and engineering; bachelor's degrees in social work, psychology, commerce, and engineering; and at least 15 years of relevant experience. About one–quarter of the manpower is spent in general counseling (remedial/developmental, individual/group), and three–quarters in career counseling, education, and placement services. The workers have to be fluent in English (the medium of instruction), Cantonese Chinese (the main dialect of the region), and Putonghua or Mandarin (the national Chinese language.) Written communication (such as announcements, e-mails, letters, and training materials) is primarily in English, with some supplement in Chinese. Oral communication is chiefly in Cantonese for locals, but Putonghua is used for nonlocals (for example, students from Eastern and Northern China), and English for nonChinese students. Other than individual consultation, group programs are the primary means of service delivery. These include mentoring programs, career talks or exhibitions, Pathfinders forums (inside guide to winning jobs in specific industries), recruitment talks or job fairs, interview and aptitude test practicums, preselection exercises, a web-based advising system linking students with alumni (called "Honorary Advisors in Career Education"), entrepreneurial and international career programs, study missions covering major industrial manufacturers in the Pearl River Delta and companies in major Chinese cities, and internships in the Chinese Mainland or foreign countries. Career services are provided in close partnership with academic departments or school offices via their undergraduate and postgraduate career coordinators. Student societies or associations, alumni, employers, and government and non-government organizations are ongoing partners in our programs.

The following characteristics and trends have been found:

- The use of tests developed outside Hong Kong continues to pose a challenge for career counselors. While Hong Kong is fairly "Westernized," the deep Chinese cultural roots and values remind counselors to interpret with caution popular instruments like the Strong Interest Inventory or Self-Directed Search. Many assessment tools have not been contextualized or indigenized for cross cultural application.

- While career resources in print, video, or electronic forms are still available at our Career Center, service delivery has rapidly increased via the Center Web site. In particular, HKUST has led the public universities in Hong Kong by establishing, managing, and operating the web-based Joint Institution of Job Information System for free use by employers in recruitment and students in job search. Since its inception in 2001, eligible users have paid almost 5 million visits to the site.

- Hong Kong changed from a British colony to a Special Administrative Region of China in 1997. The Chinese sovereignty, under the "one country, two systems" arrangement, is creative but complicated. Occupational concerns and career development are no longer restricted to the small region but should be considered in the context of the whole country. In particular, many jobs are available in the Chinese Mainland, but Hong Kong graduates are reluctant or not ready to take them. Career counseling and service have to be very adaptive and innovative in helping students to work and live in the post-1997 era.

- With increased unemployment in a fluctuating economy of Hong Kong, university graduates have seen a drop of 30% in median starting salary since 2000. Great is the psychological impact, greater is the courage needed to face reality, and greatest is the flexibility required for job placement. When jobs are abundant, career counseling seems easier. When jobs are scarce, personalized placement that was previously for the elite is now crucial for the least competitive among the graduates. Reduction of the unemployment rate among the graduates can readily be a performance indicator for career counselors or for the institution in budgetary consideration.

- Not all graduate students in master's programs will pursue doctoral studies. Some of them enroll in such programs as a shelter or transition in a difficult job market while some intend to take the master's as their destination degree. Possessing an advanced degree or a delay in entering the world of work does not mean they are ready to do so. Career counseling and education have become more important for graduate students with little or no full time work experience outside their academic setting.

Career Counseling in Jordan

Prepared by: Marisabel Abu-Jaber, PhD

Information submitted by: Abdel-Rahim Abdel-Jaber
Assistant Director General for Technical Affairs
Vocational Training Corporation, Amman, Jordan

Vocational Training Corporation

The Vocational Training Corporation (VTC) was established in Jordan in 1976. Its main roles include providing vocational training opportunities for technical workforce preparation and upgrade workforce in different programs (VTC, 2001).

In order to implement the functions and activities assigned, the VTC has established 35 training centers and institutes all over the country. In 2003, 12 new centers were under construction (A. R. Abdel-Jaber, personal communication, June 22, 2003).

The VTC serves a female and male population, who range from 16 years of age and older. The educational requirements for the different programs vary. Some programs require that the trainee be able to read and write, and some other programs require, as a minimum, a Secondary School Certificate. Most of the trainees graduating from the VTC's programs are self-employed or they are recruited by the private sector (A. R. Abdel-Jaber, personal communication, June 22, 2003).

Some of the major activities of the VTC include testing, job placement, training, and counseling. The VTC staff provides assistance and training to small and medium enterprises in different occupations. They prepare vocational guidance and counseling programs with the aim of increasing the acceptance of vocational education by society, and they also organize the occupation work in the labor market by classifying occupational workplaces and workers (A. R. Abdel-Jaber, personal communication, June 22, 2003, VTC, 2001).

VTC's trainees main career issues are related to training needs, work-related skills, educational information, orientation, and preparation for standardized placement tests. In the last 2 years, the VTC has experienced an increased demand for training in the field of hotel services and information technology (A. R. Abdel-Jaber, personal communication, June 22, 2003).

Career Guidance in a Scottish Borders School

Written by: Bob Holmes
Stow, Scotland

The school that I work in (a state-funded school) has a student population of 1,000. The age range is 12 to 18 and the school serves a rural and urban community—rural in the sense that about 20% of our students live in the country, farms and outlying villages, while the remainder live in the town, which is in itself a rural community being fairly distant from the nearest city. The town itself has a population of 15,000.

It is worth noting that the town, some 20 years ago, was a vibrant and prosperous town based around traditional industries. Students who left school at that time were virtually guaranteed employment. Thus, education had a relatively low priority and career guidance was almost nonexistent. However, all of that has changed. The traditional industry is almost all gone. The town is falling on hard times and is depopulating because families need to find work elsewhere.

Further, the attitude of the younger people has changed. Where previously there was a reluctance to leave the community, many young people are now leaving to learn new skills—but are not returning.

The major activities of the school are to deliver the National Curriculum to all students and to prepare older students for national examinations so that some of them will have adequate qualification for entry into further education (college and vocational courses) and higher education (university). The education the students receive is very much in the Scottish tradition—a broad base initially, then narrowing gradually into specialisms. These specialisms often provide the basis for college and university courses, and, very often, the future career.

Career guidance is delivered through a number of avenues and approaches. Firstly, it is delivered to groups of students of all ages through the school's Personal and Social Development Programme. Every student has 40 minutes each week of this. Essentially, the focus is on raising self-awareness. During this process all students complete a nationally accredited Progress File.

At critical times in the students' development through school—we call it Choice of Course (at 14 and 16 years of age)—the students are given specific time and support from their own guidance teacher to make the most appropriate choices. This can take the form of counselling but mostly it is in the form of advice. This is, in turn, supported by input from the school's careers adviser who delivers group guidance and is available for one-on-one sessions with students and their parents.

In addition, there are often visiting speakers who deliver talks to larger groups of students (probably a group of 200) on a specific career. The Armed Services is a good example here. Colleges and universities also present this kind of information and they hold fairs or conventions that students and their parents can attend and talk directly to the college or university staff.

In addition, both the school and the Careers Services Department offer specific courses for more disaffected students to help them make appropriate career choices. These courses are often experiential and deliver information in a different way. These are very effective courses. For example, the school's own course includes a residential component that is very highly thought of by the students. We have discovered, for example, that in going on this residential component, it is the very first time (age 15) that some students have been out of the town and away from home overnight. "Taster" courses are also offered; in which students can try a particular course for a week or two at the local college. This way, they can decide if college is for them and if that kind of course is also for them.

Every student who has reached year 4 in the school is entitled to one week's work experience. Here the student can choose to work in a particular placement for a week and be treated as one of the employees. This can serve several purposes: The student has a taste of work. The student can decide whether this kind of work may form part of a career choice. Equally, as a result of the experience, the student may decide that work in this area is not for them; or that delaying going to find work and working toward further academic qualifications is the better option. In whatever case, we have found work experience to be valuable in helping students to appreciate the kind of skills and attributes required for the workplace.

For the oldest students in the school we offer challenge weekends and weeks. These are opportunities for the students to challenge themselves individually and collectively in a different setting. These challenges are personal and intellectual as well as academic—and assist the students in making more appropriate career choices. The Armed Services as well as nationally known industries sometimes help us deliver these courses, as well as organisations who specialise in delivering challenge courses to adolescents.

There is no one particular career issue discussed in school. The issue is that we deliver career advice to a very diverse student population—some who will aspire to a career in Academia; some who will be artisans; and some of whom may be unemployable. It is a very comprehensive school. The issue then is one of appropriateness—trying to ensure that the best and most current information, advice, and support is delivered to each and every student according to his and her needs. We also try to ensure that the support every student is offered is ongoing and that they feel supported all through their school career.

Equally, there is no preferred career. As was explained earlier, the traditional industries formerly met all of the town's employment needs. Now the students have to go looking much further afield. So, in that sense, a small town in Scotland is becoming a part of the global village. The students are venturing further out into the world seeking opportunities.

Beyond these levels of support, the school's library has a significant part of its resource devoted to career literature. In addition, every student in the school has access to the world wide web. We are finding that more and more students are accessing this resource to help them find the most appropriate course at the University or the best kind of career opportunity that suits their needs. Indeed, most students now apply to a college or university electronically and are supported through this process by their own guidance teacher.

Finally, it is worth concentrating for a moment on the role of the student's Tutor and Guidance Teacher. Every student is a member of a tutor group and the tutor takes a daily—but brief—interest in the continuing development of the members of that group. The tutor will work in partnership with each students' guidance teacher in sharing and passing on information and advice to the student. The guidance teacher, however, has a pivotal role in supporting students all through school. The student will usually be assigned the same guidance teacher for their entire time at school. The guidance teacher is a person who takes a very special interest in the pupil in three ways:

- in terms of personal and social development
- in terms of monitoring curricular development
- in terms of vocational support and advice

It would be good to be able to describe this relationship as a counseling relationship, but that does not really happen too often. The essential relationship is student/teacher, and while some of the barriers can be removed, there is yet a long way to go.

So, in building relationships with their students through every year in school, the guidance teacher (in understanding the needs and abilities of the student) can help ensure that the student leaves school with the best possible chance of realising their career potential.

A GLOBAL CREDENTIAL FOR CAREER COUNSELORS

Recently, the Center for Credentialing and Education Incorporated began to offer the Global Career Development Facilitator credential for those who meet the requirements. This credential provides standardized training requirements and recognizes the trained professional who works as a career counselor. The qualifications for receiving the credential cover the basic career skills that career counselors need in order to effectively provide services to their clients. The twelve competencies required to qualify are as follows (Kennedy, 2004):

1. helping skills
2. labor market information and resources
3. working with diverse populations
4. technology and career development
5. ethical and legal issues
6. employability skills
7. consultation and supervision
8. training clients and peers
9. career development theories and models
10. program management and implementation
11. assessment
12. promotion and public relations

SUMMARY

In the 21st century, the move toward globalization is a significant economic characteristic that affects work and workers around the world. This movement has, of course, had tremendous impact on both the American workforce and the individual worker. Significant among these impacts is the departure from many of the traditions that guided work and workers in the United States in much of the 20th century to rapid changes, uncertainties, and constant challenges for the individual in the 21st century. These challenges include changes where one works, changes in what one does and how one does it, as well as changes in lifestyles. Counselors assisting clients with career needs must recognize the impact of these dramatic changes on their clients and must learn to think and understand globalization and its implications for practice. This would include being active in international professional networks and associations.

DISCUSSION QUESTIONS

1. International recreational travel increased significantly in the last half of the 20th century. What foreign countries, if any, have you visited? Did you encounter language difficulties? Did you have an impression of workers and workplaces in these countries?

2. Are there any foreign countries you have not previously visited that you would like to tour? Why?

3. If you could have a one-year international working internship in any country (other than the United States), what country would you choose? Why? If it had to be non-English speaking which one would you choose? Why?

4. How many members of the class own foreign-made automobiles? Why did you purchase a foreign model?

CLASS ACTIVITIES

1. If possible, invite three to five workers in your community or area, who immigrated to the United States for employment, to participate in a panel discussion of why they came, adjustments they had to make, and other comments.
2. Write a brief paper describing under what conditions you would accept employment in another country.
3. Read a foreign newspaper. Note any articles dealing with labor issues. Also review the adver-

tising and note U.S. products advertised, if any. Report your findings to the class.
4. Discuss, in small groups, employment trends noted in your home towns. What effect do these have on the career planning of students and young people in the community?
5. In small groups, discuss the impact, direct or indirect, of globalization on employment and careers in your home town.

READINGS OF INTEREST

Challenges for career counseling in Asia. (2002). [Special section]. *The Career Development Quarterly, 50*(3), 209–284.

Clawson, T. W., & Jordan, J. (2001). Globalization of professions: A U.S. perspective with the cyberworld in mind. *Eric/Cass Digest*, September. (EDO-CG-01-02)

Clawson, T. W. (2000). Expanding professions globally: The United States as a marketplace for global credentialing and cyberapplications. In J. W. Bloom, & G. R. Walz, (Eds.) *Cybercounseling and cyberlearning: Strategies and resources for the millennium* (pp. 29–37). Alexandria, VA: American Counseling Association and CAPS, Inc., in association with the ERIC Counseling

and Student Services Clearinghouse, Greensboro, NC.

Daalder, I. H., & Lindsay, J. M. (2003, Winter). The globalization of politics. *Brookings Review, 21*(1), 12–17.

Judy, R. W., & D'Amico, C. D. (1997). *Work force 2020: Work and workers in the 21st century*. Indianapolis, IN: Hudson Institute. (Chapter One: The forces shaping the American economy).

Kennedy, A. (2004, January). Career counselors can benefit from earning global credential. *Counseling Today*, 27.

Rifkin, J. (1995). *The end of work: The decline of the global labor force and the dawn of the post-market era*. New York: Tracher/Putnam.

Stigler, J. W., & Hiebert, J. (1999). *The teaching gap: Best ideas from the world's teachers for improving education in the classroom.* New York: The Free Press.

Useem, J. (2001, November 26). Globalization. *Fortune, 144*(11), 76–84.

Walz, G. R., & Reedy, L. S. (2000). The international career development library: The use of virtual libraries to promote counselor learning. In J. W. Bloom and G. R. Walz (Eds.) *Cybercounseling and cyberlearning: Strategies and resources for the millennium* (pp. 161–170). Alexandria, VA: American Counseling Association and CAPS, Inc., in association with the ERIC Counseling and Student Services Clearinghouse: Greensboro, NC.

Yuen, M. (2003). Exploring Hong Kong Chinese guidance teachers' positive beliefs: A focus group study. *International Journal for the Advancement of Counseling, 24,* 169–182.

Chapter 3

Career Development and Technology

Globalization and technology are rapidly changing how career development is delivered. Technology can take the "distance" out of counseling, but it requires that counselors acquire a new set of technological competencies if they are to utilize the power inherent in technology to reach more clients effectively. Distance career counseling, aided by emerging new technologies such as the picture phone, needs to be one of the new competencies that counselors possess if they are to meet the needs of clients in these times of change and turmoil.

Garry R. Walz, PhD, NCC
CEO
Counseling Outfitters/CAPS Press
Former Director of the ERIC Clearinghouse
on Counseling and Student Services
Professor Emeritus
University of Michigan

OBJECTIVES

To provide readers with an understanding of:

1. An overview of the dramatic developments in the field of technology and their effects on the world of work
2. The impact of the new technologies on professional counseling in general and career counseling specifically

INTRODUCTION

As noted in Chapter 2, globalization has been facilitated by the tremendous advances in the field of technology in the past 20 years. Developments such as the computer, the Internet, e-mail, and faxes, have made communications among nations and peoples almost instantaneous. These communication advancements, as well as the refinement of the jet engine, have also accelerated international traffic to the point where hours, not weeks, separate travelers from one country to another. It is clear that counselors must not only think globally and be aware of global developments as they occur, but that they must also be competent in the technologies of today's and tomorrow's interconnected world. In this regard, the Association for Counselor Education and Supervision (1999) established a list of minimum technological competencies needed by counselor education students upon the completion of their graduate degree programs:

- Be able to use productivity software to develop Web pages, group presentations, letters, and reports.
- Be able to use such audiovisual equipment as video recorders, audio recorders, projection equipment, videoconferencing equipment, and playback units.
- Be able to use computerized statistical packages.
- Be able to use computerized testing, diagnostic, and career decision-making programs with clients.
- Be able to use e-mail.
- Be able to help clients search for various types of counseling-related information via the Internet, including information about careers, employment opportunities, educational and training opportunities, financial assistance/scholarships, treatment procedures, and social and personal information.
- Be able to subscribe, participate in, and sign off counseling-related listserves.
- Be knowledgeable of the legal and ethical codes that relate to counseling services via the Internet.
- Be knowledgeable of the strengths and weaknesses of counseling services provided via the Internet.
- Be able to use the Internet for finding and using continuing education opportunities in counseling.
- Be able to evaluate the quality of Internet information. (As cited in Bloom & Walz, 2000, pp. 429–430)

Tyler and Sabella (2004) suggest that counselors who have adequate levels of technological literacy are able to do the following:

- Understand the nature and role of technology, in both their personal and professional lives.

- Understand how technological systems are designed, used, and controlled.
- Value the benefits and assess the risks associated with technology.
- Respond rationally to ethical dilemmas caused by technology.
- Assess the effectiveness of technological solutions.
- Feel comfortable learning about and using systems and tools of technology in the home, in leisure activities, and in the workplace.
- Critically examine and question technological progress and innovation. (Tyler & Sabella, 2004, p. 5)

TERMINOLOGY

An outgrowth of the spectacular technological advancements of the 1990s and early 2000s, is a whole new vocabulary integrating itself into the daily conversations of millions of Americans. *E-mail, fax, Web sites, downloading, modems*—words that would have puzzled our grandparents—are now in common use. This section presents a brief review of the labels commonly associated with the major technological advancements in the field of communications.

Internet: A connection of computer networks for the purpose of transferring information electronically between computers.

There are thousands of free Internet service providers that offer access, both locally and nationally. The Internet enables users to read content, listen to music, or even play games. There are also a number of paid Internet service providers. For example, AT&T (American Telephone and Telegraph) offers what they label as WorldNet Service, and has several budget options to meet the needs of a variety of consumers. In fisherman's terminology, one needs to cast a wide net to catch all the information available in cyberspace. Users need to understand that they have many choices of nets. Internets, intranets, and the extranets all provide information.

Web site: One "site" in the total collection of World Wide Web (WWW) sites containing information and resources.

Web sites include home pages and links for both organizations and individuals. The World Wide Web has influenced the way we think about information. In contrast to the library, warehouses of knowledge, the Web's hypertext structure can instantly connect related ideas and materials. The Web has many sites that exist for the purpose of helping users find information on other sites.

e-mail: Electronic mail is a popular process which enables messages to be transmitted among individuals via the Internet.

Most businesses and many individuals now possess e-mail addresses. There are also e-mail messaging systems that store and forward documents.

search engines: Certain Web sites, which have the function built into them, are able to search the world wide web by using key words.

One of the popular options available currently is to search the host of job options opened up for job seekers by the World Wide Web. Job seekers may post their resumes for free viewing by thousands of prospective employers.

modems: Modems convert digital computer signals into forms that permit them to travel over phone lines.

Modems connect computers to the Internet. Although broadband or high-speed modems are increasingly popular, the older dial-up modems continue to provide an inexpensive and reliable link to the Internet.

surfing the net: A phrase used to describe the search through vast amounts of information available to find the information one needs.

Many surfers of the Web are looking for specific information but are unsure where this information might be stored. Surfing is a technique that enables one to examine many possibilities.

listserve: Electronic journals and discussions may be distributed through e-mail software by listserve providers.

CD-ROM: The storage for later use of data can be achieved through the use of compact discs known as CD-ROMs.

These discs can store audio, video, text animation, and graphics.

information highway: The integration of computers, cable television, telephones, and the Internet for the purpose of providing interactive communications and information.

distance education: The delivery of education to individuals and audiences separated by geographic distances from the source of instruction.

Audio-visual communication, as well as other electronic resources, may be used to bring instructor and learner together electronically. Distance education is becoming an increasingly popular option available from major university campuses.

As you consider the potential of today's technologies, especially the Web, in your work, also consider what Sabella (2003) suggested to help conceptualize the range of available technologies:

- *Information/Resource* In the form of words, graphics, video, and even three-dimension virtual environments, the Web remains a dynamic and rapidly growing library of information and knowledge.
- *Communication/Collaboration* Chat rooms, bulletin boards, virtual classroom environments, video conferencing, online conferences, electronic meeting services, e-mail—the Web is now a place where people connect, exchange information, and make shared decisions.
- *Interactive tools* The maturing of Web-based programming has launched a new and unforeseen level of available tools on the Internet.

Interactive tools on the Web can help counselors build and create anything ranging from a personalized business card to a set of personalized Web site links. In addition, interactive tools help counselors to process data such as calculating a GPA or the rate of inflation, converting text to speech, creating a graph, or even determining the interactive effects of popular prescription drugs.

- *Delivery of services*   Most controversial, yet growing in popularity, is how counselors use the Web to meet with clients and deliver counseling services in an online or "virtual" environment." (p. 7)

CAREER COUNSELING ON THE INTERNET

On May 22, 2001 *USA Today* published an article, by Marilyn Elias, entitled "Online Therapy Clicks." In this article it was pointed out that online counseling is a hot, new trend in therapy, although it is not without its controversy. Internet counseling was also reported as being done in what is labeled "chats." This process permits clients and their counselors to message each other back and forth as a substitute for the usual, face-to-face therapeutic conversations between a counselor and a client. One of the popular topical areas for online counseling is dealing with the career concerns of clients.

The information highway provides counselors with an opportunity to display their qualifications and also their special expertise (such as career counseling) for the potential client. Counselors using this medium may wish to indicate whether their practice is limited to online assistance or whether they also engage in the traditional face-to-face interaction in a counseling setting. Of course, in some instances, the Internet may be the only option available for individuals who cannot readily access a traditional counseling facility due to their location or a physical disability. There are also circumstances in which clients may find, with counselor direction, the Internet to be particularly helpful, such as when they are gathering information and data for decision making or job searches. In this process, clients must be cautioned that, in some instances, Internet sites may encourage premature or inappropriate decision making. With this in mind, Bowlsbey, Dikel, and Sampson, Jr., suggested a sequence of events for effective use of the Internet in individual counseling:

1. identification and clarification of the client's problem or concern
2. identification of potential Internet sites for securing information that may be appropriate for the client's needs
3. evaluation of the information secured through the Internet searches
4. application of the information to the client's concern
5. evaluation of the outcomes in terms of client satisfaction and resolution of the client's needs or concerns (1998)

Many states have created technological centers that specialize in career assistance, where counselors and individuals can secure information using the Internet (as well as e-mail, Web sites and toll-free numbers). An example, familiar to your authors, is the Indiana Career and Post-Secondary Advancement Center (ICPAC). The mission of ICPAC, as outlined by the Indiana General Assembly, is informing, encouraging, and supporting the education and career development of the people of Indiana.

Career counselors should be aware that their clients may have access to course offerings, both academic and nonacademic, through the Internet. In the instance of academic course offerings, the opportunity to earn academic credit is becoming increasingly popular, and in some instances controversial, as many such programs are being generated by organizations that have only a mailbox for their physical campus. The new technology can also provide clients with practice tests and feedback relevant to potential admission to educational institutions or for assessing a client's career interests and job placement possibilities.

> In addition to the broad-based searches, Web sites may be accessed more narrowly for specific assessment purposes. For example, interest inventories may be reached through the *Career Interests Game,* which may be found at www.missouri.edu/~cppcwww/holland.shtml. Abilities/skill inventories may be identified through the *University of Waterloo Career Services Career Development Manual* (Web site address: www.adm.uwaterloo.ca/infocecs/crc/manual-home.html and career descriptions may be accessed through the *Occupational Outlook Handbook:* http://stats.bls.gov/ocohome.htm (Gibson & Mitchell, 2003, p. 425)[1]

DISTANCE CAREER COUNSELING

As noted earlier, distance education is a process for delivering informational services from the holder of information, such as a university, library, or agency, to the individual or individuals requesting the information. These individuals are usually at an inconvenient distance from the information source. Distance education has become increasingly popular as a university outreach service since the 1990s, and it seems very likely that education is only on the threshold of the distance learning movement. In this regard, the combination of easy access to new information resources and alternatives to traditional learning strategies will become acceptable and common. This popularity may increasingly compete with the traditional campus classroom learning environments. It is highly probable that self-directed studies using the Internet will offer further nontraditional educational opportunities as these possibilities become better known to the public and more acceptable to educational institutions.

[1] *Gibson, Robert L, & Mitchell, Marianne H., Introduction to Counseling and Guidance, 6/e, © 2003. Reprinted by permission of Pearson Education, Inc., Upper Saddle River, NJ.*

In recent years distance career counseling, similar to the advent of online counseling, has also become an emerging practice. The development of this new and emerging technique for the delivery of career assistance obviously poses a number of challenges at this point. While clear guidelines will undoubtedly emerge in the near future, Malone (2002) suggested the following:

- **A Clear and Comprehensive Web site,** which fully informs potential clients about the design and delivery of services, ethical and legal issues such as privacy and confidentiality, fee structure, possible risks to confidentiality due to the service delivery media, the professional counseling relationship and other issues relevant to informed consent.
- **A Comprehensive, Technology-Assisted Pre-Counseling In-Take Registration and Assessment Protocol** which includes the use of validated Internet instruments and open-ended questionnaires.
- **Personalized Selection and Assignment of A Well-Matched Counselor,** which helps to ensure the building of an effective working alliance.
- **Technology-Assisted Strategies,** which facilitate efficient and personalized communication between counselor and client.
- **Structured Distance Career Counseling Interventions,** which appear to be quite effective for clients according to emerging research studies. The Distance Career Counselor does well to use some sort of template, such as the recursive career development process:
  assessment<>exploration <>decision-making<>self-marketing.
- **Maintaining Counselor-Client Contact Between Sessions,** which continues to support the counseling relationship.
- **Providing Clients with Thoughtful, Written Feedback from Their Counseling Sessions,** which provides a meaningful and insightful review of the counseling experience with implications for follow-up action.
- **Evaluating Distance Career Counseling Practices,** which gives clients an opportunity to express what they feel were more or less effective counselor interventions.

It is important to determine the effectiveness of all counseling practices, including those of special interest to career counselors. Sexton (1999) makes an excellent case regarding the need for professional counselors to engage in research designed to evaluate the effectiveness of career counseling practices, which would imply the inclusion of the method of distance career counseling. This is particularly relevant as we anticipate the expansion of Internet career counseling and distance career counseling in the era of frequent career changers for the majority of the workforce.

Recently, the Center for Credentialing and Education, Incorporated (CEE), an affiliate of the National Board for Certified Counselors (NBCC), established credentialing for counselors and others working in the helping professions: the distance credentialed counselor. The completion of a specialized counselor training program is required for this credential. For an explanation of the many responsibilities of a distance career counselor, see Table 3-1.

TABLE 3-1
A taxonomy of face-to-face and technology-assisted distance counseling.

Counseling
- Face-to-face counseling
  - Individual counseling
  - Couple counseling
  - Group counseling
- Technology-assisted distance counseling
  - Telecounseling
    - Telephone-based individual counseling
    - Telephone-based couple counseling
    - Telephone-based group counseling
  - Internet counseling
    - E-mail-based individual counseling
    - Chat-based individual counseling
    - Chat-based couple counseling
    - Chat-based group counseling
    - Video-based individual counseling
    - Video-based couple counseling
    - Video-based group counseling

Source: The Practice of Internet Counseling, (2001). National Board for Certified Counselors, Inc.; and Center for Credentialing and Education, Inc.; Greensboro, NC 27403-3660. p. 2. Reprinted with the permission of the National Board for Certified Counselors and Affillates, 3 Terrace Way, Suite D, Greensboro, NC 27403-3660.

THE ONLINE JOB SEARCH

One of the most significant changes for career counselors during the new technology age has been the emergence of online job search opportunities. Thanks to the world wide web, numerous new and helpful options have emerged to assist career counselors and job seekers everywhere. These include Web sites that offer individual job seekers the opportunity to post their résumés for the potential perusal of thousands of employers. Career counselors can implement such searches by helping their career clients to identify the kind of careers that meet their needs and then locating potential appropriate career opportunities. Some examples of Web sites providing career assistance for job-hunters are as follows (Winfield, 2001, 73–75):

PROFESSIONAL STAFF LTD.   This is an international group of specialist employment agencies and recruitment businesses that place professionals in science, telecommunications, information technology, and interim management (http://www.professional-staff.com).

CAREERBUILDER   This site contains opportunities in a variety of industries from employers around the world. It is also a source of employment information on the Internet for job seekers, employers, and recruiters (http://www.careerbuilder.com).

MANPOWER   Manpower claims to be the largest staffing and employment service in the world. They operate 3,500 branch offices and franchises in 54 countries (http://www.manpower.com).

EMPLOYMENT-NETCANADA.COM   The Employment Network is a network of recruitment and human resource services, offering Canadian and international jobs (http://www.employment-netcanada.com).

FEDERATION OF EUROPEAN EMPLOYERS   This is a nonprofit organization that provides access to news, consulting, briefings, and legal information about human resources (http://www.euen.co.uk).

CAREER ADVANCEMENT EMPLOYMENT SERVICES, INC.   This is a recruiting and employment services organization that specializes in permanent and contract environmental jobs, engineering positions, and financial and consulting opportunities (http://www.careeradvancement.on.ca).

STUDENT EMPLOYMENT NETWORK   This network helps current high school students and postsecondary graduates in Canada in their job searches (http://www.studentjobs.com). (Winfield, 2001, p. 73–75).

TECHNOLOGY OF THE FUTURE

Many of the technological developments discussed in this chapter did not become commonplace until the 1990s. The rapidity of their refinement and cost reduction prompted a very swift acceptance and utilization by the general public. Computers, cell phones, fax machines, and other more advanced communications devices are everywhere, and new devices are introduced on a regular basis. New inventions and improvements on older devices will continue to occur at a record pace. Undoubtedly, many of these will impact the profession and the provision of counseling, including career services, just as the computer and Internet have had such a dramatic impact over the past decade.

For example, the vision phone, which projects the images of the communicators is already being used in corporations and are spreading into personal households. Projected rocket travel between continents will shrink travel time even more and will further stimulate worker movement from country to country. (If you can return home from Scotland to Indiana on a one-hour rocket flight, why not take that job in Edinburgh?) Finally, from the Buck Rogers cartoons of yesteryear, most local travel to stores, schools, and other destinations will be airborne as air coupes and personal rocket chairs become common. Another development that will increase in popularity on the international scene is the translator phone, which enables an individual to talk into the phone in his or her native language and have it translated instantly into the language of the recipient. For example, a counselor educator in the United States could call a counterpart in China. Even though neither spoke the language of the other, they could communicate fluently and easily using the translator phone. It has been projected that such phones would have buttons representing the common languages of the world so that to send or receive in another language you would simply press the appropriate button.

Those of us who are always looking for more electrical outlets may look forward to the wireless home of the near future, as tiny chips will provide energy for our microwaves, toasters, coffee makers, computers, and other electrical devices. Tiny sensors called *smart dust* will be used to pass along related information. Sensors will also replace the current systems of audio-visual surveillance for monitoring the whereabouts and well-being of the sick, infirm, and elderly. The credit card craze of recent decades will fade into oblivion as an individual's thumb print will validate his or her identity as a basis for charging by simply pressing on the thumb pad censor at the check-out counter.

Modern medical breakthroughs are expected to continue the dramatic increases in longevity which, of course, will lead to an increasingly aging but also increasingly physically fit population. These developments will present new challenges and opportunities to the field of career counseling.

OBSERVATIONS FROM THE FIELD

As previously noted, the great technological surge of the recent generations has impacted the homes of millions of individual consumers and has also transformed the business and industrial world. A result of these developments has been a dramatic increase in educational programs reflecting the new technologies. For example, computer instruction is commonplace at all educational levels. Additionally, as will be noted in later chapters, various informational and educational services are available online to both students and nonstudents of nearly all ages and settings. Not unexpectedly, the demand for formal instruction in the fields of technology has also increased significantly, as witnessed by the increased number of applicants seeking admission to all types of technical programs and institutions.

In the spring of 2004, your authors visited three varied types of technical educational institutions: Georgia Institute of Technology (Atlanta, Georgia); Ivy Tech State College (Bloomington, Indiana); and West Virginia Institute of Technology (Montgomery, West Virginia). A summary of these visitations follows.

THE GEORGIA INSTITUTE OF TECHNOLOGY

During our visit to the Georgia Institute of Technology (Georgia Tech) in Atlanta, Georgia, we were hosted by Ralph D. Mobley, director of career services. Marge Dussich, assistant director, also participated in our discussions. Approximately 16,500 full-time students are enrolled, including over 2,800 international students. This population is distributed among the six colleges of the institution. The largest college is the college of engineering, which accounts—not unexpectedly—for more than half of the total enrollment. Other program areas in order of their enrollment are management, computing, sciences, liberal arts, and architecture.

Among the Career Services offered are the following:

- career counseling
- majors fair
- career library
- seminars
- résumé critiques
- internships
- job postings
- mock interviews
- salary surveys
- career focus
- on-campus interviews by potential employers

All entering students are given an attractive and detailed career guide describing career services at Georgia Tech. This guide assists students in each year of their undergraduate enrollment. The career services Web site offers a calendar of events, useful employment links for all majors, tips on numerous topics related to the job search process, internships, and a link to CareerBuzz. They also offer a career development guide to assist students in each year of their undergraduate enrollment. During their freshmen year, students are encouraged to begin clarifying career goals, assessing their skills, and finding out about career-related work. Sophomores are encouraged to list career choices related to their majors and to secure career-related employment. During the junior year, continuing the previous activities is encouraged, along with assuming more responsible positions and continuing to develop contacts both on- and off-campus. The career services office at Georgia Tech also suggests that juniors should become familiar with specialized areas in their chosen field and potential employers. Seniors are advised to develop a job search strategy, or if interested, apply to appropriate graduate schools.

Excellent physical facilities are available to promote the functions of the career services office at this institution. These include over 30 comfortably-equipped private interview rooms for recruiters and an attractive lounge and refreshment center also for recruiters. Additional space is available for workshops, seminars, and conferences. The sum total of these facilities and services were impressive and would ensure a high level of career services available to the students of Georgia Tech and their potential employers.

IVY TECH STATE COLLEGE

"Ivy Tech" is located in our hometown of Bloomington, Indiana. Katie T. Anderson, assistant director of career services hosted the visit. Ivy Tech is an example of a 2-year technical educational institution. Enrollment at Ivy Tech is approximately 3,500 students, of whom approximately 60% (2,100) are full time students and approximately 40% (1,400) are enrolled as part time students. Programs offered include the following:

- accounting
- business administration
- computer information systems
- criminal justice
- design technology
- early childhood education
- electronics technology
- general studies
- manufacturing and industrial technology
- associate of science nursing
- practical nursing
- office administration
- paramedic science
- paralegal science

The career services available to students at Ivy Tech on the Bloomington campus are categorized as follows:

Career Advising

- career assessments
- occupational reports
- up-to-date labor market information
- job shadowing

Employment Preparation

- résumé and cover letter writing assistance and workshops
- prospective employer lists, business brochures, and annual reports for reference
- interviewing practice and tips
- employment hotline
- career opportunity bulletin
- career expo online

Employment Opportunities

- part-time and full-time résumé referrals with area employers
- work-study—part-time, on-campus employment
- cooperative education/internships
- career expo

Among the special activities of career services at Ivy Tech are a series of career expo workshops designed to connect students and employers. Most students applying for new career opportunities would find these workshops helpful.

Anderson noted that trends impacting Ivy Tech in recent years included (a) the loss of the manufacturing sector; (b) the emergence of life sciences; (c) increased demand for skilled technicians, including drafting, electronics, and facilities technicians; and (d) an increasing demand for healthcare division programs, including nursing and a biomedical technology program.

THE WEST VIRGINIA UNIVERSITY INSTITUTE OF TECHNOLOGY

West Virginia University Institute of Technology (West Virginia Tech) is located in Montgomery, West Virginia. It offers associate's, bachelor's, and master's degrees for a student enrollment of approximately 1,800 full-time and 750 part-time. The most popular programs are engineering (32%); business management, marketing, and related subjects (23%); and engineering technology and technicians (12%).

Mr. Cantrell Miller, the director of career services at West Virginia Tech, met with us to discuss the career services provided for students of his institution. Career services offered to all students include career advising; employment opportunities, including part-time summer internships and cooperative education positions; graduate and professional school information; and online services that include résumé workshops, interview workshops, and letter-writing workshops. Student employment is assisted by an ongoing series of campus visits by employer recruiters who conduct interviews for employment.

All students are presented with a brochure listing online job database sites. These include categories by majors or fields of study, state and government jobs, local jobs, international jobs, and temporary and seasonal jobs. All students also receive a schedule of services and events sponsored by the office of career services for each semester. Each student also receives a comprehensive career services handbook.

CONCLUSIONS: OBSERVATIONS FROM THE FIELD

We can conclude from these interviews that, not unexpectedly, programs of technological education have experienced increasing popularity at all levels in recent years. Career counseling and assistance programs have also become a vital resource to both students and employers, as well as a source of employment for graduates from counselor preparation programs.

Services provided include employer information and opportunities, résumé preparation and interviewing skills, job fairs, and scheduled interviews with potential employers. Individual assistance is available at all times. Many career services are offered online as well as through the more traditional modes.

SUMMARY

Technology has, and will continue to have, a significant impact on the entire range of counselor activities, but perhaps the area of career counseling and guidance will continue to be the most affected area. This chapter has presented an overview of developments in the field of technology that affect the profession of counseling and career assistance. The competencies that should be acquired to be proficient in the various technological undertakings as prescribed by the Association of Counselor Education and Supervision (ACES) were presented, as were brief definitions of common terms such as *Internet, Web site,* and *e-mail.*

A discussion of career counseling on the Internet followed, including guidelines for effective use of the Internet. Many states have created technological centers specializing in providing career assistance. Career counselors should be aware that their clients can access both academic and nonacademic course offerings through the Internet. Another opportunity for earning academic credit is distance education, which became increasingly popular as a university outreach service in the 1990s. In recent years, even distance career counseling has become an emerging practice. Suggested guidelines to assist counselors and their clients in using the Internet effectively were presented. As job searches are one of the most popular uses of the Internet, a brief discussion of online job searches, as well as some popular resources, were included. Finally, we placed a quivering eye on the future and suggested some probable developments that would, in turn, influence the practice of counseling and the provision of career services.

DISCUSSION QUESTIONS

1. Describe how you use the computer. How do you use the Internet and the world wide web?
2. Have you had any experiences with distance education? If so, describe these and your reactions.
3. From a technology standpoint, how is your current home different from your childhood home or your parents' childhood homes?
4. What technology training, if any, should counselors receive?
5. What technology advances do you envision in the near future?

CLASS ACTIVITIES

1. List, then share with the class, your view of the ten most significant scientific or technological advances of the 20th century.
2. Read a current periodical (professional or popular) article describing a probable or predicted technological or scientific advancement. Report your findings to the class.
3. Organize into small groups—four to six members each—and plan scheduled visits to local industries, agencies, and government offices to observe their uses of technology. Has special training been necessary for employees in these settings? Share your findings with the class.

READINGS OF INTEREST

Albrecht, A. C., & Jones, D. G. (2004). Planning for cyberlearning: A framework for counselor educators. In J. W. Bloom & G. R. Walz (Eds.), *Cybercounseling & cyberlearning: An encore* (pp. 57–80). Greensboro, NC: CAPS Press and Alexandria, VA: American Counseling Association.

Bloom, J. W., & Walz, G. R. (Eds.). (2004). *Cybercounseling & cyberlearning: An encore.* Greensboro, NC: CAPS Press and Alexandria, VA: American Counseling Association.

Bloom, J. W., & Walz, G. R. (Eds.) (2000). *Cybercounseling and cyberlearning: Strategies and resources for the millennium.* Alexandria, VA: American Counseling Association and Greensboro, NC: CAPS, Inc. in association with the ERIC Counseling and Student Services Clearinghouse.

Future of Technology. [Special section]. *Business Week,* 2003, August 18–25, 64–160.

Heinlen, K. T., Welfel, E. R., Richmond, E. N., & Rak, C. F. (2003). The scope of WebCounseling: A survey of services and compliance with NBCC Standards for the Ethical Practice of WebCounseling. *Journal of Counseling & Development, 81*(1), 61–69.

Jencius, M., & Paez, S. (2004). Converting counselor Luddites: Winning over technology-resistant counselors. In J. W. Bloom & G. R. Walz (Eds.), *Cybercounseling & cyberlearning: An encore* (pp. 81–114). Greensboro, NC: CAPS Press and Alexandria, VA: American Counseling Association.

Malone, J. F., Miller, K. S., & Miller, R. M. (2004). The evolution of a distance career counseling model: Implications for training, practice, and supervision of cybercounselors. In J. W. Bloom & G. R. Walz (Eds.), *Cybercounseling & cyberlearning: An encore* (pp. 151–182). Greensboro, NC: CAPS Press and Alexandria, VA: American Counseling Association.

Manzanares, M. G., O'Halloran, T. M., McCartney, T. J., Filer, R. D., Varhely, S. C., & Calhoun, K. (2004). CD-ROM Technology for education and support of site supervisors. *Counselor Education and Supervision, 43*(3), 220–231.

Mitchell, D. L., & Murphy, L. J. (2004). E-mail rules! Organization and individuals creating ethical excellence in telemental-health. In J. W. Bloom & G. R. Walz (Eds.), *Cybercounseling & cyberlearning: An encore* (pp. 203–217). Greensboro, NC: CAPS Press and Alexandria, VA: American Counseling Association.

Sampson, J. P., Jr., Carr, D. L., Panke, J., Arkin, S., Vernick, S. H., & Minvielle, M. (2004). Implementing Internet Web sites in counseling services. In J. W. Bloom & G. R. Walz (Eds.), *Cybercounseling & cyberlearning: An encore* (pp. 247–258). Greensboro, NC: CAPS Press and Alexandria, VA: American Counseling Association.

Technology and School Counseling. (2004). [Special section]. *ASCA School Counselor, 41*(4), 10–35.

Tyler, J. M., & Guth, L. J. Understanding online counseling services through a review of definitions and elements necessary for change. In J. W. Bloom, & G. R. Walz (Eds.), *Cybercounseling and cyberlearning: An encore* (pp. 133–150). Greensboro, NC: CAPS Press and Alexandria, VA: American Counseling Association.

Tyler, J. M., & Sabella, R. A. (2004). *Using technology to improve counseling practice: A primer for the 21st century.* Alexandria, VA: American Counseling Association.

Wall, J. E. (2004). Enhancing assessment through technology. *ASCA School Counselor,* 41(4), 30–35.

Wheaton, J. E., & Granello, P. F. (2004). Designing Web pages that are usable and accessible to all. In J. W. Bloom & G. R. Walz (Eds.), *Cybercounseling and cyberlearning: An encore* (pp. 3–17). Greensboro, NC: CAPS Press and Alexandria, VA: American Counseling Association.

Chapter 4

Theories of Career Development

Not all theories are "good" theories. Although good theories have many characteristics, my suggestion is that you evaluate each of the theories in this chapter using two criteria: First, does the theory offer practical applications that can be used to promote career development and to help people with career-related issues? Second, is the theory logical, that is, would a noncounselor accept the theorist's view of the world of career choice and development? If the answers to both questions are "Yes," you have found a practical tool that will help you in your own career development.

Duane Brown, PhD
Professor of Education
University of North Carolina, Chapel Hill

OBJECTIVES

To provide readers with an understanding of:

1. The traditional and popular theories of career development and their implications for career counseling
2. The major influences on career planning and decision-making

INTRODUCTION

Why did you decide to enter the profession of counseling, teaching, social work or any other profession? We have all responded to such questions on occasion and have asked such questions of others. Curiosity about career choice is common. Why do people enter the careers they do? What are the influences on career choice? For those approaching the time to make career decisions, how can you be sure that you make the right choice? This question is one that counselors will respond to many times. In their responses they will be guided by a body of professional knowledge underpinned by research and theories relevant to career development and decision-making.

When examining theory development, let us begin by noting that all of us have values or beliefs covering a broad range of subjects and activities that in turn influence our practice in these areas. These may include what experience has taught us is the best way to train our dog or cat, how to manage a classroom of 30 challenging adolescents, or how to effectively persuade others of our point of view. Although we might label these among our theories of life, they hardly constitute true theory as defined and developed in our professional and scientific communities. They are not without value—they may very well serve as useful guidelines in certain situations. However, unlike the theories that guide our professional practices, our personal theories have neither been tested nor confirmed in an empirical sense. Research with an acceptable design has not proven them to be consistent, valid, and predictable in their outcomes.

In a professional sense, theories serve as a basis for generating research that in turn produces a valid body of knowledge to guide us in our professional practice. Theories lead to the establishment of cause-and-effect relationships between variables with the twin objectives of explaining and predicting. Empirical research tests theories and clarifies concepts used in theoretical formulations. Well-formulated theories can, therefore, enable us to derive deductions about what will happen in different situations and under specified conditions.

In their examination of personality theories, Hall and Lindzey (1957) stated a classic definition of theory that is relevant to our examination of theories of career development. They stated that "a theory is a means of organizing and interpreting all that is known concerning a related set of events" (p. 14). They assert that a theory is useful or not useful in terms of whether it is verifiable and comprehensive in the scope of the behavior it accounts for. Career development theories, therefore, are useful when helping counselors understand how their career clients experience career development, make career decisions, and adjust to career demands. They provide us with empirically tested guidelines for our professional practice.

DIFFERING THEORETICAL VIEWPOINTS

Human beings are the most diverse of all living species. Each of us is different. While we share common traits with other humans, no two of us are alike. Individuals behave differently in the same situations, have differing interests, and often have opposing preferences. There are also differing viewpoints on what constitutes normal behavior, and how people change, and so on. The circumstances under which people live their lives also change. These changes include how, where, and even why people work. It is, therefore, not surprising that theories of career development, which reflect differing or changing viewpoints have emerged; just as we also have different and changing theoretical approaches to counseling itself. However, we should note that Osipow (1990), Borgen (1991), and others have observed that theoretical systems within career counseling share much in common and are—to a degree—moving toward convergence. Borgen (1991) notes that "it is not difficult to view them as more alike than different. Moreover, over their long careers, they have adapted their concepts and methods in ways that have moved them closer together."

> Existing career theories should be seen as complementary ways of knowing, not competing, and fully-developed alternative explanations of the same behavioral set or population. There are major voids in the knowledge necessary about women, minorities, and other groups in the society whose career behavior has been particularly affected by the magnitude of social, political, and economic changes of the past quarter century, but if one takes an aggregate view of existing career theory and research, there are tentative sets of constructs and propositions that can be used to explain different patterns of career behavior for a range of subpopulations and to design differential interventions or systems of interventions. (Herr & Cramer, 1992)

> "However, such existing configurations deserve experimental treatments by goal and by client attributes that are comprehensively done and meticulously described by behavioral outcome and by the intervention process involved." (Herr, 1996, p. 29)

A paragraph discussing convergence is presented later in this chapter. In the paragraphs that follow in this chapter, we will examine some of the more traditional and popular of these theories and their applications in practice. We will also note some of the more recent theoretical developments, keeping in mind that while offering contrasting viewpoints in some areas they will also appear very similar in others.

PERSPECTIVES ON CAREER THEORIES

The traditional theories of career development have, in recent generations, been criticized due to their limited attention to racial and ethnic minorities, women, and older populations. Also, as the world of work is dramatically changing, the gap between theories developed in the past and today's theories may continue to widen. As Harmon noted (1996):

> When daily headlines proclaim corporate plans to lay off thousands of workers in the name of downsizing or retrenchment, it is increasingly clear that the concept of change must be incorporated in any definition of *career* in today's society. No longer can workers, no matter what their level of education or experience, expect to have the same job for life. For the most part, our theories have been developed from the implicit assumption that career development proceeds toward a choice of career or a career path that is relatively stable and predictable and controlled by the individual. However, the clients we see today can no longer afford to make such naive assumptions. They need to plan for change because the world of work is itself changing. (p. 37)

While new theories are being hypothesized and researched, research to update the traditional theories continue. The traditional theories can, with some caution, still provide valuable and proven guidelines for career counseling while the emerging newcomers can broaden the perspectives that counselors bring to their career clients. Regardless of theoretical orientation, career counselors should consistently remind themselves that:

- Career development is but one aspect of the individual's total development and our holistic view of the client must not be lost in our study or practice in special areas such as careers
- Many workers in the decades ahead will experience multiple careers across their working life spans. Our traditional expectancies of one career for one's life—often in one location—is a tradition of the past. Career decision making will no longer be limited to a given age span, but will occur at differing intervals across the life span. Gelatt (1989) has noted that changing one's mind will be an essential decision-making skill in the future. Keeping an open mind will be another. He proposed a new decision-making strategy called "positive uncertainty" to assist clients in dealing with ambiguity, accept inconsistency, and utilize the intuitive side of choosing. Career counselors must, therefore, be prepared to assist clients with adapting to and growing in this era of change in the world of work.
- Careers and work must be viewed in a broad perspective. We must help clients understand that a career is more than just a job description—it is a way of life. What one does affects how one lives. Further, how the client views work in their

life is also an important perspective for client and counselor exploration in career counseling. Richardson (1993) notes a need to focus on the meaning of work in people's lives in which work is considered to be a central human activity that is not tied to or solely located in our traditional occupational structure.

- While the traditional steps in career counseling—(a) self-assessment; (b) assessment of the world of work; and (c) integrating knowledge of self and the world of work—may still be appropriate, a fourth step—assistance to clients on implementing their decisions and making adjustments as needed to their new settings (school or work)—is also required.

TRADITIONAL THEORIES OF CAREER DEVELOPMENT AND DECISION-MAKING

TRAIT-FACTOR THEORY

The first theory to emerge for guiding career counseling and advice was labeled the *trait-factor theory*. It derived its label from the assumption that assessment of individual traits (i.e., interests, aptitudes, achievements, and so on) through objective measures (psychological tests) and then making comparisons or matchings to those factors typically required for successful performance in a given career area would enable the counselor to provide meaningful assistance to clients seeking career direction. This trait-factor approach was an outgrowth of Frank Parson's concept of vocational guidance as described in his book, *Choosing a Vocation,* published in 1909. In this book Parsons described three steps for the individual making a career choice:

1. A clear understanding of yourself, your attitudes, abilities, interests, ambitions, resource limitations, and their causes
2. A knowledge of the requirements and conditions of success, advantages and disadvantages, compensation, opportunities, and prospects in different lines of work
3. True reasoning on the relations of these two groups of facts (p. 5)

Trait-factor theory assumed that individuals possessed relatively stable traits or characteristics and that career factors would experience little change.

The popularity of the trait-factor approach has, over the years, stimulated the development of a multitude of psychological tests designed to measure individual's interests, aptitudes, and personality traits and identify useable and accessible descriptors and classification systems for careers. The increasingly popular computerized systems available also provide for the basic phases of a trait-factor approach. In general, most of the assessment instruments profiled individual traits and overlaid or matched these with occupational factors, which resulted in determining the degree of fit between the individual and a specific occupation. These results were then integrated into the counseling process.

In application, E. G. Williamson, a prominent advocate of the trait-factor approach in the years immediately before and after World War II, suggested the following six steps as summarize in Isaacson & Brown (2000):

1. analysis
2. synthesis
3. diagnosis
4. prognosis
5. counseling
6. follow-up

Taken consecutively, these steps require:

1. collecting data about the client from all available sources
2. organizing and summarizing the data to identify client strengths and weaknesses
3. drawing inferences from the data that help to explain the client and the client's problem
4. attempting to predict the degree of success the client might encounter
5. helping the client to understand the different possibilities and their potential likelihood of success
6. checking later with the client to ascertain what happened.

Williamson also saw career counseling clients as usually presenting one of four types of problems: no choice, uncertain choice, unwise choice, or a discrepancy between interests and aptitudes. The diagnostic step in counseling focuses on identifying which, if any, of these categories apply to the client. (Isaacson & Brown, 2000)

Another trait-factor approach may be to (a) assist the client in increasing their self-understanding, including the probable use of appropriate psychological measures; (b) directing the client to appropriate career information resources; (c) assisting the client in the process of integrating and matching knowledge of self with knowledge of career possibilities in the current world of work; and (d) examining the probable lifestyle and role of work in one's life resulting from a possible career choice.

Counselors must be aware of the following suggested cautions in the use of the trait-factor approach: as follows:

- It focuses on a given point and time rather than viewing the client developmentally.
- It tends to be limited in focus to specific test results and specific information regarding careers.
- It has a tendency to biases regarding women and minority clients.
- It places an undue emphasis on test results.
- The steps of the trait-factor approach are so simple and expeditious that clients often find themselves victims of an "assembly line" approach.

However, the modernization or transition of trait-factor into a person-environment fit, as described by Rounds and Tracey (1990), suggests that the original components of this theory, when integrated with current factual data, can continue to be useful.

> Three central assumptions underlie contemporary person-environment fit theories (Chartrand, 1991; Rounds and Tracey, 1990). First "individuals seek out and create environments . . . that provide and/or allow for behavioral

trait manifestation" (Rounds & Tracey, 1990, p. 198), that is, environments that are consistent or congruent with an individual's characteristics. Second, the degree of fit between person and environment is related to important outcomes, for both the person and the environment, and greater fit leads to better outcomes. Third, the process of person-environment fit is reciprocal: The individual shapes the environment and the environment shapes the individual. (Swanson, 1994, p. 100)

PERSONALITY THEORIES

Personality theories of career decision making emphasize the relationship between the personality traits of the individual and their influences on career choice. This theoretical orientation is most prominently represented by the theoretical presentations of Anne Roe and John Holland. Roe (1956) based much of her theory on Maslow's (1954) suggested hierarchy of basic psychological needs. These needs, in order of their importance from high to lower, were stated as follows:

1. physiological needs
2. safety needs
3. need for belongingness and love
4. need for self-esteem and self-respect
5. need for information
6. need for understanding
7. need for beauty
8. need for self-actualization

This concept suggests that, until the higher needs are met, the need or needs that follow will not be attended to. For example, those needs for maintaining life (needs 1 and 2) must be satisfied before addressing needs for love and respect (needs 3 and 4).

Roe's research led her to believe that the needs structure of the individual would be greatly influenced by early childhood experiences. This needs structure would, in turn, influence occupational categories the individual would select. Roe's extensive research into occupations led her to the development of eight occupational groups (Roe and Lunneborg, 1984).

1. service
2. business contact
3. organization
4. technology
5. outdoor
6. science
7. culture
8. arts and entertainment

These eight occupational categories were then subdivided into six classification levels as determined by degree of responsibility and abilities needed:

1. professional and managerial (independent responsibility)
2. professional and managerial (less independence or important responsibility)

3. semiprofessional and small business
4. skilled
5. semiskilled
6. unskilled

Roe's system of classification and categorization has proved useful as a framework for organizing, in a meaningful way, a multitude of occupations. Her work has had an impact on interest test development and career research.

One of the most prominent career researchers whose theory has a personality base is John Holland. Holland, similar to other personality theorists, also believes that an individual expresses their personality through their career choice. His theory is based on the following assumptions:

- In our culture, most persons can be categorized as one of six types: realistic, investigative, artistic, social, enterprising, or conventional.
- There are six kinds of environments: realistic, investigative, artistic, social, enterprising, and conventional.
- People search for environments that will let them exercise their skills and abilities, express their attitudes and values, and take on agreeable problems and roles.
- A person's behavior is determined by an interaction between his personality and the characteristics of his environment. (Holland, 1973, pp. 2–4)

In 1984 Holland added a fifth assumption: identity. For one's personal identity, it suggests a clear and stable picture of one's interests, abilities, and goals. For organizational identity, the focus is on stability, clarity, and integration of goals.

Holland's theory tends to support the viewpoint that a career is, in effect, a way of life through his emphasis on the interaction between the individual and his or her work situation. Accordingly, Holland identified six personality types analogous to six work environments. Holland's typology of personalities and work environments categorizes people and jobs as noted in Table 4-1.

Holland once believed that people of certain personality types (see Table 4-2) who work in settings where most of their fellow workers possess similar personalities are more likely to be happy, stable, and succeed in their careers. This simple construct labeled *congruence,* however, was not substantiated by studies of complex research design in recent years and has, as a result, been downplayed or demoted by Holland. On the other hand, Holland's hypothesis that individuals tend to prefer or select environments that match their personality types, has considerable empirical evidence which appears to hold for men, women, and minorities (Brown & Lent, 1992)

Holland does not believe people can be categorized in one of only six ways. He suggests, therefore, that most people would have a dominating type plus one or several additional types of lesser influence. For example, an individual could have a dominant conventional personality profile and also substantial characteristics and interests similar to those categorized as realistic and social. He further suggests that some types mesh better with each other and some less so. To reflect this consistency Holland has arranged the six types in a special order around a hexagon, which enables one to note

TABLE 4-1
Holland's personality types and work environments

- **Realistic** The work requires mechanical, manual, technical, or agricultural skills and practical, concrete problem solving. Realistic people tend to be practical, materialistic, and uninvolved with others. They value strength and tangible results and lack interpersonal skills.

- **Investigative** The work requires scientific and mathematical abilities and intellectual problem solving. Investigative people tend to be analytical, introspective, and complex. They value the scientific approach to life and lack social and leadership skills.

- **Artistic** The work requires the use of creative skills in an unsystematized environment. Artistic people are usually imaginative, expressive, sensitive, and nonconforming. They value freedom, ambiguity, and esthetics and lack skills in the orderly manipulation of data.

- **Social** The work requires social, educational, and therapeutic skills. Social people tend to be cooperative, ethical, responsible, understanding, and friendly. They value interpersonal relationships and lack mechanical and scientific skills.

- **Enterprising** The work involves persuasive, manipulative, and leadership skills. Enterprising people tend to be ambitious, extroverted, domineering, and self-confident. They value success in the political and economic fields and lack scientific abilities.

- **Conventional** The work involves the systematic organization and manipulation of data. Conventional people tend to be methodical, conforming, conscientious, unimaginative, and practical. They value organization and achievement in business and lack artistic skills.

Source: From *Career Counseling: A Psychological Approach,* p. 12, by Elizabeth B. Yost and M. Anne Corbishley. Copyright © 1987 by John Wiley & Sons, Inc. Reprinted with permission of John Wiley & Sons, Inc.

those types that are closest together and more likely to be more compatible. This model of relationships is noted in Figure 4-1.

Two psychological inventories were important outcomes of the development of Holland's theories. The currently very popular Self-Directed Search and the earlier Vocational Preference Inventory were designed to measure, in different ways, the individual's personality as related to the world of work. The dominant perspective used in career counseling today is that of person-job matching. This perspective is most popularly represented by Holland's theory.

DEVELOPMENTAL THEORY

The fields of medicine, psychology, and education began, in the early 20th century, to show an increased interest in how individual patterns of growth and development differ with age. A leader at the turn of the century, and one often cited as the founder of the field of child and adolescent development, was G. Stanley Hall, a professor of psychology at Johns Hopkins University and later president of Clark University. He

TABLE 4-2
Holland's personality types

The **Realistic** type likes realistic jobs such as automobile mechanic, aircraft controller, surveyor, farmer, electrician. Has mechanical abilities but may lack social skills. Is described as

Asocial	Inflexible	Practical
Conforming	Materialistic	Self-effacing
Frank	Natural	Thrifty
Genuine	Normal	Uninsightful
Hardheaded	Persistent	Uninvolved

The **Investigative** type likes investigative jobs such as biologist, chemist, physicist, anthropologist, geologist, medical technologist. Has mathematical and scientific ability but often lacks leadership ability. Is described as

Analytical	Independent	Rational
Cautious	Intellectual	Reserved
Complex	Introspective	Retiring
Critical	Pessimistic	Unassuming
Curious	Precise	Unpopular

The **Artistic** type likes artistic jobs such as composer, musician, stage director, writer, interior decorator, actor/actress. Artistic abilities: writing, musical, or artistic, but often lacks clerical skills. Is described as

Complicated	Imaginative	Intuitive
Disorderly	Impractical	Nonconforming
Emotional	Impulsive	Open
Expressive	Independent	Original
Idealistic	Introspective	Sensitive

The **Social** type likes social jobs such as teacher, religious worker, counselor, clinical psychiatric case worker, speech therapist. Has social skills and talents but often lacks mechanical and scientific ability. Is described as

Ascendant	Helpful	Responsible
Cooperative	Idealistic	Sociable
Empathic	Kind	Tactful
Friendly	Patient	Understanding
Generous	Persuasive	Warm

The **Enterprising** type likes enterprising jobs such as salesperson, manager, business executive, television producer, sports promoter, buyer. Has leadership and speaking abilities but often lacks scientific ability. Is described as

Acquisitive	Energetic	Flirtatious
Adventurous	Excitement-	Optimistic
Agreeable	seeking	Self-confident
Ambitious	Exhibitionistic	Sociable
Domineering	Extroverted	Talkative

The **Conventional** type likes conventional jobs such as bookkeeper, stenographer, financial analyst, banker, cost estimator, tax expert. Has clerical and arithmetic ability but often lacks artistic abilities. Is described as

Careful	Inflexible	Persistent
Conforming	Inhibited	Practical
Conscientious	Methodical	Prudish
Defensive	Obedient	Thrifty
Efficient	Orderly	Unimaginative

Source: Adapted and reproduced by special permission of the Publisher, from *The Self-Directed Search Professional Manual,* by John L. Holland, PhD Copyright ©1985, 1987, 1994 by Psychological Assessment Resources, Inc. Further reproduction is prohibited without permission from PAR, Inc. The SDS materials are available from PAR by calling (800) 331-8378.

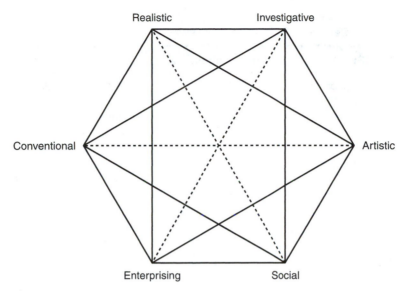

FIGURE 4-1
Holland's model of relationships among personality types and work environments
Source: From John L. Holland, *Making Vocational Choices: A Theory of Vocational Personalities and Work Environments,* 2/e. Published by Allyn and Bacon, Boston, MA. Copyright © 1984 by Pearson Education. Reprinted by permission of the publisher.

believed that development through adolescence was influenced primarily by genetic and biological factors. Hall was fascinated by the stages of development that children demonstrated as they matured. One of his students, Arthur Gesell, founded the Clinic of Child Development at Yale University in 1911. Gesell suggested that growth and development were determined by a fixed timetable of maturation.

As the result of his studies based on observations, Gesell developed time tables that describe the sequence of development through childhood for motor, visual-adaptive, language, and personal-social behavior. Another of Hall's students, Lewis Terman, was prominent in beginning the mental testing movement and believed that intelligence gradually matured and stabilized with adolescence.

Another early major contributor to developmental studies was Jean Piaget, a Swiss biologist. Piaget's viewpoint was that nature and nurture worked together in human development and that each individual is genetically programmed for biological changes that will occur during this development. Among Piaget's other beliefs were that individuals adapt to their environments while organizing their psychological structures, and that assimilation and accommodation are the two processes involved in this adaptation. Assimilation takes place when people understand something that is new and fitted into an already existing system or category. Accommodation occurs when new information causes an existing system to be altered or a new one created. Piaget's stages of cognitive development may be noted in Table 4-3.

Note: Elementary school counselors should have a clear understanding of how children make sense of the world if the counselor is to enter that world and to communicate effectively.

TABLE 4-3
Piaget's stages of cognitive development

Stage	Approximate age	Characteristics
Sensorimotor	0–2 years	Begins to make use of imitation, memory, and thought. Begins to recognize that objects do not cease to exist when they are hidden. Moves from reflex action to goal-directed activity.
Preoperational	2–7 years	Gradual language development and ability to think in symbolic form. Able to think operations through logically in one direction. Has difficulties seeing another person's point of view.
Concrete operational	7–11 years	Able to solve concrete (hands on) problems in logical fashion. Understands laws of conversation and is able to classify and seriate. Understands reversibility.
Formal operational	11–15 years	Able to solve abstract problems in logical fashion. Thinking becomes more scientific. Develops concerns about social issues, identity.

Source: From *Piaget's Theory of Cognitive and Affective Development: Foundations of Constructivism,* 4/e, by Barry J. Wadsworth. Published by Allyn & Bacon, Boston, MA. Copyright © 1990 by Pearson Education. Adapted from *Educational Psychology,* 4/e, by Anita E. Woolfolk. Published by Allyn & Bacon, Boston, MA. Copyright © 1990 by Pearson Education. Reprinted by permission of the publisher.

Another significant contributor to the understanding of child development was Erik Erikson. Erikson emphasized the influence of social environments on the individual's psychological development, which in turn provides a link between personal and social development. Erikson's theory emphasized the emergence of self, the individual's search for identity, and the significance of one's personal relationships in all stages of life. Erikson's theory provides counselors with a useful framework for understanding the dramatic impacts of school and home on the social and personal development of a child. Table 4-4 presents Erikson's stages of personal and social development.

In a procedure analogous to that used by Erikson, Havighurst has developed the concept of developmental tasks. Havighurst, a sociologist as well as an educator, was perhaps more explicit in enumerating his tasks than Erikson. The reader will find that Table 4-5 and the Erikson model or chart are complementary.

As people grow, they face a series of psychosocial crises that shape personality, according to Erik Erikson. Each crisis focuses on a particular aspect of personality and each involves the person's relationship with other people.

TABLE 4-4
Erikson's stages of personal and social development

	Approximate ages	Psychosocial crises	Significant relationships	Psychosocial emphasis
I	Birth–mo.	Trust v. mistrust	Maternal person	To get To give in return
II	18 mo.–3 yr.	Autonomy v. doubt	Parental persons	To hold on To let go
III	3–6 yr.	Initiative v. guilt	Basic family	To make (= going after) To "make like" (= playing)
IV	6–12 yr.	Industry v. inferiority	Neighborhood, school	To make things To make things together
V	12–18 yr.	Identity v. role confusion	Peer groups and models of leadership	To be oneself (or not to be) To share being oneself
VI	Young adulthood	Intimacy v. isolation	Partners in friendship, sex, competition cooperation	To lose and find oneself in another
VII	Middle adulthood	Generativity v. self-absorption	Divided labor and shared household	To take care of
VIII	Late adulthood	Integrity v. despair	"Mankind" "My kind"	To be, through having been To face not being

Source: From *Identity and the Life Cycle* by Erik H. Erikson. Copyright © 1980 by W. W. Norton & Company, Inc. Copyright © 1959 by International Universities Press, Inc. Used by permission of W. W. Norton & Company, Inc.

A knowledge of the way in which the developmental tasks of early childhood blend with those of middle childhood and preadolescence is of especial importance to elementary school counselors, although they must be seen in the *total* context of Havighurst's list of emerging tasks. The challenge to the counselor, naturally, is not to memorize the tasks but to absorb the sense of their meaning and then to interpret and to apply them as a part of his or her growing fund of developmental knowledge.

In the period following World War II, developmental theory began to emerge in the vocational or career area. The first prominent theory of career choice, from a developmental standpoint, was the outgrowth of empirical studies by a team consisting of an economist, a psychiatrist, a sociologist, and a psychologist. Though empirical in nature, these studies were seriously biased inasmuch as their population were upper-middle-class white males. Even so, this team of Ginzberg, Ginsburg, Axelrad, and Herma (1951) concluded that occupational choice is a developmental process that begins at around 11 years of age and concludes shortly after age 17. During this period the individual passes through three distinct stages: (a) fantasy; (b)

TABLE 4-5
Vocational development: A lifelong process

Stages of vocational development	Age
I. Identification with a worker Father, mother, other significant persons. The concept of Working becomes an essential part of the ego-ideal.	5–10
II. Acquiring the basic habits of industry Learning to organize one's time and energy to get a piece of work done. School work, chores. Learning to put work ahead of play in appropriate situations.	10–15
III. Acquiring identity as a worker in the occupational structure Choosing and preparing for an occupation. Getting work experience as a basis for occupational choice and for assurance of economic independence.	15–25
IV. Becoming a productive person Mastering the skills of one's occupation. Moving up the ladder with one's occupation.	25–40
V. Maintaining a productive society Emphasis shifts toward the societal and away from the individual aspect of the worker's role. The individual sees himself as a responsible citizen in a productive society. He pays attention to the civic responsibility attached to his job. The individual is at the peak of his occupational career and has time and energy to adorn it with broader types of activity. He pays attention to inducting younger people into stages III and IV.	40–70
VI. Contemplating a productive and responsible life This person is retired from work or is in the process of withdrawing from the worker's role. He looks back over his work life with satisfaction, sees that a personal social contribution has been made, and is pleased with it. While he may not have achieved all of his ambitions, he accepts life and believes in himself as a productive person.	70+

Source: Reprinted from R. J. Havighurst, *Youth in Exploration and Man Emergent* (1964), p. 216. © American Counseling Association. Reprinted with permission. No further reproduction authorized without written permission of the American Counseling Association.

tentative; and (c) realistic. These stages of the team's original theory are outlined in Table 4-6.

Originally, Ginzberg and his colleagues stated that an individual's progress through the stages was irreversible. Later, Ginzberg (1972) refuted this claim and opted instead to emphasize the importance of early career decision making. In his 1984 review of his theory, he reaffirmed that occupational choice was a lifelong process. He also noted that this (the lifelong process) would necessitate repeated reassessment for determining the best fit between an individual's changing career goals and the world of work.

TABLE 4-6
Stages or periods in the Ginzberg study

Period	Age	Characteristics
Fantasy	Childhood (before age 11)	Purely play orientation in the initial stage; near end of this stage, play becomes work-oriented
Tentative	Early adolescence (ages 11–17)	Transitional process marked by gradual recognition of work requirements; recognition of interests, abilities, work rewards, values, and time perspectives
Realistic	Middle adolescence (ages 17 to young adult)	Integration of capacities and interests; further development of values; specification of occupational choice; crystallization of occupational patterns

Source: From *Career Counseling, Applied Concepts of Life Planning,* 5/e, by Zunker. © 1998. Reprinted with permission of Wadsworth, a division of Thomson Learning: www.thomsonrights.com. Fax 800-730-2215.

Perhaps the most influential of the developmental career researchers and writers was Donald E. Super. His exploration early in his professional career of the research and writings then available on career development theory led to two publications: *Dynamics of Vocational Adjustment* (1942) and his classic book *The Psychology of Careers* (1957). Super also initiated his major research (1951–1952) investigation, known as the Career Pattern Study. This study investigated how adolescents developed their readiness to make appropriate vocational and educational choices. In the development of his theory, Super emphasized the development of vocational maturity.

The major concepts in Super's (1957) early theory development were: (a) vocational stages; (b) vocational tasks to achieve if one is to successfully pass through the stage; (c) implementation of the self-concept in developing a career identity; (d) the development of vocational maturity; and (e) career patterns.

Although these concepts remained central to Super's theory, he broadened and made revisions to his theory over the years 1957 to 1990. One of his prominent contributions during this time was labeled the Life-Career Rainbow (1980), which depicted how various roles emerge and interact across the life span. He identified nine major roles that most individuals play across their lifetime: (a) child, (b) student, (c) leisurite, (d) citizen, (e) worker, (f) spouse, (g) homemaker, (h) parent, and (i) pensioner. In addition to these roles, he identified four environments: as (a) home, (b) the community, (c) the school, and (d) the workplace. The Life-Career Rainbow is illustrated in Figure 4-2.

The concept of role salience was introduced in this rainbow model. This term refers to the combinations of the qualities of role commitment, participation, and knowledge. It is part of the effort to understand the meaning of work within an

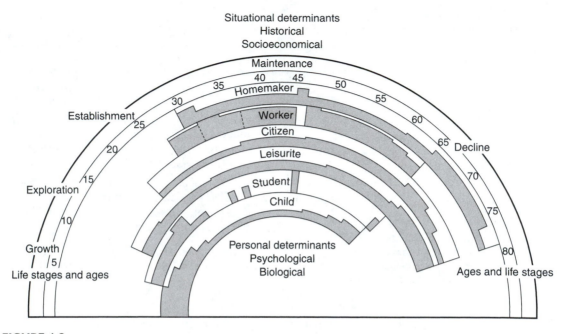

FIGURE 4-2
Super's Life-Career Rainbow: Six life roles in schematic life space
Source: From Brown, *Career Information, Career Counseling, and Career Development,* 8/e. Published by Allyn and Bacon, Boston, MA. Copyright © 2003 by Pearson Education, Inc. Reprinted by permission of the publisher.

individual's life from differing perspectives. In the early 1990s, Super presented his archway model (see Figure 4-3). Super (1990) presented his life span development theory based on the following propositions.

1. People differ in their abilities and personalities, needs, values, interests, traits, and self-concepts.

2. People are qualified, by virtue of these characteristics, each for a number of occupations.

3. Each occupation requires a characteristic pattern of abilities and personality traits—with tolerances wide enough to allow both some variety of occupations for each individual and some variety of individuals in each occupation.

4. Vocational preferences and competencies, the situations in which people live and work, and, hence, their self-concepts, change with time and experience, although self-concepts, as products of social learning, are increasingly stable from late adolescence until late maturity, providing some continuity in choice and adjustment.

5. This process of change may be summed up in a series of life stages (a "maxicycle") characterized as a sequence of growth, exploration, establishment, maintenance, and decline, and these stages may in

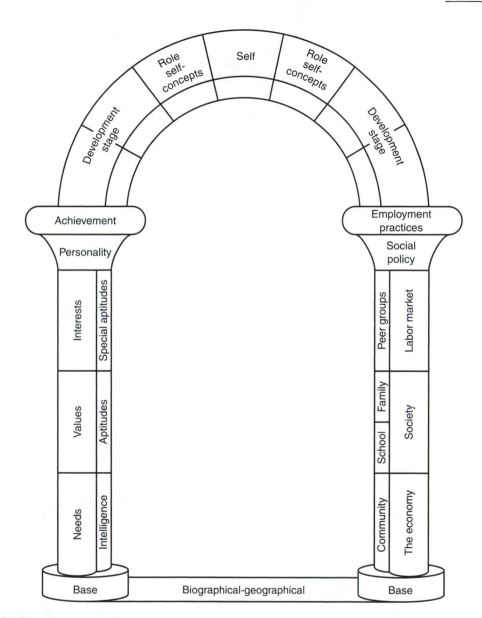

FIGURE 4-3

Segmental model of career development

Source: From "A Life-Span, Life-Space Approach to Career Development" by Donald E. Super in *Career Choice and Development: Applying Contemporary Theories to Practice,* 2/e, by Duane Brown, Linda Brooks & Associates, pp. 206–208. Copyright © 1990, by Jossey-Bass, Inc., Publishers. Reprinted by permission.

turn be subdivided into (a) the fantasy, tentative, and realistic stage. A small (mini) cycle takes place in transitions from one stage to the next or each time an individual is destabilized by a reduction in force, changes in type of personnel needs, illness or injury, or other socio-economic or personal events. Such unstable or multiple-trial careers involve new growth, reexploration, and reestablishment (recycling).

6. The nature of the career pattern—that is, the occupational level attained and the sequence, frequency, and duration of trial and stable jobs—is determined by the individual's parental socioeconomic level, mental ability, education, skills, personality characteristics (needs, values, interests, traits, and self-concepts), and career maturity and by the opportunities to which he or she is exposed.

7. Success in coping with the demands of the environment and of the organism in that context at any given life-career stage depends on the readiness of the individual to cope with these demands (that is, on his or her career maturity).

8. Career maturity is a hypothetical construct. Its operational definition is perhaps as difficult to formulate as is that of intelligence, but its history is much briefer and its achievements even less definite.

9. Development through the life stages can be guided partly by facilitating the maturing of abilities and interests and partly by aiding in reality testing and in the development of self-concepts.

10. The process of career development is essentially that of developing and implementing occupational self-concepts. It is a synthesizing and compromising process in which the self-concept is a product of the interaction of inherited aptitudes, physical makeup, opportunity to observe and play various roles, and evaluations of the extent to which the results of role playing meet the approval of superiors and fellows (interactive learning).

11. The process of synthesis of or compromise between individual and social factors, between self-concepts and reality, is one of role playing and of learning from feedback, whether the role is played in fantasy, in the counseling interview, or in such real-life activities as classes, clubs, part-time work, and entry jobs.

12. Work satisfactions and life satisfactions depend on the extent to which the individual finds adequate outlets for abilities, needs, values, interests, personality traits, and self-concepts. They depend on establishment in a type of work, a work situation, and a way of life in which one can play the kind of role that growth and exploratory experiences have led one to consider congenial and appropriate.

13. The degree of satisfaction people attain from work is proportional to the degree to which they have been able to implement self-concepts.

14. Work and occupation provide a focus for personality organization for most men and women, although for some persons this focus is peripheral, incidental, or even nonexistent. Then other foci, such as

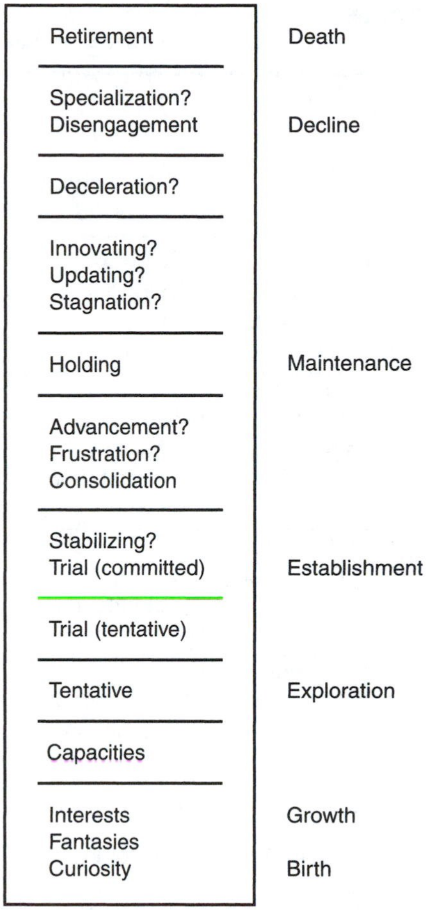

Retirement	Death
Specialization? Disengagement	Decline
Deceleration?	
Innovating? Updating? Stagnation?	
Holding	Maintenance
Advancement? Frustration? Consolidation	
Stabilizing? Trial (committed)	Establishment
Trial (tentative)	
Tentative	Exploration
Capacities	
Interests Fantasies Curiosity	Growth Birth

FIGURE 4-4
Ladder model of life-career stages, developmental tasks, and behaviors

Source: From "A Life-Span, Life-Space Approach to Career Development" by Donald E. Super in *Career Choice and Development: Applying Contemporary Theories to Practice,* 2/e, by Duane Brown, Linda Brooks & Associates, p. 214. Copyright © 1990 by Jossey-Bass, Inc., Publishers. Reprinted by permission.

leisure activities and homemaking, may be central. (Social traditions, such as gender-role stereotyping and modeling, racial and ethnic biases, and the opportunity structure, as well as individual differences, are important determinants of preferences for such roles as worker, student, leisurite, homemaker, and citizen.) (pp. 206–208)[1]

Super's ladder model (see Figure 4-4) is another way of depicting his classical sequence of life stages, their characteristic tasks, and the ages at which they typically occur.

Finally, Table 4-7 depicts Super's idea of the cycling and recycling of the developmental tasks through the life span. This figure stems from the ladder and is designed to show how one cycles and recycles through the life stages and how one faces essentially the same developmental tasks in different forms as one moves across one's life span.

[1] Reprinted from "A Life-Span, Life-Space Approach to Career Development" by Donald E. Super in *Career Choice and Development: Applying Contemporary Theories to Practice,* 2/e, by Duane Brown, Linda Brooks & Associates, pp. 206–208. Copyright © 1990 by Jossey-Bass, Inc., Publishers. Reprinted by permission.

TABLE 4-7
Cycling and recycling of developmental tasks throughout the life span

Life stage	Age: Adolescence 14–25	Age: Early adulthood 25–45	Age: Middle adulthood 45–65	Age: Late adulthood 65 and over
Decline Developmental tasks at each age	Giving less time to hobbies	Reducing sports participation	Focusing on essentials	Reducing working hours
Maintenance Tasks at each age	Verifying current occupational choice	Making occupational position secure	Holding one's own against competition	Keeping what one enjoys
Establishment Tasks at each age	Getting started in a chosen field	Settling down in a suitable position	Developing new skills	Doing things one has wanted to do
Exploration Tasks at each age	Learning more about more opportunities	Finding desired opportunity	Identifying new tasks to work on	Finding a good retirement place
Growth Tasks at each age	Developing a realistic self-concept	Learning to relate to others	Accepting one's own limitations	Developing and valuing nonoccupational roles

Source: From "A Life-Span, Life-Space Approach to Career Development" by Donald E. Super, Mark L. Savickas, & Charles M. Super in *Career Choice and Development,* 3/e, by Duane Brown, Linda Brooks & Associates, p. 136. Copyright © 1996 by Jossey-Bass, Inc., Publishers. Reprinted by permission.

SOCIAL-LEARNING THEORY

Social learning theory is an outgrowth of efforts by John Krumboltz (1979, 1990) and his associates to adapt Bandura's behavioral theory to career decision-making. Social-learning theory suggests that four categories of factors are influential in people's career development and decision-making as follows:

1. **genetic endowment and special abilities** These include certain inherited characteristics such as race and physical characteristics. These and other inherited traits may set limits or offer opportunities that influence career choices.

2. **environmental conditions and events**   Environmental influences include those provided by nature (such as natural resources that attract industries) and those developed by humankind (i.e., training programs, social policies, and neighborhood influences).
3. **learning experiences**   Two kinds of learning experiences are identified. These are (a) the instrumental, whereby the individual behaves in a certain way as the outgrowth of an experience and results in certain consequences; and (b) associate learning experiences, which are those that result from the pairing of two events in time or location such as reading career information and attending a job fair.
4. **task approach skills**   Task approach skills represent how an individual may approach a task such as setting goals, examining alternatives, or gathering career information.

These four influences may, in turn, lead to major outcomes such as:

• Self-observation generalizations or making observations about their ability to perform specific tasks based on prior information and experiences.
• World view generalizations are those derived by the individual from the world in which they live and the people who share that world.
• Task approach skills represent an influence on and outcome of one's career development and the application of what they have learned to career decision-making.
• Entry behaviors, those actions such as choosing a major or applying for a job, and similar behaviors result in consequences that affect future behaviors.

WORK ADJUSTMENT THEORY

Work adjustment theory suggests that positive career development and decision-making is an outgrowth of a "person-environment" (P-E) fit. Two major complimentary sets of constructs describe this P-E relationship between the work personality and the work environment. The degree to which this decision-making and hence work-adjustment, is satisfactory is indicated by the length of time in the career. Satisfaction and satisfactoriness are key predictors of this adjustment. *Satisfaction* is how satisfied the individual is with what he or she does while *satisfactoriness* refers to how satisfied the employer is with the employee's job performance. In other words, work adjustment is dependent on reciprocity (the worker likes his job—the employer likes the worker). The four basic psychological concepts on which the theory is founded include (a) person-environment fit, (b) satisfaction, (c) ability as a predictor of potential job performance, and (d) reinforcement value as reflected by the reinforcer's importance or power in reinforcing the worker's behavior.

Rene Davis and Lloyd Lofquist have been prominent in the development and refinement of this theory. They defined work adjustment as a "continuous and dynamic process by which a worker seeks to achieve and maintain correspondence with a work environment" (1984, p. 237). In the application of this theory, ability and value assessment of the individual are measured and contrasted with abilities and values needed in various careers. Work adjustment theory may also be applied to determine the types of on-the-job adjustment problems the individual may have. For example, skills or abilities may not be adequate for the job or the personal values and psychological needs of the worker may not be met by the work environment.

PSYCHODYNAMIC THEORY

Psychodynamic theory, as the label would imply, is the application of Freud's classic theory to the world of work. Psychoanalytical approaches have primarily treated work as a method of satisfying impulses and providing outlets for subliminal wishes (Osipow, 1983). A notable application of Freudian concepts to career development and decision-making has resulted from the research and writings of E. S. Bordin and his various associates. Bordin (1984) suggested the need to examine job performance as a way of life. He also proposed that the extent to which a person succeeds in fusing work and play is an important determinant of the degree to which career choice is determined and expressed by personality.

OTHER THEORIES

SOCIOLOGICAL THEORIES

Chance Theory   Perhaps the most popular of the sociological views of careers is one that suggests that chance—more than deliberate planning or steady progress—is a chief occupational determinant. Chance factors in career choices would include acting on impulse, sudden emotional reactions, and unexpected experiences and/or opportunities. Consider, for example, the individual who, on an apparent impulse, walks out of a good management job in a city to buy and work on a farm in a rural area. If we need current examples of the chance theory, newspapers and television reports constantly remind us of individuals who seem to be in the right place at the right time and apparently, for no other reason, end up in an unanticipated career.

A recent publication, *Luck is No Accident,* by John D. Krumboltz and A. S. Levin (2004), points out that chance occurrences more often are the determinants of life decisions, including career choices, than the careful planning we do. The authors also encourage readers to anticipate and take advantage of the unexpected. Your authors also noted in their *Introduction to Counseling and Guidance* (6th ed.) that "counselors must assist clients to recognize that unforeseen or chance factors may, on occasion, alter career planning" (2003, p. 321).

As we recognize the fact that change and chance will be increasingly affected by the rapidity of technological and global developments in the upcoming generations of the 21st century, we, as career counselors, must assist our clients at all levels to make the most of the inevitable array of opportunities that will confront them. In this regard, then, we can provide assistance and guidance to:

- Prepare clients for the possibility of chance and change.
- Help clients to be flexible and receptive to good opportunities.
- Help clients recognize that education increases options and opportunities.

- Emphasize the importance of enjoying what one does, where one does it, and with whom one does it.
- Seek and ye shall find, **but,** if you can't find it—create it.

Chance Theory

An actual example is the case of Lewis, currently a successful and highly-respected general manager of a large resort hotel. In the summer of his freshmen year in college, Lewis, a mathematics major, decided to follow his girlfriend, who was moving to a new community over 500 miles away.

Upon his arrival in this city, he went seeking summer employment and was hired on as a waiter and bus boy at a local hotel. During this temporary summer employment, Lewis volunteered his assistance to the restaurant and beverage manager who was finding the task of bookkeeping associated with his job overly demanding. By the conclusion of the summer, Lewis had proven his value in this role and was asked to remain as a regular employee assisting the foods and beverage manager. Lewis decided to do so "temporarily" because his girlfriend was still residing there. Lewis continued to experience success in this position and when the restaurant and beverage manager was advanced to a hotel management position, Lewis was appointed as his replacement. Two girlfriends later Lewis was thriving in his new position, found that he liked hotel work, and when he was offered the opportunity to become an assistant manager at another hotel he readily accepted. In a comparatively short period of time, Lewis continued his advance through the ranks of hotel management to his present position as a general manager of a large, prestigious resort hotel. He is also happily married!

ECONOMIC THEORIES

Economic theories suggest the importance that economic factors play in an individual's career choice. Such factors would include job availability versus number of qualified workers available, monetary awards associated with a particular job or career, benefits and job security, and, for some workers, retirement plans.

Prominent among the economic theories is *decision-making theory*. This theory suggests that careers are selected from alternatives on the basis of which choice promises to be the most rewarding and of value to the individual (although not necessarily in just a monetary sense).

VALUES THEORY

In the latter decades of the 20th century, the role of values in lifestyles and life's decisions, including career choices, were given considerable attention. Values education courses and values clarification workshops were becoming popular, and the impact of values in career choice and planning were increasingly researched. In 1996 Duane Brown developed and published a value-based theory of career development, which recognizes that individuals act and make decisions that are influenced by their value orientation. For example, the rules by which societies live tend to be value-based and these in turn become rules that many individuals use to judge their own behaviors. Values are also influential in rationalizing how we behave and the goals we establish for our lives.

Brown (2003) also has suggested that the interaction between inherited traits and experiences are instrumental and central in the individual's development. Brown (2003) also suggested that values are prioritized according to their importance as guidelines to behavior in the individual's environment. Seven basic propositions of this theory were stated as follows:

1. Highly prioritized work values are the most important determinants of career choice for people who value individualism (i.e., the individual is the most important unit) if their work values are crystallized and prioritized. Such individuals feel unconstrained to act on their work values; at least one occupational option is available that will satisfy the values held; values-based information about occupational options is available; the difficulty level of implementing the options is approximately the same; and the financial resources available are sufficient to support the implementation of the preferred option.

    a. Factors that limit the number of occupational options considered for people who value individualism are low SES [socio-economic status], minority status, mental health problems, physical disabilities, gender (Gottfredson, 1996), low scholastic aptitude, perception that they will be discriminated against in the occupation, and lack of values-based information. Women, minorities, people from lower SES levels, and people with mental or physical limitations who value individualism choose occupations consistent with their work values, but they are likely to choose from a more restricted range of occupations than white European American males.

    b. Self-efficacy becomes a constraining factor in the occupational decision-making process of individuals who value individualism when the options being considered require widely divergent skills and abilities.

2. Individuals who hold collective social values and come from families and/or groups who hold the same social values either defer to the wishes of the group or family members or are heavily influenced by them in the occupational decision-making process. The result is that the occupations chosen correlate less with the individual's work values than is the case with individuals who value individualism and make their own occupational choices.

    a. Gender is a major factor in the occupations entered by individuals who value collectivism because of decision makers' sex-stereotyped perceptions of occupations. The result is that occupational choices are more likely to be stereotypically male or female. Women who value collectivism enter a more restricted range of occupations than men who value collectivism.

    b. Perceptions that discrimination may occur if an occupation is chosen is a deterrent to choosing that occupation by decision makers who value collectivism.

    c. Perceptions regarding resources available to implement an occupational choice are a major limiting factor in the occupational decision-making process of individuals who value collectivism.

   d. The outcome of the occupational decision-making process for people who value collectivism is less influenced by the availability of the values-based occupational information than it is by the work values of their family or group.

3.   When taken individually, cultural values regarding activity (doing, being, being-in-becoming) do not constrain the occupational decision-making process. People who value individualism and have both a future/past-future time value and a doing/activity value are more likely to make decisions at important transition points such as graduation from high school and act on those choices than people who value either collectivism or individualism and being or being-in-becoming.

4.   Because of differing values systems, males and females and people from differing cultural groups enter occupations at varying rates.

5.   The process of choosing an occupation value involves a series of "estimates." These include estimates of (a) one's abilities and values, (b) the skills and abilities required to be successful in an occupation, and (c) the work values that the occupational alternatives being considered satisfy. For people who value individualism, the ability to make accurate estimates is a critical factor in their occupational successes and satisfaction. For individuals who value collateral, estimates made by the decision makers are the key factors in their occupational success and satisfaction.

   a. Individuals who value individualism and who come from backgrounds where little emphasis is placed on feedback about individual strengths, weaknesses, and personal traits and who make their own occupational decisions make more errors in the process as defined by mismatches between their values and those values satisfied by the job. The result is lowered job satisfaction, lower levels of success, and shorter job tenure. In the case of people who value collateral; satisfaction, success, and tenure are based on the ability of the decision maker to make their estimates.

6.   Occupational success is related to job-related skills acquired in formal and informal educational settings, job-related aptitudes and skills, SES, participation in the work role, and the extent to which discrimination is experienced regardless of which social relationship value is held.

   a. Because success in the occupational role requires an awareness of future events and the ability to accommodate the dynamic changes that occur in the workplace, success in the occupational role is related to time and activity values, with individuals with future or past/future values paired with doing/activity values being the most successful.

7. Occupational tenure is partially the result of the match between the cultural and work values of the worker, supervisors, and colleagues. (Brown, 2003, 51–53)[2]

In 2002 Brown examined the role of values in a cultural context and suggested that the process of occupational choice-making by minorities has, for the most part, been unaddressed and that a theory seeking to explain both the occupational choice-making and the adaptation process for all groups was needed. It was further proposed that culture and work values were primary factors in career choices and the outcomes of such choices. The need for research focusing on the role of values in general, and cultural values in particular, as they impact the career decision-making process was also highlighted by Brown.

THEORY OF CIRCUMSCRIPTION AND COMPROMISE

Gottfredson, in 1996, proposed a theory that focused on the development of aspirations based on four assumptions:

1. Career choice is a developmental process beginning in childhood.
2. Occupational aspirations reflect people's efforts to implement their self-concepts.
3. Satisfaction with career choice depends on how well that choice fits the self-concept. (p. 181)
4. People hold *images of occupations* which influence them in selecting occupations. (p. 184)

Gottfredson believed that a major influence on the choice of a career is guided by the desire to establish a social identity based on the career. One's first career choice, however, may be a compromise when an individual passes over his or her preferred choices to choose a career that is more readily available.

CONVERGENT THEORY

In recent years, increasing attention has been given to examining how the differing career theories might converge or could be made to bridge with each other. In the Savickas and Lent (1994) publication *Convergence in Career Development Theories*, five prominent career theorists representing the theories of development (Super), psychodynamic (Bordin), personality (Holland), social learning (Krumboltz), and work adjustment (Davis) examined how their theories might converge with others. This publication was the outgrowth of a project on convergence stimulated by a series of articles written on the occasion of the 20th anniversary of the *Journal of Vocational Development* in 1990. The initial thrust toward exploration of convergence of theories appears to have been stimulated by a career convergence project with contributions from prominent theorists (John Krumboltz, Rene Davis, John Holland, Edward Bordin, and Donald Super). While no appreciable progress was reported on convergence, useful distinctions among the major theories were reaffirmed and theoretical deficiencies and features that need renovation were noted.

Samuel Osipow and Donald Super were early leaders in encouraging the exploration of convergence theories, which led to the career convergence project and a conference on the topic attended by your authors at The Ohio State University in the spring of 1994.

THEORIES OF COUNSELING AND CAREER DEVELOPMENT

While traditional counseling theories may also provide career-related insights, counseling theories are in no way competitive or at odds with popular career theories. In fact, quite to the contrary, counseling theories and career theories generally complement each other. The counselor will utilize his or her preferred counseling theory as the broad framework within which the career client is counseled. Within this context the counselor will apply the career theory of choice for responding to the career needs of the client. Additionally, both counseling theories and career theories are frequently related to subsets of personality theories. Therefore, as noted by Sharf (1992) "since personality, counseling, and career development theory are highly interrelated, it is natural that counselors who prefer a certain personality theory or theory of counseling are likely to be drawn to a similar career development theory" (p. 4). Finally, some of the earlier theories placed an emphasis on initial career decision-making rather than a life span and adjustment approach.

REVIEW AND IMPLICATIONS

A review of the previously discussed major theories would note that the trait-factor approach suggests the importance of the individual's abilities and interest in career choice. Personality theories suggest a relationship between career decisions and personality traits such as self-concept. Developmental theories emphasize the importance of human development and maturity in readiness and reality in career decision-making. Social learning theory recognizes the influences of heredity, special abilities, environment, learning experiences, and task approach skills. Work adjustment theory underscores the importance of the person-environment fit. Psychodynamic career theory views work as an outlet for the subliminal wishes of the individual. The most prominent sociological theory emphasizes the role that chance plays in the career decisions of individuals. Economic theories underscore the importance of economic factors in career choices. Values theory believes that the individual's values and the values of their society are important in establishing career goals.

These theories can lead us to conclude that career development is a process leading to a decision; there are stages through which one passes en route to career maturity and decision-making; individuals should accomplish certain tasks at each stage of their development; and personality traits and values are related to career decision making. Additionally, there are environmental constraints that may limit or expand the careers to which one aspires. Finally, the individual's best laid plans may be altered by chance factors.

Gibson and Mitchell (2003) indicate that:

> The characteristics of these theories have certain implications for counseling clients with career development or adjustment needs:
>
> - Counselors must understand the process and characteristics of human development, including readiness to learn, and successfully complete particular tasks at certain developmental stages.
> - Counselors must understand the basic human needs as well as the special needs of persons and their relationship to career development and decision-making.
> - Counselors must be able to assess and interpret individual traits and characteristics and to apply these assessments to a variety of counselee career-related needs.
> - Counselors must assist clients to recognize that unforeseen or chance factors may, on occasion, alter career planning.
> - Counselors must recognize that the rapid changes in the way people work and live in this high-tech era require a constant examination and updating of the theory and research we use as a basis for our career counseling efforts (pp. 320–321)[4]

OTHER INFLUENCES ON CAREER DEVELOPMENT

Although the previous sections of this chapter have discussed theories of career development that counselors may use to guide them when providing career assistance to clients, they must also recognize that clients are likely to bring a reservoir of influences from outside the counseling environment that have influenced and will probably continue to influence their planning and decision-making. While many of these influences are accounted for in one or more of the major theories, we would especially note the following:

- **environmental influences and limitations** Many clients will be influenced by careers, that are prominent or promising, which they witness in their environment. They also may be limited in careers that they consider due to environmental restrictions. In some instances, they will not even be aware of some careers that exist in environments with which they are not familiar.

---

[4] *Gibson, Robert L., & Mitchell, Marianne H.*, Introduction to Counseling and Guidance, 6/e, © 2003. *Reprinted by permission of Pearson Education, Inc., Upper Saddle River, NJ.*

- **experience influences**   Some clients will be influenced by career-related experiences. For example, many highly-successful high school athletes will set their career sites—usually unrealistically—on professional careers in the sport in which they excel. Youthful individuals who have worked part time in a medical setting, a business setting, or a service setting may explore careers in these respective areas.
- **significant individuals**   Clients are often influenced in their choice of career by individuals who have been role models to them or have been positive influences in other ways. Parents and teachers are common examples of individuals who significantly influence the career planning of others.
- **peer pressures**   We often see examples of individuals making their career choice based on the fact that the majority of their peers are entering a given field. This seems to be particularly true in environments where career choices are somewhat limited for youth graduating from high school or are limited by the higher education options available to them. For example, if everyone is going to work at Wallace Electronics or if everyone is planning to enter Georgia Tech this fall.
- **financial limitations**   Financial limitations are obvious elements that may influence career choice at the post secondary school level. If one's financial capacities are limited and there are no institutions of higher education within commuting distance, one may feel compelled to make a career choice that does not require further education. At another level, the expenses of acquiring degrees in medicine or law, or other degrees, serve as detriments to many who might wish to pursue careers in these areas.
- **self-awareness**   As they mature, many individuals, become increasingly aware of their capabilities and areas of interest. For example, the high school actress realizes that being successful in high school productions does not automatically lead to stardom, especially when she was turned down for roles in her college productions. She may also discover that acting is not the only area that appeals to her as a career. Therefore, she begins to explore other options, perhaps in fields such as public relations or sales.

In recent years, several national surveys have shown a discrepancy between actual career choice and the "preferred," ideal career. In an unscientific ministudy, your authors asked 103 Indiana University graduate students enrolled in counseling courses what career they would prefer to be in—assuming they had the talent to be successful in that career. The results were as follows.

The first choice in this study was a career as an actor or actress (this is consistent with national surveys.) The second choice represented a variety of medical specialties. Not surprisingly, the professional athlete was the third choice among our population. A novelist or a writer, and business and industrial tycoon rounded out the top five.

As may be noted, only a small percentage (5.06%) actually indicated that counseling was their ideal choice. All of the sample felt that they not only could succeed as counselors, but would enjoy a career in this area. This and similar studies simply indicate that—although many individuals do not even consider pursuing their so-called "ideal" career—they can find satisfaction and achievement in thoughtful alternatives.

CASE STUDIES

Shelley

Shelley grew up in a very small, rural community in the coastal South where she attended elementary and secondary school (all in the same building). In secondary school, she participated in a wide range of activities—from Honor's Society to cheerleading. She also was the coeditor of the school yearbook. One of her significant role models was an older cousin who consistently broke barriers in male-dominated careers (e.g., she was the first female school bus driver in her state and later was employed at the U.S. Bureau of Hearings and Appeals). Following high school graduation Shelley continued her enrollment in small institutions, by attending a small teacher education and liberal arts college near her hometown, to become an elementary school teacher. Although there was no career assistance program in the college, Shelley became very interested in human behavior, particularly that of young children. Her interest had become further stimulated by undergraduate psychology courses in which she was enrolled.

As she began her elementary school teaching career, her interest in the behavior of children became even more intense, motivating her to enter a counselor education program at the master's degree level. Shortly after receiving her master's degree in counseling, she was appointed to a position as a school counselor. Her resourceful and innovative programs soon attracted wide attention, resulting in her being named school counselor of the year in her state, which in turn resulted in her being invited to participate in state and national professional associations and conferences. At one of these presentations, she was discovered by faculty from a major Midwest university and was offered a scholarship in their counselor education program, which she promptly accepted. Following a highly successful experience as a doctoral student, Shelley found employment in a series of high-profile human

services positions, where high achievement still characterizes her life.

Edith

Edith is an only child, raised in a single-parent (mother) home, in a small Appalachian community. She has never known her father who, since her early childhood, has spent his life in a state penitentiary, and her mother is employed as a sales clerk in a small local business. Despite what some might label "disadvantages," Edith grew up as a happy, energetic child and young woman. In her elementary school years she did not recall any career preferences, although she did, as a very young child, enjoy playing the role of a nurse or doctor and later, in the upper elementary grades, she was one of three upper grade students labeled "nurse assistants" to the school nurse on the occasion of her weekly visit to the school.

In high school Edith was a popular, active student. She also secured steady part-time employment as a clerical worker in a business office in the community's only "big" business (a small manufacturing corporation employing 62 workers). Her hobbies in high school were reading, dancing, and club activities. In discussions with her secondary school counselor, Edith indicated that, while she would like to go to college, she feels that it is unlikely that she will have the financial resources necessary to pay the tuition. The school counselor noted that Edith has indicated that her most enjoyable subjects were math and science, and despite the fact that she has a part-time clerical job, the subjects she has enjoyed the least were shorthand and typing. She says these are not challenging subjects. Edith's class rank is second out of 138 students and when the counselor pointed out that she took the college preparatory program, Edith simply replied that this would be the most helpful for her in whatever she did after high school. The counselor noted that the various occupational interest inventories Edith completed showed that she consistently scored highest in the sciences and medical services (nursing). The counselor decided that he would secure several teachers' recommendations in hopes of getting some scholarship help for Edith to attend college. Typical of these recommendations are the following from the school's assistant principal and the head of the school's mathematics department: "The best student we have . . . what more can I say?" "One of the most outstanding students in the 18 years I have been employed at this high school—and not just in academic ability. She is simply outstanding in everything she undertakes and also is a delightful young adolescent."

With this information and her academic background the school counselor was able to secure for Edith a college scholarship, which she enthusiastically accepted. She enrolled in the university's nursing program, from which she graduated as an honor student and where she continued to be a popular and active student. Following graduation she was employed as a nurse in a nearby, medium-sized hospital. In her fourth year in this position, she was cited as the "distinguished nurse of the year" by the hospital. Six years later, she became the head of the nursing staff and was also employed as a part-time instructor in the nurses' training program at a nearby university.

Emory (alias "Tinker")

Tinker showed an interest in mechanical things from an early age. According to his parents, he loved to take his toys apart and then try to put them back together. Later, in his junior high school years, he began mowing the neighbors' yards for spending money. He also seemed to enjoy working on everyone's lawn mower and other small appliances. When Tinker entered high school he enrolled in the college preparation program because, as he put it, "everyone else was." His grades through high school were adequate but not outstanding. He enrolled in elective auto mechanics courses and did very well. His counselor also indicated that, on the Kuder Vocational Preference Inventory, his highest score was in the mechanical area. After graduating from high school his parents were prepared to send him to college, but Tinker delayed saying he wanted to get a little serious work experience first. He began working full-time as a service station attendant and auto mechanic at his uncle's service station. His reputation seemed to spread in the geographic area served by the station. After four years working for his uncle he was hired as a mechanic for the largest automobile dealership in the community. Seven years later he was promoted to head of the service area of the agency.

SUMMARY

Career theories serve as a basis for professional counselors assisting clients in their career planning and decision-making. The empirical research supporting these theories will enable counselors and their clients to make deductions about what will happen in different situations and under specified conditions. Although traditional theories of career development have sometimes been criticized for generally not being up-to-date or inclusive of differing populations, they can still, with some cautions, provide valuable and proven guidelines for career counseling. These traditional theories include trait-factor, personality, development, social learning, economics, and values, as well as recent attempts at a convergent theory. The preceding section discussed other practical considerations that influence one's career decision making.

Because the starting point in providing career assistance to clients is usually an assessment of their abilities, interests, and background, Chapter 5 discusses standardized and nonstandardized assessment techniques as they relate to career counseling.

DISCUSSION QUESTIONS

1. Discuss the different careers you considered (from elementary school to present) and why you considered them.
2. What were the significant influences on your current decision to prepare for a career as a counselor?
3. What theory of career development seems most appropriate to your own personal experience?
4. Do you anticipate favoring any particular career development theory when providing career counseling for your clients?
5. Will the career theories developed in the 20th century be relevant in the 21st century? Why or why not?

CLASS ACTIVITIES

1. Interview a practicing counselor in a career-oriented setting (such as a university career center, an employment office, an EAP (employee assistance program), regarding his or her theoretical orientation and how they arrived at their preference (if any).
2. Have each member of the class identify the significant influences on their career planning and eventual decision making. In small groups, share these influences with other members and discuss the career choice theory that seems most appropriate to each individual's experiences.
3. Have each class member interview three different individuals about the significant influences on their career choice. Gather the results and discuss them with the class.
4. Using stick figures, draw a career map using newsprint and felt tip pens. With simple drawings, go from lower left to upper right to depict the significant events in your career development experiences.
5. Choose a historically significant individual, past or present, and determine the major influences on his or her career choice by perusing his or her biography or autobiography. Report to class, and discuss your findings with the class.

READINGS OF INTEREST

Beale, A. V. (2001). Emerging career development theories: A test for school counselors. *Professional School Counseling, 5*(1), 1–5.

Brown, D. (2002). The role of work and cultural values in occupational choice, satisfaction, and success: A theoretical statement. *Journal of Counseling and Development, 80*(1), 48–56.

Flores, L. Y., Scott, A. B., Wang, Y. W., Yakushko, O., McCloskey, C. M., Spencer, K. G., et al. (2003). Practice and research in career counseling and development. 2002. *The Career Development Quarterly, 52*(2), 98–131.

Gerber, S. (2001). Where has our theory gone? Learning theory and intentional intervention. *Journal of Counseling & Development, 79*(3), 282–291.

Krumboltz, J. D., & Levin, A. S. (2004). *Luck is no accident: Making the most of happenstance in your life and career.* Atascadero, CA: Impact Publishers.

Lapan, R. T., Gysbers, N. C., & Petroski, G. F. (2001). Helping seventh graders be safe and successful: A statewide study of the impact of comprehensive guidance and counseling programs. *Journal of Counseling and Development, 79*(3), 320–330.

Schultheiss, D. E. P. (2003). A relational approach to career counseling: Theoretical integration and practical application. *Journal of Counseling and Development, 81*(3), 301–310.

Weinrach, S. G., Ellis, A., MacLaren, C., DiGiuseppe, R., Vernon, A., Wolfe, J., et al. (2001). Rational Emotive Behavior Therapy successes and failures: Eight personal perspectives. *Journal of Counseling and Development, 79*(3), 259–268.

Chapter 5

Assessment for Career Planning

Historically, assessment has played an important role in the career counseling process. With the rapid changes in our society, it becomes even more critical that counselors learn about career assessments and the diverse instruments that can be used with various clients.

Sue Whiston, PhD
Professor of Education
Indiana University

OBJECTIVES

To provide readers with an understanding of:

1. The important role of assessment in career planning
2. Career assessment techniques and their appropriate utilization for an individual's career planning

INTRODUCTION

The objectives of this chapter are to acquaint you with (a) the role of assessment and (b) the methods of assessment for career counseling. We begin by noting, again, the historical relationship between assessment and career counseling and guidance, beginning with the early years of the counseling and guidance movement in the United States. In these years, Frank Parsons in his early (1908) organization of the Boston Vocational Bureau and in his landmark publication *Choosing a Vocation* (1909) highlighted the role of assessment in career planning and decision-making. Even today, few would find fault with the role of assessment as stated in his three factors necessary for a wise choice of a vocation:

> (1) a clear understanding of yourself, your aptitudes, abilities, interests, ambitions, resources, limitations, and other causes; (2) a knowledge of the requirements and conditions of success, advantages and disadvantages, compensation, opportunities, and prospects in different lines of work; and (3) true reasoning on the relations of these two groups of fact. (Parsons, 1909, p. 5)

Parsons also emphasized the important role of the client in his or her own self-assessment. In fact, he suggested an extensive self-study by answering questions on a "schedule of personal data." The counselor then fills in the details by reading between the lines. Parsons states that this approach will give clues to possible flaws such as defective verbal memory and slow auditory reactions. Such a client would make a poor stenographer, or as he puts it "would have difficulty in becoming an expert stenographer" (p. 7). The inventory suggested by Parsons includes such items as: "How far can you walk? Habits as to smoking? Drinking? Use of drugs? Other forms of dissipation? How often do you bathe" (p. 7)?

An unusual feature of the intake interview were observations that Parsons suggests regarding the client's physical appearance:

> While I am questioning the applicant about his probable health, education, reading, experience, et cetera, I carefully observe the shape of his head, the relative development above, before, and behind the ears, his features and expression, color, vivacity, voice, manner, pose, general air of vitality, enthusiasm, et cetera.
>
> If the applicant's head is largely developed behind the ears, with big neck, low forehead, and small upper head, he is probably of an animal type, and if the other symptoms coincide, he should be dealt with on that basis." (Parsons, 1909, p. 7)

Parsons advises getting the client to see himself or herself exactly as others do, and giving the client recommendations about methods that can be used for self-improvement. For example, he may suggest reading suitable books to develop analytical power or using biographies of famous people and finding commonalities with the client in biographic details as a form of inspiration (Gibson & Mitchell, 2003, p. 5).

In addition to Parsons' pioneering guidelines, the early trait-factor theoretical approach to career counseling placed a heavy emphases, as noted in Chapter 4, on the importance of assessment in career planning and decision making.

The role of assessment in career counseling and guidance can be noted within the framework of certain assumptions:

1. Virtually everyone will eventually enter the world of work.
2. Career development always precedes career entry and is a natural part of human growth and development.
3. The individual's career development and potential may be measured by assessment techniques.
4. This career development is now recognized as a lifelong process requiring, for most workers, multiple career decisions across the life span.
5. Career decisions are most satisfying and productive when consistent with one's abilities, interests, self-concept, environmental preferences, values, and the role of work in one's life.
6. Assessment techniques can assist individuals in making appropriate career decisions.
7. Multiple methods, including assessment techniques, are available to maximize one's career development.

GOALS FOR CAREER ASSESSMENT

The goals of career assessment may also be viewed from several dimensions. From a human development standpoint, two appropriate goals of assessment would be to assist: (a) the identification and development of the individual's potential and (b) the development of the human resource potential of the society. From a counseling relationship standpoint, the goals of assessment could be (a) to assist client self-understanding and (b) to improve counselor understanding of client traits. Expanding on the previously stated goal of assisting or expanding the client's self-understanding, goals for career assessment can also be identified as including the following:

1. **identifying**   career possibilities, maturity level, readiness
2. **confirming**   career interests, abilities, values
3. **broadening**   career horizons, options
4. **motivating**   career exploration and planning
5. **educating**   improved self-understanding, understanding of the world of work.

Assessment is beneficial to the counselor as well by enabling him or her to better understand the client and the client's needs. Assessment should also enable the counselor to more quickly, and probably more accurately, gain useful insights.

APPROACHES TO CAREER ASSESSMENT

Any approach to career assessment must be based on client needs. It should also be an approach that views the client and his or her needs within a holistic context. Further, the emerging and rapidly-changing world of work of the present and near future will demand changing concepts of assessment. A case in point is the significant impact of computerized career assessment systems. Further, the concept of career development across the life span, along with gender and multicultural needs, have broadened the range of career assessment. Increasing attention to the role of environment, the importance of leisure, and managing stress are just a few of the emerging influences on career assessment. Many of these recent developments are already reflected in some of the more traditional approaches to career assessment and standardized measurement. In addition to standardized measures, this chapter also examines some of the traditional, nonstandardized techniques (such as interviews, biographical data, and rating scales) and will look at some of the emerging assessment trends.

STANDARDIZED ASSESSMENT

Standardized assessment is primarily represented in practice by standardized testing. In a measurement sense, the term *standardized* refers to (a) specific conditions and procedures to be uniformly followed when administering, scoring, and interpreting the assessment instrument and (b) the measurement by the instruments of standards of performance, interests, and so on, through the creation of norms or expected patterns of response or performance for specific populations.

As noted earlier, standardized assessment has been popular in career counseling since the early years of the movement. Over the years these instruments have become much more numerous, more diverse in what they measure, more precise and valid in their measurements, and often more controversial. Modern career counselors have an extraordinarily wide range of options available for each area of standardized measurement. This section will only highlight some popular examples of standardized tests available for career counseling purposes, recognizing that there may be many other equally-appropriate instruments.

APTITUDE TESTING

Aptitude tests are designed to measure traits that characterize an individual's ability to perform in a given area or to potentially acquire the learning necessary for performance in a given area. It presumes the individual's inherent capacity to develop, or maximize through learning, a specific potential. This potential, however, cannot be expanded beyond a certain point—even by learning. Although this may be a controversial concept, this is the basis on which aptitude tests are developed. Career counselors should, therefore, understand the theoretical premise underlying their development. Thus, aptitude tests are designed to predict one's capacity to profit from the educational experience or the possibility of succeeding in a specific career or preparatory course of study. We are certain that you have already experienced aptitude tests purporting to assess your potential for academic work or graduate study in specific fields. In addition to academic aptitude tests there are a wide range of aptitude tests that are designed to predict for specific careers. These tests may assist the counselor and his or her client in (a) identifying or confirming client career-related aptitudes, (b) providing information that can help the individual to make a more appropriate career and/or related educational decision, and (c) motivating individuals to develop potential or special aptitudes they may possess.

While anticipating considerable individual differences across a range of aptitudes, counselors must also be alert to the possibility that an individual will not measure at the same level for a specific aptitude every time. For example, a track star may run a mile in 4 minutes one day and the same distance, under similar conditions, in 4 minutes and 10 seconds the next day. Aptitude measures are thus *actuarial* rather than *absolute*. These aptitude measures are available as special aptitude tests or as vocational aptitude batteries. Special aptitude tests are those that measure an individual's capacity for a specific career or specialized type of activity. These measures are usually referred to as single aptitude tests or component ability tests, because they only secure a measure for one specific aptitude or special ability. Tests of special aptitudes have declined in popularity in recent generations as aptitude batteries have increased in sophistication and popularity. Single aptitude tests are now most frequently used in various graduate and professional schools and, on occasion, to help determine mechanical, clerical, or artistic aptitude.

Multiple aptitude batteries are outgrowths of factorial studies of intelligence. Anastasi (1996) discusses the objectives of factor analysis as follows:

> The principle objective of factor analysis is to simplify the description of data by reducing the number of necessary variables, or dimensions. Thus, if we find that 5 factors are sufficient to account for all the common variance in a battery of 20 tests, we can for most purposes substitute 5 scores for the original 20 without sacrificing any essential information. The usual practice is to retain, from among the original tests, those providing the best measures of each of the factors. (p. 303)

Aptitude batteries offer a series of subtests based on the assumption that different career fields have their own sets of unique criteria. Thus, the subtests in varying combinations are related to a series of occupations or occupationally-related activities. The aptitude battery can thus enable a counselor and his or her client to compare potential in a variety of occupational areas. A technical advantage of the battery is that all of the subtests are normed on the same population, which would not be true for a comparable selection of individual aptitude tests.

General Aptitude Test Battery   The General Aptitude Test Battery (GATB) was originally developed and is administered by the U.S. Employment Service. However, it is available to nonprofit institutions such as schools for counseling purposes. The U.S. Department of Labor has conducted extensive and continuous studies on the validity and reliability of this battery, thus making it the most extensively researched instrument of its type. The GATB measures nine aptitudes including: general learning ability, verbal aptitude, numerical aptitude, spatial aptitude, form perception, clerical perception, motor coordination, finger dexterity, and manual dexterity.

The GATB is considered appropriate to administer for grades 9 through 12 and adult populations. It enables counselors to match test scores to aptitude levels published in the *National Occupational Classification Career Handbook*. This battery, like most aptitude batteries, enables counselors and their clients to examine the relative scores in a variety of different aptitude areas.

Differential Aptitude Test (DAT)   The Differential Aptitude Test (DAT), consists of a battery of eight subtests and currently features two levels: level 1 for students in grades 7 through 9 and level 2 for students in grades 10 through 12.[1] The publishers suggest that both versions may be appropriate to older populations as well. Versions of the DAT include a computerized adaptive form and a short form for use in employee selection and placement. The subtests of the DAT are verbal reasoning, numerical ability, abstract reasoning, clerical speed and accuracy, mechanical reasoning, space relations, spelling, and language usage. This battery has been one of the most popular in common use in schools as a means of assisting career counseling. The DAT does appear to be a good predictor of high school and college grades. However, the DAT has been extensively researched with mixed results.

The Flanagan Aptitude Classification Test (FACT)   The Flanagan Aptitude Classification Test (FACT) consists of 16 subtests: arithmetic, assembly, coding, components, coordination, expression, ingenuity, inspection, judgment and comprehension, mechanics, memory, patterns, precision, reasoning, scales, and tables. Each of these tests measures behaviors that have been identified as critical to job performance. While the entire battery is commonly administered in practice, selected groups of tests may also be used. In other words, each test measures special skills that are important for particular occupations. The FACT is designed primarily for high school students and adults.

Armed Services Vocational Aptitude Battery (ASVAB)   Since 1972, over one million high school students per year have taken the Armed Services Vocational Aptitude Battery (ASVAB). The ASVAB consists of eight tests: general science, arithmetic reasoning, word knowledge, paragraph comprehension, mathematics knowledge, electronics information, auto and shop information, and mechanical comprehension. Three special career exploration scores—verbal skills, math skills, and science and technical skills—are derived from these tests, which students use to explore the world of work. This battery is available to local high schools at no cost or obligation to either the school or the student, although the armed services hope for recruitment benefits from this service. The armed services provide the test administrator for this battery but encourages the use of monitors from the faculty or staff of the school involved. The ASVAB is also

---

[1] *Published by the Psychological Corporation, 1991.*

used throughout the military services and the U.S. Department of Defense. Military and civilian careers that have the same labels are not necessarily the same. This test has also been extensively researched with somewhat controversial results.

Scholastic Aptitude Tests   Scholastic or academic aptitude tests indirectly and (often directly) influence career planning, especially where higher education is required, because these tests are popularly used to influence collegiate admissions. Scholastic or academic aptitude tests propose to measure an individual's potential for performing in academic situations; hence, they are frequently used by institutions of higher education in determining not only entry into the institution but also entry into specific professional schools or career paths. Such tests as those that constitute the Scholastic Aptitude Test (SAT) and the formerly named American College Testing (ACT) Assessment have merit insofar as predicting academic performance at higher education levels. However, one must keep in mind that this prediction of future academic achievement tends to be on the basis of past learning rather than native aptitude. These are the two most popular tests used by institutions of higher education for admission and placement as well as counseling.

INTEREST INVENTORIES

Such statements as "I'd like to become an airline pilot"; "I've always been interested in teaching"; or "I know I would enjoy selling cars" are statements that are not uncommon to those we hear from teenagers. We also hear statements from adults on occasion such as "I always thought I would enjoy being a dentist"; "if I had the time I would plan to become an accountant"; or "in my next life I am going to be an architect." Such pronouncements of career interest are common across all ages. Equally common in today's rapidly-changing world of work are statements of uncertainty and frustration regarding individual career choices. Statements such as "I haven't got a clue as to what career I should enter"; and "I can't make up my mind between biology and chemistry as a major"; or "I am really upset because I think they are phasing my job out and I don't know what to do next" are not uncommon. These and similar comments indicate a need for some specific direction in career planning. For many years, interest testing has been a popular psychometric tool used to assist individuals, from adolescence through adulthood, in career planning.

In recent years there has also been an increased use of interest measurements for older adults considering career changes. While the exploration of careers, through literature and discussions, can be a valuable aid in career planning, there are also values that may result from standardized interest inventories. These potential values include:

1. a comparative and contrasting inventory of a person's interests
2. verification of a person's claimed interest or tentative choice
3. identification of previously unrecognized interests
4. identification of the possible level of interests for various (usually career) activities
5. contrast of interest with abilities and achievements
6. identification of problems associated with career decision making (no areas of adequate interest; high stated interest versus low inventoried interest in a career field)
7. a stimulus for career exploration or career counseling

If the values of interest inventories are to be realized, certain cautions should be observed by career counselors:

- It is important for counselors to remind clients that interest inventories measure interests only—**not** abilities. Although we recognize that interest and abilities are frequently related, interest inventories are just what they indicate: an inventory of interest only.
- The results of interest inventories will have less long-range predictability with younger clients because many of their interests will change dramatically as they mature.
- Interest inventories measure interests in terms of broad categories rather than fine distinctions. For example, an interest inventory may indicate that an individual has a high interest in outdoor activities or careers, but it does not distinguish between agriculture, forestry, or recreation.

Interest inventories also must be used cautiously with individuals who are under a great deal of stress or emotional trauma. Counselors should address the client's emotional difficulties before suggesting that career interest testing take place. Hood and Johnson (1997) pointed out that:

- Counselors should keep in mind that interest inventories measure likes and dislikes, **not** abilities. . . .
- Second, clients should be positively motivated to participate in the assessment process. . . .
- Third, general interest inventories are of limited value for people who must make rather fine distinctions, such as choosing between civil and electrical engineering. . . .
- Fourth, interest inventories may be inappropriate for people with emotional problems (Brandt & Hood, 1968). Disturbed people make more negative responses and endorse more passive interests than do people who are not disturbed (Drasgow & Carkhuff, 1964). Personal issues can interfere with decision making. Counselors usually must address the emotional difficulties before career planning can take place.
- Fifth, scores on interest inventories can show significant changes for clients who are young or after long time periods (Johansson & Campbell, 1971). . . .
- Finally, counselors may wish to use an interest card sort instead of an interest inventory if they are interested in the underlying reasons for the client's choices (Slaney, Moran, & Wade, 1994, pp. 153–154).

Counselors should understand how interest inventories have been developed in order to appropriately interpret them in their practice. Popular inventories evolved from studies that indicated that people in a given occupational area seem to share a cluster of common interests that distinguish them from people in other occupational areas. These differences in interests extended beyond those associated with job performance and individuals in a given occupational or career area also have similar nonvocational interests as well (e.g., hobbies or recreational activities). As a result, interest inventories could be designed to assess one's interests and then relate those interests to those of different occupational areas. Two of the earliest and still most popular of these inventories were those developed by Kuder and Strong.

Kuder Inventories   The Kuder Preference Record is the original, and still the most popular, of the various Kuder inventories. This inventory provides a series of interest items arranged in triads. Respondents then must choose the one that they prefer the most and the one that they would like the least. The results are scored and profiled for the occupational areas of outdoor activities, mechanical, computational, scientific, persuasive, artistic, literary, musical, postal service, and clerical. A list of occupations correlated with each scale is provided. A *V* score (verification scale) is also provided and indicates whether the score might be of questionable validity.

The Kuder General Interest Survey was extended downward to the sixth grade by revisions of the original Kuder Preference Record. These revisions employ a simpler vocabulary that requires only a sixth grade reading level. The original version was usually considered appropriate for use in grades 9 through 12.

In still another version, the Kuder Occupational Interest Survey provides scores showing similarities with occupational and college level areas. This form differs from the previous Kuder inventories by displaying a person's score on each occupational scale as a correlation between his or her interest patterns and the pattern of a particular occupational group. Lack of experience or understanding of the world of work can result in low scores on the occupational scales or the *V* score. The National Career Assessment Service in Adel, Iowa publishes all Kuder instruments.

Strong Interest Inventory   The Strong Interest Inventory has replaced the well-known Strong/Campbell Interest Inventories.[2] This inventory is based on the assumption that an individual whose interests are similar to those workers in a specific occupation is more likely to find that specific occupation satisfactory than a person who does not have these common interests. This interest inventory yields six general occupational theme scales based on Holland's six types. Scores are also provided for 207 occupational scales. This inventory is suggested for grades 11 through adulthood. It is related to the Pathfinder career decision-making system using interactive video. A computerized version is available.

Ohio Vocational Interest Survey   The Ohio Vocational Interest Survey is designed to assist students and adults with their career and educational planning. It yields data on 253 job activities derived from 23 interest scales. A student information questionnaire is provided, as well as a student report folder and a guide to career exploration. The latter is designed to link interests to the world of work and are optional. The Survey is published by several publishing companies, including the Psychological Corporation.

Self-Directed Search (SDS)   Another approach to the assessment of career interests is the Self-Directed Search (SDS). This instrument was developed by John Holland,

---

[2] *Published by the Consulting Psychologists Press.*

whose hexagonal model of six occupational themes is represented in the six summary scores of realistic, investigative, artistic, social, enterprising, and conventional. Accordingly, there are also six work environments populated by workers of the related personality type. Holland's popular theory suggests that career choices that reinforce one's personality type will be most satisfying and successful.

The SDS is designed to be self-administered, self-scored, and self-interpreted. When an individual completes the SDS, he or she uses a summary code comprising the types that rank first and second across all the subtests. Using this code, he or she refers to a job finder, which presents information about 456 jobs listed in terms of two-letter SDS codes. Once a person finds his or her lists of careers that match a summary code, suggested next steps are listed for his or her organized career planning.[3]

The summary form for Holland's theory describing the personality characteristics of six occupational categories and the career or work environments related to each of these categories is presented in Chapter 4. Holland's popular SDS is based on this theory. It is not suggested that these categories are mutually exclusive or that a individual would fit into only one of the six described psychological types.

The Career Maturity Inventory   The Career Maturity Inventory, although it is not precisely an interest inventory, has been designed to measure the maturity of attitudes and competencies that are involved in career decision making. The attitude scale surveys five attitudinal clusters: (a) involvement in the career choice process, (b) orientation toward work, (c) independence in decision making, (d) preference for career choice factors, and (e) conceptions of the career choice process. In contrast, the competency text measures the more cognitive variables involved in choosing an occupation. The five parts of the competency test are (a) self-appraisal, (b) occupational information, (c) goal selection, (d) planning, and (e) problem solving.[4]

Career Attitudes and Strategies Inventory (CASI)   This self-administered self-scoring inventory, developed by John Holland and Gary Gottfredson in 1994, is used to measure employed and unemployed adults' beliefs about their career problems, job satisfaction, reaction to change, work strategies, and other career issues. The inventory consists of a checklist for common career obstacles and 150 multiple choice items grouped into the following nine scales:[5]

1. **job satisfaction**   High scoring persons are satisfied with and committed to their jobs
2. **work involvement**   High scoring individuals are devoted to their careers
3. **skill development**   High scorers try to improve their job performance and sharpen their skills

---

[3] *The SDS is published by Psychological Assessment Resources, P. O. Box 998, Odessa, FL 33556.*

[4] *The Career Maturity Inventory is available from Chronicle Guidance Publications, Inc., 66 Aurora St., Moravia, NY 13118-1190.*

[5] *The Career Attitudes and Strategies Inventory (CASI) is available through Psychological Assessment Resources, Inc.*

4. **dominant style**   High scorers tend to take charge when something needs to be done at work
5. **career worries**   Low scoring individuals are relatively free from anxiety about their careers
6. **interpersonal abuse**   This scale explores past intimidation, harassment, and perceived mistreatment at work
7. **family commitment**   High scoring persons have dual role responsibilities. They are committed to and responsible for a family as well as a career
8. **risk-taking style**   High scorers are willing to take risks to further their careers
9. **geographical barriers**   High scores on this scale indicate freedom to relocate for a job

The U.S. Employment Office Interest Inventory (II)   The U.S. Employment Office Interest Inventory, developed in 1982, is an entry instrument for clients' assessment and career exploration. It is used to give direction to career planning and is usually given together with the General Aptitude Test Battery by employment office counselors. This instrument yields interest scores for the artistic, scientific, plants and animals, protective, mechanical, industrial, business retail, selling, accomodatory, humanitarian leading, influencing, and physical performing occupational areas. This test is appropriate for individuals in grade 9 through adulthood.

The Jackson Vocational Interest Survey   The Jackson Vocational Interest Survey is designed for high school, college, and adult age groups. The instrument consists of 289 pairs of statements that describe job-related activities. These statements, when scored, are profiled along 34 basic interest scales that cover career role dimensions relevant to a variety of careers and work style scales indicative of work environment preferences.[6]

The Gibson/Mitchell Nonstandardized Interest Inventory   Figure 5-1 displays a nonstandardized interest exploratory instrument that was developed and is used by your authors. Once completed by a client, this instrument should be discussed between the client and his or her counselor for its career implications.

PERSONALITY MEASURES

Introduction   Of all the areas of standardized testing, none is more intriguing or perhaps more controversial—than the area of personality testing. From do-it-yourself tests found in daily newspapers to sophisticated projective techniques that require highly specialized psychological training, personality testing represents our continual quest to probe the secrets of one's personality and to satisfy our curiosity about what makes someone "tick." We see the individual's personality frequently associated with career potential. For example, he has the personality to be a great lawyer, she has

[6] *The Jackson Vocational Interest Survey (1995) is published by Sigma Assessment Systems, Inc., Port Huron, MI.*

<table>
<tr><td colspan="4" align="center">**Interest Assessment**</td></tr>
<tr>
<td>Significant <u>People</u> in your life and their occupation</td>
<td><u>Places</u> (environments) that you enjoy</td>
<td><u>Things</u> (material items) of value to you</td>
<td>Great <u>Experiences</u> in your life (such as camping out, making new friends, or traveling)</td>
</tr>
</table>

Recommended careers

1. _____

2. _____

3. _____

I.D. Number _____

FIGURE 5-1
The Gibson/Mitchell nonstandardized interest inventory

such a caring personality she should consider going into medicine, or I won't hire anyone in sales that does not have an engaging personality.

While many personality tests were initially designed to measure psychopathology, in recent generations their potential values in career counseling have been increasingly explored. Certainly, Holland's hexagonal model relating personality types to work environments has been a major influence, as has Super's (1990) emphasis on the importance of self-concept in career decision-making.

Caution: Personality—A Changing Variable   As personality tests are increasingly used for career counseling purposes, counselors must consider four questions that have been traditionally asked within the context of personality measurement:

1. What is personality? While dictionaries, psychologists, and psychiatrists may arrive at reasonably common definitions or descriptions of the components of personality, there will be a much broader range of responses if the question is put to the general public. It is, therefore, important in personality measurement that personality—as defined by the instrument itself—be understood and recognized by those administering and interpreting the instrument.

2. What is normal personality? While some personality instruments define *normal* in terms of generally acceptable behavioral patterns or norms, these measures may still erroneously suggest that individuals who deviate from these norms are classified as abnormal. It is the arbitrary designation of certain points of deviation

from the norms as becoming abnormal that brings criticism of some personality measures. For example, an extremely extroverted person might be measured as abnormal on a personality scale but would be viewed as very likeable and popular by most individuals who know him or her.

3. Can personality be measured? Many people will be unable to accurately analyze some aspects of their own personality. Some individuals may deliberately falsify their responses on a personality measure to reflect a view that is more socially acceptable than perhaps their own true response might be.

4. How stable are individual personalities? Not only is the human personality difficult to measure accurately, and in view of the wide variations in human behavior to ascertain normalcy, it is also important to recognize that needs and preferences do change over the life span and that patterns of these changes are difficult to predict. Therefore, one's personality today may not be one's personality next year. However, as one ages, dramatic personality changes are less likely to occur. Some of the more popular personality tests include the following:

Edwards Personal Preference Schedule   The Edwards Personal Preference Schedule (EPPS) measures 15 personality variables based on Murray's manifest needs (1938). This schedule is designed to measure normal personality variables and to show the relative importance to the individual of 15 key needs or motives: achievement, affiliation, nurturance, deference, introspection, change, order, succorance, endurance, exhibition, dominance, heterosexuality, autonomy, abasement, and aggression.

All of these measures can be related to career needs. For example, *achievement* indicates the need to achieve or to accomplish tasks; *order* indicates the need to plan well and to be organized; *succorance* indicates the need for support and encouragement or motivation; and *aggression* indicates a need to express one's opinion or to be critical and assertive.

16 Personality Factor Questionnaire (16 PF)   The 16 PF (5th ed.), developed by R. B. Cattell, A. Karen Cattell, and Heather E. P. Cattell, provides a measure of 16 personality dimensions. These may be interpreted to suggest potential influences on career choices. The 16 PF instrument assesses an individual's personality against 16 key scales: warmth, vigilance, reasoning, abstractedness, emotional stability, privateness, dominance, apprehension, liveliness, openness to change, rule consciousness, self-reliance, social boldness, perfectionism, sensitivity, and tension. It is a factor-analytical derived questionnaire for assessing an individual's personality. These personality characteristics are represented in a set of attitudes, preferences, social and emotional reactions, and habits.

VALUES INVENTORIES

In recent years, family values have received a considerable amount of attention in political platforms, on editorial pages, and at school board meetings. While no consensus has been reached on what constitutes desirable values, these discussions have contributed to an awakening of the general public to the importance of values in motivating behavior, influencing choices, and determining practices. Values give meaning and direction to one's life and because one's career also may give meaning and direction to one's life, the relationship between personal values and career choice are of great significance. An individual's career choice offers the opportunity to enhance and perpetuate his or her own values. The similarity between true values and a true or good career choice is frequently noted as both require the opportunity to choose freely, to have options from which to choose, to choose after consideration and reflection, to affirm publicly, and to practice or incorporate the choice into daily life.

The increasing awareness of the importance of values in career selection has resulted in more attention to values assessment, resulting in turn in the stimulation of research in the area, as well as heightened interest in the use of values measures in career counseling. Three examples of these measures are briefly noted.

Work Values Inventory   The Work Values Inventory, developed by Donald E. Super, is appropriate for use in grades 7 through 12 and for adults. This instrument is designed to assess satisfaction, which individuals look for in their careers. This inventory measures 12 work values as including: creativity, work environment, prestige, independence, mental challenge, variety, income, supervision, coworkers, achievement, lifestyle, and security.

The Minnesota Importance Questionnaire   The Minnesota Importance Questionnaire (MIQ) is an instrument, developed in 1981, that assesses vocational needs and values, which are important aspects of worker satisfaction. It measures 20 worker needs and six values associated with these needs: achievement, altruism, autonomy, comfort, safety, and status validity.

The Study of Values   The development of this instrument (by Allport, Vernon, and Linzey) was based on Spranger's six types of personality: theoretical, economic, aesthetic, social, political, and religious. Questions were designed to measure the values believed to be represented in Spranger's personality types. This inventory was primarily developed for college students and adults but norms are now available for high school students as well. The inventory consists of two parts. In the first part, individuals indicate disagreement or preference for controversial statements, and in the second part, individuals respond to multiple choice questions, the answers to which reflect their attitudes.

TEST SELECTION

The proliferation of standardized tests available to counselors necessitates the recognition and application of criteria in test selection. In Appendix A, the Association for Assessment in Counseling presents what is referred to as the RUST Statement, regarding the responsibilities of users of standardized tests. Appendix B presents The Code of Fair Testing Practices in Education (2002), prepared by the Joint Committee on Testing Practices (American Psychological Association). Appendix C presents Standards for Multicultural Assessment (2nd ed.), prepared by the Association for Assessment in Counseling (a division of the American Counseling Association).

The importance of selecting tests that are accurate measures, that provide for predictability, and are within the counselor's competencies of interpretation are critical considerations. Errors in measurement or interpretation have the disastrous potential to lead to an error in client decision-making.

The critical criterion in test selection is test validity. Validity is the degree to which an instrument measures what it claims to measure or is used to measure. For example, does the test being considered really measure one's aptitude for artistic careers and activities or does it reflect one's previous experiences in the areas being tested or one's vocational interests in the area?

When establishing a test's validity, counselors may review the appropriateness of test questions and situational samples to the measurement objectives. Because all possible questions or situations cannot be included, those that are included must be representative and must also be appropriate for the individual under study and the given circumstances. When an instrument meets these conditions, it is said to have *content validity.* When content validity cannot be provided, the test developers may cite *construct validity,* which refers to the adequacy or concept underlying the measurement instrument. It involves a logical determination of the psychological attributes that account for variations in test scores. Construct validity is reported in terms of the kinds of responses the instrument should elicit and the ways in which these responses should be interpreted in view of the logical inferences about the behavior the test is designed to measure.

The second major criterion used in the selection of standardized tests is *reliability.* This criterion represents the consistency with which the test obtains the same results from the same population, but on different testing occasions. The measure of reliability enables the counselor to determine predictions that can be made based on the established consistency of the particular test.

In addition to the significant criteria of validity and reliability, the counselor must also determine the *practicality* of an instrument. The most important practical consideration is whether the counselor is competent to interpret the particular standardized test under consideration. The importance of the counselor's understanding the fine points of interpretation cannot be overemphasized. Other practical factors that enter into test selection include the ease of administering and scoring, the expense, and the time required for administration.

MULTICULTURAL AND GENDER BIAS IN TEST SELECTION

Counselors involved in using standardized measures for career assessment must, of course, be aware of the issue and concern for cultural fairness. Recent reviews of the testing literature by J. Ronald Quinn (1993) have noted the paucity of critical reviews of specific instruments, even though acknowledging the existence of the problem. Gender bias has also been a concern in standardized measurement, and although some reviews of specific instruments have noted the existence of such bias, many questions still remain. Because the manuals accompanying specific tests are unlikely to point out any such biases, counselors must themselves attempt to discern the existence of such biases through examination of the make up of the norming population and any recent critical reviews. Also, a personal examination of instruments under consideration by knowledgeable minority or female professionals can be helpful.

INTERPRETING TEST SCORES— WHAT DO THEY MEAN?

Whenever we assess or evaluate an individual, we almost always do it in terms of some kind of comparison or point of reference. For example, we may refer to Eduardo as the best student in the class and Isaiah as the hardest worker in the hardware store. In these examples we are comparing Eduardo to all other students in the class and Isaiah to all other workers in the hardware store. Of course, predictions from this meager amount of information would hardly be justified and in fact, would probably be viewed as unreliable. A career counselor interviewing either Eduardo or Isaiah should seek additional, and more valid, data in the process of assisting them to arrive at informed career decisions.

An elementary understanding of statistics and statistically-based tests would assist the counselor in doing this. These understandings would enable the counselor to (a) compare the characteristics of these individuals to a specific group or population and (b) predict the probability of Eduardo and Isaiah succeeding or not in a given area based on their present or past behaviors. In addition to understanding comparative traits of Eduardo and Isaiah, basic understandings of educational and psychological statistics enable counselors to infer the characteristics of a population from a sample of that population. It may enable the counselor to make predictions regarding a group, plan developmental or remedial programs, and develop other special programs to meet the needs of a group.

We begin with a brief examination of statistical terms with the most common and most frequently misunderstood of all these terms: *average*. Most educational and psychological evaluation is based on the individual's relative position in a group as compared to others who constitute the group. In order to conduct this comparison, obtaining the average of the group becomes necessary. For example, when Ovella reports to her parents that she scored 65 on her biology test, should they be pleased, satisfied, or displeased? Without more information they cannot be sure how to react, because the 65 could represent 65% of the questions answered correctly, 65 answered correctly out of 70 questions, or some kind of a formula score where certain questions are worth more or less than others.

When discussing averages, we note that there are three distinguishing statistical types of averages referred to as measures of central tendency. These are the *mean*, the *median*, and the *mode*. The mean is commonly associated with average. The median is the midpoint of a set of scores, with 50% of a set of scores below and 50%

above that point. The mode represents the most frequent score in a set of scores. Of these three averages, the mean is the most common and useful while the mode has little statistical value and is the least helpful.

VARIATIONS FROM THE AVERAGE

In many instances, counselors may wish to measure the degree to which an individual varies from the average of a group. Statistical measures that enable the counselor to compute this are called *measures of variability*. The common measures of variability are the *range* and the *standard deviation*. The range represents the spread of scores from the lowest to the highest in a specific distribution. The actual statistical formula is the highest score in the group minus the lowest one, plus one. (The "plus one" in the formula extends the range to its real limits, which are half a score unit below the lowest score.) The range, while relatively simple as a measurement device, has limited descriptive value. On the other hand, the standard deviation allows for an exact determination of the distance of a score from the mean. When computed for specific test results, the mean and standard deviation would enable a counselor to determine how well individuals perform in comparison to a group.

> This interpretation is made by specifying standard deviation distance from the mean and determining the proportion of the population that will be beyond or deviate from it, assuming that the scores are normally distributed. The normally distributed population is most popularly viewed as a normal curve, as shown in Figure 5-2. (Note: Rarely are the mean, median, and mode the same.) (Gibson and Mitchell, 2003, p. 229)
>
> In Figure 5-3, the normal curve is, in effect, sliced into bands one standard deviation wide, with a fixed percentage of cases always falling in each band. Figure 5-3 then illustrates a significant fact: the mean plus and minus one standard deviation encompasses approximately 68% of a normally distributed population; the mean plus and minus two standard deviations encompasses approximately 95% of that population; and the mean plus and

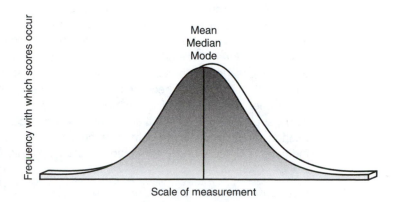

FIGURE 5-2
The normal curve
Source: R. L. Gibson and M. H. Mitchell. *Introduction to Counseling and Guidance,* 6/e, © 2003, p. 229. Reprinted by permission of Pearson Education, Inc., Upper Saddle River, New Jersey.

FIGURE 5-3

Scores in a normal distribution.

Source: R. L. Gibson and M. H. Mitchell. *Introduction to Counseling and Guidance,* 6/e, © 2003, p. 230. Reprinted by permission of Pearson Education, Inc., Upper Saddle River, New Jersey.

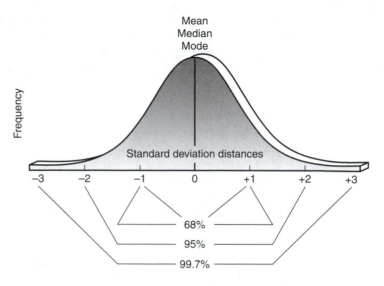

minus three standard deviations encompasses 99.7% of that population. This information, which remains constant for any normally distributed set of scores or values, makes possible a meaningful interpretation of any score in a group. As you view the normal curve and its segmentation into standard deviations, note that these facts are handy for interpreting standard scores. Furthermore, whenever you can assume a normal distribution, you can convert standard scores to percentile scores and vice versa. Thus, three basic facts for deriving a statistical evaluation of a person's performance on a psychological test are the person's raw score, mean, and standard deviation for the group with which the individual is being compared. (Gibson and Mitchell, 2003, pp. 229–230)[7]

STATISTICAL RELATIONSHIPS

Although determining the meaning of an individual's score in relation to others on the same test is important, one must also determine the other relationships of this score. An individual score will take on additional meaning when it can be related to some useful purpose. For example, if students who score high on college entrance examination tests are shown to perform at a high academic level in college, then it may be assumed that there is a relationship between scores on the entrance examination and grades in college. (There are many other variables that could influence one's grades.) As a result, their test scores become meaningful in terms of this practical purpose.

Another popular statistical method for comparing relationships between two variables, such as test scores and academic performance, is a *correlation coefficient.* Correlation coefficients range from plus one, through zero, to minus one. A plus one indicates a perfect positive correlation; that is, the rank order of those taking the college

---

[7] *Gibson, Robert L., & Mitchell, Marianne H.,* Introduction to Counseling and Guidance, *6/e, © 2003. Reprinted by permission of Pearson Education, Inc., Upper Saddle River, NJ.*

entrance examination and their academic rank order in the college program are identical. A correlation of minus one means that the scores go in exactly the reverse direction. Thus, a correlation of minus one would indicate that persons who score highest on the entrance examination achieve the lowest in college. A zero correlation would represent a complete lack of relationship between the two sets of data. A frequently-computed coefficient of correlation is the Pearson product-moment coefficient.

RAW SCORES

As previously noted, raw scores become more meaningful when converted to comparative scores. Most standardized tests, therefore, use one or more of the following common methods for converting raw scores into something more meaningful to present to the individual. The most common of these is the *percentile.* A percentile score represents the percentage of persons in the standardized sample who fall below a given raw score on the test. The individual's percentile ranking, therefore, indicates his or her relative position in a normal sample.

STANDARDIZED SCORES

A standard score represents the individual's distance from the mean in terms of the standardized deviation of the distribution. For example, let us look at Dinorah, Felix, and Abraham and their scores on a test:

Mean of the test takers	75
Standard deviation	15
Dinorah's score	90
Felix's score	65
Abraham's score	45

Using the formula $\dfrac{X \text{ (raw score)} - M \text{ (mean)}}{SD \text{ (standard deviation)}}$, the following standard scores are obtained

$$\text{Dinorah:} \ \frac{90 - 75}{15} = +1.0$$

$$\text{Felix:} \ \frac{65 - 75}{15} = -0.7$$

$$\text{Abraham:} \ \frac{45 - 75}{15} = -2.0$$

Because both decimal points and plus and minus signs may be confusing or easily misplaced, they can be transformed into a more convenient form by multiplying each standard score with some constant. For example, if we multiply these scores by 10, we have +10, –7, and –20. We can then eliminate the plus and minuses by adding a constant of 100. Thus, Dinorah's score becomes 110, Felix's 93, and Abraham's 80.

NORMS

The term *norm* or *normal* is a popular one, commonly used to indicate what we can reasonably anticipate. The concept of normal or norm, as used in standardized testing terminology, also implies normal or average performance. The norms for a test are derived during the process of standardizing the instrument. In this process, the instrument is administered to a sample that is representative of the population for whom the test is designed. This sample or group comprises the standardization population for establishing the norm of the instrument. These norms reflect the average performances and also the relative frequency of varying degrees of deviation from the average.

NONSTANDARDIZED ASSESSMENT

INTRODUCTION

Because of the extensive use of standardized assessment in career counseling, there may be a tendency to overlook the potential contributions of nonstandardized or qualitative assessment. However, career counselors should be familiar with the various qualitative or subjective techniques available to them and the possible benefits of qualitative assessment. Goldman (1990) noted the following:

1. Qualitative methods tend to foster an **active role** for the client in the process of collecting and teasing meaning out of data, rather than the role of a passive responder who is being measured, predicted, placed, or diagnosed. This, to me, is one of the hallmarks of counseling psychology as contrasted with clinical psychology, for example. This distinction goes along with calling people clients rather than patients, which is much more than a small semantic point.

2. Qualitative assessment emphasizes **holistic study** of the individual rather than the isolation and precise measurement of narrowly defined discrete elements of ability, interest, or personality. Naturally, the results of qualitative assessment tend to appear somewhat vague and subjective as contrasted with the products of standardized tests. As I have argued elsewhere, however, the seeming precision and definiteness of standardized tests are greatly exaggerated (Goldman, 1972). This becomes evident when one critically examines some of the typical characteristics of standardized tests: the inadequacies of most norm groups; the ambiguities of many test items, especially in the realm of personality; and, perhaps most telling of all, the fact that the score on any given scale makes a completely unfounded assumption that we know what the individual understood each item to mean and what he or she meant by the yes-no or multiple choice response to each of those items. The statistical foundation of

standardized tests becomes less impressive when one examines the
reality of what can be stated for an individual from validity coefficients of even .60, especially when they are based on criteria that are
themselves of questionable validity.

3. Qualitative assessment methods tend to emphasize the concepts of
    learning about oneself and understanding oneself in a **developmental**
    framework. These concepts are most harmonious with the spirit of
    counseling psychology, as contrasted with other traditions where diag-
    nosis and placement are emphasized.

4. Qualitative assessment methods often **work well in groups** of
    clients and, in fact, are often at their best in a group setting, where
    each individual may learn something about individual differences as
    well as understanding him- or herself better, through the comparison
    with others in the group. Such developmental and growth groups
    and workshops are distinctive, positive features of counseling
    psychology in many of its settings.

5. Qualitative assessment **reduces the distinction between assessment
    and counseling**. Counseling interactions are stimulated by the assess-
    ment methods rather than hampered by them, which is a problem with
    so many standardized tests—where the very process of testing inter-
    rupts the counseling process and disturbs the counseling relationship.

6. At a time when professional psychology as a whole is called upon to
    relate more effectively to persons of **different cultural and ethnic
    groups, socioeconomic levels, sexual identities, and to people
    with disabilities**, the qualitative methods are especially valuable.
    Most qualitative methods may readily be modified in their contents
    without a negative effect on their usefulness. Vocabulary may be
    modified so that it is understandable to the particular client or popu-
    lation. The specific situation used for a simulation may be altered or
    recast so that it fits the life experiences of the client or group. Be-
    cause the qualitative methods do not attempt precise measurement
    or numerical comparison with normative samples, they may be
    modified and adapted in both their content and interpretation in
    order to take into account experience or lack of it, reading ability,
    and, in fact, any pertinent life experience of the population being
    assessed. (Goldman, 1990, 205–207)[8]

When striving for the most complete picture of the client and his or her career
needs, counselors should utilize all techniques—standard or nonstandard—that can,
within a reasonable timeframe, be utilized to formulate this picture. Included in these
techniques are interviewing, observation and observation reports, self-reported descriptions, checklists, scales, and questionnaires.

---

[8] Leo Goldman. Qualitative Assessment. "The Counseling Pyschologist", pp. 205–213, copyright © 1990 by Sage
Publications, Inc. Reprinted by Permission of Sage Publications, Inc.

INTERVIEWS

Interviewing is a common practice in the world of work for determining an individual's potential for employment or advancement to a particular position. Initial interviews are often referred to as *intake interviews*. In career settings, an intake interview is typically used to obtain general information related to the client's history, including previous employment experiences, education, and career aspirations. Many counselors may prefer to structure the interview. Structured interviews enable counselors to obtain specific information to serve a particular purpose. When designing a structured interview, the counselor first determines the purpose(s) and then designs questions that are suitable for obtaining the desired information for serving the purpose(s) of the interview. These questions would be arranged in a logical sequence, although the interviewer must have the flexibility to alter the sequence and nature of the questions should circumstances warrant.

An example of a structured interview for a client who has expressed the desire to change careers follows:

1. Explain the purpose and procedures for the interview.
2. Would you give me a brief review of your employment experiences?
3. What is your educational background?
4. Do you have any unique experiences or interests that might be related to the choice of a career, such as hobbies or special interests?
5. Why have you decided, at this time, to change careers?
6. Tell me about your ideas regarding a new or different career.
7. How can I (as your career counselor) be helpful?

It is important initially to explain the purpose and procedures for the interview. This will usually help to put the client more at ease and facilitate the interviewing process. It is also important to structure the questions so as to generate discussion and possibly feelings rather than eliciting a simple, and limiting, "yes" or "no" answer. Finally, the structured questions are designed to get the interview off to a meaningful start and are not intended to limit the interview. The counselor must have the flexibility to go beyond the set questions if deemed desirable.

OBSERVATION

Of all the techniques used for the assessment and understanding of others, none is more popular than observation. In our daily lives we hear expressions such as "He looks like a very determined person," "You could just tell by looking at her that she was the one for the job," "You knew by their walk that they were very confident," and "I've been observing him for weeks and he deserves the promotion." Although we recognize that these informal and unscientific observations may have little validity, we nonetheless make these casual analyses of others on a daily basis.

In career counseling we are concerned with what we can learn about our clients through observation and what our clients may learn about themselves through their being observed by others. When used within a professional counseling context, observation must not be haphazard and informal but must have purpose and format. In other words, some sort of observational guidelines and a means of reporting observations must be devised if the observations are to have any basis in fact. Purpose precedes the selection or design of an observation instrument. The most commonly employed observation instruments for career assessment or assistance are rating scales and checklists.

Rating scales are popular assessment tools in the career world. They are frequently used as at least a partial basis for employment, placement, advancement, selection for training or, in some instances, dismissal. In career counseling they may be used to assist clients in career planning, career decision making, placement or, in school settings, as an aid to career development needs. Rating scales consist of items to be observed, usually a description of the items to guide the observer, and scales for recording judgments of the observation.

Rating scales should only be completed by raters who have been in a position to observe the client being rated in significant, relevant settings (i.e., school, work, or home) over a sufficient period of recent time to be able to render knowledgeable judgments. Examples of items that are popular on general career-oriented rating scales are as follows:

- industry
- promptness
- sense of responsibility
- accuracy
- neatness
- good work habits
- attention to details
- desire to achieve
- cooperativeness
- acceptance of criticism

Checklists are also popular tools for directing and recording observations. Checklists direct an observer's attention to specific observable traits and require the observer to simply check those traits that he or she observes, usually without indicating the extent or degree to which the trait is present.

OTHER ASSESSMENT TECHNIQUES

In addition to those techniques designed to record observations, there are written response techniques for eliciting information or opinions from career clients. These techniques may contribute further to the assessment and planning process. In this regard, the questionnaire is a particularly popular choice; one commonly found in employment offices, college admissions and placement offices, and in various counseling offices. The questionnaire has the advantage of collecting information in a relatively short time. It also has the advantage of being a client participation technique. Questionnaires may be designed to collect a broad range of general information or may be narrowly designed to focus on a specific area such as work values or future career plans. Questionnaires are also sometimes designed for the purpose of validating already available information. The usefulness of the instrument will be determined, at least to a degree, by the appropriateness of its design and the skill of its administration, which will be reflected to a large degree by client receptivity to and understanding of the instrument and its purpose. Questionnaire characteristics such as directions, design, item content, and length are important considerations.

How important are the following in your job choice:

Important		**Not Important**
_____	Must be in commuting distance of where I now reside	_____
_____	Must be within 30 minutes commute from my residence	_____
_____	Must have a mild climate (year round)	_____
_____	Must be in or near a large population center	_____
_____	Working under direct supervision	_____
_____	Working night shift	_____
_____	More education needed	_____
_____	A job you've never considered	_____
_____	Monotonous repeat work	_____
_____	Working on your own	_____
_____	Working in a setting with many others	_____
_____	Attractive work environment	_____
_____	Supervising others	_____
_____	Involves a lot of travel	_____
_____	Involves selling	_____
_____	Involves working odd hours	_____
_____	Benefits package	_____
_____	Annual vacation plan	_____
_____	Requires one year commitment (yours)	_____
_____	Interesting work	_____

FIGURE 5-4
Career planning checklist

Some self-reporting instruments may be designed to solicit broader client responses than the questionnaire. These would include self-descriptors such as the career autobiography, brief self-descriptors, and self-expression papers regarding a specific topic such as "my ideal job," "what I enjoy doing," or "my values."

SAMPLES OF NONSTANDARDIZED ASSESSMENT TOOLS

In addition, there are a number of more narrowly defined instruments that counselors may use to elicit client information. These might include a career planning checklist (see Figure 5-4) in which the client indicates the relative importance of various factors in choosing a career. The Career Value Survey, Figure 5-5 is another example of a nonstandardized instrument for exploring a client's values as they may relate to career or specific employment choice.

Rate According to Importance	1–10
Geographic area where I live	____
Size and type of community where I live	____
Owning my own home	____
Cost of living	____
What I do (career of my choice)	____
People with whom I work (on-the-job associates)	____
"Bosses" for whom I work	____
Salary I earn	____
Opportunities to advance	____
Job security and benefits	____
Leisure time opportunities in the area	____
Vacation time	____
Educational system in the community	____
Opportunities to worship in my own religion	____
Closeness to family	____
Other	____

7–10	Very important (a decisive factor)
4–6	Average importance
1–3	Minimal importance

FIGURE 5-5
Career value survey

DSM-IV-TR (TEXT REVISED)

The most popular diagnostic system in the United States is the *Diagnostic and Statistical Manual of Mental Disorders - IV-TR,* published by the American Psychiatric Association in 1994. This manual contains authoritative information and official opinions about a range of mental health problems. Although the manual itself presents a standardized system of recording observations, the judgments on which these recordings are made will frequently be subjective.

The *DSM-IV* characterizes a mental disorder as a clinically significant behavior or psychological syndrome or pattern that occurs in an individual. According to the *DSM-IV,* one of the following must be present to diagnose a client as having a mental disorder:

- **AXIS I**   Clinical disorders and other conditions that may be the focus of clinical attention
- **AXIS II**   Personality disorders, mental retardation, borderline intellectual functioning, and other disorders with less severe symptoms
- **AXIS III**   General medical conditions
- **AXIS IV**   Psychological and environmental problems that may be impacting the client
- **AXIS V**   Global assessment of functioning (using a rating scale form)

The mental disorders and conditions covered in the *DSM-IV* are divided into 17 categories as follows:

1. Disorders usually first diagnosed in infancy, childhood, or adolescence
2. Delirium, dementia, amnestic, and other cognitive disorders
3. Mental disorders due to a general medical condition
4. Substance-related disorders
5. Schizophrenia and other psychotic disorders
6. Mood disorders
7. Anxiety disorders
8. Somatoform disorders
9. Factitious disorders
10. Diassociative disorders
11. Sexual and gender identity disorders
12. Eating disorders
13. Sleep disorders
14. Impulse-control disorders not elsewhere classified
15. Adjustment disorders
16. Personality disorders
17. Other conditions that may be a focus of clinical attention

Counselors using the *DSM-IV* should have special preparation and supervised experience.

While the *DSM-IV* is not specifically designed for career assessment, counselors are often requested by employers to determine if specific problems, such as depression or substance abuse, exist in job applicants. Such problems may handicap their performance on the job.

TECHNOLOGY AND ASSESSMENT

The use of technology for individual assessment has become extremely popular with the continued refinement of computers. The dramatically increased use stimulated by the lowering costs of computers has resulted in its infusion into nearly every aspect of business and education, including counseling. Its most popular use in the counseling field has been easily accessing educational and occupational information and individual assessment. In the area of assessment, computers are widely used in standardized testing for the administration, scoring, profiling, and interpretation of tests. In many instances computerized testing offers the complete package of test administration, scoring, profiling, and interpretation. Computerized guidance systems such as the SIGI PLUS (System of Interactive Guidance and Information) and the Discover system not only provide individual assessment information, but also provides linkages to related follow-up information desirable for career decision-making. There are several advantages of computer and Internet use for assessment. Probably the most obvious is the ready accessibility of instruments and the immediate feedback of results. With many populations, especially school-aged youth, there appear to be psychological advantages as well, because the computer to many seems like a nonthreatening and even fun way to give and receive information. These programs have also stimulated the outreach efforts of counseling offices, especially to the disabled and those who live in isolated geographic regions.

In order to effectively use technology for assessment purposes, Wall, in Bloom and Walz (2000), suggests that educators—including counselors—should:

- understand the advantages and pitfalls of technology use, particularly as they relate to the use of assessment tools with clients and students
- follow the assessment standards and policies of applicable professional associations
- use the best practices . . . to better assure good service to their clientele
- stay updated on topics related to assessment and technology (Wall, 2000, p. 238)

SUMMARY

Assessment and career assistance have been inextricably linked since the early beginnings and throughout the development of the counseling movement in the United States. Throughout this development, the major assessment emphasis has been on identifying the abilities and interests of clients relevant to career possibilities. Since World War II, personality variables and values have also received increased attention in career assessment. Although the overwhelming majority of assessment techniques have focused on standardized testing, nonstandardized methods such as interviews, rating scales, and other observation techniques have come into play. Also, as noted in the preceding section, the *DSM-IV* has become very popular as a nonstandardized but systematic approach to individual assessment.

Typically, upon the completion of the assessment process, the counselor and client are ready to explore possible career options. Dramatic changes have occurred, in just the past decade, to techniques that clients and counselors may use to instantly access and explore a wide range of career and related educational information and options. Some of these will be noted in Chapter 6, which describes career counseling activities in school settings.

DISCUSSION QUESTIONS

1. Identify any standardized test that you have taken that influenced your planning or decision making.
2. Identify any autobiographies you have read that were written by famous people. Discuss any special insights they provided you regarding the author.
3. Design a standardized testing program for screening candidates for admission to counselor preparation programs. Share and defend your program.
4. When you meet someone for the first time, what traits or characteristics do you particularly notice?
5. If you were to write your autobiography, what title would you use?

CLASS ACTIVITIES

1. Develop an interest checklist for identifying potential counselors.
2. In small groups, develop a checklist and a questionnaire that might be used for assessing candidates applying to master's level counselor preparation programs.
3. Develop an assessment program designed to screen candidates for sales positions in a large marketing firm.
4. Design a rating scale to measure the social interaction skills of 6th grade pupils and a second rating scale to measure 12th grade students.
5. In small groups, go out and observe three strangers unknown to any of the group members. Upon returning to the class, each observer should share his or her observations with the other members of their small group.

READINGS OF INTEREST

Jones, W. P. (2004). Testing and counseling: A marriage saved by the Internet? In J. W. Bloom & G. R. Walz (Eds.). *Cybercounseling & Cyberlearning: An Encore.* Alexandria, VA: American Counseling Association and Greensboro, NC: CAPS, Inc.

Kennedy. R. B., & Kennedy, D. A. (2004). Using the Myers-Briggs Type Indicator in career counseling. *Journal of Employment Counseling, 41*(1), 38–44.

Perrone, K. M., Sedlacek, W. E., & Alexander, C. M. (2001). An investigation of Holland types and the

Sixteen Personality Factor Questionnaire—Fifth Edition. *The Career Development Quarterly, 50*(2), 179–188

Thorngren, J. M., & Feit, S. S. (2001). The Career-O-Gram: A postmodern career intervention. *The Career Development Quarterly, 49*(4), 291–303.

Vacc, N. A., Juhnke, G. A., & Nilsen, K. A. (2001). Community mental health service providers' codes of ethics and the Standards for Educational and Psychological Testing. *Journal of Counseling & Development, 79*(2), 217–224

Wnuk, S. M., & Amundson, N. E. (2003). Using the Intelligent Careers Card Sort with university students. *The Career Development Quarterly, 51*(3), 274–284.

Chapter 6

Career Counseling Across the Life Span: School Populations

Career counseling, like all counseling, is both personal and developmental—with an emphasis on career choice and development goals. Students at all levels of education can be helped to achieve career development if the interventions are developmentally appropriate. And, experiencing success in one's career counseling efforts can be both exciting and rewarding.

Stanley B. Baker, PhD
Professor of Counselor Education
North Carolina State University at Raleigh

OBJECTIVES

To provide readers with an understanding of:

1. Basic counseling skills and their applications to career counseling
2. Concepts of human development
3. Characteristics of students and schools at the elementary, middle, secondary and higher education levels and their implications for career assistance programs at these levels
4. Provisions for career counseling and guidance in elementary, middle, and secondary school settings

INTRODUCTION: THE CAREER COUNSELOR IS A COUNSELOR

As we begin our discussions of career counseling across the life span, we will first review basic counseling techniques. We will then discuss career counseling across the school ages from elementary through college.

The hallmark of any profession is that its members embrace and engage in the basic activity, the centerpiece, of that profession. Thus, counselors are expected to, first and foremost, counsel. Assessment and providing information enhance the counseling process but do not replace it. In career counseling, although the subject may be the client's career, the process of assisting the client is still considered counseling. Although career counseling *is* counseling, we can distinguish it from other forms of counseling because it has more specific standardized assessment instruments available; it offers computerized assistance systems that assist counselors and clients in career decision-making; the counselor gives more information than in many areas of counseling; and is also more able to connect the client with career opportunities in differing environments.

As we consider the significance of professional counseling in the context of career counseling, we should remind ourselves of the basic skills expected of all counselors: (a) attending behavior; (b) reflection of feelings; (c) unconditional positive regard for our clients; (d) respect; (e) empathy; (f) facilitative communication; and (g) genuineness. Counselors should also exemplify good human relationship skills and should watch for opportunities to advocate for fairness and ethical behavior.

In addition to individual counseling, career counselors frequently use groups in the process of facilitating career development, exploration, and decision-making. These groups should be conducted within the professional framework of group counseling. This means that attention may be given to the selection of group members, the appropriateness of topics for group member needs, and logistical considerations such as mutual convenience of meeting times. A group counselor must conduct himself or herself in an open, honest, sincere, and ethical manner at all times. He or she must also accept the input of all group members who wish to contribute but should not demand that individuals respond on occasions when they prefer not to. A group counselor, as in individual counseling, must recognize and reflect the contributions of group members, aid in clarification, and when appropriate, he or she should encourage questions and the examination of information. A group counselor should mirror the feelings of individual members and the group as a whole and should provide a summary and some sort of feedback at the conclusion of each group session.

Baker and Gerler (2004) also suggested that school counselors in the 21st century will probably be more effective if they are able to provide proactive programs that meet and enhance developmental needs as well as reacting to the more traditional demands for intervention when required (p. 36).

SHORT-TERM COUNSELING

A significant number of clients seeking career assistance can be, and probably desire to be, served in a relatively short period of time. This somewhat abbreviated time frame has often been labeled *short-term counseling* or *therapy*. Reinforcing this approach is a considerable amount of evidence indicating that short-term counseling is at least as effective as the more traditional long-term counseling, in terms of the durability of results. Short-term counseling is characterized by: (a) prompt attention to a client's needs; (b) rapid assessment of and focus on the client's needs; and (c) successful assistance in a short period of time.

Another attribute of short-term counseling is that typical clients hope for relatively brief assistance with their target problems. Candidates that will react best to short-term approaches are those who: (a) are motivated to change or make decisions; (b) expect only a short period of time with a counselor; (c) can establish personal relationships easily and readily; and (d) are not psychologically impaired. Short-term career assistance will be possible when a client seeks routine information or interpretations of information.

COACHING

Coaching has long been associated with the sporting world and with legendary coaches like Vince Lombardi, Newt Rockne, John Wooden, and Casey Stengel. These distinguished coaches are familiar names to most sports fans. So are counselors now *coaches*? Perhaps they are. The title could fit. An athletic coach may condition his or her players physically but counselors condition their clients psychologically. Athletic coaches draw up game plans for their teams to execute but counselors draw up game plans intended to assist their clients with lifelong fulfillment—winning the game of life.

The use of the *coaching* label to distinguish a particular and unique relationship between counselors and clients is relatively new; it is a product of the last years of the 20th century. Auerbach (2001) noted that the essential difference most frequently cited between psychotherapy and coaching is that psychotherapy usually focuses on resolving mental illnesses or trauma and coaching focuses on enhancing achievement and fulfillment in well-functioning individuals.

The Professional and Personal Coaches Association, now the International Coach Federation, describes coaching as follows:

> Coaching is an ongoing relationship, between the professional coach and the client, which focuses on the client taking action towards the realization of his or her vision, goals, or desires. Coaching uses a process of inquiry

and personal discovery to build the client's level of awareness and responsibility and provides the client with structure, support, and feedback." (Auerbach, 2001, p. 6)

Gallwey defines coaching as "a powerful alliance designed to forward and enhance the lifelong process of human learning, effectiveness, and fulfillment." (as cited in Auerbach, p. 6)

As we view these definitions and the current literature describing nonathletic coaching, we might conclude that it is a process in which the coach motivates the client to develop and utilize the client's potential across his or her life span. We believe that a goal of professional counseling is to help clients to become the best they can become.

When examining steps in the coaching process one can note their similarity to those of the counseling process:

1. **relationship establishment**   The coach exhibits understanding and human relationship skills designed to promote comfort and trust in the relationship.
2. **assessment**   The coach seeks information to help him or her understand the client's current situation. The coach also seeks information that will help gain an understanding of the client's strengths, weaknesses, values, and goals.
3. **goal identification**   The coach works with the client to identify his or her ideal self and lifelong goals. The coach and client work together to establish these goals and to determine the appropriate role for the coach. The goals themselves should be attainable but they should also be challenging. It is not uncommon to write the agreed-upon goals down in a contract form for the signatures of both the coach and the client.
4. **preparation to achieve goals**   The client and coach work together to identify the most appropriate procedures or activities that help with goal achievement. Time lines should be specified and an evaluation process must be agreed upon.
5. **action to achieve goals**   This step is essentially the implementation of the procedural plan for goal achievement within the agreed-upon time limits. The coach may suggest homework to facilitate the process. The coach will also provide support, encouragement, and ongoing evaluation and accountability. This process may include the necessity of learning new skills and may necessitate attitudinal change.
6. **continued reinforcement**   The coach will continue to lend support to the client, monitor the client's progress, and provide advice and counsel.

CONSULTATION

The term *consultation* is a popular one and is used in a wide variety of fields ranging from used car consultants to financial consultants. The term *consultation,* and the activity it represents, originated in the medical profession in the 19th century and became an accepted activity for counselors in the latter years of the 20th century. A consultant is an individual who possesses expertise, skills, and knowledge in a specific field and who assists other individuals or groups when this expertise is requested by a third party (such as a homeroom teacher, a community agency, or a business organization). The consultant becomes the helper in a triad that includes the consultee and the object of the consultation.

In school settings, school counselors will frequently serve as consultants to teachers, school administrators, parents, and student groups. A school counselor should, through training and experience, have an understanding of the educational environment and its influences. School counselors should also have the human relationship and communication skills necessary to easily and effectively consult with those school-related populations most likely to seek consultation assistance. Group skills are also useful in facilitating consultation that involves group motivation and change. School consultants must have an understanding of human growth and development, including problems and processes of adjustment, appropriate to the age group they are serving. A consultant's role is advisor rather than a supervisor.

When counselors function as consultants, there are certain basic guidelines appropriate to the consultation process:

1. The identified need cannot be adequately dealt with by the organization or individual seeking consultation assistance.
2. The consultant possesses the expertise and skills necessary to appropriately address the need.
3. The party in need, once requesting the aid of the consultant, has the capacity to implement the consultant's recommendations.
4. The consultant possesses or acquires an adequate understanding of the organization and environmental context within which his or her recommendations will be carried out. The consultant is also aware of possible consequences once the problem has been solved.

CAREER COUNSELING IN SCHOOLS

We should first remind ourselves that all aspects of human development—social, physical, emotional, psychological, and educational—are only parts of an individual's total development. Although these parts are interwoven and may often be difficult to distinguish from each other, we recognize that they all contribute to the career development of an individual. It is important that the many aspects be recognized when designing and implementing programs that provide career counseling and assistance over the life span and that are critical to the development of an individual's human potential.

Five concepts of development related to career counseling and the development of the individual's human potential are noted as follows.

1. Development occurs across the life span of the individual. Significant in this development is the maturing process, which is related to the mastery of developmental tasks at each life stage. Career counseling should reflect an awareness of this process and the developmental tasks to provide those experiences and information that enable the individual to master these tasks at the highest level of one's potential.

2. Environment is a significant factor influencing the development of one's potential. Career counseling seeks to accent the favorable factors in an individual's environment and compensate for or intervene with those unfavorable factors that might limit one's capacity to develop to the fullest.

3. Career development should recognize the different life age-stages through which the individual progresses and provide the experiences and learnings that are appropriate for each.

4. As individuals develop, the aptitudes and interests in which they excel should be enhanced by experiences and other strategies designed to assist them in developing their full potential.

5. Programs designed to optimize the development of the individual must also work to inhibit factors that might prevent such full development. This suggests that prevention and early intervention programs should be designed to compensate for negative factors that could possibly influence the individual's development in a negative way. (Gibson & Mitchell, 2003, pp. 321–322)[1]

In the exploration of career development across the life span, careers offer probably the greatest opportunity for individuals to achieve what they are capable of achieving. Career counselors can play a continuous role in this process by assisting and encouraging their clients to challenge the limits of their potential. The paragraphs that follow discuss ways in which counselors in school settings may undertake these important tasks.

Some principles that guide the practice of career counseling in schools include: (a) the opportunity to develop an unbiased basis for later career decision-making; (b) the early and continuous development of positive attitudes toward school *and* work; (c) developing an understanding of the relationship between work and education; and (d) experiencing opportunities to test, consult, experience, and develop the client's potential. As the ultimate goal of every individual seeking career counseling should be to enter into and progress in some worthwhile rewarding and enjoyable work, career counseling seeks to facilitate this goal. Counselors help clients to make appropriate choices, learn how to make decisions, and develop investigative strategies. Because every individual who seeks career counseling anticipates working in his or her adult life, the overwhelming majority of our population can benefit from career counseling and assistance at some point in their life.

---

[1] *Gibson, Robert L., & Mitchell, Marianne H., Introduction to Counseling and Guidance, 6/e, © 2003. Reprinted by permission of Pearson Education, Inc., Upper Saddle River, NJ.*

CAREER DEVELOPMENT IN ELEMENTARY SCHOOLS

The development of an individual's potential begins, in a formal and programmatic sense, in the elementary school and will continue throughout his or her lifetime. The great potential of the individual and the collective potential of humankind is important to consider. We have only to look at the achievements of our species—from the discovery of fire to the walk on the moon—to remind ourselves of our ever-present potential. Each individual possesses multiple potentials and, while some may never be fully explored, we must—as counselors—accept the challenge to stimulate each individual's exploration of their potential.

The elementary school has long been accepted by most adult residents of the United States as the most effective tool, fashioned by the culture, for shaping our youth. In this regard, elementary schools have been expected to provide the foundations for each individual's future learning, including their responsibilities as productive citizens in the workforce of society and for their socialization into the society. Whereas the instructional program in elementary schools seeks to provide for the teaching and learning of those basic skills that provide the essential foundations for lifelong learning, counseling programs in elementary schools provide the needed foundations, in a child's development, for lifelong living. The latter includes the acquisition of basic social and personal foundations, including career development.

Counseling programs represent a significant educational effort of elementary schools. They represent the ultimate effort of a school system to foster the fulfillment of human potential of its elementary school pupils and to assure their positive future as productive citizens. The broad and ideal goals of elementary school counseling programs are to help both the individual pupil and the school itself to become the best that they can be. Table 6-1 indicates benefits of counseling programs in elementary schools.

In the development of counseling programs, it is important to understand the characteristics of the target population the program is designed to serve. However, the difficulties of characterizing an elementary school population in general, and a typical elementary school student specifically (even if restricted to a particular age or grade level), is nearly impossible. The difficulty can be even more appreciated by teachers and parents who have daily contact with elementary school children. Therefore, any attempt to discuss the characteristics of elementary school students then must be prefaced by a warning: Children in this age range exhibit wide differences and variations in their characteristics and also in their individual needs and any given listing could not be equally applicable to every individual.

There have been innumerable studies completed, and many volumes written, about the needs of elementary school children. The brief discussion in this chapter will neither attempt to summarize or highlight even the most significant of these studies nor attempt to summarize the multitude of studies available in this area. For our purposes, and as a basis for examining career development in the elementary school, we may view these studies and our need to understand student development from two standpoints: (a) those basic needs that continuously demand satisfaction; and (b) those developmental needs that must be met during different life stages. The basic needs of humankind that must be constantly satisfied were presented by

TABLE 6-1
Benefits of counseling programs in elementary schools

The elementary school exists to provide:	The counseling program in the elementary school can contribute by:	This implies the following:
1. Foundations for learning and living	1. Providing classroom (c/r) guidance to enhance learning and relate learning to preparation	1.1 Classroom guidance 1.2 Consultation with teachers and administrators
2. Transmission of our culture and historical heritage	2. Developing multicultural awareness: pride in our cultural diversity; and respect for the uniqueness of all cultural/ethnic groups	2.1 Classroom guidance activities 2.2 Consultation with teachers and administrators 2.3 Group guidance and counseling
3. Development as a social-psychological being	3. Providing for the socialization (social development) of all children, including respect for self and others	3.1 Group guidance and group counseling focusing on prevention, development, and remediation 3.2 Individual counseling 3.3 Consultation with parent
4. Preparation for citizenship	4. Providing for the development of each individual's human potential	4.1 Career development 4.2 Individual assessment 4.3 Talent and skill enhancement

Source: From R. L. Gibson, M. H. Mitchell, & S. K. Basile, *Counseling in the Elementary School: A Comprehensive Approach,* p. 20. Copyright © 1993. Reprinted by permission of Allyn & Bacon.

Maslow (1954) in a hierarchy or priority ordering (previously noted in Chapter 4) in which the higher order needs demand satisfaction prior to the lower order needs.

A prominent career theorist, Anne Roe, believed that the need structure of the individual (as previously noted in Chapter 4) would be greatly influenced by one's early childhood experiences. These needs would influence, in turn, the career categories the individual would consider or select. Within this context, as we view the elementary school student and his or her ability to become self-actualized and develop their potential, including their career potential, we must be concerned with and aware of the degree to which the individual's higher order needs are being met.

A second and equally important consideration is the need to meet the developmental needs of the individual during different life stages. These developmental needs have been well presented by Havighurst (1953) in his popular developmental tasks. He identifies the following developmental tasks for middle childhood:

1. learning physical skills necessary for ordinary games
2. building wholesome attitudes toward oneself as a growing organism
3. learning to get along with age mates

4. learning an appropriate masculine or feminine social role
5. developing fundamental skills in reading, writing, and calculation
6. developing concepts necessary for everyday living
7. developing conscience, morality, and a scale of values
8. achieving personal independence
9. developing attitudes toward social groups and situations (Gibson & Mitchell, 2003, p. 76)[2]

Relevant to Havighurst's developmental tasks are the results of a study of the most frequently mentioned mental health needs of elementary school students, as identified in a survey, of 57 elementary school teachers, conducted by your authors. These high-priority mental health needs were identified, in order, as follows:

1. coping skills
2. social skills
3. behavior management
4. being responsible
5. motivation

These skills are obviously significant to an individual's success in his or her adult years in the world of work. Just as obviously, the development of these skills must begin in the formative/elementary school years of the individual's life. Elementary school counselors and teachers must plan and work together to ensure that these important developmental skills are not left to chance.

Two other important viewpoints of child development should also be noted: (a) Piaget's stages of cognitive development; and (b) Erikson's stages of personal and social development. Piaget believed that dramatic changes occurred in sequential stages in an individual's thinking process. His four stages of cognitive development are sensory and motor, preoperational, concrete operational, and formal operational. These stages are associated with approximate ages, although knowing the age of the child does not guarantee that they are using their thinking abilities associated with the stage. Piaget's stages are simply general descriptions of the way children think. In fact, some children may think at one stage and, at the same time, be utilizing another stage for other thought processes.

Erik Erikson emphasized the importance of the social environment on each individual's psychological development, which provides, a meaningful link between personal and social development. His theory, therefore, is called a *psycho-social theory*. It emphasizes how the self emerges, one's search for identity, and the importance of one's personal relationships in all stages of life, and provides counselors with a helpful framework for understanding the dynamic impact of school and home environments on personal and social development. Erikson identified eight psycho-social stages from birth through death. Each of these stages consists of a developmental crisis that must be resolved. Depending on the reactions of individuals, a conflict involved with each crisis will be resolved in a positive or negative way. Successful

---

[2] *Gibson, Robert L., & Mitchell, Marianne H.,* Introduction to Counseling and Guidance, *6/e, © 2003. Reprinted by permission of Pearson Education, Inc., Upper Saddle River, NJ.*

accomplishments in early stages will contribute to the individual's ability to resolve future crises, thus creating an interdependence among the stages. On the other hand, an undesirable or unhealthy resolution of a psycho-social crisis can result in difficulties throughout one's later life. However, an unsatisfactory resolution may later be altered to satisfactory outcomes when proper conditions present themselves. Erikson's and Piaget's stages are labeled and contrasted in Figure 6-1.

The viewpoints of Maslow, Havighurst, Piaget, and Erikson stressed the personal, cultural, cognitive, and social/emotional needs of children as they grow and develop. These theories, in turn, imply developmental tasks for the elementary schools themselves. The tasks of providing appropriate learning, social, and other developmental experiences to meet the basic and developmental needs of elementary school students would thus appear to be the responsibility of the elementary school. Among the developmental needs of students is the need to attend to career

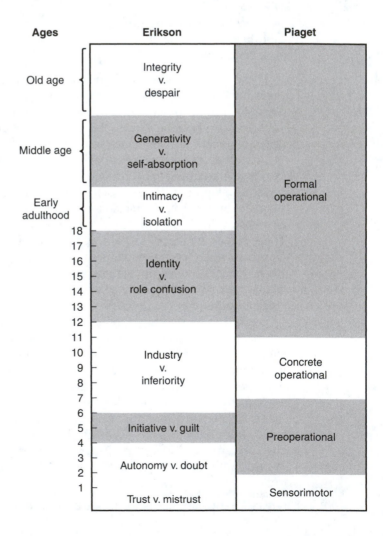

FIGURE 6-1
Stages in personal and cognitive development

Source: From Slavin, Robert E. *Education Psychology: Theory Into Practice,* 3/e. Published by Allyn and Bacon, Boston, MA. Copyright © 1991 by Pearson Education. Reprinted by permission of the publisher.

development. Some general characteristics of elementary school children, which should be considered in the development of a responsive and relevant career program, are as follows:

- Elementary school students experience continuous growth, development, and change.
- Elementary school students constantly integrate their experiences.
- Elementary school students are relatively limited in the ability to verbalize.
- The reasoning powers of elementary school students are not yet fully developed.
- The ability of elementary school students to concentrate over long periods of time is limited.
- Enthusiasm and interest can be easily aroused in elementary school children.
- Decisions and goals tend to serve immediate purposes rather than long-range plans.
- The feelings of elementary school children are displayed openly.

Few would argue that the elementary years are the most important for preparing youth to make appropriate career and educational decisions and related personal and social adjustments. These are years of curiosity and inquiry, trial and exploration, and relative freedom from prejudice. As such, the elementary grades encompass the natural years for developing appropriate career foundations. It is within the role of the school counseling and guidance program to see that these opportunities are not lost.

CHARACTERISTICS OF ELEMENTARY SCHOOLS

Educational planners have long recognized that educational programs and the institutions that house them must reflect the characteristics of the students they are designed to serve. Although elementary and secondary schools share certain characteristics in common, each is a unique institution in its own right and reflects both its place on the educational continuum and the growth and developmental characteristics of the student population it is designed to serve. It is therefore important that the career development program in the elementary school reflect the general objectives and characteristics of the elementary school itself as well as the characteristics and needs of its student population. Having noted the characteristics of elementary school children, which have implications for the career development program in the elementary school, it is important to recognize the characteristics of the elementary school itself as the contextual framework within which a career guidance program will be planned to meet the needs of each student.

The elementary school is organized for the general purposes of (a) initiating and orienting the child to the educational environment and processes and (b) providing the child with basic academic foundations in the essential content fields. The characteristics of the elementary school itself are important when organizing and developing any program at that level—including career development programs. The first of these characteristics to note is that the elementary school is homeroom/teacher-centered. Elementary school students will usually have a homeroom assignment and be with a homeroom teacher for much of the school day. Further, elementary school children are with this teacher for at least one, and often two, academic years. Many of the students' activities—social as well as academic—tend to originate in the homeroom. The homeroom serves another important objective of the elementary school: to facilitate the socialization of the children. In this setting the elementary teacher is a major influence on the behavior, adjustment, and development of the children. As a result, teacher/pupil relationships are more intimate in the elementary school than in the higher grades because of their close association, and teachers and students have the opportunity to get to know each other better. Elementary school teachers frequently become listening stations for student concerns and friends to elementary students in need. Elementary school children know that he or she can communicate with his or her teacher and that the teacher will be a receptive and understanding listener. Additionally, elementary schools are laboratories for living. The elementary setting provides the child with the opportunity for developing self-understanding, responsibilities, concern for others, and the ability to relate to others and to make appropriate decisions.

Elementary schools emphasize learning through seeing and doing—more than at any other educational level. Learning is stimulated through student observation, participation, and activity. Role playing, field trips, and physical exercises related to learning are common student experiences in elementary schools. Another characteristic of elementary schools is that they are usually smaller and less complex than the middle schools or junior or senior high schools into which the students will eventually matriculate. Curricular patterns and physical facilities are relatively simple. In addition, elementary school children are members of a reasonably stable group because they may be with many of the same classmates throughout the elementary school years.

The elementary school setting encourages a greater feeling of security and encourages the student to explore and experiment. Also, parental interest and involvement tends to be greater at the elementary school level. At the time of a child's first significant separation from the home, and during the initial experiences of the son or daughter in formal education, it is only natural that more parents will be more involved than in the student's later educational years. This involvement also promises potential contributions to the student's career understandings by making them more aware of their parents' careers and the careers of their friends' parents.

CAREER DEVELOPMENT GUIDELINES FOR ELEMENTARY SCHOOLS

The previously-stated characteristics of elementary school children and elementary schools provide the basis or implications for principles upon which career development programs in elementary schools can be based. These implications are stated with the uniqueness of each elementary student's developmental needs and the educational setting of the elementary school in mind:

- Students should be provided with the opportunity to develop an unbiased base from which they can make their later occupational/educational decisions.
- The early and continuous development of a positive student attitude toward education is critical.

- As a corollary to the first two statements, elementary students must be taught to view a career as a way of life and view education as preparation for life.
- Elementary students must have help to develop an adequate understanding of themselves and must be prepared to relate this understanding to both their social/personal development and their career educational planning.
- Students must be provided with an understanding of the relationships between education and career. Students need an understanding of both where they are and why they are at a given point on the educational continuum at a given time.
- Elementary school students must have career-oriented experiences that are appropriate for their levels of readiness and that are simultaneously meaningful and realistic.
- Students must have opportunities to test concepts, skills, and roles in order to develop values that may have future career application.
- Elementary school career guidance programs are centered in the classroom, with coordination and consultation by school counselors and participation by parents.
- An elementary school's program of career guidance is integrated into the functioning guidance and total educational programs of the institution.

COMPETENCIES FOR ELEMENTARY SCHOOL STUDENTS CAREER DEVELOPMENT

The developmental approach to the career development of an elementary school student is the appropriate and desired approach. This approach is based on the identification of competencies that elementary school children should acquire during their elementary school years. They are the desired outcomes for the school's comprehensive career development and guidance program. The competencies themselves provide a good basis for planning activities, which should be a cooperative enterprise between counselors and faculty. Suggested career development competencies for elementary and middle schools appear in Table 6-2.

CAREER DEVELOPMENT PROGRAMS IN ELEMENTARY SCHOOLS

A career development program for an elementary school must provide the appropriate experiences along with the relevant resources that recognize a child's growth and development characteristics at each level. Elementary school counselors will find that there are many opportunities for experiences that utilize natural and prepared resources available to facilitate elementary school students' career development. One viewpoint for examining these potential resources is a chronological one that presumes that a child's early experiences will occur, in all probability, primarily in the home, secondarily in his or her elementary school, and thirdly in the community where the pupil resides. Figure 6-2 depicts the resource pool for career development experiences.

The career development team for an elementary school child should place the parent/teacher and counselor on the "first string." All of these adults have important roles to play in the child's early career development and preliminary career planning. Each will be less effective without major involvement from the others.

TABLE 6-2
Career development competencies

Type of grade school	Sample indicators that competency has been developed
Elementary school:	*Student can:*

Elementary school:

1. Knowledge of the importance of a positive self-concept to career development
2. Skills for interacting with others*
3. Awareness of the importance of emotional and physical development on career decision making
4. Awareness of the importance of educational achievement to career opportunities*
5. Awareness of interrelationship of work and learning*
6. Skills for understanding and using career information*
7. Awareness of the interrelationship of personal responsibility, good work habits, and career opportunities*
8. Awareness of how careers relate to needs and functions of society
9. Understanding of how to make decisions and choose alternatives related to tentative educational and career goals*
10. Awareness of the interrelationship of life roles and careers*
11. Awareness of changing male/female roles in different occupations
12. Awareness of career planning process*

Student can:

1. Describe positive characteristics about self
2. Demonstrate skills in resolving conflicts
3. Identify ways to express and deal with feelings
4. Implement a plan of action for improving academic skills
5. Describe how one's role as a student is like that of an adult worker
6. Describe jobs in his/her community
7. Describe the importance of cooperation among workers for accomplishing a task
8. Describe how careers can satisfy personal needs
9. Describe how decisions affect self and others
10. Identify the value of leisure activities for enriching one's lifestyle
11. Describe the changing roles of men and women in the workplace
12. Describe the importance of planning

Middle school/junior high school:

1. Knowledge of the influence of positive self-concept on career development
2. Skills for interacting with others*
3. Knowledge of the importance of emotional and physical development on career decision making
4. Knowledge of the relationship of educational achievement to career opportunities*
5. Skills for locating, understanding, and using career information*
6. Knowledge of skills necessary to seek and obtain a job*
7. Understanding of the attitudes necessary for success in work and learning*
8. Understanding how careers relate to needs and functions of the economy and society
9. Skills in making decisions and choosing alternatives in planning for and pursuing tentative educational and career goals*
10. Knowledge of the interrelationship of life roles and careers*
11. Understanding of changing male/female roles
12. Understanding of the process of career planning*
13. Understanding the relationship between work and learning*

Student can:

1. Describe personal likes and dislikes
2. Demonstrate an appreciation for similarities and differences in people
3. Identify internal and external sources of stress and conflict
4. Relate one's aptitudes and abilities to broad occupational areas
5. Identify various ways occupations can be classified
6. Compile a job application form in a satisfactory manner
7. Demonstrate effective learning habits and skills
8. Discuss the variety and complexity of occupations
9. Describe one's current life context as it relates to career decisions
10. Describe the interrelationships among family, career, and leisure
11. Describe problems, adjustments, and advantages of entering a nontraditional career
12. Identify tentative life and career goals
13. Demonstrate effective learning habits

*These competencies are also included in the *National Standards for School Counseling Programs,* by C. A. Campbell and C. A. Dahir, 1997, Alexandria, VA: American School Counselors Association.

Source: From Brown, *Career Information, Career Counseling, and Career Development,* 8/e. Published by Allyn and Bacon, Boston, MA. Copyright © 2003 by Pearson Education. Reprinted by permission of the publisher.

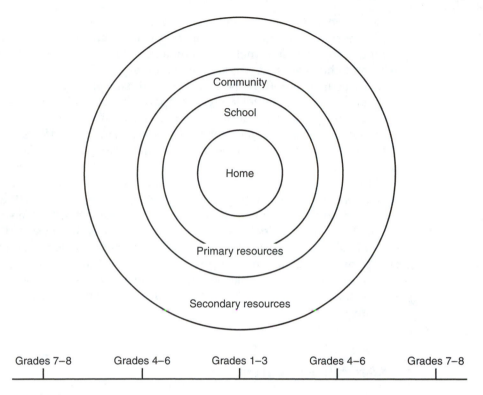

FIGURE 6-2
Pool of resources

Source: From R. L. Gibson, M. H. Mitchell, and S. K. Basile, *Counseling in the Elementary School: A Comprehensive Approach*, p. 205. Copyright © 1993. Reprinted by permission of Allyn and Bacon.

Usually, adults at home provide elementary school students with the most persistent, as well as important, contact with a worker. In this setting, children have the opportunity to do a detailed study of their parents' careers, to learn the role of work and its importance in the life of adults, and to understand work's impact on the family's way of life and daily living. Further, children's homes convey values appropriate to careers and the world of work and, unfortunately, biases that may prejudice children as they consider options in the world of work.

In many family settings, elementary school students become cognizant of the dramatic and rapid changes affecting the world of work and workers such as their parents. For example, many working parents will experience multiple careers over their working lifetime as opposed to the traditional single career pattern of the past. They will be a resource to other pupils who may be experiencing more traditional family-work lives. Parents are continuous influences on children, but classroom teachers, and sometimes counselors, will change as the pupils move through the elementary school grades. Continuity of a student's career development program is thus enhanced when parents are aware of and are involved in the program.

Some techniques for parental involvement include: (a) teacher/counselor/parent conferences; (b) parental participation in career guidance activities; (c) providing parents with career information and materials; (d) making parents aware of special skills and characteristics of their child; and (e) explaining the school's program of career guidance. In return, the counselor and teacher may anticipate: (a) additional pupil data and (b) parental interest, support, and possible participation as consultants or program participants. The counselor is the coordinator and specialist of the team who must recognize the teacher as the key in-school person, and the parent as the key out-of-school person in an effective program of elementary school career guidance.

If the parents' contribution to their children's career development is to be maximized, they must be aware of their potential and the role that they may play in their children's development. It is therefore important that the parent be educated about the children's developmental characteristics and needs, including those in the career area of their children; what the school is doing or planning to do about these developmental needs; and how they can contribute. The following (Example 6-1) is an example of correspondence for the purpose of orienting parents to their potential involvement in a career development unit and seeking their assistance.

EXAMPLE 6-1: Parent Letter

Dear Parent,

Next Wednesday our third grade class will begin their study of a unit entitled "Introduction to the World of Work." I am enclosing a copy of the lesson plan for this unit for your information and also because we hope that you might be willing to assist us in making this a very meaningful learning experience for our third-grade students. You will note that your son, Joseph, has been assigned to interview you (and your spouse, if employed) about your job(s). This interview will be based on the kinds of information he and his fellow class members have decided they would like to have about workers in today's world of work. All interviewees will be asked to respond to the question "What makes a good worker?" During the week after the job interviews and discussions, we will discuss good habits at home that lead to good habits on the job, and your assistance will again be appreciated. In this latter activity, each pupil will have assignments as a "home worker." At the end of the week, you and your spouse will be asked to complete a "Home Worker Checklist" that your son will bring home to you.

Many thanks for your assistance and cooperation in these assignments. If you have any suggestions, comments, or questions, please call me.

Sincerely yours,
Ms. Ashley Spencer
Counselor

Home Worker's Checklist

Dear Parent:

Please place a check mark beside each of the following that your son/daughter accomplishes for each day of the week, beginning on Monday

	M	T	W	R	F
• arises on time					
• makes bed before departing for school					
• straightens up his or her bedroom					
• is on time for meals					
• washes face and hands before eating					
• brushes teeth after eating					
• voluntarily helps with housework					
• is polite and considerate to others					
• can be depended on					
• goes to bed at a reasonable hour					

Comments:

Please ask Joseph to bring this form to school with him on Friday, October 16. Thank you for your help.

Mr. Jake Wallace
Third Grade Teacher
Snowdeep Elementary School

As noted earlier, elementary school teachers have a crucial role to play in children's career development. In elementary schools, classroom teachers have daily contact with the student and works closest with them and therefore has the opportunity to have daily influence on the child's career attitudes and concepts and to indicate appropriate role models. Classroom teachers have the opportunity to continuously stimulate children's career curiosity and awareness. Classroom teachers can also incorporate appropriate career development learning activities into the planned program of the student's total learning experience.

In many instances, elementary school counselors will work with classroom teachers and will provide suggestions and materials and assist in the preparation of effective educational/career development activities and learning experiences. An example of a cooperative effort involving the classroom teacher and the elementary school counselor is noted in Example 6-2, a career unit prepared for utilization in an elementary school classroom.

EXAMPLE 6-2: Unit Title: Introduction to the World of Work

Unit Objectives:

1. to become more aware of the significance of the "world of work"
2. to become more knowledgeable about one specific career
3. to become aware of the many different jobs in the world of work
4. to learn about some of the characteristics that make a good worker
5. to practice good home habits that can become good work habits

Methods for Achieving Unit Objectives:

1. The film, "The World of Work," will be presented and class discussion will follow.
2. *Assignment:* Each pupil will be asked to "interview" at least one of their parents about his or her career. Class members will discuss kinds of information and questions to ask. Following the completion of the assignment, each class member will identify the career she or he explored, present findings, and answer any questions classmates may ask.
3. *Bulletin board display:* Each child will be asked to cut out an illustration, from a magazine or newspaper, which illustrates his or her parents' careers. These will be grouped by the teacher to illustrate clusters of similar careers as well as the many different jobs represented in even this relatively small group of people. The display will be studied and reacted to in class discussions.
4. The pupil will be requested to ask their parents "what makes a good worker?" Each pupil will report these responses to the class and a discussion will follow. Their teacher will conclude the discussion by presenting composite characteristics of good workers.
5. From the previous exercise, a list of good work habits will be prepared. Those that can be practiced in the home will be part of a checklist that parents will be asked to keep for a week.
6. The unit will be concluded with a review and discussion.

Period of Time for Unit: Two Weeks Related Activities

Art class: Pupils will be asked to draw pictures depicting their parents at work.

Music class: The class will learn songs about work and workers ("I've Been Working on the Railroad," "There's no Business Like Show Business").

Source: From Gibson, R. L., Mitchell, M. H., & Basile, S. K. *Counseling in the Elementary School: A Comprehensive Approach,* pp. 209–210. Published by Allyn and Bacon, Boston, MA. Copyright © 1993 by Pearson Education. Reprinted by permission of the publisher.

In the upper elementary grades, students may actually operate a school store as a real business activity. While this is a traditional activity, it is still a popular and meaningful educational activity that conveys a career message. Such stores may sell candy, inexpensive school supplies, and novelties. Students staff the store, keep track of sales, order goods as needed, and decide how to use their profits. Similarly, students will often sell magazine subscriptions, candy, or other merchandise as door-to-door salespeople to raise money for class projects. Such activities also serve as valuable prework experiences.

School newspapers are becoming increasingly popular in upper elementary grades. In this activity students assume the various occupational roles associated with the press, such as editors, sports writers, fashion columnists, reporters, cartoonists, and managers. As they develop and publish their own school or classroom newspaper, they may meet with representatives of the local press to further their understanding of their assumed "careers." In such an experience they become aware of the various careers associated with the news media, and at the same time, learn writing and English usage skills. Coauthored novels and autobiographies are other examples of activities that combine writing careers with the development of language arts.

Pupils at all grade levels enjoy playing games and those with a career flavor are no exception. The well-known television show "What's My Line?" can be adapted to the classroom. Parents or students represent certain careers, and participants and different panels of students then try to identify the career of each participant. They are limited to ten "indirect" questions. In another version of this game students may develop skits using puppets to demonstrate various careers while the class members seek to identify their "line." The popular party game, "charades," can be both fun and informative. Each student attempts to provide cues, while remaining silent, to his or her team, which can lead to the identification of careers selected by the opposing team.

Occupational crossword puzzles can be developed. Students may work on them individually or in teams of two in competition with other student teams. Occupational games in which students use dice to advance up a career ladder are informative and stimulating.

Another popular activity is a career dress-up day. On this day, pupils dress up to represent a career in which they are interested and then talk about the characteristics and training appropriate to this career. A variation on this activity can be play-acting "What am I?" and getting responses from their fellow students.

Classroom teachers may often call upon excellent resource personnel and facilities in other educational institutions of the school system. Career and technically-oriented programs should be especially mentioned. Secondary school vocational teachers and their facilities can provide small instructional and informational programs for elementary school pupils. Science teachers and their students can also be invited to plan demonstrations and exhibits.

Similarly within most communities, a wealth of resources is available to contribute to career understanding. When utilizing these resources it is important that youth develop an understanding of the interrelationships between the community, careers, and the individual, in addition to learning the specifics of certain jobs. Elementary school children should also begin to gain some understanding of employment problems that affect many of our workers and our society. The brief statements that follow suggest some of these general understandings, which the elementary school career development program should seek to foster.

Certain careers serve basic needs that are common to nearly all communities. Law enforcement personnel, teachers, doctors, grocery store managers and clerks, service station attendants, and postal clerks are familiar examples of workers needed and found in almost any community—regardless of size or geographic location. Problems that result when communities experience shortages or an absence of such basic workers might also be discussed.

Careers that are unique to a community are usually the results of a variety of interrelated factors. The development of local industries and related careers are influenced by the natural resources of the area, the geographic location, local taxes, availability of labor, and supporting industries. There are also some careers that have little direct relevance to the needs of the community in which they are performed. For example, aircraft parts may be manufactured in a community where there is no demand for the product, there are no planes, and there is not an airport.

An interesting activity is one often labeled the "Model Community Project." In this project, students identify their career interests and seek to build a model community around these jobs, noting the kinds of industries needed, critical careers where workers might have to be recruited, and other resultant problems. Example 6-3 shows what an anonymous elementary school counselor wrote based on responses of students in the upper elementary grades of his school.

EXAMPLE 6-3: Our Town Tomorrow!

This is our Town in the year of the turn of the century, 2000 AD, and our youth of today (2005) have become the citizens of tomorrow—the elementary school student of Main Street School has become the adult on our Main Street of tomorrow.

What has happened in this transition, from a typical small urban community of 1999 to something else in the year 2020? It is certainly not typical—at least not by today's standards—and even then perhaps the most unique community of its time. Let us see why.

It appears that we will have become both a movie colony and a big league sports center—with approximately one-third of our population engaged in these careers. We will be the first community of only 2,500 to support a big league ball club. Our movie colony will be typical, however, with grandfather Tom Cruise married to seven of our lovely leading ladies at the same time!

Our community will also have produced three of the busiest people in town:—one barber and two beauticians—but we hope that our one lion tamer won't be quite so busy. The one bank robber in our town will be well-chased with three policemen and other law enforcement officers on the prowl for him. We can almost hope that they will never catch him, because we have no lawyers to defend him. We will have, however, two doctors, one dentist, and four nurses to protect our health.

Both the Riverview Milling Company and the Armstrong Sheet Metal plant will be closed for lack of employees as we will have become, evidently, a residential community with only two merchants active in our shopping mall.

Still, we will be proud of our community that will have produced two generals, an astronaut, a senator, one governor, two scientists, a space explorer of Mars, two F.B.I.

agents, and the first American president of Russia. One old and perennial problem will remain—we will only have three teachers for our schools—forty less than in 1999.

Yes, our town will be different. We can't be sure why. Perhaps it will be a geographical shift of the population or automation—or could it be a poor program of career development and guidance in our schools way back in 1999?!!

CAREER DEVELOPMENT AND ASSISTANCE IN MIDDLE SCHOOLS

MIDDLE SCHOOL CHARACTERISTICS

The middle school, in some instances, has been called a play on the old numbers game! Whatever it may be, the middle school has, in most school districts replaced the previously traditional junior high school which was the initial transitional school between the elementary school and the secondary school. The middle school, then, in the current educational structure is a school that receives students from elementary school and prepares them to pass on to high school. It is, like its older counterpart the junior high, a transitional educational institution.

One of the strongest arguments for the development of middle schools were the beliefs that: (a) today's developing youth reaches social, intellectual, and physical maturity at a younger age than did previous generations and (b) that junior high schools, as typically organized, did not meet the developmental needs of today's students. It was suggested that children ten to fourteen years of age now constitute a distinct age of development involving unique emotional, social, mental, and physical characteristics. In practice, middle schools are designed to provide for more appropriate curricula for the age groups now in the middle school programs, such as fifth- and sixth-grade school students, than would have been available to them in traditional elementary schools. Also, seventh- and eighth-grade students can have more age-appropriate experiences than were previously provided the traditional junior high schools.

Coming from elementary schools, students will find a greater variety of teachers, including more specialized teachers, and a greater variety of classes. Further, there will be many courses from which choices can be made and curricula that have future educational and career implications. The middle school will typically offer a developmental and student-centered instructional program.

CHARACTERISTICS OF MIDDLE SCHOOL STUDENTS

Middle school children are difficult to characterize in terms of a single set of characteristics for a given grade/age level, much less for the entire middle school population. It is perhaps appropriate to suggest that the most universal characteristic of middle school students is that there is no universal characteristic. Middle schools foster constant growth and change. Some general characteristics of middle school children follows:

1. Physical growth tends to be rapid but uneven.
2. Girls will often mature physically ahead of boys. Sex differences also become more accentuated. It also is a period of dramatic emotional and physical change.

3. The entire middle school years are characterized by students being very physically active.
4. As they pass through middle school, students become more reasonable, insightful, and able to solve and reason through complex problems. Their vocabulary also expands and they become more expressive.
5. Peer relationships tend to be important throughout the middle school years, although older students tend to worry more and be more concerned about peer relationships.
6. Middle school years will see the emergence of values in individual children.
7. Middle school students will increasingly want autonomy.

Some studies indicate that as children progress through the grade levels, parental involvement lessens. The first significant decline often becomes apparent while their children are in middle school. However, the research is overwhelmingly clear that when parents are involved in a positive way in their children's education, they perform better in school. Positive parental assistance is characterized by positive attitudes about school and the importance of education. Counselors can assist parents in these efforts by providing them with useful communication regarding the school program at each grade level, sending them descriptors of the school counseling program and its ongoing activities, and holding regular parent conference groups to further the dissemination of information and to respond to questions and concerns that parents may have. Parent communication should be encouraged and welcomed, and parent-student-counselor conferences can be extremely beneficial during a child's middle school years. Parents can play a major role in assisting their sons and daughters to explore careers and can also contribute to the middle school's important career day programs.

CAREER DEVELOPMENT PROGRAMS IN MIDDLE SCHOOLS

In the middle school years, students will become increasingly conscious of the fact that they will, sooner rather than later, be making direct or indirect decisions related to their career choice. The middle school years will continue the exploratory phase of career development initiated during elementary school, but with increasing maturity. Activities should be designed to assist middle school children with understanding how to make decisions and recognizing the consequences of their decision-making. The interrelationships between education and careers should continue to be emphasized, especially as some students will be approaching the age/grade levels at which they give serious consideration to dropping out of school. In the middle school career development program, students should be made aware of good work habits, the importance of personal responsibility, and the dimensions of career planning. Career development groups for all students are especially beneficial during middle school, and even such traditional secondary school activities as career days and college days may be considered for some middle school populations.

As previously noted, Table 6-2 depicts career development competencies and sample indicators for the middle school/junior high school and the elementary school.

CAREER DEVELOPMENT AND ASSISTANCE IN SECONDARY SCHOOLS

CHARACTERISTICS OF SECONDARY SCHOOLS

For many years the secondary school was almost solely the source of organized career assistance in United States educational systems. The major inhabitants of secondary schools have always been adolescents. Their characteristics and characteristics of secondary schools are, in a manner of speaking, common knowledge to most citizens of this country. While we are noticing some changes and more diversification in the organizations and practices in secondary schools, they still remain, as a group across the country, similar in their educational characteristics. Some of the more obvious of these characteristics that have implications for the school's career assistance program are as follows:

1. Secondary schools are generally large, complex institutions populated by a heterogeneous student body. The size and complexity of the secondary school have implications for both counseling program development and program activities. Because the larger student bodies tend to be more heterogeneous, often representing many cultural minority groups, the identification of these groups and the response to their needs can represent a major challenge to the program.

2. Secondary school faculties represent a variety of academic specialties. The secondary school faculty member tends to concentrate on a particular subject area. As a result, the secondary school faculty represents a variety of specializations, which provides a reservoir of resources that the school counseling program may use in the career, educational, and personal/social development of students.

3. Secondary school years are important decision-making years for individual students. During a student's secondary schooling, one is usually confronted with at least two lifetime-influencing decisions. The first of these decisions that many youth make during this period of time is whether to complete their secondary schooling. Various dropout studies indicate that approximately one fourth of high school youth make the decision to leave school before finishing their secondary school program. In addition, many students make important decisions regarding careers or choice of college. The wide variety of course offerings and activities available in most secondary schools prompt a nearly continuous series of minor decisions for students as well. They may also be confronted with significant personal decisions regarding sex and marriage; use of tobacco, alcohol, and drugs; and friends and friendship.

4. Secondary schools are subject-matter oriented. Schedules and classes tend to be formal and rigidly organized in many secondary schools, with considerable emphasis on academic standards, homework, and

grades (rather than personal growth). Emphasis on standardized test achievements and school discipline can be expected. The homeroom that many students have experienced in the elementary school years ceases to exist in most high schools, except as an administrative checkpoint. As a result, at a time when students are accelerating their development as social beings, the secondary school structure often tends to inhibit this growth and development by placing them in a series of formal, academically-oriented subject-matter class experiences. At the same time, many schools fail to provide students with an organized scheduled group (such as homeroom), where they might develop social skills and attitudes. This suggests a challenge to the subject-matter teacher and the counselor to work cooperatively to incorporate social development experiences into the academic program.

5. School spirit, or esprit de corps, is usually more evident in secondary schools than in any other educational institution. This school spirit is usually reflected in the quest for winning athletic teams, championship bands, and other public indications of excellence. Often the competition among students for participation in significant school events is keen. Social divisions may often arise between those who have "made it" and those who have not in terms of these activities. On the positive side, however, school spirit in competitive activities can often be a potential factor in motivating students to remain in school, making them seek higher academic achievements, and promoting pride in the school. Recently, frequent suggestions and efforts have been made to increase the visibility of academic competition as well.

6. The school principal is the single most influential person in the secondary school setting. Decisions, policy development, and practices all emanate or are subject to the approval of the school principal. Unlike the elementary school principal, the secondary principal is frequently assisted by several assistant principals, supervisors, department heads, and specialty chairs. In addition, probably no other person is so significant in establishing the tone or atmosphere of the school and its inhabitants." (Gibson & Mitchell, 2003, pp. 79–80)[3]

CHARACTERISTICS OF SECONDARY SCHOOL STUDENTS

The secondary school student is typically classified as an adolescent, the period of growth between childhood and adulthood. Developmentally, adolescence is a period of rapid and intense changes that can drastically alter the individual's physical, intellectual, and personality characteristics. It is also a time of significant lifestyle changes for the individual. During the adolescent years, parents and teachers

---

[3] Gibson, Robert L., & Mitchell, Marianne H., Introduction to Counseling and Guidance, 6/e, © 2003. Reprinted by permission of Pearson Education, Inc., Upper Saddle River, NJ.

sometimes find it difficult to accept and understand the changing behavior of this age group—behavior that may be normal but not necessarily likeable. Specifically, these changes include:

- **physical development**   These are the most readily observed and easily measured changes. These changes are rapid, and in the short space of a few months childhood is left behind and the physical adult arrives, complete with voice changes and sexual characteristics. This new appearance is important to young high school students. Girls, particularly, are concerned about their physical appearance while boys worry about their physical growth and coordination and their general appearances of manhood.
- **intellectual development**   While the development of the adolescent's intellect is as equally startling as their physical development, it is not as readily observable. New ways of utilizing their intelligence are brought into play as adolescents solve their problems from a broader frame of reference and become more aware of alternatives. It is also a period when individuals make their own interpretations and learn to hypothesize.
- **personality development**   New behavioral and personality traits become observable during this period in the form of new interests, values, and attitudes. Adolescents also begin to imitate adult behavior in many ways. These behaviors seek to establish their own personal identity and emphasize their growing independence. This is also a time when a sense of personal responsibility and self-discipline begins to be evident.
- **goal development**   The development of worthwhile goals, including educational and occupational aspirations, occurs. The interrelationship between these two goals also becomes more evident. Further, adolescents are more inclined to seek adult assistance in these areas which, in turn, underscores the importance of effective career counseling and development programs in secondary schools.

During the adolescent changes of life, there are often behaviors associated with the normal changes of this period that are not necessarily welcomed by the adults experiencing the results of these changes. Parents and teachers are often disturbed by the aggressiveness occasionally displayed toward them. Much of the hostility will stem from the adolescent's quest for independence. Adults may also view as unacceptable certain adolescent behaviors in which they are, in effect, seeking adult experiences. For example, adolescents may be anxious to drive or own a car and to drive it in such a way as to draw attention to the fact that he or she is driving—usually fast with attention-getters like tire squeals, rapid acceleration, and horn-honking. For some, there will be a significant increase in the use of profanity, cigarette smoking, and alcohol and drug use. Sex becomes a popular topic of conversation and sexual activities dramatically increase during this period. Mood swings are also often a concern to both parents and teenagers because of their unpredictability and because of the apparent trivialities that appear to trigger them. Some parents also become concerned about the significance that peer groups acquire during this period. Parents and other adults often lament the language, dress, fads, and values of these groups. Some parents also view these groups as too predominant in the lives of their children.

CAREER DEVELOPMENT PROGRAMS IN SECONDARY SCHOOLS

A secondary school classroom teacher, similar to those in elementary and middle schools, plays a key role in the career development of adolescent students. It is important to both classroom teachers and their students to be able to relate their subject matter to the world of work. Many subject matter teachers will prepare, often with the assistance of the school counselor, an introductory unit that provides an overview of the course that they are teaching and also an overview of the relationship of the subject matter content to the world of work. In some instances, references are also made to avocational interests or hobbies related to the subject matter. Such a unit has been found to provide a reality check for students, helping them recognize the relationship of the subject matter to the real world. This will have, in many instances, a motivational effect on students and spur them to greater interest in the subject matter as well as exploration of possible career spinoffs. In addition, classroom teachers can be alert throughout the semester for appropriate times to relate the topic to workers or the world of work. Another important role that classroom teachers can play is that of watching for students that show a special aptitude or interest in their particular subject matter. They can, of course, themselves follow-up on this special interest or ability but they may also refer the student to the school counselor, who can provide special materials and information that may further assist the student's exploration of the topic.

Table 6-3 presents competencies to be developed in high school students and sample indicators.

Gati and Saka (2001) reported a study of high school students' career related decision-making difficulties. They presented these difficulties in a taxonomy of career decision-making difficulties, which are identified in Figure 6-3.

Activities of classroom's teachers should be supplemented by special activities organized by the school's counseling program. A notable example and a long time traditional activity is a career day. A career day is a special day set aside to permit students to explore their career interests within the physical confines of the school itself. The career day planning is usually initiated by a survey of the student population to determine what careers are popular among the students and should be represented on a career day program. Speakers are then invited to present these careers and a schedule is made out. Students should visit as many as three different career presentations during the course of the career day. In addition to the popular careers to be represented, it is the usual practice to invite representatives of local area major businesses and industries, representatives of the U. S. armed services, and representatives of the local employment office. Speakers are provided with guidelines for their presentations by the counseling office and are encouraged to provide adequate time for questions and discussions by the students attending their sessions. Speakers are also encouraged to bring any appropriate materials that they may have available for student distribution. Follow-up activities are important to further stimulate the career exploration initiated by the career day. Computerized programs may be helpful in this regard. In some schools, career groups have been found to be useful for follow-up discussions. The classroom itself is an appropriate setting to continue exploration of careers related to the subject matter being taught.

TABLE 6-3
Competencies to be developed in high school students and sample indicators

Competencies	Sample indicators: The student will
1. Understanding of the influence of a positive self-concept on career development	1. Demonstrate the ability to manage her/his behavior in developing and maintaining a healthy self-concept
2. Interpersonal and social skills required for positive interaction with others	2. Describe appropriate employee–employer interactions in varying situations
3. Understanding of the interrelationships of emotional and physical development and career decision making	3. Exhibit behaviors that are important to good physical and mental health
4. Understanding of the interrelationship between educational achievement and career planning, training, and placement*	4. Identify essential learning skills required in the work environment
5. Positive attitudes toward work and learning	5. Demonstrate positive work ethic and attitude
6. Skills for locating, evaluating, and interpreting information about career opportunities*	6. Describe the impact of factors such as population, climate, and geographic location on local job opportunities
7. Skills for preparing for, seeking, obtaining, maintaining, and advancing in a job*	7. Develop skills in preparing a resume and completing a job application
8. Understanding of how societal needs and functions influence the nature and structure of work	8. Demonstrate an understanding of the global economy and how it affects each individual
9. Skills in making decisions and choosing alternatives for and pursuing educational and career goals*	9. Project and describe factors that may influence educational and career decisions
10. Understanding of the interrelationships of life roles and career*	10. Describe the ways career choice may influence lifestyle
11. Understanding of the continuous changes in male/female roles and how they relate to career decisions	11. Develop attitudes, behaviors, and skills that contribute to the elimination of sex stereotypes and sex bias
12. Skills in career exploration and planning*	12. Develop career plans that include the concept that a changing world demands lifelong learning

*These competencies are also included in the *National Standards for School Counseling Programs,* C. A. Campbell and C. A. Dahir, 1997, Alexandria, VA: American School Counselor Association.

Source: From Brown, *Career Information, Career Counseling, and Career Development,* 8/e. Published by Allyn and Bacon, Boston, MA. Copyright © 2003 by Pearson Education. Reprinted by permission of the publisher.

Other traditional activities used for the exploration of careers are those of shadowing and field trips. Shadowing is an activity where a student shadows an individual working in the student's area of possible career interest. This usually involves spending the full workday, or at the very least half a workday, observing the individual who

Career decision-making difficulties

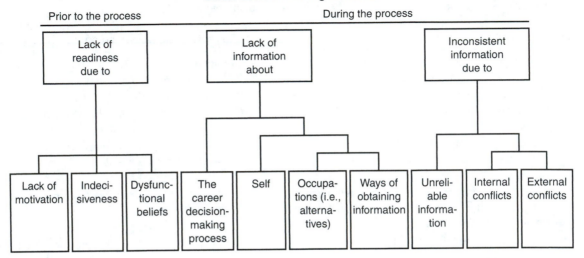

FIGURE 6-3

A taxonomy of career decision-making difficulties

Source: Reprinted from I. Gati and N. Saka, High School Students' Career-Related Decision-Making Difficulties, *Journal of Counseling and Development, 79*(3) p. 333 © American Counseling Association. Reprinted with permission. No further reproduction authorized without written permission of the American Counseling Association.

works in the student's field of career interest. In some instances, the student may also engage in light work activities.

Field trips are sometimes scheduled to special career sites such as a major local industry or employer, or a vocational-technical school. The purpose of the field trip is to provide students with a first-hand look at a career in the work setting. In recent years, both field trips and shadowing have taken on new dimensions with the development of closed-circuit television, interactive video, and the Internet. For these activities, the student may remain in the school environment but view workers in their work sites in a wide range of settings.

It is also important to prepare students for the realities of the world of work in which they are preparing to enter and progress in over the coming years. For example, speakers who address such topics as "living and working out of the country," or "perspectives of a dual career couple" address topics that workers must face today.

Recently (April, 2004), the Owen Valley School System (in Spencer, Indiana) announced plans to initiate a Career Academies Model in the 2004–2005 school year in their secondary school. Under this model, students will spend their first high school year choosing an "academy" that represents a career field such as engineering, manufacturing and industrial technology, art, human services, or health services. They will then spend the next three years following a specified course of studies consisting of four 80-minute blocks and a 55 minute period. An academy will function during three of the four longer blocks, while in the other periods students will take electives or required courses outside their academy. Within their academy, career-related electives, core subjects, and application opportunities such as internships will be provided. The objective of the model is to enhance students' options and exposure to a range of careers. Research suggests that academy students have a better attendance record, better grades, and a higher graduation rate from high school than students enrolled in traditional secondary schools. Studies also indicate that they are more likely to go on to and stay in college.

Of course, the counseling program itself is active throughout secondary school. Counselors will schedule individual career conferences with all students to provide them with assistance and information on career decision-making. In many schools, programs of career assessment are carried out by the counselors of the school using interest and/or aptitude measures and, on occasion, personality or values inventories. In addition, the counseling program will often conduct groups to assist students with preparing for employment interviews and development of their personal resumes. They may also provide activities and assistance with the selection of post secondary institutions related to the students' career field of interest.

THE SCHOOL TO WORK OPPORTUNITIES ACT OF 1994

Career development and counseling are key cornerstones of a major 1990s federal legislative act. Secondary school counselors should be very aware of the School to Work Opportunities Act of 1994, which provides a framework for creating school to work opportunities systems in all states. Career guidance and counseling is given a high priority in the provisions for state development grants. According to the announcements regarding these grants, "all funds provided under a school to work opportunities development grant must be used for activities to develop a state-wide school to work opportunities system." This may include, for example, such career development activities as:

- supporting local planning and development activities to provide guidance, training, and technical assistance for teachers, employers, mentors, counselors, administrators, and others in the development of school to work opportunities programs
- developing a training and technical support system for teachers, employers, mentors, counselors, related services personnel, and others that includes specialized training and technical support for the counseling and training of women, minorities, and individuals with disabilities for high-skill, high-wage careers in nontraditional employment. (Kososki, October, 1994, p. 3)

CAREER DEVELOPMENT AND ASSISTANCE IN INSTITUTIONS OF HIGHER EDUCATION

CHARACTERISTICS OF HIGHER EDUCATION

Institutions of higher education have, over the centuries, been viewed as the terminal preparatory institution for entry into many careers and professions. Although many youth have made the decision to go to college long before making a career decision, college is recognized as the ultimate right of passage into the career world. Many youth arrive at college doors without having finalized their career decisions. As a result, the initial career assistance usually begins with the admissions counseling process. To be effective, this process requires admissions counselors who have both expert knowledge of all the programs available to students and career counseling skills and knowledge. These counselors seek to assist and prepare students entering the portals of higher education to make the required entry decisions, which often have career implications. An entering student's choice of schools or colleges (such as arts and sciences, education, engineering, or business) often imply a career choice and may lock students into preparatory programs that narrow their career options. Faculty advisors who have appropriate knowledge and often distinguished expertise are available to provide career assistance to students upon entry and throughout their tenure at the institution of higher education.

In addition to the faculty advisory and assistance program, many colleges and schools—especially those with highly specialized training such as engineering and business—have developed their own career information and placement offices to assist their graduates with securing appropriate employment options. Further, in recent generations, we have witnessed the development of specialized career assistance centers on many college and university campuses. These centers are usually staffed by counselors who have special knowledge and skills not only in the programs of the institution of higher education but also in career assessment, career counseling, and career placement. Figure 6-4 presents a graphic view of a career development center at a large, residential campus (Indiana University, Bloomington, Indiana).

CHARACTERISTICS OF HIGHER EDUCATION STUDENTS

The popular view from the ivory tower seems to suggest a tranquil, neat, and attractive college campus with frequent focus on the football stadium, the neatly attired student body, and sometimes—although very rarely—the distinguished professor. A more serious or realistic view of most college campuses, while still confirming the existence of football stadiums and distinguished professors, would portray a student body of great diversity, representing many cultures and characterized more by differences than by similarities. As the heterogeneity of the higher education student body has increased since World War II, so has the variety of student personnel services available on most college campuses for meeting the needs of this student population. Recognizing the wide range of student characteristics, we will attempt to make a few generalizations regarding the characteristics of young adults on college campuses.

From a physical development standpoint, the college student will reach a point of maturity that will, in effect, stamp him or her for life. While later aging will have its effect on one's physical appearance it is always easier to identify someone we last saw in our college years than someone we haven't seen since grade school! In addition, young adulthood will see the peaking of many of the physical skills of the individual and for some, there may even begin to be a reduction in some of these skills.

The college years are also important for the continued social and emotional development and increasing maturity of young adults. The maturation of these

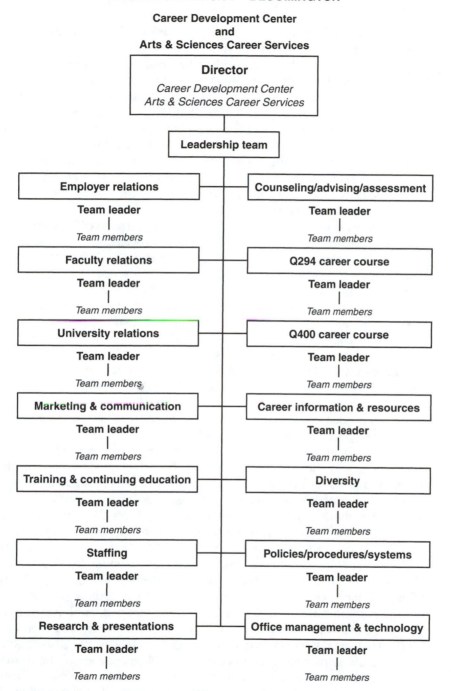

INDIANA UNIVERSITY—BLOOMINGTON

Career Development Center
and
Arts & Sciences Career Services

FIGURE 6-4
Graphic view of the setup of Indiana University's career development center
Source: Indiana University, Career Development Center and Arts & Sciences Career
Services. Permission granted by Patrick Donahue, 2004.

characteristics are important as they prepare for important commitments to marriage, family, career, initial jobs, and community responsibilities. Higher education provides the opportunities for testing social relationships and emotional development with peers. During this time there is a near complete independence from the primary family unit, which encourages individuals to further their own emotional and social development.

While college students are still somewhat idealistic, their idealism is beginning to be tempered by realism. This realism also becomes increasingly evident when seeking answers to everyday problems. Commitments also become increasingly important. Commitment to a career, marriage, to organizations, or to values are all evidence of the increasing maturity of college students. The college years are also a period of continuous physical and emotional growth and for most students, of great cognitive stimulation and curiosity as well.

There is great variety in the levels of development among college students. Likewise, there is great variation in their career maturity, expectations, and career choices. As these choices may be reflected in their college majors, it is interesting to note that little change takes place in the more popular majors of business, social sciences, education, engineering, life sciences, and health related fields. Women continue to dominate the fields of education and nursing, while men continue to dominate the traditional fields of business and engineering and the more recently developing field of computer and information sciences. From the first year to the fourth year, more students transfer to the fields of business and social sciences than any other. Not unexpectedly, the range of confidence in the initial career choices of college students range from very confident to great uncertainty. All of these factors suggest a need for readily available career assistance programs on the college campus. This need will be significantly expanded with the return of adults seeking retraining or more advanced training as a result of the significant changes in the demographics of the workforce in the coming century. Two-year technical and community colleges feed another stream of students into four-year institutions of higher education. These students are often older when they enter four-year institutions due to their part time attendance at the two-year institutions.

It is fair to conclude that over the four-year undergraduate period there is a breadth and depth to the changes that occur in the college student. The result is a graduate who is dramatically different from the one who entered as a freshman four or more years before graduation. Adult competencies, with sample indicators, are indicated in Table 6-4.

Zunker (1998) reviewed the results of a 20-year study by Pascarel and Terenzi (1991). Among their findings were that: (a) students often change their career plans; (b) significant differences in occupational status that occur between high school and college graduates are maintained over the life span; and, as shown in many studies, (c) college graduates are less likely to be unemployed than are high school graduates.

The National Career Development Association (NCDA) has developed competencies for professionals engaged in career counseling at or above the master's degree level of education. These competencies are not intended to limit the initial training and subsequent education and professional development of career counselors. In the ever-changing world of work, it must be anticipated that there will be ever-changing educational demands on career counselors. Please refer to Appendix D, which presents NCDA's competencies.

TABLE 6-4
Adult competencies and indicators

Competency	Sample indicator: The adult will
1. Maintenance of a positive view of self in terms of potential and preferences and assessment of their transferability to the world of work	1. Identify achievements related to work, learning, and leisure and state their influence on his/her perception of self
2. Ability to assess self-defeating behaviors and reduce their impact on career decisions	2. Understand physical changes that occur with age and adapt work performance to accommodate these
3. Skills for entering, adjusting to, and maintaining performance in educational and training situations	3. Document prior learning experiences and know how to use their information to obtain credit from educational institutions
4. Skills for locating, evaluating, and interpreting information about career opportunities	4. Assess how skills used in one occupation may be used in other occupations
5. Skills required for seeking, obtaining, keeping, and advancing in a job	5. Develop a resume appropriate for an identified career objective
6. Skills in making decisions about educational and career goals	6. Develop skills to assess career opportunities in terms of advancement, management styles, work environment, benefits, and other conditions of employment
7. Understanding of the impact of careers on individual and family life	7. Describe how family and leisure roles affect and may be affected by career roles and decisions
8. Skills in making career transitions	8. Accept that career transitions (e.g., reassessment of current position, job changes, or occupational changes) are a normal aspect of career development
9. Skills in retirement planning	9. Recognize the importance of retirement planning and commit to early involvement in the retirement planning process
10. Understand how the needs and functions of society influence the nature and structure of work	10. Recognize economic trends that influence workers
11. Understanding the continuing changes in male and female roles	11. Identify changes in the job and family roles held by men and women

OBSERVATIONS FROM THE FIELD

Eastern Elementary School

The following description of career activities in Eastern Elementary School resulted from a visit, by your authors, hosted by Ms. Sandi Yoho, School Counselor. Ms. Yoho was the Elementary School Counselor of the Year in Indiana in 2004. Eastern Elementary School enrolls 750 children in kindergarten through sixth grade. It was interesting to note that career units were presented at every grade level, including kindergarten. The school library also has an extensive section devoted to career materials, displayed by grade level. Additional displays of career materials and publications have been provided by representatives of Indiana Workforce Development.

The school newspaper also frequently devotes space to career activities such as applying for a job. Among the school's special career activities is a career week, which focuses on career activities related to eight major career clusters. Outside speakers (often parents of enrolled students) contribute to this week. There are also a number of special career activities such as career dress-up day (where students dress appropriately for their career choice). The school emphasizes the importance of character in the world of work. Displayed in the halls are the six pillars of character. Once each week there is a 30-minute interactive lesson integrating character and careers.

Perrysburg Junior High School (Ohio)

Submitted by: Mr. Charles Hablitzel and Mr. Tom Przybylski

Major Career Activities

Perrysburg Exempted Village Schools follow the Ohio Career Development Model. This mission of the vocational and career education system is to prepare youths and adults to make informed career choices and to successfully enter, compete in, and advance in a changing work world. This is accomplished through the following imperatives: (a) focus on lifelong individual needs; (b) provide career focused education for all students; and (c) extend and strengthen strategic alliances.

The process begins in kindergarten with the establishment of an Individual Career Plan (ICP) folder that contains a record of all career-related activities for every student. The focus of the process in grades K through five is awareness, in grades six through eight it is exploration and planning, and in grades nine through twelve it

is preparation. Topics that are included in this process include self-awareness, community involvement, decision-making/goal setting, reduction of biases, employability skills, economics (kindergarten through eighth grade), career information, self-assessment, exploration, future trends, vocational orientation, and academic planning (grade six through twelve).

In the junior high school (grades six through eight) career information is blended into all academic areas. Every subject area takes time to show how it is related to the real world of work. In addition, sixth grade students are given the Career Game by Rick Trow Productions, Inc., which has a very good basic self-assessment and interest inventory. Using the accompanying software, Counselor Tools, students can then enter their scores and print out a career report. Seventh grade students utilize the Ohio Career

Information System (OCIS) online, adding another inventory (IDEAS) and using the system for wide-ranging career investigations. During the eighth grade year, students use the ACT Discover program online to continue their career investigations. They also have the option of taking the inventories provided by ACT. In addition, all eighth grade students are given the ACT Explore test every fall, which provides an academic snapshot, a self-assessment, and an interest inventory (scores of which can be added to the ACT Discover program).

Career Preferences

Based on recent ACT Explore results, 77% of the student population is planning on attending 2- or 4-year colleges/universities. The following represents the overall career preference categories: business operations—3%; administration and sales—5%; technical—13%; social service—16%; arts—26%, and science and technology—28%.

Career Concerns

The needs assessment portion of the ACT Explore test provides us with data that correlates with career concerns. The needs assessment asked students to identify which of the following areas they felt they needed help in: writing, reading speed, reading comprehension, math skills, study skills, test-taking skills, computer use, selecting courses, higher education options, and financial aid. The five areas that students reported needing some (or a lot of) help with included: financial aid—77%; study skills—71%; higher education options—65%; math skills—62%; and test-taking skills—60%.

East Fairmont High School, West Virginia

East Fairmont High School is located in Fairmont, West Virginia. The school enrolls approximately 8,860 students in grades nine through twelve. The career services of the school are among those offered by the guidance department, chaired by Donald Boyles, assisted by Charles McClain and Linda Stalnaker. The overwhelming majority of the graduating classes (65–75%) each year enter programs of higher education. An additional eight to ten percent enlist in the military services; five to ten percent attend vocational-technical schools; and ten to fifteen percent go directly into the workforce. At East Fairmont High School, homerooms or career clusters meet for planned career-related activities for 45 minutes every two weeks. The guidance offices plan and coordinate annual career-related activities such as college and career fairs, financial aid nights, and parental information nights for all new students. Counselors also interview and advise each student, every year, in their course selection process. During this process they make up-to-date career resources available for their use. Appropriate assessment instruments are administered to all sophomores in October and the results are explained to each student by counselors. Students are presented with a handout that describes career clusters and majors with the possible occupational fields related to these clusters. Each student is also presented with a Marion County Schools career cluster/career major program.

Indiana University, Bloomington, Indiana

Indiana University is a large, major residential university, located in Bloomington, Indiana. Like many large universities the major colleges of Indiana University each have their own separate and distinct placement office. The university-wide career development center emphasizes career planning, assessment, and various outreach presentations. All entering students are informed through published brochures that career counseling is available to help all students at all times. The center also offers a two-credit, eight-week course for freshmen and sophomores in the process of choosing a major and exploring career fields. The course emphasizes self-information, research on the various majors and their career fields, decision-making, and goal setting. The center also provides career assessment, externships, career panels, and internships, as well as various career assistance workshops. Your authors secured the above information as a result of a conference with Patrick Donahue, the director of Indiana University's career development center and arts and sciences career services.

SUMMARY

This chapter began by reminding readers that a counselor, regardless of one's specialty or the special needs of one's client is, first and foremost, a counselor. The appropriateness of short term counseling for career counselors was noted as well as the more recent technique, labeled *coaching,* is also gaining in popularity in working with career clients. The process of consulting is also useful in providing career assistance. This chapter focused on career development in schools, beginning with elementary schools. The importance of elementary schools in the development of our adult population, including career development, must be recognized. In understanding this significance, important viewpoints of child development, such as Havighurst's and Piaget's, were noted. The characteristics of elementary schools and elementary school students, which enhance the delivery of career information, were also noted. Competencies were indicated for all educational levels: elementary; middle/junior high school; high school; and higher education.

DISCUSSION QUESTIONS

1. What were the influences on your career preferences in elementary school, middle school, high school, and undergraduate years in higher education?

2. Are there local environmental or community characteristics that you believe could influence high school students' career choices?

3. Identify examples of career role models that may influence career preferences among young students.

4. Do (or can) subject-matter teachers influence students to consider certain careers?

5. It is frequently suggested that a career predicts a way of life. What characteristics of a way of life would you predict for those entering the profession of counseling?

6. It has been noted that individuals have multiple potentialities. What are the implications of multipotentiality for assisting individuals in their career planning and decision-making?

CLASS ACTIVITIES

1. Draw a career map, using newsprint and felt tip pens, with stick figures and simple drawings. Go from lower left to upper right and depict significant events and influences on your career development.
2. Arrange for student panels (four to five students) representing elementary, middle, secondary, and higher education to discuss their career concerns. (Don't schedule them all on the same day.)
3. Invite school counselors from elementary, middle, and secondary schools to present an overview of their career counseling and guidance programs.
4. Plan an orientation trip to a university's career center.

READINGS OF INTEREST

Adolescent Career Development. Special section. *The Career Development Quarterly, 51*(1), (September, 2002), 36–86.

Beale, A. V. (2004). Tips for writing winning resumes: Answers to students' most frequently asked questions. *Techniques: Connecting Education and Careers, 79*(5), 22–25.

DeMato, D. S., & Curcio, C. C. (2004). Job satisfaction of elementary school counselors: A new look. *Professional School Counseling, 7*(4), 236–245.

Freeman. B. (1994). Importance of the National Career Development Guidelines to school counselors. *The Career Development Quarterly, 42*(3), 224–228.

Helwig. A. A. (2004). A ten-year longitudinal study of the career development of students: Summary findings. *Journal of Counseling & Development, 82*(1), 49–57.

Hoyt, K. B. (2001). Helping high school students broaden their knowledge of postsecondary education options. *Professional School Counseling, 5*(1), 6–12.

Raufman, L., Olson, T., Jones, R. (2002). Career development resources from California Community Colleges. In G. R. Walz, R. Knowdell, & Kirkman, C. (Eds.), *Thriving in Challenging and Uncertain Times.* Greensboro, NC: ERIC Clearinghouse on Counseling & Student Services and CAPS, Inc.

School-to-Work Transitions. (1999). (Special issue). *The Career Development Quarterly, 47*(4), 291–364.

School to Work Transition. Special section. *Phi Delta Kappan, 77*(8), (April, 1996), 528–562.

School Violence. Special section. *Professional School Counseling, 4*(2), (December, 2000), 77–133.

Stein, T. S. (1991). Career exploration strategies for the elementary school counselor. *Elementary School Guidance and Counseling Journal, 26*(2), 153–157.

Stone, J. R., III., & Alfeld, C. (2004). Keeping kids in school: The power of CTE. *Techniques: Connecting Education and Careers, 79*(4), 28–29.

Chapter 7

Career Counseling Across the Life Span: The Adult Years

Historically, career development was seen as most relevant when adolescents were finding their personal identity and contemplating their choice of a first job. However, in the last half of the twentieth century, theory and research increasingly emphasized that adulthood is comprised of dynamic change, choice dilemmas, and transitions. Induction and adjustment to the work force, midcareer changes, stress, unemployment, and underemployment have become prominent issues for career counseling in a world of constant change. Thus, as career development theory and research focus on these adaptations and challenges and their impact on the personal and work life of individuals, they describe where, when, how, and for what purpose career counseling is provided.

Edwin L. Herr, EdD
Distinguished Professor Emeritus of Education and
Associate Dean Emeritus
Pennsylvania State University

OBJECTIVES

To provide readers with an understanding of:

1. Changes in the world of work and their implications for workers and their career counseling
2. Career counseling across the adult life span from entry through retirement stages
3. The role of career counseling in adult job loss, stress, and the development of leisure pursuits

INTRODUCTION

The dramatic shift from school to work results in three of the important life decisions an individual will make. The first of these is what do we do. This means having to identify and pursue a career that we believe we are qualified for and interested in. The second important life decision is usually related to the first decision as to where we work and live. As noted earlier, these two relatively stable elements in the lives of our parents and grandparents are very tenuous today as we become aware of the predictions that many now entering the world of work will have multiple careers and live in multiple communities in their lives. Incidentally, the third important life decision for many—with whom we live—is frequently influenced by the first two. The "right" decisions in these instances are clearly important to the individual's personal growth and satisfaction in life.

CHANGES IN THE WORLD OF WORK IN THE NEW MILLENNIUM

As already stated, one of the significant changes that will dramatically affect the average worker in the United States in the new millennium is the high probability that he or she will experience anywhere from three to seven distinctly different careers over his or her working lifetime (with the possible exception of the professions). The ability to access the Internet, download e-mail, and use cell phones on the move has enabled office workers to communicate more frequently and conveniently. These technology advancements have also promoted flexibility and mobility for those working primarily alone and/or at home.

These changes will also bring not only a change in what each individual does, but a change in where and how one does it. For those preferring to work in higher skill and higher paying jobs, continuing education will be a fact of life. All indications are that there will be a high demand for talented and educated workers in the early decades of the 21st century. These demands will be reflected in careers in the engineering and technology fields, human services, computer work, teachers, and in the field of health. In other words, individuals will move from job to job, from community to community, and in and out of educational programs throughout their working life spans. Change, rather than stability, will be an ever-present characteristic of life. Workers will spend significant portions of their lives reacting to and adjusting to change. Counselors working in both noneducational and educational settings can anticipate adult clients seeking their professional assistance with accepting and adjusting to these changes. Counselors also must be aware that these changes, and adjusting to them, will often involve the worker's family as well as the worker. Counselors will also need to make themselves aware of relevant educational programs available in the geographic area in order to assist workers preparing for a transition to a new career. It may also be anticipated that dual career couples will need special assistance when one of the wage earners must make a career change that also necessitates a geographic move. In summary, the career world of the future will be complex, challenging, constantly changing, and exciting.

As the world moves into the new millennium, despite all the new advances in computer technology aiding predictions of the future, views of the world of work in the years ahead will remain cloudy. Rapid changes in workforce needs will result from increasingly rapid technological advancements and continued globalization. The impact of significant immigrant populations, as well as shifting population demographics, will also alter demands in the world of work. Changes in government policy (such as unemployment compensation requirements) will also affect the labor market. Other factors such as cost of living, increased employment of temporaries, increase in home workers, and increased educational requirements will fuel additional uncertainties in the labor market.

CAREER COUNSELING AND ADULT WORKERS

We have previously noted that, in a sense, everyone is a client for career counseling because virtually everyone enters the world of work. It might now be appropriate to suggest that nearly everyone is our potential client across their working life spans because the dramatic changes that have occurred and are occurring affect today's and tomorrow's worker. They present challenges calling for professional career counseling assistance. The paramount concern for career counselors serving working clients must be satisfaction in the worker's job. The major elements in the individual's career satisfaction are: (a) the individual likes what he or she does (career); (b) the individual likes who he or she does it for (organization); (c) the individual likes where one does it (the geographic setting for job and living); and (d) the individual feels a sense of job security and receives adequate benefits.

A worker's career also provides a framework for his or her life, which includes satisfaction from a job well done and the feeling of belonging associated with one's working peers. Economic security is also of paramount importance. Adult workers seek to avoid routine, predictable tasks. Most adult workers also prefer close association with their colleagues rather than working in isolation. Lack of supervision and feedback, as well as unrealistic demands, are among the causes of job dissatisfaction and stress. When assisting adult job seekers, counselors should consider: (a) the individual's coping styles, especially the way one relates to others; (b) the individual's relevant educational attainments and previous experiences; (c) relevant job opportunities available and their comparative geographic accessibility; (d) the relationship of a specific career opportunity to other aspects of the individual's life such as family, leisure, basic values, and self-concept; and (e) the characteristics of the potential employing organization, especially those that are personally important to the client.

Counselors working with adult career clients must also be prepared to overcome some of the potential barriers to career problem-solving, such as:

- a lack of understanding of the career counseling and assistance process and the client's role in this process
- not understanding the variables in good decision-making
- being unwilling or unable to assume the responsibility of decision-making

- inaccurate or prejudiced information
- lack of awareness of resources
- lack of motivation

As previously suggested, a counselor should employ the basic skills and processes associated with being an effective professional helper, keeping in mind that adult career clients are generally more mature and more experienced and have more responsibilities (such as family). Counselors assisting adult workers with their career needs must recognize the maturity and previous work experience of the individual. As a result, clients will be more involved in developing solutions to their needs than adolescent clients would. Also, a different set of resources are usually desirable for the mature experienced worker. For example, previous work experience may qualify an individual for jobs that would be unavailable to an entry-level worker.

ENTERING THE WORLD OF WORK

Students in school settings are usually familiar with their school counselors and the services they offer and usually display little hesitancy when approaching them with their career and personal concerns. However, once the student becomes an adult in the career world, they no longer have familiar and ready access to a professional counselor. Adults seeking the services of professional counselors may find them available in various community agencies, private practices, and perhaps their own organization's employee assistance program (EAP). Approaching these counselors is, in no way as familiar and comfortable as walking down the school hall into the office of someone you see at least incidentally several times a week—someone who probably knows your name and has a fair amount of background information on you.

In the adult world of work, counselors serving these populations must recognize that many of their clients will be apprehensive, ill-at-ease, and unsure of the process. The counselor's first job is usually to put their adult clients at ease and help them to understand what they can expect, how you hope to assist them, and what their responsibilities are. Some clients will feel they have no control over their destiny. Others will be highly frustrated and many will want immediate answers and salvation. As a counselor you will, from the onset, use your counseling skills of attending, reflecting, and facilitating the client's talking about their concerns. Eventually, the counselor will help the client to develop a coping plan. Such a plan would: (a) establish goals for the client; (b) select strategies for achieving the goals; (c) take action to implement the strategies; and (d) evaluate the outcomes.

Whereas the previous life stages were characterized by changing interests, fluctuating goals, and significant physical and psychological change, young adults are entering the beginning of a relatively stable and more mature lifestyle. This period will include more specific career and other life goals which probably include marriage and perhaps the beginning of a family. Physical characteristics tend to stabilize and physical abilities tend to reach their peak during the early adult period. Young adults tend to have confidence in their ability and life planning, even though they may be somewhat idealistic.

While these generalizations of characteristics of young adults are probably appropriate for the majority of this age group, variations from these norms will occur based on the differing demands of socioeconomic classes, ethnic groups, nationalities, and educational levels. Significant national events such as wars, economic depressions, or epidemic illnesses can also be influences.

The goal of career counseling during this important transition phase is to assist the individual with: (a) identification of appropriate opportunities that promise a happy and productive career which will enhance their human potential and (b) recognition of and consideration of those environmental characteristics important to the individual's lifestyle. The counselor helps the individual to become the best they can become and move toward achieving their potential. In preparing to enter the world of work, the individual making the transition from school to work will, in most instances, benefit from a systematic job search. This job search should be prefaced with the preparation of a resume, which includes, in addition to personal data, background information covering the applicant's educational record, past employment experiences, other significant experiences such as military service, and references or letters of recommendation.

Career clients should be made aware of the professional job placement services available to them. These would include any placement service that the secondary or postsecondary school most recently attended by the client have available, public employment services, private employment service agencies, and online job placement centers. Finally, we should not overlook the method of scanning help wanted ads in newspapers. Because many job opportunities will be influenced by personal interviews between the applicant and the potential employer, it may be helpful for the counselor to discuss and role play interviewing skills with the client.

We would conclude this section by pointing out that the World Wide Web provides a wide range of options for the job-seeker. Some of these options will permit the client to post their resume, without charge, for the review of hundreds of potential employers.

> The young adult entering the workforce for the first time can also
> encounter a number of challenges, including the following:
>
> - The individual discovers discrepancies between what he or she anticipated upon entry into the workplace and what is actually encountered. This initial letdown or disillusionment can affect the individual's initial attitude and achievements.
> - Adjusting to supervision and direction from superiors, as well as adhering to company policies, can be frustrating to those who were recently free-spirited students.
> - The assumption of complete responsibility, especially financially, for their life and lifestyle can be a burden if the individual is unprepared.
> - The possibility of marriage brings another major responsibility and dramatic change in the individual's lifestyle to mesh with his or her initial career entry.
> - The individual may suddenly have less free time and may encounter changes in the types of leisure activities he or she engages in. (Gibson & Mitchell, 2003, p. 338)[1]

[1] *Gibson, Robert L., & Mitchell, Marianne H., Introduction to Counseling and Guidance, 6/e, © 2003. Reprinted by permission of Pearson Education, Inc., Upper Saddle River, NJ.*

MIDLIFE ADULTS AND CAREER CHANGE

Midlife adults are usually between ages 35 and 55. By midlife, individuals have generally reached their physical peak and physical skills are beginning to gradually decline. Their cognitive skills, however, continue to be at their previous high levels and learning is not inhibited. They also are at the peak of their social development and have, for the most part, integrated their career life with their social life. For many, the symptoms of age are beginning to appear—such as wrinkles, gray hair, and weight problems. In the past century it was assumed that by midlife the individual was well-established in his or her career and community; raising a family; paying off a mortgage; and generally, well-settled in his or her lifestyle. However, recent years have seen dramatic changes in both the workplace and one's lifestyle, with even more significant changes predicted in the immediate future. Midlife career change is no longer viewed as the experience of a small minority, but can be anticipated by the majority of workers entering the workforce in this generation. For many who had assumed that their career patterns would be similar to those of their parents and grandparents, these changes will be traumatic. For the majority of workers, the change will result from their initial career choice no longer being in demand or its being so drastically altered that they will no longer desire to remain in the career. They may not want to seek the additional education needed to upgrade their skills to the necessary level to remain in the career.

In this climate of career change increasing numbers of workers will feel freer to explore alternate careers or alternate settings. The majority of these midlife career changers will benefit from the professional assistance career counselors can provide. Counselors working to assist clients contemplating career change should encourage them to:

- Be a continuing education buff by expanding skills and developing new ones (Don't be afraid to "enroll.")
- Become a recognized individual. Be visible, make friends, volunteer, and speak up. Be a supporter of others. Have a good attitude. Be a team player!
- Develop your own personal public relations plan. Decide who you want to know about you and how best to inform them (without seeming pushy). Don't become discouraged! Be positive *and* productive at all times.

OLDER ADULTS—STILL WORKING

Moving along the maturity continuum, the "graying of America" is another phenomenon of the recent century. Americans are now living longer and working longer. Mandatory retirement is no longer legal. While significant changes are beginning to occur in the physical capabilities and appearance of older adults, counter to popular myths, there is little change in one's personality and no appreciable decline in one's mental capacities. There are, however, major life changes: some positive, such as the advent of grandparenting; and some negative, such as loss of close friends, relatives, or spouses. There are also changes in the older adults' social roles and relationships and leisure time activities.

Studies indicate that approximately one third of older workers will ease into retirement by opting for part time employment rather than full time retirement. Others (approximately 25%), when they reach retirement age, prefer to continue working in their present job. Some may also wish to explore possible new careers that are less demanding and more commensurate with their lifestyle and physical capacities. Volunteering will also appeal to some. Counselors working with this population should be prepared to assist clients in late-life career change, counseling for retirement, assistance in identifying meaningful leisure time activities, and volunteering possibilities. Bereavement counseling will also be common, as will the stress of loneliness and isolation. Counselors should also be aware of the various government programs providing assistance in different areas for the elderly.

The Case of Jimmy: A Lifetime of Career Changes

As noted previously in Chapter 4, chance is an ever-present possibility in one's career development. Krumboltz's *Luck is No Accident* (2004) further underscores this point. With these perspectives in mind, one may conclude that the possibility of career change—often influenced by chance or luck—is also ever-present. Sometimes these changes may be so slow and subtle that they are barely noticed unless one compares the entry career with the exit career. For example: (a) star college student-athlete; (b) star professional athlete; (c) winning college coach; (d) college director of athletics; (e) college president; (f) vice president of sales and public relations with the Mushy Mattress Corporation; and (g) President and CEO of Mushy Mattress Corporation.

An example of multiple and subtle change may be noted in the career chronology of this real life career saga of "Jimmy."

Jimmy

Jimmy's initial experience was in the Navy, where he served for approximately four years and achieved the commissioned rank of Sub-Lieutenant. Shortly thereafter, Jimmy concluded his undergraduate education with a dual major in physics and mathematics and earned a postgraduate certificate in education. He then went on to earn a graduate degree in educational administration. During this period of time he was gaining teaching experience as a physics and mathematics teacher. His next position was as a principal of a secondary school. This position was followed by a short tenure as the founding president of a newly-established junior college. His next position was that as head of a school system.

This post was followed by a move out of education and into the world of finance, with his appointment as financial secretary for his country. He continued in the financial realm when, leaving government, he became the general manager of a large financial institution. He currently is serving as a CEO of an insurance consortium that operates internationally. He also serves on a number of boards and service organizations.

As the reader may note, Jimmy's work history reflects many of the previously indicated suggestions.

COMMON MISCONCEPTIONS OF ADULT CAREER CLIENTS

Not unexpectedly, most career clients bring to their counseling sessions certain misconceptions, prejudices, or expectations. Perhaps the most common of these is lack of accurate information regarding careers, their locations, and entry-level skill requirements. Many clients especially underestimate the type and extent of education needed to even qualify as a particular job applicant. It is also not uncommon that many clients fail to see the big picture as, for example, they do not consider the environment they wish to work in or live in, access to religious and leisure preferences, quality of local schools, or availability of health care.

Some clients will be impatient with the process of career counseling, especially when formalized assessment is needed. At the other extreme are those clients who are hesitant, are unsure, or lack sufficient motivation to engage in the process in a timely manner. Some experienced workers, as well as some young adults entering the workforce, tend to overestimate both their career opportunities and their worth in terms of salary. Some will also set unrealistic conditions on their employment or pursuit of employment. In some instances, such as job loss, some clients seem to be stunned into a state of inactivity.

SPECIAL CAREER CONCERNS OF ADULTS

JOB LOSS

Although it is no longer uncommon, job loss is still a traumatic experience to most individuals. The number of American workers experiencing at least temporary unemployment has risen dramatically in recent generations. Because some industries have shifted to cheap labor locations outside the country, changing public demands for goods, the computerization of America, and technology advancements resulting in the replacement of human labor, many American workers live in a state of uncertainty. However, even plant closings, with the resultant layoffs of one's entire group of coworkers, does not lessen the shock and anguish felt by the individual. Individuals who lose a job, especially when it is unexpected, almost always experience frustration, anger, and considerable unease at the prospect of starting over again. Some job loss clients also experience a considerable loss of self-esteem. Job loss frequently affects family relationships and divorce rates go up for this segment of the population. In these instances, counselors must reassure the individual of his or her self-worth and future possibilities. Once the appropriate relationship has been established, it is important to move rapidly towards assisting the client to develop clear-cut objectives and achievable goals. It is also often desirable to involve the whole family in the search for new career opportunities. (For example, the children can read the news-paper want ads. By going to the local library, they can examine newspapers in the im-mediate geographic area and search the Internet. The spouse may explore educational requirements for new career directions that he or she might think would be interesting and appropriate. The career changer may use such resources as the Discover or Sigi systems to pinpoint specific opportunities.) The counselor must also provide continuous encouragement and must follow up with the client.

STRESS MANAGEMENT

Unexpected and unanticipated job events have always caused stress for workers. Over the centuries, workers have expressed their concern regarding their conditions of work. In the recent century, various legislative measures were enacted to protect workers in the workplace. In the last half of the recent century, the complexities, in-creasing demands, and uncertainties of the workplace have placed extraordinary pres-sures on many members of the labor force. The term *burnout* was borrowed from the light bulb industry to describe the effects of these conditions on individual workers. Its anecdote, stress management, became a popular way to provide assistance to a worker suffering burnout.

While most individuals experience stress to varying degrees for work-related is-sues, burnout as a mental health issue usually refers to those clients who, because of work-related conditions, are unable to function normally and consistently in the per-formance of their daily responsibilities. The stress generators are constantly at the forefront of the individual's thinking and seriously handicap his or her ability to cope. Such individuals may also be characterized by depression, withdrawal, paranoia, and lethargy. They are likely, at times, to be atypically irritable and cynical. When assist-ing clients in need of stress relief or management, the counselor must first of all seek to identify the causes of the disorder. Some of the common causes of individual stress are:

- too many demands for the individual's time commitment
- conflict between job responsibilities and personal responsibilities
- hassles in getting things done
- constant frustration when attempting to accomplish job tasks
- a feeling of powerlessness—of being trapped without options
- failure to get ahead
- negative interpersonal relationships with supervisors and/or peers

Counselors may also recognize that candidates for burnout may be identified by the level, stage, or degree of burnout. Figure 7-1 presents a view of a possible se-quence to burnout.

When assisting clients with excessive stress, counselors should assist their clients to:

- Identify the causes.
- Discuss the causes.

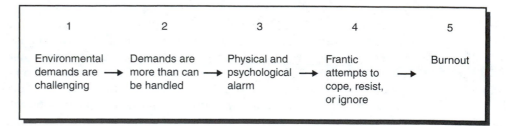

FIGURE 7-1
A possible burnout sequence

Source: From R. L. Gibson and M. H. Mitchell, *Introduction to Counseling and Guidance,* 6/e, p. 374. Copyright © 2003. Reprinted by permission of Pearson Education, Inc., Upper Saddle River, NJ.

- Explore possible anecdotes.
- Develop a stress reduction plan that may include time management, increased leisure time pursuits, taking a break and getting away from it all, and/or shaping up physically and psychologically.
- Group discussions, especially with colleagues suffering the same experiences, are frequently helpful.

Counselor feedback, follow-up, and evaluation are important.

Candidates for stress management are often individuals who have, in effect, brought the stress on themselves by becoming *workalcoholics*. To the average worker, a workalcoholic appears to be addicted to his or her job. The following characteristics are now commonly associated with a workalcoholic:

- arrives at work early and leaves late
- eats lunch while working at their work station
- frequently takes work home
- works, to the extent possible, on the commute to and from work and has a cell phone for business purposes
- rarely takes vacations (and when one *does* take a vacation, takes work along)
- rations time for children and family
- frequently volunteers for extra duties

LEISURE TIME ACTIVITIES

What was your most fun experience of the past year? If you could spend a month doing what you wanted to do, without regard to expense, what would you do? If you had an extra hour free time per day, how would you use that hour?

In all probability, none of your responses to these questions were related to your work setting. While it may be extreme to say that "Americans work so they can play," it *is* accurate that many, if not all, workers look forward to enjoyable times away from the job. Some workers will spend the work year planning for their next vacation. Others, who have less patience, will plan for the weekend ahead. Some will even identify leisure activities to pursue when the workday is over. Certainly, good mental health is enhanced by a balance between work time and leisure time. However, the evidence is—despite the media attention to recreational and leisure activities—that many American workers have failed to identify and participate in meaningful leisure time activities although leisure time has become increasingly recognized as an anecdote to worker stress.

Perhaps more workers should develop and participate in meaningful leisure time activities. A balance between work and leisure is clearly important to the mental health of an individual and the avoidance of job stress. It is also important to recognize that leisure time is just not limited to vacation time. Some leisure time activities can be participated in during after-work hours.

When assisting leisure-need clients, we can make some basic assumptions as follows:

1. Individuals satisfy their basic psychological needs through *both* work and pleasure.
2. Individuals implement (and develop) their self-concept through *both* work and leisure.
3. An individual's value system may be reflected in his or her pattern of leisure activities.
4. A balanced life includes both work and leisure, appropriately proportioned.

When providing counseling assistance to individuals who need to develop meaningful leisure time activities, it is important to distinguish between free time and leisure time. Free time tends to be described as unencumbered time to use as one chooses, whereas leisure time is time devoted to specific activities deemed to be pleasurable. When assisting clients with the identification of meaningful leisure time activities, the counselor can draw upon the same strategies used to help an individual identify a career—namely identifying what would they like to do that they feel capable of doing and deciding, where and what time they will put aside specifically to engage in the activity (a leisure development program). Follow-up questions could be: Did the client engage in the activity as planned? What degree of satisfaction did the client have? What are plans for the future?

TEMPORARY, PART TIME, AND AT HOME WORKERS

In the last decade of the 20th century, dramatic changes took place in the demographics of the workforce as increasing numbers of workers were classified as temporaries, part time employees, or at home workers. Technological changes, frequently in computer-assisted formats; uncertainties regarding future consumer demands; the impact of globalization; and the drive toward increased corporate profits all resulted in the classification of many workers as *temps* (temporaries). Business and industry justified the classification on the basis of future uncertainties prohibiting them from guaranteeing permanent jobs. As a result thousands of workers were employed on a "here today, could be gone tomorrow" basis. In addition to relieving employers of the responsibility of guaranteed employment, they also profited from the avoidance of pension plans, health care coverage, and paid vacations. These conditions can contribute to the development of stress on the part of a worker.

Part time workers have also increased as the cost of living, especially in such basic needs as cost of homes, automobiles, and health care have risen. This has resulted in many workers having more than one job. The majority of these workers work one full time job and one part time job. Some workers even have two part time jobs in addition to one full time job. Further, nearly fifty percent of all women are multiple job holders.

Continued increases in part time employees are predicted as businesses and industries continues to search for technology that will improve the efficiency of their operations, resulting in the elimination of workers replaced by the technology. A decrease in the number of hours needed by the individual worker to perform the previous full time job may also be problemmatic.

During the adult years, many workers, especially those in the professions, become comfortable with a specific career such as teacher or lawyer. For some there have been significant stepping stones that lead to the career of choice in their adult years. These stepping stones could include college preparation, a significant life experience, or chance factors.

Because there is the popular statement that "in America, anybody can become president," Table 7-1 identifies each president's educational preparation, if appropriate, and previous significant careers. In examining this table it would appear that one's chances of becoming president are significantly improved if one is a lawyer or a military hero and if one has graduated from an ivy league university. While the majority of our presidents took office years before there was any researched career theory, we can assume that most of those who ascended to the presidency via the military route could appropriately be attributed to the chance theory. It is also probable that, in retrospect, several of our presidents—especially those of recent generations—could appropriately be classified in one of Holland's categories (realistic, investigative, artistic, social, enterprising, or conventional— see Chapter 4). The several presidents who spent most of their working years prior to the presidency in government and elected offices could also be ascribed to developmental theories.

SUMMARY

Providing career assistance to adult populations has taken on new significance in view of changes taking place in the world of work in the new millennium. This chapter discussed counselors assisting adult workers from the time of their entry into the workforce through retirement. Special concerns such as job loss, stress management, and midlife career change were addressed. Comparatively new phenomena such as temporary workers, part time workers, and at home workers are also noted.

TABLE 7-1
Presidential background information

Number	Name	Education	Occupation
1	George Washington (1789–1797)		Military
2	John Adams (1797–1801)	Harvard	Law
3	Thomas Jefferson (1801–1809)	William & Mary	Law
4	James Madison (1809–1817)	Princeton	Government/law
5	James Monroe (1817–1825)	William & Mary	Law
6	John Quincy Adams (1825–1829)	Harvard	Law
7	Andrew Jackson (1829–1837)		Military
8	Martin Van Buren (1837–1841)		Law
9	William Henry Harrison (1841)		Agriculture
10	John Tyler (1841–1845)	William & Mary	Law
11	James K. Polk (1845–1849)	University of North Carolina	Law
12	Zachary Taylor (1849–1850)		Military
13	Millard Fillmore (1850–1853)		Law
14	Franklin Pierce (1853–1857)	Bowdoin College	Law
15	James Buchanan (1857–1861)	Dickinson College	Law
16	Abraham Lincoln (1861–1865)		Agriculture/law
17	Andrew Johnson (1865–1869)		Tailor
18	Ulysses S. Grant (1869–1877)	West Point	Military
19	Rutherford B. Hayes (1877–1881)	Kenyon College Harvard	Law
20	James Garfield (1881)	Western Reserve	Educator
21	Chester Arthur (1881–1885)	Union College	Law/educator

(continued)

TABLE 7-1
Presidential background information (*continued*)

Number	Name	Education	Occupation
22	Grover Cleveland (1885–1889)		Law
23	Benjamin Harrison (1889–1893)	Miami University of Ohio	Law
24	Grover Cleveland (1893–1897)		Law
25	William McKinley (1897–1901)		Educator/Law/Government
26	Theodore Roosevelt (1901–1909)		Rancher
27	William H. Taft (1909–1913)	Yale	Law
28	Woodrow Wilson (1913–1921)	Princeton University of Virginia	Law/Educator
29	Warren Harding (1921–1923)		Publisher of Newspaper
30	Calvin Coolidge (1923–1927)	Amherst College	Law
31	Herbert Hoover (1928–1937)	Stanford	Engineering
32	Franklin D. Roosevelt (1933–1945)	Harvard Columbia Law School	Government
33	Harry Truman (1945–1953)	University of Missouri	Farmer/Merchant
34	Dwight D. Eisenhower (1953–1961)	U.S. Military Academy—West Point	Military
35	John F. Kennedy (1961–1963)	Harvard	Government
36	Lyndon Johnson (1963–1969)	Southwest Texas State Teachers College	Government
37	Richard Nixon (1969–1974)	Whittier College	Law
38	Gerald Ford (1974–1977)	University of Michigan & Yale Law School	Law
39	Jimmy Carter (1977–1981)	U.S. Naval Academy	Military/Government
40	Ronald Reagan (1981–1989)	Eureka College	Actor
41	George H. W. Bush (1989–1993)	Yale University	Business—Oil/Government
42	William J. Clinton (1993–2001)	Georgetown University Yale	Law Business/Oil
43	George W. Bush (2001–)	Yale Harvard	

DISCUSSION QUESTIONS

1. Discuss the statement that "A career is a way of life" from the perspectives of a school teacher, a physician, a commercial airlines pilot, and a supermarket clerk. Would gender make any difference?

2. Discuss your favorite leisure time activities when you were in (a) elementary school and (b) high school; then discuss current leisure time activities.

3. Share with others (in small groups) part time and temporary jobs you have experienced.

CLASS ACTIVITIES

1. Interview three adult workers regarding additional education or training programs they have participated in since entering the workforce. Report to class.

2. Examine the help wanted ads in an out-of-town newspaper. Identify part time and full time jobs. Report to class.

3. Examine and compare the help-wanted and situation wanted ads in such professional publications as the *Journal for Counseling and Development*. Discuss them with the class.

4. Interview personnel at an EAP or interview industrial personnel regarding common causes of stress among their employees. Discuss them with the class.

5. Interview a retiree regarding his or her activities and report to class.

6. Discuss career concerns with adults in three different job settings and report your findings to the class.

READINGS OF INTEREST

Amundson, N. E., Borgen, W. M., Jordan, S., & Erlebach, A. C. (2004). Survivors of downsizing: Helpful and hindering experiences. *The Career Development Quarterly, 52*(3), 256–271.

Harper, M. C., & Shoffner, M. F. (2004), Counseling for continued career development after retirement: An application of the theory of work adjustment. *The Career Development Quarterly, 52*(3), 272–284.

Jepsen, D. A., & Choudhuri, E. (2001). Stability and change in 25-year occupational career patterns. *The Career Development Quarterly, 50*(1), 3–19.

Lapan, R. T., & Kosciulek, J. F. (2001). Toward a community career system program evaluation framework. *Journal of Counseling & Development, 79*(1), 3–15.

Laporte, B. J. (2002). Career development for vital agers: Meeting the challenge. In G. R. Walz, R. Knowdell, & Kirkman, C. (Eds.). *Thriving in Challenging and Uncertain Times*. Greensboro, NC: ERIC Clearinghouse on Counseling & Student Services and CAPS, Inc.

Patton, W., & Creed, P. A. (2001). Developmental issues in career maturity and career decision status. *The Career Development Quarterly, 49*(4), 336–351.

Chapter 8

Career Counseling for Diverse Populations

In our democratic society, equal access and opportunity for all people is a foundational principle. Yet how can we achieve equality in the world of work, especially when there is so much human diversity? By regarding diversity as our strength and greatness, career counselors begin by moving beyond their stereotypes and good intentions. In this chapter we learn how effective career counseling also depends on having sensitivity to both group and individual differences.

Charles R. Ridley, PhD
Professor and Associate Dean
The University Graduate School
Indiana University

OBJECTIVES

To provide readers with an understanding of:

1. The impact of culture on clients and their career needs
2. The unique career needs of women, older Americans, at-home workers, the disabled, and those infected with AIDS
3. The prevention of the underdevelopment or loss of human potential because of poverty or imprisonment, and other similar circumstances and their challenges to the counseling profession

INTRODUCTION

The United States has been known for many years as a melting pot where many cultures melted together to make our nation one of diversity and greatness. In recent years, we have witnessed a heightened awareness of the distinctly different cultures in our society and the contributions they have made to the strength and development of this country. This increased recognition of our diversity has encouraged the preservation of cultures and their characteristics and increased respect and acceptance for these differences. It is important that counselors, whether in school or nonschool settings, recognize, accept, and promote cultural integrity. Counselors must, however, recognize that there are no exact profiles for any cultural group. In fact, the only stereotype is that individual differences *do* exist in all cultures.

To further understand cultures and their impact on clients, scholars who have studied culture seem to agree on several key points:

- Culture includes all aspects of human life and is a process by which groups impose order on and meaning [on] their life experience (Erchak, 1992).
- Culture is verbal, visual, rhythmic, spatial, temporal, and symbolic (Agar, 1994). It involves communications between all the senses in patterns that are recognizable even though members of any given culture may not be able to express an awareness of the patterns to which they are responding.
- An understanding of how the language is used in a specific culture is essential to understanding the language. Language shapes experience, and experience shapes language. It predetermines modes of observation and interpretation, shaping interpretation of experiences, recreating experiences, and empowering members to imagine and create new experiences (Agar, 1994; Goodenough, 1981; Sapir, 1958).
- The most effective method for understanding one's own culture is to compare it to other cultures. This process forces a person to perceive the various systems embedded in different cultures and to use this understanding of systems, which order and impose meaning, to revisit his or her own cultural system.
- Members of a specific culture typically do not experience their culture as a humanly constructed system. They experience their cultures as "the way things are and the way things should be." This phenomenon is generally referred to as *ethnocentrism*. Individuals within a culture tend to believe that their ideas about the universe are simply "common sense" (Geertz, 1983) even though what is common sense in one culture may be unheard of or taboo in another (Okun, Fried, & Okun, 1999, p. 9).

Guidelines for counseling clients from diverse backgrounds are suggested by the Association for Multicultural Counseling and Development (1992, 1996), a division of the American Counseling Association. Also, the American Psychological Association

(APA) Council of Representatives endorsed *Multicultural Guidelines on Education and Training, Research, Practice, and Organizational Development for Psychologists* (APA, 2002), creating new policy for its members.

COUNSELING CLIENTS FROM DIVERSE BACKGROUNDS

The world of work and the workers that inhabit it are undergoing dramatic and constant changes. Demographic data available in various publications, such as *American Diversity* (Denton and Tolnay, Eds., 2002), and the Hudson Institute's report entitled *Workforce 2020* (1997) clearly depict the dramatic changes constantly occurring in the composition of the U.S. workforce. Counselors providing career assistance must be aware that these changes will result in different client opportunities, concerns, and challenges. Additionally, career counselors will need to assist employers and potential employees to understand the changes in the workplace as they affect the worker. Counselors should also be able to assist clients from all cultural backgrounds to become more employable and to understand the requirements for success in their chosen fields. Counselors should also help employers to understand and respond appropriately to the cultures represented in their workforce.

Ridley (1995) noted that clients from different cultural backgrounds frequently experience the following:

- **diagnosis**   Minority clients tend to receive a misdiagnosis, usually involving more severe psychopathology but occasionally involving less severe psychopathology, more often than is warranted.
- **staff assignment**   Minority clients tend to be assigned to junior professionals, paraprofessionals, or nonprofessionals for counseling rather than senior and more highly trained professionals.
- **treatment modality**   Minority clients tend to receive low-cost, less preferred treatment consisting of minimal contact, medication only, or custodial care rather than intensive psychotherapy.
- **utilization**   Minority clients tend to be represented disproportionately in mental health facilities. Specifically, minority clients are underrepresented in private treatment facilities and over-represented in public treatment facilities.
- **treatment duration**   Minority clients show a much higher rate of premature termination and dropout from therapy, or they are confined to much longer inpatient care.
- **attitudes**   Minority clients report more dissatisfaction and unfavorable impressions regarding treatment. (p. 9)

It is appropriate to keep in mind the inherent worth and dignity of the individual, the right of the individual to develop his or her potential, and respect for the individual's uniqueness. All clients should have the opportunities for effective counseling assistance regardless of cultural, ethnic, religious, or socioeconomic backgrounds.

THE CULTURES WE COUNSEL

The United States is a multicultural nation. With the exception of American Indians, there is no native culture. The term *multicultural* means that many cultures are represented in the United States. These many cultures have each contributed to the greatness that is America, while, at the same time, retaining their own uniqueness. As we begin to examine how to provide career counseling assistance to these various cultures, there are occasional misconceptions that must be avoided.

- The nature of being multicultural means there will be minorities.
- Some cultures have more positive characteristics than others.
- All cultures share so many characteristics in common that, from a counseling standpoint, they can be treated as a homogeneous group.

In multicultural counseling, one of the central objectives must be that the desired results of the counseling are not handicapped in any way by the cultural differences between a counselor and his or her client. In the counseling profession the basis for this desired and necessary interaction may be derived from our philosophical assumptions of the inherent worth and dignity of the individual, respect for the uniqueness of the individual, and the right of the individual to achieve his or her potential. As we view multicultural counseling, we must recognize that the prefix *multi* means *many*. As counselors we must, therefore, be sensitive to the uniqueness of many different cultures and backgrounds that will make up our client population. We also must recognize that many of the traditional characteristics of mainstream counseling, such as openness, sharing, and emotional expression, may inhibit effective counseling with some client populations. Many minority clients will also initially be anxious, prejudiced, lacking in trust, and uncertain regarding their role and the counselor's expectations in the process. From the initial contact the counselor must be respectful and aware of the cultural traditions and backgrounds of the client. The paragraphs that follow briefly discuss the most populous minorities in the United States.

AFRICAN AMERICANS

The African American population in the United States, until recently the largest minority, has historically been discriminated against and subject to prejudice. In recent generations, legislative, educational, and humanitarian efforts have been made to overcome and eliminate these abuses. While progress has been made, much remains to be done, especially in the world of work and assisting African American career clients. The counseling profession must be a vigorous advocate for equality.

Sue and Sue (2003) have offered guidelines for counseling with African Americans. They have suggested that the first few sessions are of the utmost importance to the ultimate success of the total counseling process. Their suggestions include the following:

1. Ask the client what his or her reaction is to a counselor of a different ethnic background.

2. Ascertain the expectancies of the African American client regarding the process of counseling.
3. Determine the client's view of his or her problem and the possible solutions they have identified.
4. Establish a facilitative relationship with the client. Counselor self-disclosure may be helpful, especially if the client appears hostile. It may also be helpful to discuss some noncounseling topics, such as sports or entertainment, in which the client has an interest.
5. Explore the client's responses to any discrimination and racism they have experienced.
6. Help the client identify positive assets relevant to the situation (such as family, friends, school, community, or church).
7. Help the client define goals and appropriate procedures for attaining these goals.

Although some of these suggestions may be omitted or amended, they do provide a helpful framework for assisting this client population. Within this population there will be great diversity, which again emphasizes the necessity of recognizing individual differences and avoiding cultural stereotypes.

LATIN AMERICANS

Latin Americans are the fastest growing minority in the United States. The U.S. Census Bureau, July 1, 2002, also reported that Hispanics had become the largest minority group in this country with a population of 38,800,000. Over 66% of this population are of Mexican family heritage. Hispanics are the largest minority in major league baseball. The Hispanic population in the United States is growing rapidly and is a comparatively young population. Additionally, lenient legal immigration laws will undoubtedly add to the continued increase in numbers of this group in the United States. The growth and impact of this culture suggests that members of the counseling profession need to understand its significant characteristics. It is important to recognize the predominance of the family and the significance of family values in Latin culture. Counselors must also keep in mind that the sex roles are clearly defined, with males being dominant in the traditional settings. Although males are expected to be the wage earner of the family, Latin women in the United States are becoming more prominent in the workforce. This change in role is often a source of conflict within the family and the Latin society. As with all cultures, counselors must be sensitive to the uniqueness of the culture and the client. It is, for example, important that the counselor show the Latin client respect by using the correct pronunciation of the client's name. Latin clients also seem to respond better to more direct approaches and are frequently turned off by the use of traditional assessment instruments.

ASIAN AMERICANS

The Asian American population in the United States is another rapidly growing minority. This population includes such distinctive national groups as Japanese-Americans, Chinese Americans, Filipino Americans, and Korean Americans. In each of these groups family roles and values are important. Respect for authority and restraint of emotions are also common across these cultures. However, we would again caution the counselor to avoid stereotyping this population. Counselors should be aware that mental health counselors are neither well-known nor accepted by this population. Sue and Sue (2003) have suggested the following for increasing counselor effectiveness with these populations.

1. Be aware of cultural differences between the therapist and the client as regarding counseling, appropriate goals, and process. How would they affect work with Asian Americans who have a collectivistic, hierarchical, and patriarchal orientation?

2. Build rapport by discussing confidentiality and explaining the client role and the need to coconstruct the problem definition and solutions.

3. Assess not just from an individual perspective but include family, community, and societal influences on the problem. Obtain the worldview and ethnic identity of the Asian American client.

4. Conduct a positive assets search. What strengths, skills, problem-solving abilities, and social supports are available to the individual or family?

5. Consider or reframe the problem when possible as one in which issues of culture conflict or acculturation are involved.

6. Determine whether somatic complaints are involved and assess their influence on mood and relationships.

7. Take an active role but allow Asian Americans to choose and evaluate suggested interventions.

8. Use problem-focused, time-limited approaches that have been modified to incorporate possible cultural factors.

9. With family therapy, the therapist should be aware that western-based theories and techniques may not be appropriate for Asian families. Determine the structure and communication pattern among the members. It may be helpful to address the father first and to initially have statements by family members directed to the therapist. Focus on positive aspects of parenting such as modeling and teaching. Use a solution-focused model.

10. In couples counseling, assess for societal or acculturation conflicts. Determine the way that caring, support, or affection is shown. Among traditional Asians, providing for the needs of the other is as or more important than verbalizations of affection. Obtain their perspective on the goals for better functioning.

11. With Asian children and adolescents, common problems involve acculturation conflicts with parents, feeling guilty or stressful over academic performance, negative self-image or identity issues, and struggle between interdependence and independence.

12. Among recent immigrants or refugees, assess for living situation, culture conflict, and social or financial condition. Case management skills may be needed to obtain help in obtaining food and other community resources.

13. Consider the need to act as an advocate or engage in systems-level intervention in cases of institutional racism or discrimination. (Sue & Sue, 2003, p. 342)

ARAB AMERICANS

There has been a significant increase, in recent decades, of the Arab American population. Over three million Arabs live in the United States and additionally, a student population numbering in the thousands live temporarily in this country while pursuing higher education degrees. Terrorism linked to native Arabs and the war in Iraq have resulted in increased surveillance of elements of this population. Increased discrimination and stereotyping have resulted in hostility and suspicion between many Americans and Arabs residing in this country. When members of this population *do* seek counseling, it is important that counselors are extra sensitive to the cultural background of Arab American clients.

McFadden (1993) suggested the following when working with Arab American clients.

- Marriage and children are essential for a complete and happy adult life.
- Men are the heads of their families and the designated decision makers. In other words, authority and family identification are patrilineal.
- The extended family is valued across generations. Young people owe profound respect to their elders, and often even to older siblings.
- Children are expected to care for their parents and older relatives, usually inviting them to live in their homes, particularly after an older person is widowed.
- Family honor is most easily damaged by the behavior of women, so they have a great responsibility toward the entire extended family to comport themselves in an honorable way.
- Family ties and duties have precedence over work or career aspirations.
- Religious identity and belief in God are essential. (McFadden, 1993, p. 264)

NATIVE AMERICANS

The only minority culture in the 48 contiguous states not based on immigration is that of Native Americans. This population consists of a number of Indian tribes, each of which has its own heritage and cultural traditions. The U.S. government recognizes over 500 tribes impacted by a complex mosaic of various federal laws and their interpretations. Many of these laws are aimed at ending the long and disgraceful discrimination suffered by Native Americans. There is evidence of increased counselor activity with this population in recent years. Effective counselors must recognize and respect the characteristics of the tribal system and cultures. As with many of the previously-discussed minority groups, the family and cultural values are important. Many also desire harmony with nature, and many will consider counselors to be similar to tribal elders. Because of this, counselors will, at least initially, be expected to do most of the talking and also to impart advice as requested. By explaining the counseling process, counselors may encourage the Native American client to be more active in the total process.

WOMEN IN THE WORKFORCE

Perhaps the most significant change in the U.S. workforce in the 1900s was the tremendous influx of women workers into all careers at all levels, primarily in the period following World War II. During this time, federal and state legislation stimulated both equity and opportunity for women workers. There is an abundance of evidence that equity in job choice, advancement, salaries, and other aspects of the world of work still favor males, despite legislative efforts to achieve equity among workers of both sexes. For example, the U.S. Census Bureau noted in its report of February, 2001, that female workers at all age levels, compared by school achievement levels, earned consistently less than their male counterparts. In nearly all comparisons, women of equal age and educational level were earning at least 23% less than their male equivalents. While many married women *do* work to raise the standard of living for their families, the majority of women who work do so because of economic necessity. Also, the overwhelming majority of single parent families are headed by women and over 50% of these are living in poverty.

Significant to the large-scale influx of women into the workforce are the dramatic changes in traditional family relationships and home life. The impact of both parents working on family members has become an important psychological and sociological issue that draws much attention from the many helping professions, especially those specializing in marriage and family therapy. The current pattern of both parents working has raised some interesting career dilemmas such as: (a) whose career takes precedence?; (b) what if one partner gets a lucrative advancement that requires movement to another locale?; (c) how are the traditional domestic responsibilities allocated?; and (d) in the case of children in the home, what arrangements are made for their care? If there are children in the home, are they being left alone without supervision (are they latchkey children?)?

It is important for counselors to be free of any gender prejudice and reflect this in both words and action. On some occasions career counselors may have the opportunity to consult with potential employers to encourage (with tact) the elimination of gender bias in their hiring practices.

OLDER ADULTS

Another significant change in the population of the United States, in the last half of the recent century, is the graying of America. Improved healthcare and awareness of healthy living strategies has resulted in the average longevity of the American population increasing over 30 years in the 20th century. Not only are Americans now living longer, they are also working longer. The increasing number of senior citizens in the workforce can also be attributed to such factors as: (a) antidiscrimination legislation, which includes provisions prohibiting job bias against older workers; (b) economic necessity, often stimulated by the lack of company pension plans, for older workers to continue working; and (c) many healthy seniors do not wish to retire.

Career counselors should also be aware that some older workers wish to shift from full time to part time employment. Some may also wish to experience new and different careers and may be willing to secure additional formal education in order to qualify for new opportunities. Some older workers may also seek to reenter the workforce after retirement, due to a decline in financial security, the loss of social contacts, or the death of a spouse. In fact, the majority of workers of retirement age prefer to continue working—some full time, some part time, and some in new careers. For those that do not wish to continue regular employment, volunteering appears to be popular. When providing career assistance to this population, counselors must recognize physical and other limitations that would preclude certain job opportunities.

The personal adjustment for many older Americans, which comes with retirement and withdrawal from their social groups, when entering a new career and social setting must be addressed. In some instances, clients may also need assistance with planning for meaningful leisure time activities. Counselors must also be active in overcoming bias and prejudice against older workers and, in some instances, counterattacking this bias within the older worker himself or herself.

Access to this older population is not typically available through the usual channels of school programs and community employment agencies. In response to older workers' needs, some businesses and industries are beginning to include retirement counseling as an activity of their EAPs. Smaller businesses, and sometimes consortiums of these, are beginning to hire career counseling consultants to assist their older workers. Outreach programs, through community service agencies, are also worthy of consideration. Counselors—regardless of setting—assisting retirees must be aware of appropriate career opportunities, and educational programs that retrain retirees for new opportunities. It is also important to consider the wide range of volunteer opportunities available in most communities.

HOME ALONE AND WORKING

In recent years a number of circumstances such as financial need, premature retirement trends, and boredom have resulted in increasing numbers of individuals exploring "home careers." Working out of one's home has been stimulated by use of computers, e-mail, the Internet, cell phones, and other technological developments that are increasing access to information and speeding up communication. Many home-start businesses grow into full time ventures complete with an outside facility.

Career counselors can assist clients interested in developing a career based on working at home by assessing the client's interests, abilities, and experience background and matching these variables with career opportunities that lend themselves to working in the home. In this process, it is important to identify home careers that clients will enjoy and that can be managed from the home. It is probably appropriate to remind clients that they may need a business license, and local zoning laws must be checked to be certain that their business activity does not cause conflict. Some examples of home-run businesses that are currently successful are bookkeeping and accounting for small businesses, lawn care and landscaping, information search and retrieval, copy editing, foreign language translation, day care, pet sitting, personal services, and bed and breakfast businesses. There are many more options.

PEOPLE WITH DISABILITIES

There are approximately 6 million Americans of working age who have varying degrees of physical or mental disabilities. As a population, their human potential is seriously underdeveloped and nearly two thirds of this group are unemployed. Additionally, many are subtly discriminated against despite the Americans with Disabilities Act (ADA). This comprehensive law identifies disabled individuals as follows:

- An individual with a disability is a person who has a physical or mental impairment that substantially limits one or more "major life activities," or has a record of such an impairment, or is regarded as having such an impairment.
- Examples of physical or mental impairments include, but are not limited to, such contagious and noncontagious diseases and conditions as orthopedic, visual, speech, and hearing impairments; cerebral palsy, epilepsy, muscular dystrophy, multiple sclerosis, cancer, heart disease, diabetes, mental retardation, emotional illness, specific learning disabilities, HIV disease (whether symptomatic or asymptomatic), tuberculosis, drug addiction, and alcoholism. Homosexuality and bisexuality are not physical or mental impairments under the ADA.
- "Major life activities" include functions such as caring for oneself, performing manual tasks, walking, seeing, hearing, speaking, breathing, learning, and working.
- Individuals who currently engage in the illegal use of drugs are not protected by the ADA when an action is taken on the basis of their current illegal use of drugs. (*Americans with Disabilities Act Handbook,* 1991, pp. 3–4)

The counseling profession first responded to the needs of this population after World War I with a specialty in rehabilitation counseling. This specialty grew rapidly in the period following World War II. Data from business and industrial settings indicate that employment, as well as the retention of the disabled, are enhanced with counseling. This furthers a goal of the ADA, which is to remove barriers that restrict the development of the potential of this population. When assisting disabled clients, counselors must first be aware that not all disabilities are visible. Also, just because an individual cannot perform all aspects of one job does not necessarily mean he or she will not be able to perform all aspects of another job. When working with this population, counselors should be knowledgeable about appropriate and inappropriate job opportunities and careers and relevant training programs. Disabled clients may also benefit from personal adjustment counseling in such areas as self-concept development, career development, and social development. Support groups and support systems, such as family, are important. Counselors may also be alert to assisting disabled clients who have been subtly discriminated against or find themselves the victims of personal prejudice. Although legislative enactments have increased public awareness and strengthened employment opportunities for the disabled, counselors can and should play a key role in the still-needed advancement of people who have disabilities.

PEOPLE WHO HAVE HIV/AIDS

AIDS became widely recognized as a disease and epidemic in some parts of the world in the 1980s and 1990s. Some estimates have predicted over 2 million deaths worldwide from HIV/AIDS in 2004. In the United States it is estimated that there are over 200,000 cases, of which 60% are under 35 years of age. This population, especially when individuals are identified, faces extreme discrimination in society in general and the workplace in particular. Most of this population feels isolated, punished, and discriminated against. They tend to have low self-esteem. As a result of all of these factors, many will not disclose their condition, which creates other problems. For counselors working with clients who have AIDS, it is important to educate both employers and fellow employees by using group techniques. Counselors can help AIDs victims focus on life and living by developing adequate coping styles and identifying careers in which they can achieve. As we enter the new century there is an international recognition of the epidemic nature of AIDS, especially in the African countries, and there have been renewed and vigorous efforts around the world to find a cure.

THE LOSS OF HUMAN POTENTIAL: A CHALLENGE TO SOCIETY AND TO CAREER COUNSELING

PEOPLE IN POVERTY

In 1998 over 34 million people in the United States were living below government poverty levels ($17,050 annual income or less for a family of four). Over 23 million are white, 9 million black and 8 million are Hispanics. The poverty population tends to be centered in large, metropolitan, industrial areas and those rural settings that have very few natural resources. These settings seem to perpetuate a cycle of poverty as children are born to parents of poverty and grow up to become adults in the same environment. For many, these settings appear to be so restrictive and without opportunities that individuals simply give up because they see no way out. The public schools in these areas are usually poor, which results in little educational stimulation and preparation of the young. All too often the general public appears to be blind, deliberately or otherwise, to the circumstances and this population has little political influence. In recent years, however, there have been encouraging results in the efforts of some cities to overcome inner-city poverty. A report in the May 19, 2003, issue of *USA Today* (Dennis Cauchon) showed declines in the percentage of people living in poverty in 10 metropolitan areas decreasing from 74% (Detroit) to 35% (New Orleans). While many workers moved from welfare poor to working poor, others found the means to move out and individuals who had better paying jobs moved in.

Counseling programs are rare in these settings, and where they *do* exist they are often viewed with suspicion. Efforts are being made to place more counselors in inner-city and other poverty area schools. However, simply being there does not guarantee effective services. To be effective in these settings, counselors must first of all understand the culture of the poor. This is essential to the development of a public information program that will bring about desired results. Both individual and group work will be enhanced when counselors recognize the unique characteristics and problems of the poverty population.

Counseling assistance should not only be available to school populations but should be provided to adult populations through community agencies. When assisting this population counselors must, in addition to being sensitive about the environment and the circumstances it has created, deal with the frequent feelings of hopelessness and worthlessness on the part of the client. The counselor must provide practical, realistic, and helpful information regarding career opportunities and find appropriate training programs that can be accessed by this population.

The poorest of the poor are generally the homeless. Included in their numbers are many children and young adults. Members of this population are often frequent victims of discrimination and crime. They are, more frequently than other populations, ravaged by disease and sickness. They achieve little in the way of education and their one major goal is simply to survive. Society pays little attention to this group, except from a law enforcement standpoint, which only serves to stimulate feelings of helplessness and worthlessness. Educational and counseling outreach programs are suggested for assisting this population, but unfortunately these are few and far between. Here again is an example of a total loss of human potential.

CRIMINAL OFFENDERS

A tragic loss of human potential, as well as the individual's well-being, is reflected in the over 6,300,000 adults in either prison or on probation (U.S. Bureau of Justice Statistics, 2001, p. 202). Additionally, over 1,700,000 juveniles are in jail, on probation, or have a criminal record (National Center for Juvenile Justice, 2001, p. 1998). These numbers represent violators of specific criminal statutes and do not take into consideration unreported violations of the law—crimes for which the perpetrators have not been caught and thousands of cases of unreported domestic violence. The most serious and populous crime areas are located in urban areas in metropolitan cities that have high levels of poverty, unemployment, noise, and environmental problems. Although rural poverty areas experience increasing crime, especially where unemployment is high, the inner cities continue to be the chief breeding grounds for criminals.

A contributory condition recognized by most sociologists, educators, and law enforcement specialists is the quality and availability of schooling. The majority of schools, both inner city and rural, are faced with major problems associated with inadequate financing. Among the shortcomings of these schools is the lack of school counseling programs. An additional contributing cause is the lack of parental involvement in the students' school life and after-school activities. Gangs are common in urban settings, and these seem to stimulate the use of drugs and alcohol and other more serious criminal activities.

Although there are no clear-cut personality profiles of the criminal-to-be, there *are* indicators that appear frequently enough to alert counselors that these individuals need special attention. One such indicator is that a person's home life was disruptive, problem-centered, nonsupportive or abusive. A second factor was frequent trouble in school, sometimes leading to suspension or being labeled as a loner or antisocial. These students may blame others for their problems. Many criminal-bound students are hostile, aggressive, impulsive, and lack self-control. Of course, there were some who enter careers in crime because of the desire for money or the goods of others and also because it seems easy and they feel no sense of guilt. The majority of this population never considered or never were counseled about careers of worth that could be rewarding and enjoyable to them.

In addition to the population heading for careers in crime, approximately 625,000 who served time in penal institutions were released from prison in 2003. This critical mass faced crushing obstacles to finding full time employment. This difficulty will contribute to more than 60% of these releasees being returned to prison within 3 years, as reported by the U.S. Department of Justice in 2003.

Prevention is the best anecdote to the crime waves our country has been experiencing. Each year we notice state, local, and federal governments complaining about the increased amount of money that they must spend for building additional prison facilities. A small portion of this amount would enable schools and social agencies to target high-crime and high-poverty areas for counselors and social workers to concentrate preventive efforts with at-risk populations of youth. Most counselors coming from middle- or upper-class backgrounds will have difficulty meeting the needs of at-risk youth simply because they do not have an adequate knowledge of the backgrounds, environmental and personal, of those in need. This understanding gap will be further accentuated for counselors seeking to assist at-risk racial and ethnic minorities. Many at-risk youth hold lower career expectations, which does not seem to be unwarranted. In too many of these cases there is a true lack of opportunity for employment tied to a perpetual cycle of poverty and multiple social disadvantages. These disadvantages can be further exacerbated by alcohol and drug abuse.

Theory and research in the field has not provided many guidelines for effective intervention practices that would change the experiences and expectations for these at-risk populations. Clearly, more research is needed. We must examine the environmental realities that at-risk youth encounter, including limited career opportunities, and we must discover what intervention strategies project promise for assisting at-risk youth.

While many prison systems do have career placement activities designed to find appropriate jobs for inmates upon their release, the task is often difficult and the high percentage of those reentering the field of crime suggests that many opt out of honest careers shortly after their release from prison.

Some prison populations will receive career assistance from offender workforce development specialists. These specialists will help prisoners plan for careers upon their release from prison. This should increase the likelihood that former prisoners will stay out of prison following their release. The National Career Development Association (NCDA) arranges for the training of these facilitators at the state level.

SUMMARY

This chapter reviewed many cultures that make up the population of the United States and the impact these cultures have on clients. Counselors assisting career clients must be aware of the implications of the client's cultural background. The cultures of Latin Americans, Asian Americans, Native Americans, African Americans, and Arab Americans were briefly summarized. Additionally, the characteristics of women in the workforce, older adults, home workers, people with disabilities, and HIV/AIDS patients were noted. The chapter concluded by looking at that segment of our population that has lost its human potential through poverty and crime.

DISCUSSION QUESTIONS

1. What minority group do you feel is most discriminated against in the job marketplace? How would you, as a professional counselor, try to counteract this discrimination?
2. What minority group do you feel you have the least contact with or understanding of? How do you plan to remedy this?
3. Do you know any home workers? What do they do? Why did they decide on the home as their work setting? Are they satisfied?
4. At what age do you believe you might retire? What do you plan to do to occupy your time in retirement?
5. Do you personally know anyone who became "employed" in a career of crime? What were the causative factors in their choice?

CLASS ACTIVITIES

1. Divide into small groups. In each small group, discuss what cultural biases and assumptions are held and have group members challenge unfounded biases and stereotypes.
2. Divide into pairs. Take turns describing times when you each exhibited intentional or unintentional racism and what you could have done differently to avoid exhibiting the racist behavior. Then discuss your own experiences with being a victim of racism. Finally, discuss times you exhibited cultural sensitivity.
3. A recent immigrant to this country is seeking assistance with securing a job. This individual has limited command of the English language and, although he is a high school graduate in his native country, he did not receive any

specific career preparation. Assume that the setting is in the community in which you now reside. How would you proceed to assist this client.

4. Divide into small groups. In each group, have each person answer the following questions: (a) What foreign countries would I select if I were to move out of the United States to seek employment? (b) What would I identify as my ethnicity?

READINGS OF INTEREST

Capuzzi, D., & Gross, D. R. (2004) *Youth at risk: A prevention resource for counselors, teachers, parents* (4th. ed). Alexandria, VA: American Counseling Association.

Clements, C. B. (1999). Psychology, attitude shifts, and prison growth. *American Psychologist, 54*(9), 785.

Egisdottir, S., & Gerstein, L. H. (2000). Icelandic and American students' expectations about counseling. *Journal of Counseling & Development, 78*(1), 44–53.

Garrett, M. T., & Pichette, E. F. (2000). Red as an apple: Native American acculturation and counseling with or without reservation. *Journal of Counseling & Development, 78*(1), 3–13.

Granello, P. F., & Hanna, F. J. (2003). Incarcerated and court-involved adolescents: Counseling an at-risk population. *Journal of Counseling & Development, 81*(1), 11–18.

Hunt, B., Jaques, J., Niles, S. G., & Wierzalis, E. (2003). Career concerns for people living with HIV/AIDS. *Journal of Counseling & Development, 81*(1), 55–60.

Luzzo, A. D., & McWhirter, E. H. (2001). Sex and ethnic differences in the perception of educational and career-related barriers and levels of coping efficacy. *Journal of Counseling & Development, 79*(1), 61–67.

Multicultural Counseling Competencies. (2004). (Special section). *Journal of Mental Health Counseling, 26*(1), 39–93.

Nassar-McMillan, S. C., & Hakim-Larson, J. (2003). Counseling considerations among Arab Americans. *Journal of Counseling and Development, 81*(2), 150–159.

O'Brien, T. P., & Jones, D. J. (1999). A balanced approach for corrections policy needed. *American Psychologist, 54*(9), 784.

Petersen, S. (2000). Multicultural perspective on middle-class women's identity development. *Journal of Counseling & Development, 78*(1), 63–71.

Rowley, W. J., & MacDonald, D. (2001). Counseling and the law: A cross-cultural perspective. *Journal of Counseling & Development, 79*(4), 422–429.

Sue, D. W., Bingham, R. P., Porche-Burke, L., & Vasquez, M. (1999). The diversification of psychology: A multicultural revolution. *American Psychologist, 54*(12), 1061–1069.

Sue, S. Science, ethnicity, and bias: Where have we gone wrong? (1999). *American Psychologist, 54*(12), 1070–1077.

Utsey, S. O., Ponterotto, J. G., Reynolds, A. M., & Cancelli, A. A. (2000). Racial discrimination, coping, life satisfaction, and self-esteem among African Americans. *Journal of Counseling & Development, 78*(1), 72–80.

Weinrach, S. G. (2002). The counseling profession's relationship to Jews and the Issues that concern them: More than a case of selective awareness. *Journal of Counseling & Development, 80*(3), 300–314.

Yeh, C. J., & Arora, A. G. (2003). Multicultural training and interdependent and independent self-construal as predictors of universal-diverse orientation among school counselors. *Journal of Counseling & Development, 81*(1), 78–83.

Chapter 9

Guidelines: Legal, Ethical, and Program Management

As the authors of this book suggest, career counselors must emphasize for workers in our society "flexibility and both the capacity and willingness to change." Professional counselors must take a lesson from what they teach. To be professional and wise, counselors must understand basic ethical and legal principles, and must be prepared for these guidelines to change on a regular basis. This chapter summarizes important ethical, legal, and professional issues in counseling, and importantly, provides a look to the future.

Theodore P. Remley, Jr., JD, PhD
Professor and Chair
Department of Educational Leadership,
Counseling, and Foundations
College of Education
University of New Orleans

OBJECTIVES

To provide readers with an understanding of:

1. Legal enactments significant to the profession of counseling and providing career assistance
2. The importance and content of codes of ethics for the profession of counseling and the practice of counselors
3. Program planning, development, and management and its impact on the provision of effective, efficient, and accountable counseling services

INTRODUCTION

The corporate scandals of recent years have reminded Americans of the importance of legal guidelines and ethical standards for those who serve and advise the public. These guidelines are not limited to the corporate and political worlds. Counselors and potential counselors *must* be aware that, as a profession, we must recognize the hallmarks that identify a true profession. First and foremost is an academic training program that leads to a recognized degree from a reputable institution. Further, true professions provide for licensure or certification, as well as their periodic renewal, for practitioners in the field. In addition, professionals should be alert to those legal enactments that pertain to their professional activities. Professions also adopt codes of ethics and standards for practice to guide the professional performance of their members. A profession takes responsibility for regulating and enforcing policies among its membership to ensure that the appropriate legal and ethical responsibilities are adhered to. This strict adherence to the ethical standards and relevant legal enactments is important to gaining the public's trust and acceptance of the profession as a profession. This final chapter focuses on the legal and ethical responsibilities that you, as a professional counselor, will be expected to assume and also underscores the meaning of *professionalism*.

LEGAL GUIDELINES

Regardless of their professional setting, professional counselors function in a complex legal environment. In their professional work, a variety of laws and regulations apply to the counselor and the practice of counseling. These include national, state, and local legal guidelines and for those in educational settings, possibly school board regulations are included as well. During the recent decades, few aspects of the counselor's role and function, regardless of setting, have remained untouched by legislative or judicial activities. For example, there has been a virtual landslide of legislation dealing with substance abuse, including alcoholism; violence, especially in school settings; spouse abuse; treatment of the chronically mentally ill; discrimination in a wide variety of settings; and bullying in schools.

Although following professional guidelines may shield counselors from actions that would lend themselves to criminal or civil liability, all counselors must be aware that, on those rare occasions when they may encroach upon the limitations the law allows, they could risk legal liability. For example, criminal liability could occur when a counselor (a) is guilty of failure to report suspected child abuse; (b) fails to report a crime or is an accessory to a crime; (c) is guilty of misconduct of a sexual nature; (d) contributes to the delinquency of minors; or (e) takes action deemed injurious (mental or physical) to children.

Civil liability may result from negligence or malpractice that results in injury (mentally or physically) or damages. A prime example of civil liability has been the tremendous increase in malpractice suits against members of the helping professions in the past several decades. Although high profile and expensive lawsuits against medical practitioners have been prominent in the public eye, none of the helping professions, including counseling, have been exempt from frequent charges of negligence and malpractice. Malpractice suits are usually based on (a) the failure of the practitioner to provide reasonably competent services to the client as a result of negligence or (b) lack of knowledge of the appropriate procedures, which result in damages to the client. Counseling professionals should meet the standards of competent practice as reflected by their guidelines and standards for practice. Licensing laws may also be significant, even though many do not specify areas of responsibility and standards of care that must be met in the eyes of the law.

LEGISLATIVE ENACTMENTS OF SIGNIFICANCE TO CAREER COUNSELORS

Over the years, the U.S. Congress has been active in passing legislation designed to protect, enhance, or define rights of workers and those seeking to work. Perhaps the first significant federal laws that especially impacted women in the workforce were Title VII of the Civil Rights Act of 1964 and Title IX of the Educational Amendments of 1972. These enactments prohibit discrimination on the basis of gender as it relates to educational opportunities, employment opportunities, or payment received for work. Title VII also prohibited discrimination against employees on the basis of race, color, religion, gender, or national origin. Title IX is significant to career advisees seeking higher educational opportunities because it prohibits discrimination for admission and recruitment of students. It also addresses appropriate discrimination for denial of admission to institutions of higher education and differing criteria for other benefits, including services in programs or activities.

Additionally, the Vocational Rehabilitation Act of 1973 and the Americans with Disabilities Act of 1990 furthered the protection originally offered in Titles VII and IX. Counselors assisting disabled clients, as well as potential employers of these clients, should be familiar with the Americans with Disabilities Act. Please refer to chapter 8.

State rehabilitation agencies usually provide counseling to disabled clients who are eligible for such assistance. Counselors in rehabilitation agencies and other settings should have an understanding of various disabilities and their career implications and should be knowledgeable in terms of appropriate resources for identifying career opportunities and relevant training programs.

Of particular interest to school counselors is the Carl D. Perkins Vocational Education Act (Public Law 98-524) of 1984, which mandated programs designed to assist individual students with developing self-assessment, career planning, career decision-making, and employability skills. Two other provisions for career assistance to youth as they prepare to enter the workforce were (a) the amendments in 1992 to the Job Training Partnerships Act, a partnership of federal, state and local agencies, with school systems, employers and their community, to help youth acquire the skills and knowledge they need to assume full participation in their society and (b) the School to Work Transition Act of 1994, which provided funding to bring together schools, pupils, parents, communities, and businesses to develop the country's future workforce. The School to Work Transition Act provides for career counseling and mandates career exploration in schools in order to make the connection from school to work a realistic one.

LEGAL CONSIDERATIONS FOR SCHOOL COUNSELORS

At times it may seem to counselors working in educational settings that they are about to be overwhelmed by local edicts, school board rulings, professional dictates, and a variety of federal, state, and local laws. Perhaps the most important laws relating to educational settings are two constitutional provisions that are highly relevant to education. These are contained in the 14th Amendment to the U.S. Constitution, which provides for the right of individuals to due process and equal protection under the law. For school counselors assisting clients with career needs, this means that these clients must be treated fairly and equally, without discrimination. School counselors should also be aware of the provisions of the First Amendment to the U.S. Constitution, which provides for freedom of speech.

One of the most consistent concerns of school counselors is whether state laws protect the confidentiality of the counselor and client relationship. Although there may be many situations in career counseling where this is not of particular concern, there will also be many where it can be an issue. Confidentiality is usually viewed as an ethical commitment on the part of the counselor to not reveal—without the client's consent—the information disclosed by the client during counseling sessions. School counselors also need to be aware of whether or not they are protected by state laws on issues of privileged communication, inasmuch as privileged communication is a legal concept that protects the content of counselor and client communication from being disclosed in a court of law without the consent of the client.

The Family Educational Rights and Privacy Act of 1974, commonly referred to as the Buckley Amendment, applies to all public educational institutions and any private school receiving federal monies. This act gives parents of students two rights: the right to (a) inspect and review their child's educational records and even to challenge their contents; and (b) have their written consent obtained before copies of their child's educational records can be transferred to a third party. This has significant implications for placement of students with employers who wish to review the applicant's educational record and for college admissions offices who typically request such records prior to admission decisions. Antidiscrimination legislation must also be considered. In school settings it is important for counselors to keep in mind, in their career counseling, that racial, sex, and age discrimination may not even be inferred.

The various legislative enactments will influence counselor actions. Counselors must be knowledgeable and up-to-date in this complicated arena. Because most school corporations retain legal counsel for their school districts, it would be advisable for school counselors to meet with the appropriate legal representative on at least an annual basis to be updated and educated regarding the counselor's legal obligations.

ETHICAL GUIDELINES

A profession's code of ethics represents the standard of conduct expected for the members of that profession. The code of ethics provides guidelines for members of the profession to follow in their professional practice. It also assures the public that their welfare will be protected during their interaction with members of the profession.

For members of the counseling profession, at least two basic documents guide the practice and behavior of the counselor. These may be viewed in Appendix E: Code of Ethics and Standards of Practice of the American Counseling Association (1995) and Appendix F: Ethical Principles of Psychologists and Code of Conduct of the American Psychological Association (2002).

Among the ethical issues to which members of the profession must respond are the following: (a) confidentiality and privileged communication; (b) competence; and (c) relationships with clients.

CONFIDENTIALITY AND PRIVILEGED COMMUNICATION

As discussed earlier in this chapter, confidentiality is usually viewed as the ethical responsibility to protect and safeguard information that the client has shared with the counselor. This means that the counselor cannot reveal this information to others without the explicit permission of the client, unless he or she is required to do so by law. This is a very complex issue and may involve legal as well as ethical considerations. Privacy is broader in its interpretation and refers to an individual's right to decide what information about themselves will be shared with others. Confidentiality and privileged communication both apply to the professional relationship between counselor and client. Privileged communication is the narrowest of the three terms and is regarded as a legal concept. For a communication to be privileged, a statute must have been enacted that grants this privilege to a profession and those who members of the profession serve. The exceptions to confidentiality and privileged communication are noted in Figure 9-1.

COMPETENCE

The issue of competence begins when the counselor applies for a position as a professional. The counselor must present his or her qualifications based on training and experience honestly to a potential employer (who also has the responsibility to

FIGURE 9-1

Exceptions to confidentiality and privileged communication

Source: From Remley, Thoeodore P.; Herlihy, Barbara; *Ethical, Legal, and Professional Issues in Counseling,* 1st Edition, p. 107. Copyright © 2001. Reprinted by permission of Pearson Education, Inc., Upper Saddle River, NJ.

Sharing information with subordinates or fellow professionals is permissible under the following circumstances:

- Clerical or other assistants handle confidential information.
- A counselor consults with colleagues or experts.
- The counselor is working under supervision.
- Other professionals are involved in coordinating client care.

Protecting someone who is in danger may require disclosure of confidential information when the following conditions exist:

- The counselor suspects abuse or neglect of children or other persons presumed to have limited ability to care for themselves.
- A client poses a danger to others.
- A client poses a danger to self (is suicidal).
- A client has a fatal, communicable disease and the client's behavior is putting others at risk.

Confidentiality is compromised when counseling multiple clients, including the following:

- Group counseling
- Counseling couples or families

There are unique confidentiality and privileged communication considerations when working with minor clients:

- Counseling minor clients

Certain exceptions are mandated by law, including the following:

- Disclosure is court ordered.
- Clients file complaints against their counselors.
- Clients claim emotional damage in a lawsuit.
- Civil commitment proceedings are initiated.

---

determine whether the counselor is qualified for the position). Where licensure or certification is a possible requirement, the counselor must also specify whether they are or will be qualified for licensure. Once employed, the counselor is expected to practice within their professional limitations. Counselors should also be aware of the legal implications of practicing within their expertise, because competency for the counseling professional involves both legal and ethical considerations. From an ethical perspective, the moral principle that is most appropriate is to do no harm or stay within your levels of competency because incompetency is frequently a factor in causing a client harm. The legal term usually applied to incompetence is *nonmaleficence.* Counselors assisting clients with career needs must be knowledgeable about the career world, at least in their environmental and geographic regions, and also knowledgeable about valid assessment techniques for assisting clients to make informed career choices.

PERSONAL RELATIONSHIPS WITH CLIENTS

Codes of ethics of the helping professions indicate appropriate professional behavior in relationships with clients. These ethical guidelines establish clear limits on social interactions with clients. A major concern in this area has been the potential for sexual exploitation of clients by counselors. Such activity can result in loss of license, lawsuits, and even criminal charges. Client consent does not lessen the possibility of criminal charges or loss of license. Any social relationship with clients, which could handicap the counselor's professional judgment, should be avoided. Counseling close friends, relatives, and employees are examples of potential clients that should be avoided. Finally, clients should not be exploited for financial or social status. Although counselors are encouraged to engage in research activities, the involvement of clients in research studies must be done only with the client's full understanding and consent.

COUNSELORS AS PROFESSIONALS

It is important for all who qualify and enter the profession of counseling to assume the mantle of professionalism and conduct themselves accordingly. As a professional, the individual's professional obligations begin with membership in the appropriate professional organizations. For counselors, this would include the American Counseling Association (ACA), possibly the American Psychological Association (APA), and other associations related to the special training and interests of counselors. For those intending to practice as career counselors, membership in the National Career Development Association (NCDA) would be expected. Membership in state and local branches should also be anticipated. However, it is not enough to hold a membership card.

Professional membership implies actions or activities intended to enhance not only the individual but the profession itself. This should involve participation in professional conventions, conferences, and workshops where interaction with other professionals will take place. These present the opportunity to learn from others and to share one's own professional achievements. Another benefit of belonging to professional associations is receiving the journals, newsletters, and other publications of the organization. These are not intended to be door stops, but rather to be read as another means of keeping current. These publications also provide opportunities for individual professionals to share their ideas and accomplishments through professional writing. Professionals have an obligation to join and benefit from relationships with others and to contribute to the advancement of their profession through appropriate research and writing. All worthwhile research does not depend on exotic, mysterious, statistical formulas, but may often produce a simple solution to a simple problem that has previously gone unresolved. A true professional is also an active professional in other ways. A professional counselor should promote the public awareness of who counselors are, what they do, what competencies they possess, and how the profession can benefit the public. A true professional is also active in identifying those who need, but may not be receiving the services of the profession. Then, with the profession's help, a true professional would explore governmental and other opportunities to expand counseling services to those in need. Counselors and counseling organizations have a responsibility to be proactive at outreach, prevention, needs assessment, and legislative programs.

PROGRAM DEVELOPMENT GUIDELINES

The effectiveness of any counseling program, regardless of whether it is general or specialized, is dependent on its program planning and management. Planning involves determining the specific needs, based on factual data, to serve a specified population in an effective and efficient manner. Management involves the efficient and considered programming of personnel talents for undertaking the tasks required to effectively serve the program's clients. The five specific steps include the following:

STEP 1: IDENTIFY THE NEEDS OF THE PROGRAM'S TARGET POPULATION

This initial procedural step requires an objective, factual assessment to identify the needs of the potential clients the program seeks to serve. This needs assessment should not be viewed as a one-time activity. Instead, it should be conducted annually to update the changing needs of a potentially changing client population.

STEP 2: PROCEDURAL PLANNING

The guidelines for procedural planning should be identified in the objective statements of the goals of the counseling career development program. These goals should reflect the client population needs as identified in Step 1. Procedural planning has the two following components: (a) an environmental assessment to determine the significant environmental influences on client behavior and effective program development and (b) a determination regarding who among the professional staff will be responsible for what activities and when and how these activities will be carried out.

STEP 3: PROGRAM EVALUATION

Program effectiveness and program improvement is dependent on an assessment of program outcomes. Objective procedures, which at least annually measure the programs strengths and weaknesses, must be identified and implemented. These strengths and weaknesses will be reflected in the attainment of the program's stated objectives. This is the accountability procedure that is imperative to strengthening programs and to securing the public's support necessary for their existence. The complete process of counseling program planning and evaluation is depicted in Figure 9-2.

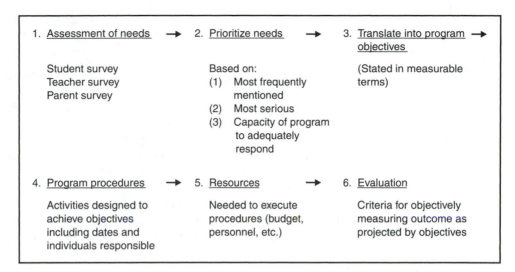

1. Assessment of needs   ➔   2. Prioritize needs   ➔   3. Translate into program ➔
                                                               objectives

   Student survey   Based on: (Stated in measurable
   Teacher survey   (1) Most frequently   terms)
   Parent survey   mentioned
                               (2) Most serious
                               (3) Capacity of program
                                    to adequately
                                    respond

4. Program procedures   ➔   5. Resources   ➔   6. Evaluation

   Activities designed to   Needed to execute   Criteria for objectively
   achieve objectives   procedures (budget,   measuring outcome as
   including dates and   personnel, etc.)   projected by objectives
   individuals responsible

FIGURE 9-2
The process of counseling program planning and evaluation

STEP 4: COMMUNICATION AND PUBLIC RELATIONS

Although counselors are known to be skilled communicators in the counseling relationship, there is evidence that we have frequently failed to adequately communicate with
our various publics. On occasion we have even been referred to as the *silent profession*.
It cannot be expected that unconditional and blind support from the various publics for
counseling programs, regardless of the setting or population they are designed to serve,
will automatically occur. The counseling profession does not have the lengthy and dynamic history that other helping professions, such as law and medicine, have experienced.
It is therefore not just desirable, but essential, that counseling programs, regardless of setting or emphasis, must give a high priority to communicating their goals, activities, and
perhaps above all, their accomplishments. These should be communicated to the various
publics that can aid and influence the profession and its programs.

Every program should develop a written communication plan that ensures appropriate and ongoing communication to all appropriate publics. This plan may target specific
populations to receive certain types of information through the most appropriate means.
This plan should not only seek to inform, but also to influence. Influence is facilitated by
factual results related to program needs and outcomes. Successful communication
plans also recognize that communication is a two-way street and that it is important to
listen, receive, to be responsive to others, and to send communication to others.

STEP 5: PROGRAM DEVELOPMENT AND RESEARCH

Every counseling program, regardless of its setting and emphasis, must be cognizant of relevant and current professional research and must be alert to research
opportunities for improving their programs and contributing to the profession. Not

only is research critical to the advancement of the profession but it can also be significant in local program improvement. The various types of research that professionals can choose to engage in include the following:

- **basic research**   In educational settings, basic research is conducted for the purpose of developing theory or for establishing some general principles. This in turn can lead to implications for solving problems.
- **applied research**   Applying or evaluating of a theory through the collection of data appropriate to the testing of the theory.
- **action research**   Action research is designed to solve problems through the application of scientific method. It provides a systematic framework for problem-solving. It can also be a model for program or practice evaluation.
- **historical research**   Historical research can involve the interpretation of documents, comparing and cross-checking differing pieces of data or information and the study of chronological events. (Gibson, Mitchell, & Basile, 1993, p. 282)
- **descriptive research**   Descriptive research seeks to test hypotheses or answer questions concerning the present. There are two major classifications of descriptive research: qualitative and quantitative. In quantitative research the investigator will observe events, probably using some coding scheme, and then will draw inferences based on what has been observed. The goal of quantitative research is to describe cause and effect relationships. On the other hand, the qualitative researcher attempts to retain the viewpoint of the individual(s) being studied. This may, for example, involve the study of video or audio recordings and an analysis of field or observational notes. The qualitative researcher, then, attempts to understand the ways that individuals give meaning to the behavior of themselves and others and to describe these understandings. (Gibson & Mitchell, 2003, p. 408)
- **experimental research**   Experimental research seeks to develop predictions of what will happen in the future, given certain specific circumstances. These circumstances or variables are established through an experimental process that leads to their identification. (Gibson, Mitchell, & Basile, 1993, p. 283)[1]

CAREER COUNSELING ACROSS THE LIFE SPAN

As frequently noted, career counseling is no longer limited to a small segment of the population encapsulated in a brief period of time. In today's complex career world, two things are evident: (a) nearly everyone, male and female, now anticipates entering the world of work and (b) due to the ever-changing characteristics of the world of

---

[1] *Source: From R. L. Gibson, M. H. Mitchell & S. K. Basile,* Counseling in the Elementary School: A Comprehensive Approach, *p. 20. Copyright © 1993. Reprinted by permission by Allyn and Bacon.*

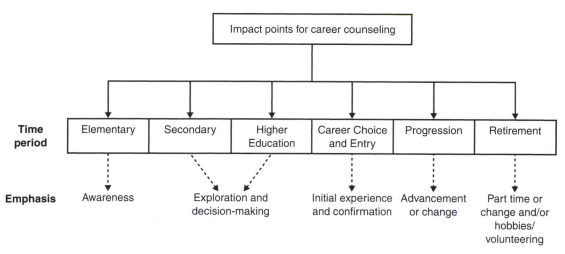

FIGURE 9-3
Career counseling across the life span

work, nearly everyone can benefit from the assistance provided by career counseling. In addition, career counseling is no longer limited to a brief span of time but is viewed as desirable and needed through the life span. As noted in Figure 9-3 there are significant impact points for career counseling beginning in elementary school and continuing through retirement years.

Although the nature of this assistance will adjust to the needs of the populations along the life span, it is nonetheless important that both the counseling profession and the general population—from elementary school children to the elderly—recognize the opportunities for and values of planned, professional career assistance.

THE FUTURE

To gain some perspective on the future, one might review the astounding technological and scientific advances and the resultant dramatic changes in daily life in the recent 20th century. Even more rapid and significant advances are being predicted for the 21st century. These changes will affect the career world in previously unexperienced ways, increasing the need and demand for career counseling. Computers, the Internet, Web sites, and distance learning have changed the way careers are explored. New assessment instruments reflecting the norms and realities of the new millennium will be required. The long-standing traditional theories of career development of the 20th century will undoubtedly be reexamined. Continuing education across the life span will become a reality for most people. Flexibility and both the capacity and willingness to change will be important to workers in all walks of life, including career counselors. Finally, we believe that the counseling profession, with its career specialty, will have unprecedented opportunities to serve. Let us hope we seize those opportunities!

SUMMARY

This chapter emphasized the importance of both legal and ethical guidelines for a profession to gaining the public's trust and acceptance. Legal guidelines, as reflected in national, state, and local legislation were reviewed. Criminal liability may occur when a counselor fails to report suspected child abuse or crimes, engages in misconduct of a social nature, or contributes to the delinquency of a minor. Civil liability may result from negligence or malpractice that results in injury or damages. A series of significant legal enactments, beginning with Title VII of the Civil Rights Act of 1964, and Title IX of the Educational Amendments of 1972, were reviewed. Legal considerations for school counselors were noted, as was the need to be aware of whether or not they are protected by state laws on such issues as privileged communication. Ethical guidelines and issues were discussed, with particular attention paid to confidentiality and privileged communication, the issue of counselor competence, and personal relationships with clients.

The importance of professional counselors assuming the mantle of professionalism was noted. A significant responsibility of counselors is to develop effective programs regardless of setting. The procedural steps for developing such programs were briefly discussed, including the responsibility to contribute to the profession through research activities. The chapter concluded by discussing career counseling across the life span and with a brief look at the future.

DISCUSSION QUESTIONS

1. Identify instances that you have read about or are otherwise aware of where individuals appear to have innocently violated criminal or civil laws.
2. Identify and discuss any new civil laws that you believe would benefit the practice and profession of counseling.
3. Identify a "problem" or issue that you might be interested in researching for more information or solutions.

CLASS ACTIVITIES

1. Discuss in small groups legislative enactments that you believe would benefit the profession of counseling.
2. Read a selected newspaper for the period of one week and identify situations that appear to be ethical violations.

3. You have been counseling a client who has admitted to you that she has a history of shoplifting. Two local policemen visit you, saying that they have reason to believe that your client has been involved in shoplifting. They want to see your counseling records. They also ask whether you know anything about this criminal activity. How would you react?

4. Luther is a 32-year-old PhD counselor in private practice. He has just concluded a series of counseling interviews with Laurie, an attractive 25-year-old single woman. Laurie, indicating that now that they are no longer counselor and client, invites Luther to come over for dinner at her place during the coming week. What should he do?

5. Invite a lawyer to visit the class for the purpose of discussing legal enactments of which counselors should be aware.

READINGS OF INTEREST

Bloom, J. W., & Walz, G. R. (Eds.) (2000). Ethical and professional challenges in cybercounseling (Special section). *Cybercounseling and cyberlearning: Strategies and resources for the millennium*. Alexandria, VA: American Counseling Association and Greensboro, NC: CAPS, in association with the ERIC Counseling and Student Services Clearinghouse.

Cottone, R. R. (2001). A social constructivism model of ethical decision making in counseling. *Journal of Counseling & Development, 79*(1), 39–45.

Cottone, R. R., & Tarvydas, V. M. (2003). *Ethical and Professional Issues in Counseling*. (2nd Ed.). Upper Saddle River, NJ: Prentice Hall.

Gale, A. U., & Austin, B. D. (2003). Professionalism's challenges to professional counselors' collective identity. *Journal of Counseling & Development, 81*(1), 3–10.

Rowley, W. J., & MacDonald, D. (2001). Counseling and the law: A cross-cultural perspective. *Journal of Counseling & Development, 79*(4), 422–429.

Walden, S. L., Herlihy, B., & Ashton, L. (2003). The evolution of ethics: Personal perspectives of ACA Ethics Committee chairs. *Journal of Counseling & Development, 81*(1), 106–110.

Appendix A

Responsibilities of Users of Standardized Tests (RUST) (3rd Edition)

Prepared by the Association for Assessment in Counseling (AAC)

Many recent events have influenced the use of tests and assessment in the counseling community. Such events include the use of tests in the educational accountability and reform movement, the publication of the *Standards for Educational and Psychological Testing* (American Educational Research Association [AERA], American Psychological Association [APA], National Council on Measurement in Education [NCME], 1999), the revision of the *Code of Fair Testing Practices in Education* (Joint Committee on Testing Practices [JCTP], 2002), the proliferation of technology-delivered assessment, and the historic passage of the *No Child Left Behind Act* (HR1, 2002) calling for expanded testing in reading/language arts, mathematics, and science that are aligned to state standards.

The purpose of this document is to promote the accurate, fair, and responsible use of standardized tests by the counseling and education communities. RUST is intended to address the needs of the members of the American Counseling Association (ACA) and its Divisions, Branches, and Regions, including counselors, teachers, administrators, and other human service workers. The general public, test developers, and policy makers will find this statement useful as they work with tests and testing issues. The principles in RUST apply to the use of testing instruments regardless of delivery methods (e.g., paper/pencil or computer administered) or setting (e.g., group or individual).

The intent of RUST is to help counselors and other educators implement responsible testing practices. The RUST does not intend to reach beyond or reinterpret the principles outlined in the *Standards for Educational and Psychological Testing* (AERA et al., 1999), nor was it developed to formulate a basis for legal action. The intent is to provide a concise statement useful in the ethical practice of testing. In addition, RUST is intended to enhance the guidelines found in ACA's *Code of Ethics and Standards of Practice* (ACA, 1997) and the *Code of Fair Testing Practices in Education* (JCTP, 2002).

Organization of Document: This document includes test user responsibilities in the following areas:

- Qualifications of Test Users
- Technical Knowledge
- Test Selection
- Test Administration
- Test Scoring
- Interpreting Test Results
- Communicating Test Results

QUALIFICATIONS OF TEST USERS

Qualified test users demonstrate appropriate education, training, and experience in using tests for the purposes under consideration. They adhere to the highest degree of ethical codes, laws, and standards governing professional practice. Lack of essential qualifications or ethical and legal compliance can lead to errors and subsequent harm to clients. Each professional is responsible for making judgments in each testing situation and cannot leave that responsibility either to clients or others in authority. The individual test user must obtain appropriate education and training, or arrange for professional supervision and assistance when engaged in testing in order to provide valuable, ethical, and effective assessment services to the public. Qualifications of test users depend on at least four factors:

- **Purposes of Testing:** A clear purpose for testing should be established. Because the purposes of testing direct how the results are used, qualifications beyond general testing competencies may be needed to interpret and apply data.
- **Characteristics of Tests:** Understanding of the strengths and limitations of each instrument used is a requirement.
- **Settings and Conditions of Test Use:** Assessment of the quality and relevance of test user knowledge and skill to the situation is needed before deciding to test or participate in a testing program.
- **Roles of Test Selectors, Administrators, Scorers, and Interpreters:** The education, training, and experience of test users determine which tests they are qualified to administer and interpret.

Each test user must evaluate his or her qualifications and competence for selecting, administering, scoring, interpreting, reporting, or communicating test results. Test users must develop the skills and knowledge for each test he or she intends to use.

TECHNICAL KNOWLEDGE

Responsible use of tests requires technical knowledge obtained through training, education, and continuing professional development. Test users should be conversant and competent in aspects of testing including:

- **Validity of Test Results:** Validity is the accumulation of evidence to support a specific interpretation of the test results. Since validity

is a characteristic of test results, a test may have validities of varying degree, for different purposes. The concept of instructional validity relates to how well the test is aligned to state standards and classroom instructional objectives.
- **Reliability:** Reliability refers to the consistency of test scores. Various methods are used to calculate and estimate reliability depending on the purpose for which the test is used.
- **Errors of Measurement:** Various ways may be used to calculate the error associated with a test score. Knowing this and knowing the estimate of the size of the error allows the test user to provide a more accurate interpretation of the scores and to support better-informed decisions.
- **Scores and Norms:** Basic differences between the purposes of norm-referenced and criterion-referenced scores impact score interpretations.

TEST SELECTION

Responsible use of tests requires that the specific purpose for testing be identified. In addition, the test that is selected should align with that purpose, while considering the characteristics of the test and the test taker. Tests should not be administered without a specific purpose or need for information. Typical purposes for testing include:

- **Description:** Obtaining objective information on the status of certain characteristics such as achievement, ability, personality types, etc. is often an important use of testing.
- **Accountability:** When judging the progress of an individual or the effectiveness of an educational institution, strong alignment between what is taught and what is tested needs to be present.
- **Prediction:** Technical information should be reviewed to determine how accurately the test will predict areas such as appropriate course placement; selection for special programs, interventions, and institutions; and other outcomes of interest.
- **Program Evaluation:** The role that testing plays in program evaluation and how the test

information may be used to supplement other information gathered about the program is an important consideration in test use.

Proper test use involves determining if the characteristics of the test are appropriate for the intended audience and are of sufficient technical quality for the purpose at hand. Some areas to consider include:

- **The Test Taker:** Technical information should be reviewed to determine if the test characteristics are appropriate for the test taker (e.g., age, grade level, language, cultural background).
- **Accuracy of Scoring Procedures:** Only tests that use accurate scoring procedures should be used.
- **Norming and Standardization Procedures:** Norming and standardization procedures should be reviewed to determine if the norm group is appropriate for the intended test takers. Specified test administration procedures must be followed.
- **Modifications:** For individuals with disabilities, alternative measures may need to be found and used and/or accommodations in test taking procedures may need to be employed. Interpretations need to be made in light of the modifications in the test or testing procedures.
- **Fairness:** Care should be taken to select tests that are fair to all test takers. When test results are influenced by characteristics or situations unrelated to what is being measured. (e.g., gender, age, ethnic background, existence of cheating, unequal availability of test preparation programs) the use of the resulting information is invalid and potentially harmful. In achievement testing, fairness also relates to whether or not the student has had an opportunity to learn what is tested.

TEST ADMINISTRATION

Test administration includes carefully following standard procedures so that the test is used in the manner specified by the test developers. The test administrator should ensure that test takers work within conditions that maximize opportunity for optimum performance. As appropriate, test takers, parents, and organizations should be involved in the various aspects of the testing process.

BEFORE ADMINISTRATION IT IS IMPORTANT THAT RELEVANT PERSONS

- are informed about the standard testing procedures, including information about the purposes of the test, the kinds of tasks involved, the method of administration, and the scoring and reporting;
- have sufficient practice experiences prior to the test to include practice, as needed, on how to operate equipment for computer-administered tests and practice in responding to tasks;
- have been sufficiently trained in their responsibilities and the administration procedures for the test;
- have a chance to review test materials and administration sites and procedures prior to the time for testing to ensure standardized conditions and appropriate responses to any irregularities that occur;
- arrange for appropriate modifications of testing materials and procedures in order to accommodate test takers with special needs; and
- have a clear understanding of their rights and responsibilities.

DURING ADMINISTRATION IT IS IMPORTANT THAT

- the testing environment (e.g., seating, work surfaces, lighting, room temperature, freedom from distractions) and psychological climate are conducive to the best possible performance of the examinees;
- sufficiently trained personnel establish and maintain uniform conditions and observe the conduct of test takers when large groups of individuals are tested;
- test administrators follow the instructions in the test manual; demonstrate verbal clarity; use verbatim directions; adhere to verbatim directions; follow exact sequence and timing; and use materials that are identical to those specified by the test publisher;
- a systematic and objective procedure is in place for observing and recording environmental, health, emotional factors, or other elements

that may invalidate test performance and results; deviations from prescribed test administration procedures, including information on test accommodations for individuals with special needs, are recorded; and

- the security of test materials and computer-administered testing software is protected, ensuring that only individuals with a legitimate need for access to the materials/software are able to obtain such access and that steps to eliminate the possibility of breaches in test security and copyright protection are respected.

AFTER ADMINISTRATION IT IS IMPORTANT TO

- collect and inventory all secure test materials and immediately report any breaches in test security; and
- include notes on any problems, irregularities, and accommodations in the test records.

These precepts represent the basic process for all standardized tests and assessments. Some situations may add steps or modify some of these to provide the best testing milieu possible.

TEST SCORING

Accurate measurement necessitates adequate procedures for scoring the responses of test takers. Scoring procedures should be audited as necessary to ensure consistency and accuracy of application.

- Carefully implement and/or monitor standard scoring procedures.
- When test scoring involves human judgment, use rubrics that clearly specify the criteria for scoring. Scoring consistency should be constantly monitored.
- Provide a method for checking the accuracy of scores when accuracy is challenged by test takers.

INTERPRETING TEST RESULTS

Responsible test interpretation requires knowledge about and experience with the test, the scores, and the decisions to be made. Interpretation of scores on any test should not take place without a thorough knowledge of the technical aspects of the test, the test results, and its limitations. Many factors can impact the valid and useful interpretations of test scores. These can be grouped into several categories including psychometric, test taker, and contextual, as well as others.

- **Psychometric Factors:** Factors such as the reliability, norms, standard error of measurement, and validity of the instrument are important when interpreting test results. Responsible test use considers these basic concepts and how each impacts the scores and hence the interpretation of the test results.
- **Test Taker Factors:** Factors such as the test taker's group membership and how that membership may impact the results of the test is a critical factor in the interpretation of test results. Specifically, the test user should evaluate how the test taker's gender, age, ethnicity, race, socioeconomic status, marital status, and so forth, impact on the individual's results.
- **Contextual Factors:** The relationship of the test to the instructional program, opportunity to learn, quality of the educational program, work and home environment, and other factors that would assist in understanding the test results are useful in interpreting test results. For example, if the test does not align to curriculum standards and how those standards are taught in the classroom, the test results may not provide useful information.

COMMUNICATING TEST RESULTS

Before communication of test results takes place, a solid foundation and preparation is necessary. That foundation includes knowledge of test interpretation and an understanding of the particular test being used, as provided by the test manual.

Conveying test results with language that the test taker, parents, teachers, clients, or general public can understand is one of the key elements in helping others understand the meaning of the test results. When reporting group results, the information needs to be supplemented with background information that can help explain the results with cautions about misinterpretations. The test user should indicate how the test results can be and should not be interpreted.

CLOSING

Proper test use resides with the test user—the counselor and educator. Qualified test users understand the measurement characteristics necessary to select good standardized tests, administer the tests according to specified procedures, assure accurate scoring, accurately interpret test scores for individuals and groups, and ensure productive applications of the results. This document provides guidelines for using tests responsibly with students and clients.

REFERENCES AND RESOURCE DOCUMENTS

American Counseling Association. (1997). *Code of ethics and standards of practice.* Alexandria, VA: Author.

American Counseling Association. (2003). *Standards for qualifications of test users.* Alexandria, VA: Author.

American Educational Research Association, American Psychological Association, National Council on Measurement in Education. (1999). *Standards for educational and psychological testing.* Washington, DC: American Educational Research Association.

American School Counselor Association & Association for Assessment in Counseling. (1998). *Competencies in assessment and evaluation for school counselors.* Alexandria, VA: Author.

Joint Committee on Testing Practices. (2000) *Rights and responsibilities of test takers: Guidelines and expectations.* Washington, DC: Author.

Joint Committee on Testing Practices. (2002). *Code of fair testing practices in education.* Washington, DC: Author.

RUST COMMITTEE

Janet Wall, Chair
James Augustin
Charles Eberly
Brad Erford
David Lundberg
Timothy Vansickle

Source: Association for Assessment in Counseling (2nd ed.), (2003). Reprinted by permission of the Association for Assessment in Counseling.

Appendix B

Code of Fair Testing Practices in Education

Prepared by the Joint Committee on Testing Practices

The Code of Fair Testing Practices in Education (*Code*) is a guide for professionals in fulfilling their obligation to provide and use tests that are fair to all test takers regardless of age, gender, disability, race, ethnicity, national origin, religion, sexual orientation, linguistic background, or other personal characteristics. Fairness is a primary consideration in all aspects of testing. Careful standardization of tests and administration conditions helps to ensure that all test takers are given a comparable opportunity to demonstrate what they know and how they can perform in the area being tested. Every test taker should have the opportunity to prepare for the test and should be informed about the general nature and content of the test. Fairness also extends to the accurate reporting of individual and group test results. Fairness is not an isolated concept, but must be considered in all aspects of the testing process.

The *Code* applies broadly to testing in education (admissions, educational assessment, educational diagnosis, and student placement) regardless of the mode of presentation, so it is relevant to conventional paper-and-pencil tests, computer based tests, and performance tests. It is not designed to cover employment testing, licensure or certification testing, or other types of testing outside the field of education. The *Code* is directed primarily at professionally developed tests used in formally administered testing programs. Although the *Code* is not intended to cover tests made by teachers for use in their own classrooms, teachers are encouraged to use the guidelines to help improve their testing practices.

The *Code* addresses the roles of test developers and test users separately. Test developers are people and organizations that construct tests, as well as those that set policies for testing programs. Test users are people and agencies that select tests, administer tests, commission test development services, or make decisions on the basis of test scores. Test developer and test user roles may overlap, for example, when a state or local education agency commissions test development services, sets policies that control the test development process, and makes decisions on the basis of the test scores.

Many of the statements in the **Code** refer to the selection and use of existing tests. When a new test is developed, when an existing test is modified, or when the administration of a test is modified, the development process should be implemented so that the resulting tests are consistent with the **Code**.

The **Code** provides guidance separately for test developers and test users in four critical areas:

A. Developing and Selecting Appropriate Tests
B. Administering and Scoring Tests
C. Reporting and Interpreting Test Results
D. Informing Test Takers

The **Code** is intended to be consistent with the relevant parts of the *Standards for Educational and Psychological Testing* (American Educational Research Association [AERA], American Psychological Association [APA], and National Council on Measurement in Education [NCME], 1999). The **Code** is not meant to add new principles over and above those in the *Standards* or to change their meaning. Rather, the **Code** is intended to represent the spirit of

selected portions of the *Standards* in a way that is relevant and meaningful to developers and users of tests, as well as to test takers and/or their parents or guardians. Organizations, institutions, and individual professionals that endorse the **Code** commit themselves to safeguarding the rights of test takers by following the principles listed. This **Code** may be adopted and promulgated by states, school districts, and organizations that develop and use tests as a sign of their commitment to fairness as a critical element of appropriate testing practice.

The **Code** has been prepared by the Joint Committee on Testing Practices, a cooperative effort among several professional organizations. The aim of the Joint Committee is to act, in the public interest, to advance the quality of testing practices. Members of the Joint Committee include the American Counseling Association (ACA), the American Educational Research Association (AERA), the American Psychological Association (APA), the American Speech-Language-Hearing Association (ASHA), the National Association of School Psychologists (NASP), the National Association of Test Directors (NATD), and the National Council on Measurement in Education (NCME).

A. DEVELOPING AND SELECTING APPROPRIATE TESTS

Test Developers	Test Users
Test developers should provide the information and supporting evidence that test users need to select appropriate tests.	Test users should select tests that meet the intended purpose and that are appropriate for the intended test takers.
A-1. Provide evidence of what the test measures, the recommended uses, the intended test takers, and the strengths and limitations of the test, including the level of precision of the test scores.	A-1. Define the purpose for testing, the content and skills to be tested, and the intended test takers. Select and use the most appropriate test based on a thorough review of available information.
A-2. Describe how the content and skills to be tested were selected and how the tests were developed.	A-2. Review and select tests based on the appropriateness of test content, skills tested, and content coverage for the intended purpose of testing.
A-3. Communicate information about a test's characteristics at a level of detail appropriate to the intended test users.	A-3. Review materials provided by test developers and select tests for which clear, accurate, and complete information is provided.
A-4. Provide guidance on the levels of skills, knowledge, and training necessary for appropriate review, selection, and administration of tests.	A-4. Select tests through a process that includes persons with appropriate knowledge, skills, and training.
A-5. Provide evidence that the technical quality, including reliability and validity, of the test meets its intended purposes.	A-5. Evaluate evidence of the technical quality of the test provided by the test developer and any independent reviewers.
A-6. Provide to qualified test users representative samples of test questions or practice tests, directions, answer sheets, manuals, and score reports.	A-6. Evaluate representative samples of test questions or practice tests, directions, answer sheets, manuals, and score reports before selecting a test.
A-7. Avoid potentially offensive content or language when developing test questions and related materials.	A-7. Evaluate procedures and materials used by test developers, as well as the resulting test, to ensure that potentially offensive content or language is avoided.
A-8. Make appropriately modified forms of tests or administration procedures available for test takers with disabilities who need special accommodations.	A-8. Select tests with appropriately modified forms or administration procedures for test takers with disabilities who need special accommodations.
A-9. Obtain and provide evidence on the performance of test takers of diverse subgroups, making significant efforts to obtain sample sizes that are adequate for subgroup analyses. Evaluate the evidence to ensure that differences in performance are related to the skills being assessed.	A-9. Evaluate the available evidence on the performance of test takers of diverse subgroups. Determine to the extent feasible which performance differences may have been caused by factors unrelated to the skills being assessed.

B. ADMINISTERING AND SCORING TESTS

Test Developers	Test Users
Test developers should explain how to administer and score tests correctly and fairly	Test users should administer and score tests correctly and fairly.
B-1. Provide clear descriptions of detailed procedures for administering tests in a standardized manner.	B-1. Follow established procedures for administering tests in a standardized manner.
B-2. Provide guidelines on reasonable procedures for assessing persons with disabilities who need special accommodations or those with diverse linguistic backgrounds.	B-2. Provide and document appropriate procedures for test takers with disabilities who need special accommodations or those with diverse linguistic backgrounds. Some accommodations may be required by law or regulation.
B-3. Provide information to test takers or test users on test question formats and procedures for answering test questions, including information on the use of any needed materials and equipment.	B-3. Provide test takers with an opportunity to become familiar with test question formats and any materials or equipment that may be used during testing.
B-4. Establish and implement procedures to ensure the security of testing materials during all phases of test development, administration, scoring, and reporting.	B-4. Protect the security of test materials, including respecting copyrights and eliminating opportunities for test takers to obtain scores by fraudulent means.
B-5. Provide procedures, materials and guidelines for scoring the tests, and for monitoring the accuracy of the scoring process. If scoring the test is the responsibility of the test developer, provide adequate training for scorers.	B-5. If test scoring is the responsibility of the test user, provide adequate training to scorers and ensure and monitor the accuracy of the scoring process.
B-6. Correct errors that affect the interpretation of the scores and communicate the corrected results promptly.	B-6. Correct errors that affect the interpretation of the scores and communicate the corrected results promptly.
B-7. Develop and implement procedures for ensuring the confidentiality of scores.	B-7. Develop and implement procedures for ensuring the confidentiality of scores.

C. REPORTING AND INTERPRETING TEST RESULTS

Test Developers	Test Users
Test developers should report test results accurately and provide information to help test users interpret test results correctly.	Test users should report and interpret test results accurately and clearly.
C-1. Provide information to support recommended interpretations of the results, including the nature of the content, norms or comparison groups, and other technical evidence. Advise test users of the benefits and limitations of test results and their interpretation. Warn against assigning greater precision than is warranted	C-1. Interpret the meaning of the test results, taking into account the nature of the content, norms or comparison groups other technical evidence, and benefits and limitations of test results.
C-2. Provide guidance regarding the interpretations of results for tests administered with modifications. Inform test users of potential problems in interpreting test results when tests or test administration procedures are modified.	C-2. Interpret test results from modified test or test administration procedures in view of the impact those modifications may have had on test results.
C-3. Specify appropriate uses of test results and warn test users of potential misuses.	C-3. Avoid using tests for purposes other than those recommended by the test developer unless there is evidence to support the intended use or interpretation.
C-4. When test developers set standards, provide the rationale, procedures, and evidence for setting performance standards or passing scores. Avoid using stigmatizing labels.	C-4. Review the procedures for setting performance standards or passing scores. Avoid using stigmatizing labels.
C-5. Encourage test users to base decisions about test takers on multiple sources of appropriate information, not on a single test score.	C-5. Avoid using a single test score as the sole determinant of decisions about test takers. Interpret test scores in conjunction with other information about individuals.
C-6. Provide information to enable test users to accurately interpret and report test results for groups of test takers, including information about who were and who were not included in the different groups being compared, and information about factors that might influence the interpretation of results.	C-6. State the intended interpretation and use of test results for groups of test takers. Avoid grouping test results for purposes not specifically recommended by the test developer unless evidence is obtained to support the intended use. Report procedures that were followed in determining who were and who were not included in the groups being compared and describe factors that might influence the interpretation of results.
C-7. Provide test results in a timely fashion and in a manner that is understood by the test taker.	C-7. Communicate test results in a timely fashion and in a manner that is understood by the test taker.
C-8. Provide guidance to test users about how to monitor the extent to which the test is fulfilling its intended purposes.	C-8. Develop and implement procedures for monitoring test use, including consistency with the intended purposes of the test.

D. INFORMING TEST TAKERS

Under some circumstances, test developers have direct communication with the test takers and/or control of the tests, testing process, and test results. In other circumstances the test users have these responsibilities.

Test developers or test users should inform test takers about the nature of the test, test taker rights and responsibilities, the appropriate use of scores, and procedures for resolving challenges to scores.
D-1. Inform test takers in advance of the test administration about the coverage of the test, the types of question formats, the directions, and appropriate test-taking strategies. Make such information available to all test takers.
D-2. When a test is optional, provide test takers or their parents/guardians with information to help them judge whether a test should be taken—including indications of any consequences that may result from not taking the test (e.g., not being eligible to compete for a particular scholarship)—and whether there is an available alternative to the test.
D-3. Provide test takers or their parents/guardians with information about rights test takers may have to obtain copies of tests and completed answer sheets, to retake tests, to have tests rescored, or to have scores declared invalid.
D-4. Provide test takers or their parents/guardians with information about responsibilities test takers have, such as being aware of the intended purpose and uses of the test, performing at capacity, following directions, and not disclosing test items or interfering with other test takers.
D-5. Inform test takers or their parents/guardians how long scores will be kept on file and indicate to whom, under what circumstances, and in what manner test scores and related information will or will not be released. Protect test scores from unauthorized release and access.
D-6. Describe procedures for investigating and resolving circumstances that might result in canceling or withholding scores, such as failure to adhere to specified testing procedures.
D-7. Describe procedures that test takers, parents/guardians, and other interested parties may use to obtain more information about the test, register complaints, and have problems resolved.

Note: The membership of the Working Group that developed the *Code of Fair Testing Practices in Education* and of the Joint Committee on Testing Practices that guided the Working Group is as follows:

Peter Behuniak, PhD
Lloyd Bond, PhD
Gwyneth M. Boodoo, PhD
Wayne Camara, PhD
Ray Fenton, PhD
John J. Fremer, PhD (Co-Chair)
Sharon M. Goldsmith, PhD
Bert F. Green, PhD
William G. Harris, PhD
Janet E. Helms, PhD

Stephanie H. McConaughy, PhD
Julie P. Noble, PhD
Wayne M. Patience, PhD
Carole L. Perlman, PhD
Douglas K. Smith, PhD (deceased)
Janet E. Wall, EdD (Co-Chair)
Pat Nellor Wickwire, PhD
Mary Yakimowski, PhD

Lara Frumkin, PhD, of the APA
served as staff liaison.

The Joint Committee intends that the Code be consistent with and supportive of existing codes of conduct and standards of other professional groups who use tests in educational contexts. Of particular note are the Responsibilities of Users of Standardized Tests (Association for Assessment in Counseling, 1989), APA Test User Qualifications (2000), ASHA Code of Ethics (2001), Ethical Principles of Psychologists and Code of Conduct (1992), NASP Professional Conduct Manual (2000), NCME Code of Professional Responsibility (1995), and Rights and Responsibilities of Test Takers: Guidelines and Expectations (Joint Committee on Testing Practices, 2000).

Appendix C

Standards for Multicultural Assessment

Association for Assessment in Counseling

OTHER PUBLICATIONS BY THE ASSOCIATION FOR ASSESSMENT IN COUNSELING

Association for Assessment in Counseling (2002). *Applying the Standards for Educational and Psychological Testing—What a Counselor Needs to Know,* Author.

Special Issue of Measurement and Evaluation in Counseling and Development on High Stakes Testing (November 2002).

Wall, Janet E. (2003). *A Parent's Survival Guide to School Testing,* Alexandria, VA: Association for Assessment in Counseling.

For ordering information contact: Dr. Brian Glaser, AAC Treasurer at bglaser@coe.uga.edu or visit the AAC website at http://aac.ncat.edu to download order forms.

ACKNOWLEDGEMENTS

AAC would like to thank AERA for permission to quote selected standards from *Standards for Educational and Psychological Testing* for this publication. The full publication can be ordered from AERA at http://www.aera.net/products/standards.htm. AAC would also like to thank the American Counseling Association (ACA) for permission to reprint portions of their ethics statements. This document is based on a previous publication created by AAC, but published by ACA; we wish to thank ACA for its willingness to allow AAC to revamp and disseminate this new publication.

Cover by Reynold Wong, Monterey, CA

PREFACE

The Association for Assessment in Counseling (AAC) is an organization of counselors, counselor educators, and other professionals that advances the counseling profession by providing leadership, training, and research in the creation, development, production, and use of assessment and diagnostic techniques.

The increasing diversity in our society offers a special challenge to the assessment community, striving always to assure fair and equitable treatment of individuals regardless of race, ethnicity, culture, language, age, gender, sexual orientation, religion or physical ability. This is especially important given the increased emphasis place on assessment spawned by national and state legislation and educational reform initiatives.

This document, *Standards for Multicultural Assessment,* is an attempt to create and maintain an awareness of the various assessment standards that have been produced by various professional organizations. It is a compilation of standards produced by several professional associations.

This publication is based on a study completed by the Committee on Diversity in Assessment under the direction of the AAC Executive Council. The first version of this document was published in 1992, and was also published as an article in *Measurement and Evaluation in Counseling and Development* (Prediger, 1994). The original publication was prompted by a request from Jo-Ida Hansen, Chair of the 1991–1992 Committee on Testing of the American Association for Counseling and Development (now ACA). The original publication was prepared by Dale Prediger under the direction of the AAC Executive Council.

Because of advances in professional standards in the past decade, it was necessary to update and expand upon the first version. This revised document was created by a committee of members from the AAC, chaired by Dr. Wendy Charkow-Bordeau along with committee members, Drs. Debbie Newsome and Marie Shoffner. This publication was commissioned by the Executive Council of the Association for Assessment in Counseling.

AAC also wishes to thank Drs. Pat Nellor Wickwire and Janet Wall for their care and assistance in finalizing this document and coordinating its production.

AAC hopes that all counselors, teachers, and other assessment professionals find this document to be useful in improving their assessment practices.

Standards for Multicultural Assessment (2nd Ed.)

TABLE OF CONTENTS

PURPOSE

The Association for Assessment in Counseling (AAC), a division of the American Counseling Association (ACA), presents this revised compilation of professional standards. Although AAC believes that tests, inventories, and other assessment instruments can be beneficial for members of all populations, AAC recognizes that the increasing diversity in client backgrounds presents special challenges for test users. The standards assembled here address many of these challenges that are specifically related to the assessment of multicultural populations.

Although a number of standards in this compilation have relevance for the use of assessment instruments in psychological screening, personnel selection, and placement, they were selected because they have special relevance for counseling and for multicultural and diverse populations. Standards that apply in the same way for all populations (e.g., general standards for norming, scaling, reliability, and validity) are not included. Readers may consult the source documents and other publications for universal testing standards.

AAC urges all counselors to subscribe to these standards and urges counselor educators to include this compilation in programs preparing the "culturally competent counselor" (Sue, Arredondo, & McDavis, 1992, p. 447). Finally, AAC supports other professional organizations in advocating the need for a multicultural approach to assessment, practice, training, and research.

DEFINITION OF MULTICULTURAL AND DIVERSE POPULATIONS

A precise definition of multicultural and diverse populations is evolving. The multicultural competencies outlined by Sue et al. (1992), and then revised by Arredondo and Toporek (1996), define the following five major cultural groups in the United States and its territories: African/Black, Asian, Caucasian/European, Hispanic/Latino, and Native American. Arredondo and Toporek differentiated between these cultural groups, which are based on race and ethnicity, and diversity, which applies to individual differences based on age, gender, sexual orientation, religion, and ability or disability.

In revising the *Standards for Multicultural Assessment,* an inclusive definition of multiculturalism and diversity was used. For the purposes of this document, multicultural and diverse populations include persons who differ by race, ethnicity, culture, language, age, gender, sexual orientation, religion, and ability.

SOURCE DOCUMENTS

Five documents which include professional standards for assessment in counseling were used as sources for this compilation.

1. *Code of Fair Testing Practices in Education* (2nd ed) (CODE) (Joint Committee on Testing Practices [JCTP], 2002. Available for download at http://aac.ncat.edu.
2. *Responsibilities of Users of Standardized Tests* (3rd ed) (RUST). (ACA & AAC, 2003 Available for download at http://aac.ncat.edu.
3. *Standards for Educational and Psychological Testing* (2nd ed.) (SEPT). (American Educational Research Association, APA, & National Council on measurement in Education, 1999). Ordering information is available from APA, 750 First Street N.E., Washington, D.C. 20002-4242 or on-line at http://www.apa.org/science/standards.html.
4. *Multicultural Counseling Competencies and Standards* (COMPS). (Association for Multicultural Counseling and Development, 1992). These standards can be viewed in the 1996 article by Arredondo and Toporek. Full reference information is listed below in the reference section.
5. *Code of Ethics and Standards of Practice of the American Counseling Association* (ETHICS). (ACA, 1996). Ordering information can be obtained from ACA, 5999 Stevenson Avenue, Alexandria, VA, 22304-3300. The ethical code and standards of practice may also be viewed on-line at http://www.counseling.org/resources/ethics.htm.

CLASSIFICATION OF STANDARDS

Sixty-eight standards specifically relevant to the assessment of multicultural and diverse populations were identified in a reading of the five source documents. The content and intent of these standards were analyzed and classified. Assessment roles, functions, and tasks cited in these standards were clustered into three major groups.

Selection of Assessment Instruments
  Content and Purpose (n = 13)
  Norming, Reliability, and Validity (n = 18)
Administration and Scoring of Assessment Instruments (n = 16)
Interpretation and Application of Assessment Results (n = 21)

THE STANDARDS

The 68 standards are listed below by cluster and source.

SELECTION OF ASSESSMENT INSTRUMENTS: CONTENT AND PURPOSE

1. Evaluate procedures and materials used by test developers, as well as the resulting test, to ensure that potentially offensive content or language is avoided. (CODE, Section A-7)
2. Select tests with appropriately modified forms or administration procedures for test takers with disabilities who need special accommodations. (CODE, Section A-8)
3. For individuals with disabilities, alternative measures may need to be found and used.
4. Care should be taken to select tests that are fair to all test takers. (RUST)
5. Test developers should strive to identify and eliminate language, symbols, words, phrases, and content that are generally regarded as offensive by members of racial, ethnic, gender, or other groups, except when judged to be necessary for adequate representation of the domain. (SEPT 7.4)
6. In testing applications where the level of linguistic or reading ability is not part of the construct of interest, the linguistic or reading demands of the test should be kept to the minimum necessary for the valid assessment of the intended construct. (SEPT, Standard 7.7)
7. Linguistic modifications recommended by test publishers, as well as the rationale for

modifications, should be described in detail in the test manual. (SEPT, Standard 9.4)

8. In employment and credentialing testing, the proficiency language required in the language of the test should not exceed that appropriate to the relevant occupation or profession. (SEPT, Standard 9.8)

9. Inferences about test takers' general language proficiency should be based on tests that measure a range of language features, and not on a single linguistic skill. (SEPT, Standard 9.10)

10. Tests selected for use in individual testing should be suitable for the characteristics and background of the test taker. (SEPT, Standard 12.3)

11. Culturally competent counselors understand how race, culture, and ethnicity may affect personality formation, vocational choices, manifestation of psychological disorders, help-seeking behavior, and the appropriateness or inappropriateness of counseling approaches. (COMPS, 13)

12. Culturally competent counselors have training and expertise in the use of traditional assessment and testing instruments. They not only understand the technical aspects of the instruments but also are aware of the cultural limitations. This allows them to use test instruments for the welfare of clients from diverse cultural, racial, and ethnic groups. (COMPS, 29)

13. Counselors are cautious when selecting tests for culturally diverse populations to avoid inappropriateness of testing that may be outside of socialized behavioral or cognitive patterns. (ETHICS, Section III.C.5)

SELECTION OF ASSESSMENT INSTRUMENTS: NORMING, RELIABILITY, AND VALIDITY

1. Evaluate the available evidence on the performance of test takers of diverse subgroups. Determine to the extent feasible which performance differences may have been caused by factors unrelated to skills being assessed. (CODE, Section A-9).

2. Technical information should be reviewed to determine if the test characteristics are appropriate for the test taker (e.g., age, grade level, language, cultural background). (RUST)

3. Where there are generally accepted theoretical or empirical reasons for expecting that reliability coefficients, standard errors of measurement, or test information functions will differ substantially for various subpopulations, publishers should provide reliability data as soon as feasible for each major population for which the test is recommended. (SEPT, Standard 2.11)

4. If a test is proposed for use in several grades or over a range of chronological age groups and if separate norms are provided for each grade or age group, reliability data should be provided for each age or grade population, not solely for all grades or ages combined. (SEPT, Standard 2.12)

5. When significant variations are permitted in test administration procedures, separate reliability analyses should be provided for scores produced under each major variation if adequate sample sizes are available. (SEPT, Standard 2.18)

6. Norms, if used, should refer to clearly described populations. These populations should include individuals or groups to whom test users will ordinarily wish to compare their own examinees. (SEPT, Standard 4.5)

7. When credible research reports that test scores differ in meaning across examinee subgroups for the type of test in question, then to the extent feasible, the same forms of validity evidence collected for the examinee population as a whole should also be collected for each relevant subgroup. Subgroups may be found to differ with respect to appropriateness of test content, internal structure of test responses, the relation of test scores to other variables, or the response processes employed by the individual examinees. Any such findings should receive due consideration in the interpretation and use of scores as well as in subsequent test revisions. (SEPT, Standard 7.1)

8. When credible research reports differences in the effects of construct-irrelevant variance across subgroups of test takers on performance on some part of the test, the test should be used if at all only for the subgroups for which evidence indicates that valid inferences can be drawn from test scores. (SEPT, Standard 7.2)

9. When empirical studies of differential prediction of a criterion for members of different subgroups are conducted, they should include regression equations (or an appropriate equivalent) computed separately for each group or treatment under consideration or an analysis in which group or treatment variables are entered as moderator variable. (SEPT, Standard 7.6)

10. When a construct can be measured in different ways that are approximately equal in their degree of construct representation and freedom from construct-irrelevant variance, evidence of mean score differences across relevant subgroups of examinees should be considered in deciding which test to use. (SEPT, Standard 7.11)

11. When credible research evidence reports that test scores differ in meaning across subgroups of linguistically diverse test takers, then to the extent feasible, test developers should collect for each linguistic group studied the same form of validity evidence collected for the examinee population as a whole. (SEPT, Standard 9.2)

12. When a test is translated from one language to another, the methods used in establishing the adequacy of translation should be described, and empirical and logical evidence should be provided for score reliability and the validity of the translated test's score inferences for the uses intended in the linguistic groups to be tested. (SEPT, Standard 9.7)

13. When multiple language versions of a test are intended to be comparable, test developers should report evidence of test comparability. (SEPT, Standard 9.9)

14. When feasible, tests that have been modified for use with individuals with disabilities should be pilot tested on individuals who have similar disabilities to investigate the appropriateness and feasibility of the modifications. (SEPT, Standard 10.3)

15. When sample sizes permit, the validity of inferences made from test scores and the reliability of scores on tests administered to individuals with various disabilities should be investigated and reported by the agency or publisher that makes the modification. Such investigations should examine the effects of modifications made for people with various disabilities on resulting scores, as well as the effects of administering standard unmodified tests to them. (SEPT, Standard 10.7)

16. When relying on norms as a basis for score interpretation in assisting individuals with disabilities, the norm group used depends upon the purpose of testing. Regular norms are appropriate when the purpose involves the test taker's functioning relative to the general population. If available, normative data from the population of individuals with the same level or degree of disability should be used when the test taker's functioning relative to individuals with similar disabilities is at issue. (SEPT, Standard 10.9)

17. When circumstances require that a test be administered in the same language to all examinees in a linguistically diverse population, the test user should investigate the validity of the score interpretations for test takers believed to have limited proficiency in the language of the test. (SEPT, Standard 11.22)

18. Counselors carefully consider the validity, reliability, psychometric limitations, and appropriateness of instruments when selecting tests for use in a given situation or with a particular client. (ETHICS, Section E.6.a)

ADMINISTRATION AND SCORING OF ASSESSMENT INSTRUMENTS

1. Provide and document appropriate procedures for test takers with disabilities who need special accommodations or those with diverse linguistic backgrounds. Some accommodation may be required by law or regulation. (CODE, Section B-2)

2. For individuals with disabilities, accommodations in test taking procedures may need to be employed. Appropriate modifications of testing materials and procedures in order to accommodate test takers with special needs are to be arranged. (RUST)

3. Include notes on any problems, irregularities, and accommodations in the test records. (RUST)

4. A systematic and objective procedure is in place for observing and recording environmental, health, emotional factors, or other elements

that may invalidate test performance and results; deviations from prescribed test administration procedures, including information on test accommodations for individuals with special needs, are recorded. Carefully observe, record, and attach to the test record any deviation from the prescribed test administration procedures. Include information on test accommodations for individuals with special needs. (RUST)

5. The testing or assessment process should be carried out so that test takers receive comparable and equitable treatment during all phases of the testing or assessment process. (SEPT, Standard 7.12)

6. Testing practice should be designed to reduce threats to the reliability and validity of test score inferences that may arise from language differences. (SEPT, Standard 9.1)

7. When testing an examinee proficient in two or more languages for which the test is available, the examinee's relative language proficiencies should be determined. The test generally should be administered in the test taker's most proficient language, unless proficiency in the less proficient language is part of the assessment. (SEPT, Standard 9.3)

8. When an interpreter is used in testing, the interpreter should be fluent in both the language of the test and the examinee's native language, should have expertise in translating, and should have a basic understanding of the assessment process. (SEPT, Standard 9.11)

9. People who make decisions about accommodations and test modifications for individuals with disabilities should be knowledgeable of existing research on the effects of the disabilities in question on test performance. Those who modify tests should also have access to psychometric expertise for so doing. (SEPT, Standard 10.2)

10. If a test developer recommends specific time limits for people with disabilities, empirical procedures should be used, whenever possible, to establish time limits for modified forms of timed tests rather than simply allowing test takers with disabilities a multiple of the standard time. When possible, fatigue should be investigated as a potentially important factor when time limits are extended. (SEPT, Standard 10.6)

11. Those responsible for decisions about test use with potential test takers who may need or may request specific accommodations should (a) possess the information necessary to make an appropriate selection of measures, (b) have current information regarding the availability of modified forms of the test in question, (c) inform individuals, when appropriate, about the existence of modified forms, and (d) make these forms available to test takers when appropriate and feasible. (SEPT, Standard 10.8)

12. Any test modifications adopted should be considered appropriate for the individual test taker, while maintaining all feasible standardized features. A test professional needs to consider reasonably available information about each test taker's experiences, characteristics, and capabilities that might impact test performance, and document the grounds for the modification. (SEPT, Standard 10.10)

13. If a test is mandated for persons of a given age or all students in a particular grade, users should identify individuals whose disabilities or linguistic background indicates the need for special accommodations in test administration and ensure that those accommodations are employed. (SEPT, Standard 11.23)

14. Counselors provide for equal access to computer applications in counseling services. (ETHICS, Section A. 12.c)

15. When computer applications are used in counseling services, counselors ensure that: (1) the client is intellectually, emotionally, and physically capable of using the computer application; (2) the computer application is appropriate for the needs of the client; (3) the client understands the purpose and operation of the computer applications; and (4) a follow-up of client use of a computer application is provided to correct possible misconceptions, discover inappropriate use, and assess subsequent needs. (ETHICS, Section A. 12.a)

16. Prior to assessment, counselors explain the nature and purposes of assessment and the specific use of results in language the client (or other legally authorized person on behalf of the client) can understand, unless an explicit

exception to this right has been agreed upon in advance. (ETHICS, Section E. 3.a)

INTERPRETATION AND APPLICATION OF ASSESSMENT RESULTS

1. Interpret the meaning of the test results, taking into account the nature of the content, norms or comparison groups, other technical evidence, and benefits and limitations of test results. (CODE, Section C-1)
2. Review the procedures for setting performance standards or passing scores. Avoid using stigmatizing labels. (CODE, Section C-4)
3. For individuals with disabilities, interpretations need to be made in light of the modifications in the test or testing procedures. (RUST)
4. When test results are influenced by irrelevant test taker characteristics (e.g., gender, age, ethnic background, cheating, availability of test preparation programs) the use of the resulting information is invalid and potentially harmful. (RUST)
5. Factors such as the test taker's group membership and how that membership may impact the results of the test is a critical factor in the interpretation of test results. Specifically, the test user should evaluate how the test taker's gender, age, ethnicity, race, socioeconomic status, marital status, and so forth, impact on the individual's results. (RUST)
6. If local examinees differ materially from the population to which the norms refer, a user who reports derived scores based on the published norms has the responsibility to describe such differences if they bear upon the interpretation of the reported scores. (SEPT, Standard 4.7)
7. In testing applications involving individualized interpretations of test scores other than selection, a test taker's score should not be accepted as a reflection of standing on a characteristic being assessed without consideration of alternate explanations for the test taker's performance on that test at that time. (SEPT, Standard 7.5)
8. When scores are disaggregated and publicly reported for groups identified by characteristics such as gender, ethnicity, age, language proficiency, or disability, cautionary statements

should be included whenever credible research reports that test scores may not have comparable meaning across different groups. (SEPT, Standard 7.8)

9. When tests or assessments are proposed for use as instruments of social, educational, or public policy, the test developers or users proposing the test should fully and accurately inform policymakers of the characteristics of the tests as well as any relevant and credible information that may be available concerning the likely consequences of test use. (SEPT, Standard 7.9)
10. When the use of a test results in outcomes that affect the life chances or educational opportunities of examinees, evidence of mean test score differences between relevant subgroups of examinees should, where feasible, be examined for subgroups for which credible research reports mean differences for similar tests. Where mean differences are found, an investigation should be undertaken to determine that such differences are not attributable to a source of construct underrepresentation or construct-irrelevant variance. While initially the responsibility of the test developer, the test user bears responsibility for users with groups other than those specified by the developer. (SEPT, Standard 7.10).
11. When score reporting includes assigning individuals to categories, the categories should be chosen carefully and described precisely. The least stigmatizing labels, consistent with accurate representation, should always be assigned. (SEPT, Standard 8.8)
12. When there is credible evidence of score comparability across regular and modified administrations, no flag should be attached to a score. When such evidence is lacking, specific information about the nature of the modification should be provided, if permitted by law, to assist test users properly to interpret and act on test scores. (SEPT, Standard 9.5 and 10.11)
13. In testing persons with disabilities, test developers, test administrators, and test users should take steps to ensure that the test score inferences accurately reflect the intended construct rather than any disabilities and their associated characteristics extraneous to the intent of the measurement. (SEPT, Standard 10.1)

14. In testing individuals with disabilities for diagnostic and intervention purposes, the test should not be used as the sole indicator of the test taker's functioning. Instead, multiple sources of information should be used. (SEPT, Standard 10.12)

15. Agencies using tests to conduct program evaluations or policy studies, or to monitor outcomes, should clearly describe the population the program or policy is intended to serve and should document the extent to which the sample of test takers is representative of that population. (SEPT, Standard 15.5)

16. Reports of group differences in average test scores should be accompanied by relevant contextual information, where possible, to enable meaningful interpretation of these differences. Where appropriate contextual information is not available, users should be cautioned against misinterpretation. (SEPT, Standard 15.12)

17. Culturally competent counselors possess knowledge about their social impact on others. They are knowledgeable about communication style differences, how their style may clash or facilitate the counseling process with minority clients, and how to anticipate the impact it may have on others. (COMPS, 7)

18. Culturally competent counselors have knowledge of the potential bias in assessment instruments and use procedures and interpret findings keeping in mind the cultural and linguistic characteristics of the clients. (COMPS, 22)

19. Counselors recognize that culture affects the manner in which clients' problems are defined. Clients' socioeconomic and cultural experience is considered when diagnosing mental disorders. (ETHICS, Section E.5.b)

20. Counselors are cautious in using assessment techniques, making evaluations, and interpreting the performance of populations not represented in the norm group on which an instrument was standardized. They recognize the effects of age, color, culture, disability, ethnic group, gender, race, religion, sexual orientation, and socioeconomic status on test administration and interpretation and place test results in proper perspective with other relevant factors. (ETHICS, Section E.8)

21. In reporting assessment results, counselors indicate any reservations that exist regarding validity or reliability because of the circumstances of the assessment or the inappropriateness of the norms for the person tested. (ETHICS, Section E.9.a)

REFERENCES

American Counseling Association. (1996). *Code of ethics and standards of practice.* Alexandria, VA: Author.

American Counseling Association and Association for Assessment in Counseling. (2003). *Responsibilities of users of standardized tests.* Alexandria, VA: Author.

American Educational Research Association, American Psychological Association, and National Council on Measurement in Education. (1999). *Standards for educational and psychological testing* (2nd ed.). Washington, DC: American Educational Research Association.

Arredondo, P., & Toporek, R. (1996). Operationalization of the multicultural counseling competencies [Electronic version]. *Journal of Multicultural Counseling and Development, 24,* 42–79.

Association for Multicultural Counseling and Development. (1992) *Multicultural counseling competencies and standards.* Alexandria, VA: American Counseling Association.

Joint Committee on Testing Practices. (2002). *Code of fair testing practices in education.* Washington, DC: Author.

Prediger, D. J. (1992) *Standards for multicultural assessment.* Alexandria, VA: Association for Assessment in Counseling.

Prediger, D. J. (1994). Multicultural assessment standards: A compilation for counselors. *Measurement and evaluation in counseling and development, 27,* 68–73.

Sue, D. W., Arredondo, P., & McDavis, R. (1992). Multicultural counseling competencies and standards: A call to the profession. *Journal of counseling and development, 70,* 477–486.

AAC EXECUTIVE COUNCIL

Secretary—Dr. Debbie Newsome, Wake Forest
University
Treasurer—Dr. Brian Glaser, University of Georgia
Member-at-Large Publications—Dr. David Jepsen,
University of Iowa
Member-at-Large Awards—Dr. Claire Miner, As-
sessment and Counseling Services
Member-at-Large Membership—Dr. Donna Gibson,
The Citadel
Governing Council Representative—Dr. F. Robert
Wilson, University of Cincinnati

ASSOCIATION FOR ASSESSMENT IN COUNSELING

Vision: The Association for Assessment in Counseling (AAC) is an organization of counselors,
counselor educators, and other professionals that
advances the counseling profession by providing
leadership, training, and research in the creation,
development, production, and use of assessment
and diagnostic techniques.

Mission: The mission of AAC is to promote and
recognize scholarship, professionalism, leadership,
and excellence in the development and use of assessment and diagnostic techniques in counseling.

Purposes: AAC is positioned to fulfill seven fundamental purposes:

- **Administration and Management:** to provide long range planning, policies, organizational structure, operating procedures, and
  resources to fulfill AAC's missions;

- **Professional Development:** to promote professional development which enhances competence in assessment, evaluation,
  measurement, and research for counselors,
  counselor educators, and other professionals
  who develop or use assessment and diagnostic tools and techniques;

- **Professionalization:** to promote the professionalization of counseling through the appropriate use of assessment;

- **Research and Knowledge:** to promote the
  development and dissemination of knowledge
  regarding assessment procedures used in
  counseling;

- **Human Development:** to promote concern
  for human rights as integral to all assessment
  activities and to serve as a resource to counselors, counselor educators, and other professionals concerning the assessment aspects of
  human development;

- **Public Awareness and Support:** to promote
  and support public policies and legislation that
  advance the appropriate use of assessment in
  optimizing human potential;

- **International and Interprofessional Collaboration:** to promote communication and
  collaboration between AAC and other
  professional organizations (national and
  international) in order to address common,
  assessment-related concerns.

Contact: 3gibsond@citadel.edu for membership
information

Source: Association for Assessment in Counseling (2nd ed.), (2003). Reprinted by permission of the Association for
Assessment in Counseling.

Appendix D

Career Counseling Competencies

Revised Version, 1997

INTRODUCTION TO CAREER COUNSELING COMPETENCY STATEMENTS

These competency statements are for those professionals interested and trained in the field of career counseling. For the purpose of these statements, career counseling is defined as the process of assisting individuals in the development of a life-career with focus on the definition of the worker role and how that role interacts with other life roles.

NCDA's Career Counseling Competencies are intended to represent minimum competencies for those professionals at or above the Master's degree level of education. These competencies are reviewed on an ongoing basis by the NCDA Professional Standards Committee, the NCDA Board, and other relevant associations.

Professional competency statements provide guidance for the minimum competencies necessary to perform effectively a particular occupation or job within a particular field. Professional career counselors (Master's degree or higher) or persons in career development positions must demonstrate the knowledge and skills for a specialty in career counseling that the generalist counselor might not possess. Skills and knowledge are represented by designated competency areas, which have been developed by professional career counselors and counselor educators. The Career Counseling Competency Statements can serve as a guide for career counseling training programs or as a checklist for persons wanting to acquire or to enhance their skills in career counseling.

MINIMUM COMPETENCIES

In order to work as a professional engaged in Career Counseling, the individual must demonstrate minimum competencies in 11 designated areas. These 11 areas are: Career Development Theory, Individual and Group Counseling Skills, Individual/Group Assessment, Information/Resources, Program Management and Implementation, Consultation, Diverse Populations, Supervision, Ethical/Legal Issues, Research/Evaluation, and Technology. These areas are briefly defined as follows:

- **Career Development Theory:** Theory base and knowledge considered essential for professionals engaging in career counseling and development.
- **Individual and Group Counseling Skills:** Individual and group counseling competencies considered essential for effective career counseling.
- **Individual/Group Assessment:** Individual/ group assessment skills considered essential for professionals engaging in career counseling.
- **Information/Resources:** Information/ resource base and knowledge essential for professionals engaging in career counseling.
- **Program Promotion, Management and Implementation:** Skills necessary to develop, plan, implement, and manage comprehensive career development programs in a variety of settings.
- **Coaching, Consultation, and Performance Improvement:** Knowledge and skills considered essential in enabling individuals and organizations to impact effectively upon the career counseling and development process.
- **Diverse Populations:** Knowledge and skills considered essential in providing career counseling and development processes to diverse populations.
- **Supervision:** Knowledge and skills considered essential in critically evaluating counselor performance, maintaining and improving professional skills, and seeking assistance for others when needed in career counseling.

- **Ethical/Legal Issues:** Information base and knowledge essential for the ethical and legal practice of career counseling.
- **Research/Evaluation:** Knowledge and skills considered essential in understanding and conducting research and evaluation in career counseling and development.
- **Technology:** Knowledge and skills considered essential in using technology to assist individuals with career planning.

Please Note: Highlighted competencies are those that must be met in order to obtain the Master Career Counselor Special Membership Category.

PROFESSIONAL PREPARATION

The competency statements were developed to serve as guidelines for persons interested in career development occupations. They are intended for persons training at the Master's level or higher with a specialty in career counseling. However, this intention does not prevent other types of career development professionals from using the competencies as guidelines for their own training. The competency statements provide counselor educators, supervisors, and other interested groups with guidelines for the minimum training required for counselors interested in the career counseling specialty. The statements might also serve as guidelines for professional counselors who seek in-service training to qualify as career counselors.

ETHICAL RESPONSIBILITIES

Career development professionals must only perform activities for which they "possess or have access to the necessary skills and resources for giving the kind of help that is needed" (see NCDA and ACA Ethical Standards). If a professional does not have the appropriate training or resources for the type of career concern presented, an appropriate referral must be made. No person should attempt to use skills (within these competency statements) for which he/she has not been trained. For additional ethical guidelines, refer to the NCDA Ethical Standards for Career Counselors.

CAREER COUNSELING COMPETENCIES AND PERFORMANCE INDICATORS

CAREER DEVELOPMENT THEORY

Theory base and knowledge considered essential for professionals engaging in career counseling and development. Demonstration of knowledge of:

1. Counseling theories and associated techniques.
2. Theories and models of career development.
3. Individual differences related to gender, sexual orientation, race, ethnicity, and physical and mental capacities.
4. Theoretical models for career development and associated counseling and information-delivery techniques and resources.
5. Human growth and development throughout the life span.
6. Role relationships which facilitate life-work planning.
7. Information, techniques, and models related to career planning and placement

INDIVIDUAL AND GROUP COUNSELING SKILLS

Individual and group counseling competencies considered essential to effective career counseling. Demonstration of ability to:

1. Establish and maintain productive personal relationships with individuals.
2. Establish and maintain a productive group climate.
3. Collaborate with clients in identifying personal goals.
4. Identify and select techniques appropriate to client or group goals and client needs, psychological states, and developmental tasks.
5. Identify and understand clients' personal characteristics related to career.
6. Identify and understand social contextual conditions affecting clients' careers.
7. Identify and understand familial, subcultural and cultural structures and functions as they are related to clients' careers.
8. Identify and understand clients' career decision-making processes.
9. Identify and understand clients' attitudes toward work and workers.

10. Identify and understand clients' biases toward work and workers based on gender, race, and cultural stereotypes.
11. Challenge and encourage clients to take action to prepare for and initiate role transitions by:
    • locating sources of relevant information and experience.
    • obtaining and interpreting information and experiences, and acquiring skills needed to make role transitions.
12. Assist the client to acquire a set of employability and job search skills.
13. Support and challenge clients to examine life-work roles, including the balance of work, leisure, family, and community in their careers.

INDIVIDUAL/GROUP ASSESSMENT

Individual/group assessment skills considered essential for professionals engaging in career counseling. Demonstration of ability to:

1. Assess personal characteristics such as aptitude, achievement, interests, values, and personality traits.
2. Assess leisure interests, learning style, life roles, self-concept, career maturity, vocational identity, career indecision, work environment preference (e.g., work satisfaction), and other related life style/development issues.
3. Assess conditions of the work environment (such as tasks, expectations, norms, and qualities of the physical and social settings).
4. Evaluate and select valid and reliable instruments appropriate to the client's gender, sexual orientation, race, ethnicity, and physical and mental capacities.
5. Use computer-delivered assessment measures effectively and appropriately.
6. Select assessment techniques appropriate for group administration and those appropriate for individual administration.
7. Administer, score, and report findings from career assessment instruments appropriately.
8. Interpret data from assessment instruments and present the results to clients and to others.
9. Assist the client and others designated by the client to interpret data from assessment instruments.
10. Write an accurate report of assessment results.

INFORMATION/RESOURCES

Information/resource base and knowledge essential for professionals engaging in career counseling. Demonstration of knowledge of:

1. Education, training, and employment trends; labor market information and resources that provide information about job tasks, functions, salaries, requirements and future outlooks related to broad occupational fields and individual occupations.
2. Resources and skills that clients utilize in life-work planning and management.
3. Community/professional resources available to assist clients in career planning, including job search.
4. Changing roles of women and men and the implications that this has for education, family, and leisure.
5. Methods of good use of computer-based career information delivery systems (CIDS) and computer-assisted career guidance systems (CACGS) to assist with career planning.

PROGRAM PROMOTION, MANAGEMENT, AND IMPLEMENTATION

Knowledge and skills necessary to develop, plan, implement, and manage comprehensive career development programs in a variety of settings. Demonstration of knowledge of:

1. Designs that can be used in the organization of career development programs.
2. Needs assessment and evaluation techniques and practices.
3. Organizational theories, including diagnosis, behavior, planning, organizational communication, and management useful in implementing and administering career development programs.
4. Methods of forecasting, budgeting, planning, costing, policy analysis, resource allocation, and quality control.
5. Leadership theories and approaches for evaluation and feedback, organizational change, decision-making, and conflict resolution.
6. Professional standards and criteria for career development programs.

7. Societal trends and state and federal legislation that influence the development and implementation of career development programs. *Demonstration of ability to:*
8. Implement individual and group programs in career development for specified populations.
9. Train others about the appropriate use of computer-based systems for career information and planning.
10. Plan, organize, and manage a comprehensive career resource center.
11. Implement career development programs in collaboration with others.
12. Identify and evaluate staff competencies.
13. Mount a marketing and public relations campaign in behalf of career development activities and services.

COACHING, CONSULTATION, AND PERFORMANCE IMPROVEMENT

Knowledge and skills considered essential in relating to individuals and organizations that impact the career counseling and development process. Demonstration of ability to:

1. Use consultation theories, strategies, and models.
2. Establish and maintain a productive consultative relationship with people who can influence a client's career.
3. Help the general public and legislators to understand the importance of career counseling, career development, and life-work planning.
4. Impact public policy as it relates to career development and workforce planning.
5. Analyze future organizational needs and current level of employee skills and develop performance improvement training.
6. Mentor and coach employees.

DIVERSE POPULATIONS

Knowledge and skills considered essential in relating to diverse populations that impact career counseling and development processes. Demonstration of ability to:

1. Identify development models and multicultural counseling competencies.
2. Identify developmental needs unique to various diverse populations, including those of different

gender, sexual orientation, ethnic group, race, and physical or mental capacity.

3. Define career development programs to accommodate needs unique to various diverse populations.
4. Find appropriate methods or resources to communicate with limited-English-proficient individuals.
5. Identify alternative approaches to meet career planning needs for individuals of various diverse populations.
6. Identify community resources and establish linkages to assist clients with specific needs.
7. Assist other staff members, professionals, and community members in understanding the unique needs/characteristics of diverse populations with regard to career exploration, employment expectations, and economic/social issues.
8. Advocate for the career development and employment of diverse populations.
9. Design and deliver career development programs and materials to hard-to-reach populations.

SUPERVISION

Knowledge and skills considered essential in critically evaluating counselor or career development facilitator performance, maintaining and improving professional skills. Demonstration of:

1. Ability to recognize own limitations as a career counselor and to seek supervision or refer clients when appropriate.
2. Ability to utilize supervision on a regular basis to maintain and improve counselor skills.
3. Ability to consult with supervisors and colleagues regarding client and counseling issues and issues related to one's own professional development as a career counselor.
4. Knowledge of supervision models and theories.
5. Ability to provide effective supervision to career counselors and career development facilitators at different levels of experience.
6. Ability to provide effective supervision to career development facilitators at different levels of experience by:
   - knowledge of their roles, competencies, and ethical standards
   - determining their competence in each of the areas included in their certification

- further training them in competencies, including interpretation of assessment instruments
- monitoring and mentoring their activities in support of the professional career counselor; and scheduling regular consultations for the purpose of reviewing their activities

ETHICAL/LEGAL ISSUES

Information base and knowledge essential for the ethical and legal practice of career counseling. Demonstration of knowledge of:

1. Adherence to ethical codes and standards relevant to the profession of career counseling (e.g. NBCC, NCDA, and ACA).
2. Current ethical and legal issues which affect the practice of career counseling with all populations.
3. Current ethical/legal issues with regard to the use of computer-assisted career guidance systems.
4. Ethical standards relating to consultation issues.
5. State and federal statutes relating to client confidentiality.

RESEARCH/EVALUATION

Knowledge and skills considered essential in understanding and conducting research and evaluation in career counseling and development. Demonstration of ability to:

1. Write a research proposal.
2. Use types of research and research designs appropriate to career counseling and development research.
3. Convey research findings related to the effectiveness of career counseling programs.
4. Design, conduct, and use the results of evaluation programs.
5. Design evaluation programs which take into account the need of various diverse populations, including persons of both genders, differing sexual orientations, different ethnic and racial backgrounds, and differing physical and mental capacities.
6. Apply appropriate statistical procedures to career development research.

TECHNOLOGY

Knowledge and skills considered essential in using technology to assist individuals with career planning. Demonstration of knowledge of:

1. Various computer-based guidance and information systems as well as services available on the Internet.
2. Standards by which such systems and services are evaluated (e.g. NCDA and ACSCI).
3. Ways in which to use computer-based systems and Internet services to assist individuals with career planning that are consistent with ethical standards.
4. Characteristics of clients which make them profit more or less from use of technology-driven systems.
5. Methods to evaluate and select a system to meet local needs.

NCDA opposes discrimination against any individual on the basis of race, ethnicity, gender, sexual orientation, age, mental/physical disability, or creed.

Revised by the NCDA Board of Directors, April 1994.

Source: National Career Development Association. (1997). Reprinted by permission of the National Career Development Association.

Appendix E

ACA Code of Ethics and Standards of Practice

New: Ethical Standards for Internet Online Counseling

ACA Code of Ethics
ACA Standards of Practice
References
Policy and Procedures for Processing Complaints of Ethical Violations

ACA CODE OF ETHICS PREAMBLE

The American Counseling Association is an educational, scientific, and professional organization whose members are dedicated to the enhancement of human development throughout the life-span. Association members recognize diversity in our society and embrace a cross-cultural approach in support of the worth, dignity, potential, and uniqueness of each individual.

The specification of a code of ethics enables the association to clarify to current and future members, and to those served by members, the nature of the ethical responsibilities held in common by its members. As the code of ethics of the association, this document establishes principles that define the ethical behavior of association members. All members of the American Counseling Association are required to adhere to the Code of Ethics and the Standards of Practice. The Code of Ethics will serve as the basis for processing ethical complaints initiated against members of the association.

ACA CODE OF ETHICS

Section A: The Counseling Relationship
Section B: Confidentiality
Section C: Professional Responsibility
Section D: Relationships with Other Professionals
Section E: Evaluation, Assessment, and Interpretation
Section F: Teaching, Training, and Supervision
Section G: Research and Publication
Section H: Resolving Ethical Issues

SECTION A: THE COUNSELING RELATIONSHIP

A.1. Client Welfare

    a. *Primary Responsibility.* The primary responsibility of counselors is to respect the dignity and to promote the welfare of clients.

    b. *Positive Growth and Development.* Counselors encourage client growth and development in ways that foster the clients' interest and welfare; counselors avoid fostering dependent counseling relationships.

    c. *Counseling Plans.* Counselors and their clients work jointly in devising integrated, individual counseling plans that offer reasonable promise of success and are consistent with abilities and circumstances of clients. Counselors and clients regularly review counseling plans to ensure their continued viability and effectiveness, respecting clients' freedom of choice. (See A.3.b.)

d. *Family Involvement.* Counselors recognize that families are usually important in clients' lives and strive to enlist family understanding and involvement as a positive resource, when appropriate.

e. *Career and Employment Needs.* Counselors work with their clients in considering employment in jobs and circumstances that are consistent with the clients' overall abilities, vocational limitations, physical restrictions, general temperament, interest and aptitude patterns, social skills, education, general qualifications, and other relevant characteristics and needs. Counselors neither place nor participate in placing clients in positions that will result in damaging the interest and the welfare of clients, employers, or the public.

A.2. Respecting Diversity

a. *Nondiscrimination.* Counselors do not condone or engage in discrimination based on age, color, culture, disability, ethnic group, gender, race, religion, sexual orientation, marital status, or socioeconomic status. (See C.5.a., C.5.b., and D.1.i.)

b. *Respecting Differences.* Counselors will actively attempt to understand the diverse cultural backgrounds of the clients with whom they work. This includes, but is not limited to, learning how the counselor's own cultural/ethnic/racial identity impacts her or his values and beliefs about the counseling process. (See E.8. and F.2.i.)

A.3. Client Rights

a. *Disclosure to Clients.* When counseling is initiated, and throughout the counseling process as necessary, counselors inform clients of the purposes, goals, techniques, procedures, limitations, potential risks, and benefits of services to be performed, and other pertinent information. Counselors take steps to ensure that clients understand the implications of diagnosis, the intended use of tests and reports, fees, and billing arrangements. Clients have the right to expect confidentiality and to be provided with an explanation of its limitations, including supervision and/or treatment team professionals; to obtain clear information about their case records; to participate in the ongoing counseling plans; and to refuse any recommended services and be advised of the consequences of such refusal. (See E.5.a. and G.2.)

b. *Freedom of Choice.* Counselors offer clients the freedom to choose whether to enter into a counseling relationship and to determine which professional(s) will provide counseling. Restrictions that limit choices of clients are fully explained. (See A.1.c.)

c. *Inability to Give Consent.* When counseling minors or persons unable to give voluntary informed consent, counselors act in these clients' best interests. (See B.3.)

A.4. Clients Served by Others
If a client is receiving services from another mental health professional, counselors, with client consent, inform the professional persons already involved and develop clear agreements to avoid confusion and conflict for the client. (See C.6.c.)

A.5. Personal Needs and Values

a. *Personal Needs.* In the counseling relationship, counselors are aware of the intimacy and responsibilities inherent in the counseling relationship, maintain respect for clients, and avoid actions that seek to meet their personal needs at the expense of clients.

b. *Personal Values.* Counselors are aware of their own values, attitudes, beliefs, and behaviors and how these apply in a diverse society, and avoid imposing their values on clients. (See C.5.a.)

A.6. Dual Relationships

a. *Avoid When Possible.* Counselors are aware of their influential positions with respect to clients, and they avoid exploiting the trust and dependency of clients. Counselors make every effort to avoid dual relationships with clients that could impair professional judgment or increase the risk of harm to clients. (Examples of such relationships include, but are not limited to, familial, social, financial, business, or close personal relationships with clients.) When a dual relationship cannot be avoided, counselors take appropriate professional precautions such as informed consent, consultation, supervision, and documentation to ensure that judgment is not impaired and no exploitation occurs. (See F.1.b.)

b. *Superior/Subordinate Relationships.* Counselors do not accept as clients superiors or subordinates with whom they have administrative, supervisory, or evaluative relationships.

A.7. Sexual Intimacies with Clients

a. *Current Clients.* Counselors do not have any type of sexual intimacies with clients and do not counsel persons with whom they have had a sexual relationship.

b. *Former Clients.* Counselors do not engage in sexual intimacies with former clients within a minimum of 2 years after terminating the counseling relationship. Counselors who engage in such relationship after 2 years following termination have the responsibility to examine and document thoroughly that such relations did not have an exploitative nature, based on factors such as duration of counseling, amount of time since counseling, termination circumstances, client's personal history and mental status, adverse impact on the client, and actions by the counselor suggesting a plan to initiate a sexual relationship with the client after termination.

A.8. Multiple Clients

When counselors agree to provide counseling services to two or more persons who have a relationship (such as husband and wife, or parents and children), counselors clarify at the outset which person or persons are clients and the nature of the relationships they will have with each involved person. If it becomes appar-

ent that counselors may be called upon to perform potentially conflicting roles, they clarify, adjust, or withdraw from roles appropriately. (See B.2. and B.4.d.)

A.9. Group Work

a. *Screening.* Counselors screen prospective group counseling/therapy participants. To the extent possible, counselors select members whose needs and goals are compatible with goals of the group, who will not impede the group process, and whose well-being will not be jeopardized by the group experience.

b. *Protecting Clients.* In a group setting, counselors take reasonable precautions to protect clients from physical or psychological trauma.

A.10. Fees and Bartering (See D.3.a. and D.3.b.)

a. *Advance Understanding.* Counselors clearly explain to clients, prior to entering the counseling relationship, all financial arrangements related to professional services including the use of collection agencies or legal measures for nonpayment. (See A.11.c.)

b. *Establishing Fees.* In establishing fees for professional counseling services, counselors consider the financial status of clients and locality. In the event that the established fee structure is inappropriate for a client, assistance is provided in attempting to find comparable services of acceptable cost. (See A.10.d., D.3.a., and D.3.b.)

c. *Bartering Discouraged.* Counselors ordinarily refrain from accepting goods or services from clients in return for counseling services because such arrangements create inherent potential for conflicts, exploitation, and distortion of the professional relationship. Counselors may participate in bartering only if the relationship is not exploitative, if the client requests it, if a clear written contract is established, and if such arrangements are an accepted practice among professionals in the community. (See. A.6.a.)

d. *Pro Bono Service.* Counselors contribute to society by devoting a portion of their professional activity to services for which there is little or no financial return (pro bono).

A.11. Termination and Referral

 a. *Abandonment Prohibited.* Counselors do not abandon or neglect clients in counseling. Counselors assist in making appropriate arrangements for the continuation of treatment, when necessary, during interruptions such as vacations, and following termination.

 b. *Inability to Assist Clients.* If counselors determine an inability to be of professional assistance to clients, they avoid entering or immediately terminate a counseling relationship. Counselors are knowledgeable about referral resources and suggest appropriate alternatives. If clients decline the suggested referral, counselors should discontinue the relationship.

 c. *Appropriate Termination.* Counselors terminate a counseling relationship, securing client agreement when possible, when it is reasonably clear that the client is no longer benefiting, when services are no longer required, when counseling no longer serves the client's needs or interests, when clients do not pay fees charged, or when agency or institution limits do not allow provision of further counseling services. (See A.10.b. and C.2.g.)

A.12. Computer Technology

 a. *Use of Computers.* When computer applications are used in counseling services, counselors ensure that (1) the client is intellectually, emotionally, and physically capable of using the computer application; (2) the computer application is appropriate for the needs of the client; (3) the client understands the purpose and operation of the computer applications; and (4) a follow-up of client use of a computer application is provided to correct possible misconceptions, discover inappropriate use, and assess subsequent needs.

 b. *Explanation of Limitations.* Counselors ensure that clients are provided information as a part of the counseling relationship that adequately explains the limitations of computer technology.

 c. *Access to Computer Applications.* Counselors provide for equal access to computer applications in counseling services. (See A.2.a.)

SECTION B: CONFIDENTIALITY

B.1. Right to Privacy

 a. *Respect for Privacy.* Counselors respect their clients right to privacy and avoid illegal and unwarranted disclosures of confidential information. (See A.3.a. and B.6.a.)

 b. *Client Waiver.* The right to privacy may be waived by the client or his or her legally recognized representative.

 c. *Exceptions.* The general requirement that counselors keep information confidential does not apply when disclosure is required to prevent clear and imminent danger to the client or others or when legal requirements demand that confidential information be revealed. Counselors consult with other professionals when in doubt as to the validity of an exception.

 d. *Contagious, Fatal Diseases.* A counselor who receives information confirming that a client has a disease commonly known to be both communicable and fatal is justified in disclosing information to an identifiable third party, who by his or her relationship with the client is at a high risk of contracting the disease. Prior to making a disclosure the counselor should ascertain that the client has not already informed the third party about his or her disease and that the client is not intending to inform the third party in the immediate future. (See B.1.c and B.1.f.)

 e. *Court-Ordered Disclosure.* When court ordered to release confidential information without a client's permission, counselors request to the court that the disclosure not be required due to potential harm to the client or counseling relationship. (See B.1.c.)

 f. *Minimal Disclosure.* When circumstances require the disclosure of confidential information, only essential information is revealed. To the extent possible, clients are informed before confidential information is disclosed.

g. *Explanation of Limitations.* When counseling is initiated and throughout the counseling process as necessary, counselors inform clients of the limitations of confidentiality and identify foreseeable situations in which confidentiality must be breached. (See G.2.a.)

h. *Subordinates.* Counselors make every effort to ensure that privacy and confidentiality of clients are maintained by subordinates including employees, supervisees, clerical assistants, and volunteers. (See B.1.a.)

i. *Treatment Teams.* If client treatment will involve a continued review by a treatment team, the client will be informed of the team's existence and composition.

B.2. Groups and Families

a. *Group Work.* In group work, counselors clearly define confidentiality and the parameters for the specific group being entered, explain its importance, and discuss the difficulties related to confidentiality involved in group work. The fact that confidentiality cannot be guaranteed is clearly communicated to group members.

b. *Family Counseling.* In family counseling, information about one family member cannot be disclosed to another member without permission. Counselors protect the privacy rights of each family member. (See A.8., B.3., and B.4.d.)

B.3. Minor or Incompetent Clients

When counseling clients who are minors or individuals who are unable to give voluntary, informed consent, parents or guardians may be included in the counseling process as appropriate. Counselors act in the best interests of clients and take measures to safeguard confidentiality. (See A.3.c.)

B.4. Records

a. *Requirement of Records.* Counselors maintain records necessary for rendering professional services to their clients and as required by laws, regulations, or agency or institution procedures.

b. *Confidentiality of Records.* Counselors are responsible for securing the safety and confidentiality of any counseling records they create, maintain, transfer, or destroy whether the records are written, taped, computerized, or stored in any other medium. (See B.1.a.)

c. *Permission to Record or Observe.* Counselors obtain permission from clients prior to electronically recording or observing sessions. (See A.3.a.)

d. *Client Access.* Counselors recognize that counseling records are kept for the benefit of clients, and therefore provide access to records and copies of records when requested by competent clients, unless the records contain information that may be misleading and detrimental to the client. In situations involving multiple clients, access to records is limited to those parts of records that do not include confidential information related to another client. (See A.8., B.1.a., and B.2.b.)

e. *Disclosure or Transfer.* Counselors obtain written permission from clients to disclose or transfer records to legitimate third parties unless exceptions to confidentiality exist as listed in Section B.1. Steps are taken to ensure that receivers of counseling records are sensitive to their confidential nature.

B.5. Research and Training

a. *Data Disguise Required.* Use of data derived from counseling relationships for purposes of training, research, or publication is confined to content that is disguised to ensure the anonymity of the individuals involved. (See B.1.g. and G.3.d.)

b. *Agreement for Identification.* Identification of a client in a presentation or publication is permissible only when the client has reviewed the material and has agreed to its presentation or publication. (See G.3.d.)

B.6. Consultation

a. *Respect for Privacy.* Information obtained in a consulting relationship is discussed for professional purposes only with persons clearly concerned with the case. Written and oral reports present data germane to the purposes of the consultation, and every effort is made to protect client identity and avoid undue invasion of privacy.

b. *Cooperating Agencies.* Before sharing information, counselors make efforts to ensure that there are defined policies in other agencies serving the counselor's clients that effectively protect the confidentiality of information.

SECTION C: PROFESSIONAL RESPONSIBILITY

C.1. Standards Knowledge
Counselors have a responsibility to read, understand, and follow the Code of Ethics and the Standards of Practice.

C.2. Professional Competence
a. *Boundaries of Competence.* Counselors practice only within the boundaries of their competence, based on their education, training, supervised experience, state and national professional credentials, and appropriate professional experience. Counselors will demonstrate a commitment to gain knowledge, personal awareness, sensitivity, and skills pertinent to working with a diverse client population.

b. *New Specialty Areas of Practice.* Counselors practice in specialty areas new to them only after appropriate education, training, and supervised experience. While developing skills in new specialty areas, counselors take steps to ensure the competence of their work and to protect others from possible harm.

c. *Qualified for Employment.* Counselors accept employment only for positions for which they are qualified by education, training, supervised experience, state and national professional credentials, and appropriate professional experience. Counselors hire for professional counseling positions only individuals who are qualified and competent.

d. *Monitor Effectiveness.* Counselors continually monitor their effectiveness as professionals and take steps to improve when necessary. Counselors in private practice take reasonable steps to seek out peer supervision to evaluate their efficacy as counselors.

e. *Ethical Issues Consultation.* Counselors take reasonable steps to consult with other counselors or related professionals when they have questions regarding their ethical obligations or professional practice. (See H.1.)

f. *Continuing Education.* Counselors recognize the need for continuing education to maintain a reasonable level of awareness of current scientific and professional information in their fields of activity. They take steps to maintain competence in the skills they use, are open to new procedures, and keep current with the diverse and/or special populations with whom they work.

g. *Impairment.* Counselors refrain from offering or accepting professional services when their physical, mental, or emotional problems are likely to harm a client or others. They are alert to the signs of impairment, seek assistance for problems, and, if necessary, limit, suspend, or terminate their professional responsibilities. (See A.11.c.)

C.3. Advertising and Soliciting Clients
a. *Accurate Advertising.* There are no restrictions on advertising by counselors except those that can be specifically justified to protect the public from deceptive practices. Counselors advertise or represent their services to the public by identifying their credentials in an accurate manner that is not false, misleading, deceptive, or fraudulent. Counselors may only advertise the highest degree earned which is in counseling or a closely related field from a college or university that was accredited when the degree was awarded by one of the regional accrediting bodies recognized by the Council on Postsecondary Accreditation.

b. *Testimonials.* Counselors who use testimonials do not solicit them from clients or other persons who, because of their particular circumstances, may be vulnerable to undue influence.

c. *Statements by Others.* Counselors make reasonable efforts to ensure that statements made by others about them or the profession of counseling are accurate.

d. *Recruiting Through Employment.* Counselors do not use their places of employment or institutional affiliation to recruit or gain clients, supervisees, or consultees for their private practices. (See C.5.e.)

e. *Products and Training Advertisements.* Counselors who develop products related to their profession or conduct workshops or training events ensure that the advertisements concerning these products or events are accurate and disclose adequate information for consumers to make informed choices.

f. *Promoting to Those Served.* Counselors do not use counseling, teaching, training, or supervisory relationships to promote their products or training events in a manner that is deceptive or would exert undue influence on individuals who may be vulnerable. Counselors may adopt textbooks they have authored for instruction purposes.

g. *Professional Association Involvement.* Counselors actively participate in local, state, and national associations that foster the development and improvement of counseling.

C.4. Credentials

a. *Credentials Claimed.* Counselors claim or imply only professional credentials possessed and are responsible for correcting any known misrepresentations of their credentials by others. Professional credentials include graduate degrees in counseling or closely related mental health fields, accreditation of graduate programs, national voluntary certifications, government-issued certifications or licenses, ACA professional membership, or any other credential that might indicate to the public specialized knowledge or expertise in counseling.

b. *ACA Professional Membership.* ACA professional members may announce to the public their memberships status. Regular members may not announce their ACA membership in a manner that might imply they are credentialed counselors.

c. *Credential Guidelines.* Counselors follow the guidelines for use of credentials that have been established by the entities that issue the credentials.

d. *Misrepresentation of Credentials.* Counselors do not attribute more to their credentials than the credentials represent, and do not imply that other counselors are not qualified because they do not possess certain credentials.

e. *Doctoral Degrees from Other Fields.* Counselors who hold a master's degree in counseling or a closely related mental health field, but hold a doctoral degree from other than counseling or a closely related field, do not use the title "Dr." in their practices and do not announce to the public in relation to their practice or status as a counselor that they hold a doctorate.

C.5. Public Responsibility

a. *Nondiscrimination.* Counselors do not discriminate against clients, students, or supervisees in a manner that has a negative impact based on their age, color, culture, disability, ethnic group, gender, race, religion, sexual orientation, or socioeconomic status, or for any other reason. (See A.2.a.)

b. *Sexual Harassment.* Counselors do not engage in sexual harassment. Sexual harassment is defined as sexual solicitation, physical advances, or verbal or nonverbal conduct that is sexual in nature, that occurs in connection with professional activities or roles, and that either (1) is unwelcome, is offensive, or creates a hostile workplace environment, and counselors know or are told this; or (2) is sufficiently severe or intense to be perceived as harassment to a reasonable person in the context. Sexual harassment can consist of a single intense or severe act or multiple persistent or pervasive acts.

c. *Reports to Third Parties.* Counselors are accurate, honest, and unbiased in reporting their professional activities and judgments to appropriate third parties including courts, health insurance companies, those who are the recipients of evaluation reports, and others. (See B.1.g.)

d. *Media Presentations.* When counselors provide advice or comment by means of public lectures, demonstrations, radio or television programs, prerecorded tapes, printed articles, mailed material, or other media, they take reasonable precautions to ensure that (1) the statements are based on appropriate professional counseling literature and practice; (2) the statements are otherwise consistent with the Code of Ethics and the Standards of Practice; and (3) the recipients of the information are not encouraged to infer that a professional counseling relationship has been established. (See C.6.b.)

e. *Unjustified Gains.* Counselors do not use their professional positions to seek or receive unjustified personal gains, sexual favors, unfair advantage, or unearned goods or services. (See C.3.d.)

C.6. Responsibility to Other Professionals

a. *Different Approaches.* Counselors are respectful of approaches to professional counseling that differ from their own. Counselors know and take into account the traditions and practices of other professional groups with which they work.

b. *Personal Public Statements.* When making personal statements in a public context, counselors clarify that they are speaking from their personal perspectives and that they are not speaking on behalf of all counselors or the profession. (See C.5.d.)

c. *Clients Served by Others.* When counselors learn that their clients are in a professional relationship with another mental health professional, they request release from clients to inform the other professionals and strive to establish positive and collaborative professional relationships. (See A.4.)

SECTION D: RELATIONSHIPS WITH OTHER PROFESSIONALS

D.1. Relationships with Employers and Employees

a. *Role Definition.* Counselors define and describe for their employers and employees the parameters and levels of their professional roles.

b. *Agreements.* Counselors establish working agreements with supervisors, colleagues, and subordinates regarding counseling or clinical relationships, confidentiality, adherence to professional standards, distinction between public and private material, maintenance and dissemination of recorded information, work load, and accountability. Working agreements in each instance are specified and made known to those concerned.

c. *Negative Conditions.* Counselors alert their employers to conditions that may be potentially disruptive or damaging to the counselor's professional responsibilities or that may limit their effectiveness.

d. *Evaluation.* Counselors submit regularly to professional review and evaluation by their supervisor or the appropriate representative of the employer.

e. *In-Service.* Counselors are responsible for in-service development of self and staff.

f. *Goals.* Counselors inform their staff of goals and programs.

g. *Practices.* Counselors provide personnel and agency practices that respect and enhance the rights and welfare of each employee and recipient of agency services. Counselors strive to maintain the highest levels of professional services.

h. *Personnel Selection and Assignment.* Counselors select competent staff and assign responsibilities compatible with their skills and experiences.

i. *Discrimination.* Counselors, as either employers or employees, do not engage in or condone practices that are inhumane, illegal, or unjustifiable (such as considerations based on age, color, culture, disability, ethnic group, gender, race, religion, sexual orientation, or socioeconomic status) in hiring, promotion, or training. (See A.2.a. and C.5.b.)

j. *Professional Conduct.* Counselors have a responsibility both to clients and to the agency or institution within which services are performed to maintain high standards of professional conduct.

k. *Exploitative Relationships.* Counselors do not engage in exploitative relationships with individuals over whom they have supervisory evaluative, or instructional control or authority.

l. *Employer Policies.* The acceptance of employment in an agency or institution implies that counselors are in agreement with its general policies and principles. Counselors strive to reach agreement with employers as to acceptable standards of conduct that allow for changes in institutional policy conducive to the growth and development of clients.

D.2. Consultation (See B.6.)

a. *Consultation as an Option.* Counselors may choose to consult with any other professionally competent persons about their clients. In choosing consultants, counselors avoid placing the consultant in a conflict of interest situation that would preclude the consultant being a proper party to the counselor's efforts to help the client. Should counselors be engaged in a work setting that compromises this consultation standard, they consult with other professionals whenever possible to consider justifiable alternatives.

b. *Consultant Competency.* Counselors are reasonably certain that they have or the organization represented has the necessary competencies and resources for giving the kind of consulting services needed and that appropriate referral resources are available.

c. *Understanding with Clients.* When providing consultation, counselors attempt to develop with their clients a clear understanding of problem definition, goals for change, and predicted consequences of interventions selected.

d. *Consultant Goals.* The consulting relationship is one in which client adaptability and growth toward self-direction are consistently encouraged and cultivated. (See A.1.b.)

D.3. Fees for Referral

a. *Accepting Fees from Agency Clients.* Counselors refuse a private fee or other remuneration for rendering services to persons who are entitled to such services through the counselor's employing agency or institution. The policies of a particular agency may make explicit provisions for agency clients to receive counseling services from members of its staff in private practice. In such instances, the clients must be informed of other options open to them should they seek private counseling services. (See A.10.a., A.11.b., and C.3.d.)

b. *Referral Fees.* Counselors do not accept a referral fee from other professionals.

D.4. Subcontractor Arrangements

When counselors work as subcontractors for counseling services for a third party, they have a duty to inform clients of the limitations of confidentiality that the organization may place on counselors in providing counseling services to clients. The limits of such confidentiality ordinarily are discussed as part of the intake session. (See B.1.e. and B.1.f.)

SECTION E: EVALUATION, ASSESSMENT, AND INTERPRETATION

E.1. General

a. *Appraisal Techniques.* The primary purpose of educational and psychological assessment is to provide measures that are objective and interpretable in either comparative or absolute terms. Counselors recognize the need to interpret the statements in this section as applying to the whole range of appraisal techniques, including test and nontest data.

b. *Client Welfare.* Counselors promote the welfare and best interests of the client in the development, publication, and utilization of educational and psychological assessment techniques. They do not misuse assessment results and interpretations and take reasonable steps to prevent others from misusing the information these techniques provide. They respect the client's right to know the results, the interpretations made, and the bases for their conclusions and recommendations.

E.2. Competence to Use and Interpret Tests

    a. *Limits of Competence.* Counselors recognize the limits of their competence and perform only those testing and assessment services for which they have been trained. They are familiar with reliability, validity, related standardization, error of measurement, and proper application of any technique utilized. Counselors using computer-based test interpretations are trained in the construct being measured and the specific instrument being used prior to using this type of computer application. Counselors take reasonable measures to ensure the proper use of psychological assessment techniques by persons under their supervision.

    b. *Appropriate Use.* Counselors are responsible for the appropriate application, scoring, interpretation, and use of assessment instruments, whether they score and interpret such tests themselves or use computerized or other services.

    c. *Decisions Based on Results.* Counselors responsible for decisions involving individuals or policies that are based on assessment results have a thorough understanding of educational and psychological measurement, including validation criteria, test research, and guidelines for test development and use.

    d. *Accurate Information.* Counselors provide accurate information and avoid false claims or misconceptions when making statements about assessment instruments or techniques. Special efforts are made to avoid unwarranted connotations of such terms as IQ and grade equivalent scores. (See C.5.c.)

E.3. Informed Consent

    a. *Explanation to Clients.* Prior to assessment, counselors explain the nature and purposes of assessment and the specific use of results in language the client (or other legally authorized person on behalf of the client) can understand, unless an explicit exception to this right has been agreed upon in advance. Regardless of whether scoring and interpretation are completed by counselors, by assistants, or by computer or other outside services, counselors take reasonable steps to ensure that appropriate explanations are given to the client.

    b. *Recipients of Results.* The examinee's welfare, explicit understanding, and prior agreement determine the recipients of test results. Counselors include accurate and appropriate interpretations with any release of individual or group test results. (See B.1.a and C.5.c.)

E.4. Release of Information to Competent Professionals

    a. *Misuse of Results.* Counselors do not misuse assessment results, including test results, and interpretations, and take reasonable steps to prevent the misuse of such by others. (See C.5.c.)

    b. *Release of Raw Data.* Counselors ordinarily release data (e.g., protocols, counseling or interview notes, or questionnaires) in which the client is identified only with the consent of the client or the client's legal representative. Such data are usually released only to persons recognized by counselors as competent to interpret the data. (See B.1.a.)

E.5. Proper Diagnosis of Mental Disorders

    a. *Proper Diagnosis.* Counselors take special care to provide proper diagnosis of mental disorders. Assessment techniques (including personal interview) used to determine client care (e.g., locus of treatment, type of treatment, or recommended follow-up) are carefully selected and appropriately used. (See A.3.a. and C.5.c.)

    b. *Cultural Sensitivity.* Counselors recognize that culture affects the manner in which clients' problems are defined. Clients' socioeconomic and cultural experience is considered when diagnosing mental disorders.

E.6. Test Selection
  a. *Appropriateness of Instruments*. Counselors carefully consider the validity, reliability, psychometric limitations, and appropriateness of instruments when selecting tests for use in a given situation or with a particular client.
  b. *Culturally Diverse Populations*. Counselors are cautious when selecting tests for culturally diverse populations to avoid inappropriateness of testing that may be outside of socialized behavioral or cognitive patterns.

E.7. Conditions of Test Administration
  a. *Administration Conditions*. Counselors administer tests under the same conditions that were established in their standardization. When tests are not administered under standard conditions or when unusual behavior or irregularities occur during the testing session, those conditions are noted in interpretation, and the results may be designated as invalid or of questionable validity.
  b. *Computer Administration*. Counselors are responsible for ensuring that administration programs function properly to provide clients with accurate results when a computer or other electronic methods are used for test administration. (See A.12.b.)
  c. *Unsupervised Test Taking*. Counselors do not permit unsupervised or inadequately supervised use of tests or assessments unless the tests or assessments are designed, intended, and validated for self-administration and/or scoring.
  d. *Disclosure of Favorable Conditions*. Prior to test administration, conditions that produce most favorable test results are made known to the examinee.

E.8. Diversity in Testing
  Counselors are cautious in using assessment techniques, making evaluations, and interpreting the performance of populations not represented in the norm group on which an instrument was standardized. They recognize the effects of age, color, culture, disability, ethnic group, gender, race, religion, sexual orientation, and socioeconomic status on test administration and interpretation and place test results in proper perspective with other relevant factors. (See A.2.a.)

E.9. Test Scoring and Interpretation
  a. *Reporting Reservations*. In reporting assessment results, counselors indicate any reservations that exist regarding validity or reliability because of the circumstances of the assessment or the inappropriateness of the norms for the person tested.
  b. *Research Instruments*. Counselors exercise caution when interpreting the results of research instruments possessing insufficient technical data to support respondent results. The specific purposes for the use of such instruments are stated explicitly to the examinee.
  c. *Testing Services*. Counselors who provide test scoring and test interpretation services to support the assessment process confirm the validity of such interpretations. They accurately describe the purpose, norms, validity, reliability, and applications of the procedures and any special qualifications applicable to their use. The public offering of an automated test interpretations service is considered a professional-to-professional consultation. The formal responsibility of the consultant is to the consultee, but the ultimate and overriding responsibility is to the client.

E.10. Test Security
  Counselors maintain the integrity and security of tests and other assessment techniques consistent with legal and contractual obligations. Counselors do not appropriate, reproduce, or modify published tests or parts thereof without acknowledgment and permission from the publisher.

E.11. Obsolete Tests and Outdated Test Results
  Counselors do not use data or test results that are obsolete or outdated for the current

purpose. Counselors make every effort to prevent the misuse of obsolete measures and test data by others.

E.12. Test Construction
Counselors use established scientific procedures, relevant standards, and current professional knowledge for test design in the development, publication, and utilization of educational and psychological assessment techniques.

SECTION F: TEACHING, TRAINING, AND SUPERVISION

F.1. Counselor Educators and Trainers
    a. *Educators as Teachers and Practitioners.* Counselors who are responsible for developing, implementing, and supervising educational programs are skilled as teachers and practitioners. They are knowledgeable regarding the ethical, legal, and regulatory aspects of the profession, are skilled in applying that knowledge, and make students and supervisees aware of their responsibilities. Counselors conduct counselor education and training programs in an ethical manner and serve as role models for professional behavior. Counselor educators should make an effort to infuse material related to human diversity into all courses and/or workshops that are designed to promote the development of professional counselors.
    b. *Relationship Boundaries With Students and Supervisees.* Counselors clearly define and maintain ethical, professional, and social relationship boundaries with their students and supervisees. They are aware of the differential in power that exists and the student's or supervisee's possible incomprehension of that power differential. Counselors explain to students and supervisees the potential for the relationship to become exploitive.
    c. *Sexual Relationships.* Counselors do not engage in sexual relationships with students or supervisees and do not subject them to sexual harassment. (See A.6. and C.5.b.)
    d. *Contributions to Research.* Counselors give credit to students or supervisees for their contributions to research and scholarly projects. Credit is given through coauthorship, acknowledgment, footnote statement, or other appropriate means, in accordance with such contributions. (See G.4.b. and G.4.c.)
    e. *Close Relatives.* Counselors do not accept close relatives as students or supervisees.
    f. *Supervision Preparation.* Counselors who offer clinical supervision services are adequately prepared in supervision methods and techniques. Counselors who are doctoral students serving as practicum or internship supervisors to master's level students are adequately prepared and supervised by the training program.
    g. *Responsibility for Services to Clients.* Counselors who supervise the counseling services of others take reasonable measures to ensure that counseling services provided to clients are professional.
    h. *Endorsement.* Counselors do not endorse students or supervisees for certification, licensure, employment, or completion of an academic or training program if they believe students or supervisees are not qualified for the endorsement. Counselors take reasonable steps to assist students or supervisees who are not qualified for endorsement to become qualified.

F.2. Counselor Education and Training Programs
    a. *Orientation.* Prior to admission, counselors orient prospective students to the counselor education or training program's expectations, including but not limited to the following: (1) the type and level of skill acquisition required for successful completion of the training, (2) subject matter to be covered, (3) basis for evaluation, (4) training components that encourage self-growth or self-disclosure as part of the training process, (5) the type of supervision settings and requirements of the sites for required clinical field experiences,

(6) student and supervisee evaluation and dismissal policies and procedures, and (7) up-to-date employment prospects for graduates.

b. *Integration of Study and Practice.* Counselors establish counselor education and training programs that integrate academic study and supervised practice.

c. *Evaluation.* Counselors clearly state to students and supervisees, in advance of training, the levels of competency expected, appraisal methods, and timing of evaluations for both didactic and experiential components. Counselors provide students and supervisees with periodic performance appraisal and evaluation feedback throughout the training program.

d. *Teaching Ethics.* Counselors make students and supervisees aware of the ethical responsibilities and standards of the profession and the students' and supervisees' ethical responsibilities to the profession. (See C.1. and F.3.e.)

e. *Peer Relationships.* When students or supervisees are assigned to lead counseling groups or provide clinical supervision for their peers, counselors take steps to ensure that students and supervisees placed in these roles do not have personal or adverse relationships with peers and that they understand they have the same ethical obligations as counselor educators, trainers, and supervisors. Counselors make every effort to ensure that the rights of peers are not compromised when students or supervisees are assigned to lead counseling groups or provide clinical supervision.

f. *Varied Theoretical Positions.* Counselors present varied theoretical positions so that students and supervisees may make comparisons and have opportunities to develop their own positions. Counselors provide information concerning the scientific bases of professional practice. (See C.6.a.)

g. *Field Placements.* Counselors develop clear policies within their training program regarding field placement and other clinical experiences. Counselors provide clearly stated roles and responsibilities for the student or supervisee, the site supervisor, and the program supervisor. They confirm that site supervisors are qualified to provide supervision and are informed of their professional and ethical responsibilities in this role.

h. *Dual Relationships as Supervisors.* Counselors avoid dual relationships such as performing the role of site supervisor and training program supervisor in the student's or supervisee's training program. Counselors do not accept any form of professional services, fees, commissions, reimbursement, or remuneration from a site for student or supervisee placement.

i. *Diversity in Programs.* Counselors are responsive to their institution's and program's recruitment and retention needs for training program administrators, faculty, and students with diverse backgrounds and special needs. (See A.2.a.)

F.3. Students and Supervisees

a. *Limitations.* Counselors, through ongoing evaluation and appraisal, are aware of the academic and personal limitations of students and supervisees that might impede performance. Counselors assist students and supervisees in securing remedial assistance when needed, and dismiss from the training program supervisees who are unable to provide competent service due to academic or personal limitations. Counselors seek professional consultation and document their decision to dismiss or refer students or supervisees for assistance. Counselors ensure that students and supervisees have recourse to address decisions made to require them to seek assistance or to dismiss them.

b. *Self-Growth Experiences.* Counselors use professional judgment when designing training experiences conducted by the counselors themselves that require student and supervisee self-growth or self-disclosure. Safeguards are provided so that students and supervisees are aware of the ramifications their self-disclosure may have on counselors whose primary role as teacher, trainer, or supervisor requires acting on ethical obligations to the profession. Evaluative components of experiential training experiences explicitly delineate predetermined academic standards that are separate and do not depend on the student's level of self-disclosure. (See A.6.)

c. *Counseling for Students and Supervisees.* If students or supervisees request counseling, supervisors or counselor educators provide them with acceptable referrals. Supervisors or counselor educators do not serve as counselor to students or supervisees over whom they hold administrative, teaching, or evaluative roles unless this is a brief role associated with a training experience. (See A.6.b.)

d. *Clients of Students and Supervisees.* Counselors make every effort to ensure that the clients at field placements are aware of the services rendered and the qualifications of the students and supervisees rendering those services. Clients receive professional disclosure information and are informed of the limits of confidentiality. Client permission is obtained in order for the students and supervisees to use any information concerning the counseling relationship in the training process. (See B.1.e.)

e. *Standards for Students and Supervisees.* Students and supervisees preparing to become counselors adhere to the Code of Ethics and the Standards of Practice. Students and supervisees have the same obligations to clients as those required of counselors. (See H.1.)

SECTION G: RESEARCH AND PUBLICATION

G.1. Research Responsibilities

a. *Use of Human Subjects.* Counselors plan, design, conduct, and report research in a manner consistent with pertinent ethical principles, federal and state laws, host institutional regulations, and scientific standards governing research with human subjects. Counselors design and conduct research that reflects cultural sensitivity appropriateness.

b. *Deviation From Standard Practices.* Counselors seek consultation and observe stringent safeguards to protect the rights of research participants when a research problem suggests a deviation from standard acceptable practices. (See B.6.)

c. *Precautions to Avoid Injury.* Counselors who conduct research with human subjects are responsible for the subjects' welfare throughout the experiment and take reasonable precautions to avoid causing injurious psychological, physical, or social effects to their subjects.

d. *Principal Researcher Responsibility.* The ultimate responsibility for ethical research practice lies with the principal researcher. All others involved in the research activities share ethical obligations and full responsibility for their own actions.

e. *Minimal Interference.* Counselors take reasonable precautions to avoid causing disruptions in subjects' lives due to participation in research.

f. *Diversity.* Counselors are sensitive to diversity and research issues with special populations. They seek consultation when appropriate. (See A.2.a. and B.6.)

G.2. Informed Consent

a. *Topics Disclosed.* In obtaining informed consent for research, counselors use language that is understandable to research participants and that (1) accurately explains the purpose and procedures to be followed; (2) identifies any procedures that are experimental or relatively untried; (3) describes the attendant discomforts and risks; (4) describes the benefits or changes in individuals or organizations that might be reasonably expected; (5) discloses appropriate alternative procedures that would be advantageous for subjects; (6) offers to answer any inquiries concerning the procedures; (7) describes any limitations on confidentiality; and (8) instructs that subjects are free to withdraw their consent and to discontinue participation in the project at any time. (See B.1.f.)

b. *Deception.* Counselors do not conduct research involving deception unless alternative procedures are not feasible and the prospective value of the research justifies the deception. When the methodological requirements of a study necessitate concealment or deception, the investigator is required to explain clearly the reasons for this action as soon as possible.

c. *Voluntary Participation.* Participation in research is typically voluntary and without any penalty for refusal to participate. Involuntary participation is appropriate only when it can be demonstrated that participation will have no harmful effects on subjects and is essential to the investigation.

d. *Confidentiality of Information.* Information obtained about research participants during the course of an investigation is confidential. When the possibility exists that others may obtain access to such information, ethical research practice requires that the possibility, together with the plans for protecting confidentiality, be explained to participants as a part of the procedure for obtaining informed consent. (See B.1.e.)

e. *Persons Incapable of Giving Informed Consent.* When a person is incapable of giving informed consent, counselors provide an appropriate explanation, obtain agreement for participation, and obtain appropriate consent from a legally authorized person.

f. *Commitments to Participants.* Counselors take reasonable measures to honor all commitments to research participants.

g. *Explanations after Data Collection.* After data are collected, counselors provide participants with full clarification of the nature of the study to remove any misconceptions. Where scientific or human values justify delaying or withholding information, counselors take reasonable measures to avoid causing harm.

h. *Agreements to Cooperate.* Counselors who agree to cooperate with another individual in research or publication incur an obligation to cooperate as promised in terms of punctuality of performance and with regard to the completeness and accuracy of the information required.

i. *Informed Consent for Sponsors.* In the pursuit of research, counselors give sponsors, institutions, and publication channels the same respect and opportunity for giving informed consent that they accord to individual research participants. Counselors are aware of their obligation to future research workers and ensure that host institutions are given feedback information and proper acknowledgment.

G.3. Reporting Results

a. *Information Affecting Outcome.* When reporting research results, counselors explicitly mention all variables and conditions known to the investigator that may have affected the outcome of a study or the interpretation of data.

b. *Accurate Results.* Counselors plan, conduct, and report research accurately and in a manner that minimizes the possibility that results will be misleading. They provide thorough discussions of the limitations of their data and alternative hypotheses. Counselors do not engage in fraudulent research, distort data, misrepresent data, or deliberately bias their results.

c. *Obligation to Report Unfavorable Results.* Counselors communicate to other counselors the results of any research judged to be of professional value. Results that reflect unfavorably on institutions, programs, services, prevailing opinions, or vested interests are not withheld.

d. *Identity of Subjects.* Counselors who supply data, aid in the research of another person, report research results, or make original data available take due care to disguise the identity of respective subjects in the absence of specific authorization from the subjects to do otherwise. (See B.1.g. and B.5.a.)

e. *Replication Studies.* Counselors are obligated to make available sufficient original research data to qualified professionals who may wish to replicate the study.

G.4. Publication

    a. *Recognition of Others*. When conducting and reporting research, counselors are familiar with and give recognition to previous work on the topic, observe copyright laws, and give full credit to those to whom credit is due. (See F.1.d. and G.4.c.)

    b. *Contributors*. Counselors give credit through joint authorship, acknowledgment, footnote statements, or other appropriate means to those who have contributed significantly to research or concept development in accordance with such contributions. The principal contributor is listed first and minor technical or professional contributions are acknowledged in notes or introductory statements.

    c. *Student Research*. For an article that is substantially based on a student's dissertation or thesis, the student is listed as the principal author. (See F.1.d. and G.4.a.)

    d. *Duplicate Submission*. Counselors submit manuscripts for consideration to only one journal at a time. Manuscripts that are published in whole or in substantial part in another journal or published work are not submitted for publication without acknowledgment and permission from the previous publication.

    e. *Professional Review*. Counselors who review material submitted for publication, research, or other scholarly purposes respect the confidentiality and proprietary rights of those who submitted it.

SECTION H: RESOLVING ETHICAL ISSUES

H.1. Knowledge of Standards

Counselors are familiar with the Code of Ethics and the Standards of Practice and other applicable ethics codes from other professional organizations of which they are members, or from certification and licensure bodies. Lack of knowledge or misunderstanding of an ethical responsibility is not a defense against a charge of unethical conduct. (See F.3.e.)

H.2. Suspected Violations

    a. *Ethical Behavior Expected*. Counselors expect professional associates to adhere to the Code of Ethics. When counselors possess reasonable cause that raises doubts as to whether a counselor is acting in an ethical manner, they take appropriate action. (See H.2.d. and H.2.e.)

    b. *Consultation*. When uncertain as to whether a particular situation or course of action may be in violation of the Code of Ethics, counselors consult with other counselors who are knowledgeable about ethics, with colleagues, or with appropriate authorities.

    c. *Organization Conflicts*. If the demands of an organization with which counselors are affiliated pose a conflict with the Code of Ethics, counselors specify the nature of such conflicts and express to their supervisors or other responsible officials their commitment to the Code of Ethics. When possible, counselors work toward change within the organization to allow full adherence to the Code of Ethics.

    d. *Informal Resolution*. When counselors have reasonable cause to believe that another counselor is violating an ethical standard, they attempt to first resolve the issue informally with the other counselor if feasible, providing that such action does not violate confidentiality rights that may be involved.

    e. *Reporting Suspected Violations*. When an informal resolution is not appropriate or feasible, counselors, upon reasonable cause, take action such as reporting the suspected ethical violation to state or national ethics committees, unless this action conflicts with confidentiality rights that cannot be resolved.

    f. *Unwarranted Complaints*. Counselors do not initiate, participate in, or encourage the filing of ethics complaints that are unwarranted or intend to harm a counselor rather than to protect clients or the public.

H.3. Cooperation with Ethics Committees

Counselors assist in the process of enforcing the Code of Ethics. Counselors cooperate with investigations, proceedings, and requirements of the ACA Ethics Committee or ethics committees of other duly constituted associations or boards having jurisdiction over those charged with a violation. Counselors are familiar with the ACA Policies and Procedures and use it as a reference in assisting the enforcement of the Code of Ethics.

ACA STANDARDS OF PRACTICE

All members of the American Counseling Association (ACA) are required to adhere to the Standards of Practice and the Code of Ethics. The Standards of Practice represent minimal behavioral statements of the Code of Ethics. Members should refer to the applicable section of the Code of Ethics for further interpretation and amplification of the applicable Standard of Practice.

Section A: The Counseling Relationship
Section B: Confidentiality
Section C: Professional Responsibility
Section D: Relationship With Other Professionals
Section E: Evaluation, Assessment and Interpretation
Section F: Teaching, Training, and Supervision
Section G: Research and Publication
Section H: Resolving Ethical Issues

SECTION A: THE COUNSELING RELATIONSHIP

Standard of Practice One (SP-1): Nondiscrimination. Counselors respect diversity and must not discriminate against clients because of age, color, culture, disability, ethnic group, gender, race, religion, sexual orientation, marital status, or socioeconomic status. (See A.2.a.)

Standard of Practice Two (SP-2): Disclosure to Clients. Counselors must adequately inform clients, preferably in writing, regarding the counseling process and counseling relationship at or before the time it begins and throughout the relationship. (See A.3.a.)

Standard of Practice Three (SP-3): Dual Relationships. Counselors must make every effort to avoid dual relationships with clients that could impair their professional judgment or increase the risk of harm to clients. When a dual relationship cannot be avoided, counselors must take appropriate steps to ensure

that judgment is not impaired and that no exploitation occurs. (See A.6.a. and A.6.b.)

Standard of Practice Four (SP-4): Sexual Intimacies with Clients. Counselors must not engage in any type of sexual intimacies with current clients and must not engage in sexual intimacies with former clients within a minimum of 2 years after terminating the counseling relationship. Counselors who engage in such relationship after 2 years following termination have the responsibility to examine and document thoroughly that such relations did not have an exploitative nature.

Standard of Practice Five (SP-5): Protecting Clients During Group Work. Counselors must take steps to protect clients from physical or psychological trauma resulting from interactions during group work. (See A.9.b.)

Standard of Practice Six (SP-6): Advance Understanding of Fees. Counselors must explain to clients, prior to their entering the counseling relationship, financial arrangements related to professional services. (See A.10. a.-d. and A.11.c.)

Standard of Practice Seven (SP-7): Termination. Counselors must assist in making appropriate arrangements for the continuation of treatment of clients, when necessary, following termination of counseling relationships. (See A.11.a.)

Standard of Practice Eight (SP-8): Inability to Assist Clients. Counselors must avoid entering or immediately terminate a counseling relationship if it is determined that they are unable to be of professional assistance to a client. The counselor may assist in making an appropriate referral for the client. (See A.11.b.)

SECTION B: CONFIDENTIALITY

Standard of Practice Nine (SP-9): Confidentiality Requirement. Counselors must keep information related to counseling services confidential unless disclosure is in the best interest of clients, is required for the welfare of others, or is required by law. When disclosure is required, only information that is essential is revealed and the client is informed of such disclosure. (See B.1. a.+f.)

Standard of Practice Ten (SP-10): Confidentiality Requirements for Subordinates. Counselors must take measures to ensure that privacy and confidentiality of clients are maintained by subordinates. (See B.1.h.)

Standard of Practice Eleven (SP-11): Confidentiality in Group Work. Counselors must clearly communicate to group members that confidentiality cannot be guaranteed in group work. (See B.2.a.)

Standard of Practice Twelve (SP-12): Confidentiality in Family Counseling. Counselors must not disclose information about one family member in counseling to another family member without prior consent. (See B.2.b.)

Standard of Practice Thirteen (SP-13): Confidentiality of Records. Counselors must maintain appropriate confidentiality in creating, storing, accessing, transferring, and disposing of counseling records. (See B.4.b.)

Standard of Practice Fourteen (SP-14): Permission to Record or Observe. Counselors must obtain prior consent from clients in order to record electronically or observe sessions. (See B.4.c.)

Standard of Practice Fifteen (SP-15): Disclosure or Transfer of Records. Counselors must obtain client consent to disclose or transfer records to third parties, unless exceptions listed in SP-9 exist. (See B.4.e.)

Standard of Practice Sixteen (SP-16): Data Disguise Required. Counselors must disguise the identity of the client when using data for training, research, or publication. (See B.5.a.)

SECTION C: PROFESSIONAL RESPONSIBILITY

Standard of Practice Seventeen (SP-17): Boundaries of Competence. Counselors must practice only within the boundaries of their competence. (See C.2.a.)

Standard of Practice Eighteen (SP-18): Continuing Education. Counselors must engage in continuing education to maintain their professional competence. (See C.2.f.)

Standard of Practice Nineteen (SP-19): Impairment of Professionals. Counselors must refrain from offering professional services when their personal problems or conflicts may cause harm to a client or others. (See C.2.g.)

Standard of Practice Twenty (SP-20): Accurate Advertising. Counselors must accurately represent their credentials and services when advertising. (See C.3.a.)

Standard of Practice Twenty-One (SP-21): Recruiting Through Employment. Counselors must not use their place of employment or institutional affiliation to recruit clients for their private practices. (See C.3.d.)

Standard of Practice Twenty-Two (SP-22): Credentials Claimed. Counselors must claim or imply only professional credentials possessed and must correct any known misrepresentations of their credentials by others. (See C.4.a.)

Standard of Practice Twenty-Three (SP-23): Sexual Harassment. Counselors must not engage in sexual harassment. (See C.5.b.)

Standard of Practice Twenty-Four (SP-24): Unjustified Gains. Counselors must not use their professional positions to seek or receive unjustified personal gains, sexual favors, unfair advantage, or unearned goods or services. (See C.5.e.)

Standard of Practice Twenty-Five (SP-25): Clients Served by Others. With the consent of the client, counselors must inform other mental health professionals serving the same client that a counseling relationship between the counselor and client exists. (See C.6.c.)

Standard of Practice Twenty-Six (SP-26): Negative Employment Conditions. Counselors must alert their employers to institutional policy or conditions that may be potentially disruptive or damaging to the counselor's professional responsibilities, or that may limit their effectiveness or deny clients' rights. (See D.1.c.)

Standard of Practice Twenty-Seven (SP-27): Personnel Selection and Assignment. Counselors must select competent staff and must assign responsibilities compatible with staff skills and experiences. (See D.1.h.)

Standard of Practice Twenty-Eight (SP-28): Exploitative Relationships With Subordinates. Counselors must not engage in exploitative relationships with individuals over whom they have supervisory, evaluative, or instructional control or authority. (See D.1.k.)

SECTION D: RELATIONSHIP WITH OTHER PROFESSIONALS

Standard of Practice Twenty-Nine (SP-29): Accepting Fees From Agency Clients. Counselors must not accept fees or other remuneration for consultation with persons entitled to such services through the counselor's employing agency or institution. (See D.3.a.)

Standard of Practice Thirty (SP-30): Referral Fees. Counselors must not accept referral fees. (See D.3.b.)

SECTION E: EVALUATION, ASSESSMENT AND INTERPRETATION

Standard of Practice Thirty-One (SP-31): Limits of Competence. Counselors must perform only testing and assessment services for which they are competent. Counselors must not allow the use of psychological assessment techniques by unqualified persons under their supervision. (See E.2.a.)

Standard of Practice Thirty-Two (SP-32): Appropriate Use of Assessment Instruments. Counselors must use assessment instruments in the manner for which they were intended. (See E.2.b.)

Standard of Practice Thirty-Three (SP-33): Assessment Explanations to Clients. Counselors must provide explanations to clients prior to assessment about the nature and purposes of assessment and the specific uses of results. (See E.3.a.)

Standard of Practice Thirty-Four (SP-34): Recipients of Test Results. Counselors must ensure that accurate and appropriate interpretations accompany any release of testing and assessment information. (See E.3.b.)

Standard of Practice Thirty-Five (SP-35): Obsolete Tests and Outdated Test Results. Counselors must not base their assessment or intervention decisions or recommendations on data or test results that are obsolete or outdated for the current purpose. (See E.11.)

SECTION F: TEACHING, TRAINING, AND SUPERVISION

Standard of Practice Thirty-Six (SP-36): Sexual Relationships with Students or Supervisees. Counselors must not engage in sexual relationships with their students and supervisees. (See F.1.c.)

Standard of Practice Thirty-Seven (SP-37): Credit for Contributions to Research. Counselors must give credit to students or supervisees for their contributions to research and scholarly projects. (See F.1.d.)

Standard of Practice Thirty-Eight (SP-38): Supervision Preparation. Counselors who offer clinical supervision services must be trained and prepared in supervision methods and techniques. (See F.1.f.)

Standard of Practice Thirty-Nine (SP-39): Evaluation Information. Counselors must clearly state to students and supervisees in advance of training the levels of competency expected, appraisal methods, and timing of evaluations. Counselors must provide students and supervisees with periodic performance appraisal and evaluation feedback throughout the training program. (See F.2.c.)

Standard of Practice Forty (SP-40): Peer Relationships in Training. Counselors must make every effort to ensure that the rights of peers are not violated when students and supervisees are assigned to lead counseling groups or provide clinical supervision. (See F.2.e.)

Standard of Practice Forty-One (SP-41): Limitations of Students and Supervisees. Counselors must assist students and supervisees in securing remedial assistance, when needed, and must dismiss from the training program students and supervisees who are unable to provide competent service due to academic or personal limitations. (See F.3.a.)

Standard of Practice Forty-Two (SP-42): Self-Growth Experiences. Counselors who conduct experiences for students or supervisees that include self-growth or self-disclosure must inform participants of counselors' ethical obligations to the profession and must not grade participants based on their nonacademic performance. (See F.3.b.)

Standard of Practice Forty-Three (SP-43): Standards for Students and Supervisees. Students and supervisees preparing to become counselors must adhere to the Code of Ethics and the Standards of Practice of counselors. (See F.3.e.)

SECTION G: RESEARCH AND PUBLICATION

Standard of Practice Forty-Four (SP-44): Precautions to Avoid Injury in Research. Counselors must avoid causing physical, social, or psychological harm or injury to subjects in research. (See G.1.c.)

Standard of Practice Forty-Five (SP-45): Confidentiality of Research Information. Counselors must keep confidential information obtained about research participants. (See G.2.d.)

Standard of Practice Forty-Six (SP-46): Information Affecting Research Outcome. Counselors must report all variables and conditions known to the investigator that may have affected research data or outcomes. (See G.3.a.)

Standard of Practice Forty-Seven (SP-47): Accurate Research Results. Counselors must not distort or misrepresent research data, nor fabricate or intentionally bias research results. (See G.3.b.)

Standard of Practice Forty-Eight (SP-48): Publication Contributors. Counselors must give appropriate credit to those who have contributed to research. (See G.4.a. and G.4.b.)

SECTION H: RESOLVING ETHICAL ISSUES

Standard of Practice Forty-Nine (SP-49): Ethical Behavior Expected. Counselors must take appropriate action when they possess reasonable cause that raises doubts as to whether counselors or other mental health professionals are acting in an ethical manner. (See H.2.a.)

Standard of Practice Fifty (SP-50): Unwarranted Complaints. Counselors must not initiate, participate in, or encourage the filing of ethics complaints that are unwarranted or intended to harm a mental health professional rather than to protect clients or the public. (See H.2.f.)

Standard of Practice Fifty-One (SP-51): Cooperation with Ethics Committees. Counselors must cooperate with investigations, proceedings, and requirements of the ACA Ethics Committee or ethics committees of other duly constituted associations or boards having jurisdiction over those charged with a violation. (See H.3.)

REFERENCES

The following documents are available to counselors as resources to guide them in their practices. These resources are not a part of the Code of Ethics and the Standards of Practice.

American Association for Counseling and Development/Association for Measurement and Evaluation in Counseling and Development. (1989). The responsibilities of users of standardized tests (rev.). Washington, DC: Author.

American Counseling Association. (1988) (Note: This is ACA's previous edition of its ethics code). Ethical standards. Alexandria, VA: Author.

American Psychological Association. (1985). Standards for educational and psychological testing (rev.). Washington, DC: Author.

Joint Committee on Testing Practices. (1988). Code of fair testing practices in education. Washington, DC: Author.

National Board for Certified Counselors. (1989). National Board for Certified Counselors code of ethics. Alexandria, VA: Author.

Prediger, D.J. (Ed.). (1993, March). Multicultural assessment standards. Alexandria, VA: Association for Assessment in Counseling.

Appendix F

Ethical Principles of Psychologists and Code of Conduct 2002

CONTENTS

INTRODUCTION AND APPLICABILITY

The American Psychological Association's (APA's) Ethical Principles of Psychologists and Code of Conduct (hereinafter referred to as the Ethics Code) consists of an Introduction, a Preamble, five General Principles (A–E), and specific Ethical Standards. The Introduction discusses the intent, organization, procedural considerations, and scope of application of the Ethics Code. The Preamble and General Principles are aspirational goals to guide psychologists toward the highest ideals of psychology. Although the Preamble and General Principles are not themselves enforceable rules, they should be considered by psychologists in arriving at an ethical course of action. The Ethical Standards set forth enforceable rules for conduct as psychologists. Most of the Ethical Standards are written broadly, in order to apply to psychologists in varied roles, although the application of an Ethical Standard may vary depending on the context. The Ethical Standards are not exhaustive. The fact that a given conduct is not specifically addressed by an Ethical Standard does not mean that it is necessarily either ethical or unethical.

This Ethics Code applies only to psychologists' activities that are part of their scientific, educational, or professional roles as psychologists. Areas covered include but are not limited to the clinical, counseling, and school practice of psychology; research; teaching; supervision of trainees; public service; policy development; social intervention; development of assessment instruments; conducting assessments; educational counseling; organizational consulting; forensic activities; program design and evaluation; and administration. This Ethics Code applies to these activities across a variety of contexts, such as in person, postal, telephone, internet, and other electronic transmissions. These activities shall be distinguished from the purely private conduct of psychologists, which is not within the purview of the Ethics Code.

Membership in the APA commits members and student affiliates to comply with the standards of the APA Ethics Code and to the rules and procedures used to enforce them. Lack of awareness or misunderstanding of an Ethical Standard is not itself a defense to a charge of unethical conduct.

The procedures for filing, investigating, and resolving complaints of unethical conduct are described in the current Rules and Procedures of the APA Ethics Committee. APA may impose sanctions on its members for violations of the standards of the Ethics Code, including termination of APA membership, and may notify other bodies and individuals of its actions. Actions that violate the standards of the Ethics Code may also lead to the imposition of sanctions on psychologists or students whether or not they are APA members by bodies other than APA, including state psychological associations, other professional groups, psychology boards, other state or federal agencies, and payors for health services. In addition, APA may take action against a member after his or her conviction of a felony, expulsion or suspension from an affiliated state psychological association,

or suspension or loss of licensure. When the sanction to be imposed by APA is less than expulsion, the 2001 Rules and Procedures do not guarantee an opportunity for an in-person hearing, but generally provide that complaints will be resolved only on the basis of a submitted record.

The Ethics Code is intended to provide guidance for psychologists and standards of professional conduct that can be applied by the APA and by other bodies that choose to adopt them. The Ethics Code is not intended to be a basis of civil liability. Whether a psychologist has violated the Ethics Code standards does not by itself determine whether the psychologist is legally liable in a court action, whether a contract is enforceable, or whether other legal consequences occur.

The modifiers used in some of the standards of this Ethics Code (e.g., *reasonably, appropriate, potentially*) are included in the standards when they would (1) allow professional judgment on the part of psychologists, (2) eliminate injustice or inequality that would occur without the modifier, (3) ensure applicability across the broad range of activities conducted by psychologists, or (4) guard against a set of rigid rules that might be quickly outdated. As used in this Ethics Code, the term *reasonable* means the prevailing professional judgment of psychologists engaged in similar activities in similar circumstances, given the knowledge the psychologist had or should have had at the time.

In the process of making decisions regarding their professional behavior, psychologists must consider this Ethics Code in addition to applicable laws and psychology board regulations. In applying the Ethics Code to their professional work, psychologists may consider other materials and guidelines that have been adopted or endorsed by scientific and professional psychological organizations and the dictates of their own conscience, as well as consult with others within the field. If this Ethics Code establishes a higher standard of conduct than is required by law, psychologists must meet the higher ethical standard. If psychologists' ethical responsibilities conflict with law, regulations, or other governing legal authority, psychologists make known their commitment to this Ethics Code and take steps to resolve the conflict in a responsible manner. If the conflict is unresolvable via such means, psychologists may adhere to the requirements of the law, regulations, or other governing authority in keeping with basic principles of human rights.

PREAMBLE

Psychologists are committed to increasing scientific and professional knowledge of behavior and people's understanding of themselves and others and to the use of such knowledge to improve the condition of individuals, organizations, and society. Psychologists respect and protect civil and human rights and the central importance of freedom of inquiry and expression in research, teaching, and publication. They strive to help the public in developing informed judgments and choices concerning human behavior. In doing so, they perform many roles, such as researcher, educator, diagnostician, therapist, supervisor, consultant, administrator, social interventionist, and expert witness. This Ethics Code provides a common set of principles and standards upon which psychologists build their professional and scientific work.

This Ethics Code is intended to provide specific standards to cover most situations encountered by psychologists. It has as its goals the welfare and protection of the individuals and groups with whom psychologists work and the education of members, students, and the public regarding ethical standards of the discipline.

The development of a dynamic set of ethical standards for psychologists' work-related conduct requires a personal commitment and lifelong effort to act ethically; to encourage ethical behavior by students, supervisees, employees, and colleagues; and to consult with others concerning ethical problems.

GENERAL PRINCIPLES

This section consists of General Principles. General Principles, as opposed to Ethical Standards, are aspirational in nature. Their intent is to guide and inspire psychologists toward the very highest ethical ideals of the profession. General Principles, in contrast to Ethical Standards, do not represent obligations and should not form the basis for imposing sanctions. Relying upon General Principles for either of these reasons distorts both their meaning and purpose.

PRINCIPLE A: BENEFICENCE AND NONMALEFICENCE

Psychologists strive to benefit those with whom they work and take care to do no harm. In their professional actions, psychologists seek to safeguard the welfare and rights of those with whom they interact professionally and other affected persons, and the welfare of animal subjects of research. When conflicts occur among psychologists' obligations or concerns, they attempt to resolve these conflicts in a responsible fashion that avoids or minimizes harm. Because psychologists' scientific and professional judgments and actions may affect the lives of others, they are alert to and guard against personal, financial, social, organizational, or political factors that might lead to misuse of their influence. Psychologists strive to be aware of the possible effect of their own physical and mental health on their ability to help those with whom they work.

PRINCIPLE B: FIDELITY AND RESPONSIBILITY

Psychologists establish relationships of trust with those with whom they work. They are aware of their professional and scientific responsibilities to society and to the specific communities in which they work. Psychologists uphold professional standards of conduct, clarify their professional roles and obligations, accept appropriate responsibility for their behavior, and seek to manage conflicts of interest that could lead to exploitation or harm. Psychologists consult with, refer to, or cooperate with other professionals and institutions to the extent needed to serve the best interests of those with whom they work. They are concerned about the ethical compliance of their colleagues' scientific and professional conduct. Psychologists strive to contribute a portion of their professional time for little or no compensation or personal advantage.

PRINCIPLE C: INTEGRITY

Psychologists seek to promote accuracy, honesty, and truthfulness in the science, teaching, and practice of psychology. In these activities psychologists do not steal, cheat, or engage in fraud, subterfuge, or intentional misrepresentation of fact. Psychologists strive to keep their promises and to avoid unwise or unclear commitments. In situations in which deception may be ethically justifiable to maximize benefits and minimize harm, psychologists have a serious obligation to consider the need for, the possible consequences of, and their responsibility to correct any resulting mistrust or other harmful effects that arise from the use of such techniques.

PRINCIPLE D: JUSTICE

Psychologists recognize that fairness and justice entitle all persons to access to and benefit from the contributions of psychology and to equal quality in the processes, procedures, and services being conducted by psychologists. Psychologists exercise reasonable judgment and take precautions to ensure that their potential biases, the boundaries of their competence, and the limitations of their expertise do not lead to or condone unjust practices.

PRINCIPLE E: RESPECT FOR PEOPLE'S RIGHTS AND DIGNITY

Psychologists respect the dignity and worth of all people, and the rights of individuals to privacy, confidentiality, and self-determination. Psychologists are aware that special safeguards may be necessary to protect the rights and welfare of persons or communities whose vulnerabilities impair autonomous decision making. Psychologists are aware of and respect cultural, individual, and role differences, including those based on age, gender, gender identity, race, ethnicity, culture, national origin, religion, sexual orientation, disability, language, and socioeconomic status and consider these factors when working with members of such groups. Psychologists try to eliminate the effect on their work of biases based on those factors, and they do not knowingly participate in or condone activities of others based upon such prejudices.

ETHICAL STANDARDS

1. **Resolving Ethical Issues**
   1.01 **Misuse of Psychologists' Work** If psychologists learn of misuse or misrepresentation of their work, they take reasonable steps to correct or minimize the misuse or misrepresentation.
   1.02 **Conflicts Between Ethics and Law, Regulations, or Other Governing Legal Authority** If psychologists' ethical responsibilities conflict with law, regulations, or other governing legal authority, psychologists make known their commitment to the Ethics Code and take steps to resolve the conflict. If the conflict is unresolvable via such means, psychologists may adhere to the requirements of the law, regulations, or other governing legal authority.
   1.03 **Conflicts Between Ethics and Organizational Demands** If the demands of an organization with which psychologists are affiliated or for whom they are working conflict with this Ethics Code, psychologists clarify the nature of the conflict, make known their commitment to the Ethics Code, and to the extent feasible, resolve the conflict in a way that permits adherence to the Ethics Code.
   1.04 **Informal Resolution of Ethical Violations** When psychologists believe that there may have been an ethical violation by another psychologist, they attempt to resolve the issue by bringing it to the attention of that individual, if an informal resolution appears appropriate and the intervention does not violate any confidentiality rights that may be involved. (See also Standards 1.02, Conflicts Between Ethics and Law, Regulations, or Other Governing Legal Authority, and 1.03, Conflicts Between Ethics and Organizational Demands.)
   1.05 **Reporting Ethical Violations** If an apparent ethical violation has substantially harmed or is likely to substantially harm a person or organization and is not appropriate for informal resolution under Standard 1.04, Informal Resolution of Ethical Violations, or is not resolved properly in that fashion, psychologists take further action appropriate to the situation. Such action might include referral to state or national committees on professional ethics, to state licensing boards, or to the appropriate institutional authorities. This standard does not apply when an intervention would violate confidentiality rights or when psychologists have been retained to review the work of another psychologist whose professional conduct is in question. (See also Standard 1.02, Conflicts Between Ethics and Law, Regulations, or Other Governing Legal Authority.)

1.06 **Cooperating With Ethics Committees**
Psychologists cooperate in ethics investigations, proceedings, and resulting requirements of the APA or any affiliated state psychological association to which they belong. In doing so, they address any confidentiality issues. Failure to cooperate is itself an ethics violation. However, making a request for deferment of adjudication of an ethics complaint pending the outcome of litigation does not alone constitute noncooperation.

1.07 **Improper Complaints** Psychologists do not file or encourage the filing of ethics complaints that are made with reckless disregard for or willful ignorance of facts that would disprove the allegation.

1.08 **Unfair Discrimination Against Complainants and Respondents** Psychologists do not deny persons employment, advancement, admissions to academic or other programs, tenure, or promotion, based solely upon their having made or their being the subject of an ethics complaint. This does not preclude taking action based upon the outcome of such proceedings or considering other appropriate information.

2. **Competence**

2.01 **Boundaries of Competence**

(a) Psychologists provide services, teach, and conduct research with populations and in areas only within the boundaries of their competence, based on their education, training, supervised experience, consultation, study, or professional experience.

(b) Where scientific or professional knowledge in the discipline of psychology establishes that an understanding of factors associated with age, gender, gender identity, race, ethnicity, culture, national origin, religion, sexual orientation, disability, language, or socioeconomic status is essential for effective implementation of their services or research, psychologists have or obtain the training, experience, consultation, or supervision necessary to ensure the competence of their services, or they make appropriate referrals, except as provided in Standard 2.02, Providing Services in Emergencies.

(c) Psychologists planning to provide services, teach, or conduct research involving populations, areas, techniques, or technologies new to them undertake relevant education, training, supervised experience, consultation, or study.

(d) When psychologists are asked to provide services to individuals for whom appropriate mental health services are not available and for which psychologists have not obtained the competence necessary, psychologists with closely related prior training or experience may provide such services in order to ensure that services are not denied if they make a reasonable effort to obtain the competence required by using relevant research, training, consultation, or study.

(e) In those emerging areas in which generally recognized standards for preparatory training do not yet exist, psychologists nevertheless take reasonable steps to ensure the competence of their work and to protect clients/patients, students, supervisees, research participants, organizational clients, and others from harm.

(f) When assuming forensic roles, psychologists are or become reasonably familiar with the judicial or administrative rules governing their roles.

2.02 **Providing Services in Emergencies** In emergencies, when psychologists provide services to individuals for whom other mental health services are not available and for which psychologists have not obtained the necessary training, psychologists may provide such services in order to ensure that services are not denied. The services are discontinued as soon as the emergency has ended or appropriate services are available.

2.03 **Maintaining Competence** Psychologists undertake ongoing efforts to develop and maintain their competence.

2.04 **Bases for Scientific and Professional Judgments** Psychologists' work is based upon established scientific and professional knowledge of the discipline. (See also Standards 2.01e, Boundaries of Competence, and 10.01b, Informed Consent to Therapy.)

2.05 **Delegation of Work to Others** Psychologists who delegate work to employees, supervisees, or research or teaching assistants or who use the services of others, such as interpreters, take reasonable steps to (1) avoid delegating such work to persons who have a multiple relationship with those being served that would likely lead to exploitation or loss of objectivity; (2) authorize only those responsibilities that such persons can be expected to perform competently on the basis of their education, training, or experience, either independently or with the level of supervision being provided; and (3) see that such persons perform these services competently. (See also Standards 2.02, Providing Services in Emergencies; 3.05, Multiple Relationships; 4.01, Maintaining Confidentiality; 9.01, Bases for Assessments; 9.02, Use of Assessments; 9.03, Informed Consent in Assessments; and 9.07, Assessment by Unqualified Persons.)

2.06 **Personal Problems and Conflicts**
(a) Psychologists refrain from initiating an activity when they know or should know that there is a substantial likelihood that their personal problems will prevent them from performing their work-related activities in a competent manner.
(b) When psychologists become aware of personal problems that may interfere with their performing work-related duties adequately, they take appropriate measures, such as obtaining professional consultation or assistance, and determine whether

they should limit, suspend, or terminate their work-related duties. (See also Standard 10.10, Terminating Therapy.)

3. **Human Relations**

3.01 **Unfair Discrimination** In their work-related activities, psychologists do not engage in unfair discrimination based on age, gender, gender identity, race, ethnicity, culture, national origin, religion, sexual orientation, disability, socioeconomic status, or any basis proscribed by law.

3.02 **Sexual Harassment** Psychologists do not engage in sexual harassment. Sexual harassment is sexual solicitation, physical advances, or verbal or nonverbal conduct that is sexual in nature, that occurs in connection with the psychologist's activities or roles as a psychologist, and that either (1) is unwelcome, is offensive, or creates a hostile workplace or educational environment, and the psychologist knows or is told this or (2) is sufficiently severe or intense to be abusive to a reasonable person in the context. Sexual harassment can consist of a single intense or severe act or of multiple persistent or pervasive acts. (See also Standard 1.08, Unfair Discrimination Against Complainants and Respondents.)

3.03 **Other Harassment** Psychologists do not knowingly engage in behavior that is harassing or demeaning to persons with whom they interact in their work based on factors such as those persons' age, gender, gender identity, race, ethnicity, culture, national origin, religion, sexual orientation, disability, language, or socioeconomic status.

3.04 **Avoiding Harm** Psychologists take reasonable steps to avoid harming their clients/patients, students, supervisees, research participants, organizational clients, and others with whom they work, and to minimize harm where it is foreseeable and unavoidable.

3.05 **Multiple Relationships**
(a) A multiple relationship occurs when a psychologist is in a professional

role with a person and (1) at the same time is in another role with the same person, (2) at the same time is in a relationship with a person closely associated with or related to the person with whom the psychologist has the professional relationship, or (3) promises to enter into another relationship in the future with the person or a person closely associated with or related to the person.

A psychologist refrains from entering into a multiple relationship if the multiple relationship could reasonably be expected to impair the psychologist's objectivity, competence, or effectiveness in performing his or her functions as a psychologist, or otherwise risks exploitation or harm to the person with whom the professional relationship exists.

Multiple relationships that would not reasonably be expected to cause impairment or risk exploitation or harm are not unethical.

(b) If a psychologist finds that, due to unforeseen factors, a potentially harmful multiple relationship has arisen, the psychologist takes reasonable steps to resolve it with due regard for the best interests of the affected person and maximal compliance with the Ethics Code.

(c) When psychologists are required by law, institutional policy, or extraordinary circumstances to serve in more than one role in judicial or administrative proceedings, at the outset they clarify role expectations and the extent of confidentiality and thereafter as changes occur. (See also Standards 3.04, Avoiding Harm, and 3.07, Third-Party Requests for Services.)

3.06 **Conflict of Interest** Psychologists refrain from taking on a professional role when personal, scientific, professional, legal, financial, or other interests or relationships could reasonably be expected to (1) impair their objectivity, competence, or effectiveness in performing their functions as psychologists or (2) expose the person or organization with whom the professional relationship exists to harm or exploitation.

3.07 **Third-Party Requests for Services** When psychologists agree to provide services to a person or entity at the request of a third party, psychologists attempt to clarify at the outset of the service the nature of the relationship with all individuals or organizations involved. This clarification includes the role of the psychologist (e.g., therapist, consultant, diagnostician, or expert witness), an identification of who is the client, the probable uses of the services provided or the information obtained, and the fact that there may be limits to confidentiality. (See also Standards 3.05, Multiple Relationships, and 4.02, Discussing the Limits of Confidentiality.)

3.08 **Exploitative Relationships** Psychologists do not exploit persons over whom they have supervisory, evaluative, or other authority such as clients/patients, students, supervisees, research participants, and employees. (See also Standards 3.05, Multiple Relationships; 6.04, Fees and Financial Arrangements; 6.05, Barter With Clients/Patients; 7.07, Sexual Relationships With Students and Supervisees; 10.05, Sexual Intimacies With Current Therapy Clients/Patients; 10.06, Sexual Intimacies With Relatives or Significant Others of Current Therapy Clients/Patients; 10.07, Therapy With Former Sexual Partners; and 10.08, Sexual Intimacies With Former Therapy Clients/Patients.)

3.09 **Cooperation With Other Professionals** When indicated and professionally appropriate, psychologists cooperate with other professionals in order to serve their clients/patients effectively and appropriately. (See also Standard 4.05, Disclosures.)

3.10 **Informed Consent**

    (a) When psychologists conduct research or provide assessment, therapy, counseling, or consulting services in person or via electronic transmission or other forms of communication, they obtain the informed consent of the individual or individuals using language that is reasonably understandable to that person or persons except when conducting such activities without consent is mandated by law or governmental regulation or as otherwise provided in this Ethics Code. (See also Standards 8.02, Informed Consent to Research; 9.03, Informed Consent in Assessments; and 10.01, Informed Consent to Therapy.)

    (b) For persons who are legally incapable of giving informed consent, psychologists nevertheless (1) provide an appropriate explanation, (2) seek the individual's assent, (3) consider such persons' preferences and best interests, and (4) obtain appropriate permission from a legally authorized person, if such substitute consent is permitted or required by law. When consent by a legally authorized person is not permitted or required by law, psychologists take reasonable steps to protect the individual's rights and welfare.

    (c) When psychological services are court ordered or otherwise mandated, psychologists inform the individual of the nature of the anticipated services, including whether the services are court ordered or mandated and any limits of confidentiality, before proceeding.

    (d) Psychologists appropriately document written or oral consent, permission, and assent. (See also Standards 8.02, Informed Consent to Research; 9.03, Informed Consent in Assessments; and 10.01, Informed Consent to Therapy.)

3.11 **Psychological Services Delivered to or Through Organizations**

    (a) Psychologists delivering services to or through organizations provide information beforehand to clients and when appropriate those directly affected by the services about (1) the nature and objectives of the services, (2) the intended recipients, (3) which of the individuals are clients, (4) the relationship the psychologist will have with each person and the organization, (5) the probable uses of services provided and information obtained, (6) who will have access to the information, and (7) limits of confidentiality. As soon as feasible, they provide information about the results and conclusions of such services to appropriate persons.

    (b) If psychologists will be precluded by law or by organizational roles from providing such information to particular individuals or groups, they so inform those individuals or groups at the outset of the service.

3.12 **Interruption of Psychological Services**
Unless otherwise covered by contract, psychologists make reasonable efforts to plan for facilitating services in the event that psychological services are interrupted by factors such as the psychologist's illness, death, unavailability, relocation, or retirement or by the client's/patient's relocation or financial limitations. (See also Standard 6.02c, Maintenance, Dissemination, and Disposal of Confidential Records of Professional and Scientific Work.)

4. **Privacy and Confidentiality**

    4.01 **Maintaining Confidentiality** Psychologists have a primary obligation and take reasonable precautions to protect confidential information obtained through or stored in any medium, recognizing that the extent and limits of confidentiality may be regulated by law or established by institutional rules or professional or scientific relationship. (See also Standard 2.05, Delegation of Work to Others.)

4.02 Discussing the Limits of Confidentiality

(a) Psychologists discuss with persons (including, to the extent feasible, persons who are legally incapable of giving informed consent and their legal representatives) and organizations with whom they establish a scientific or professional relationship (1) the relevant limits of confidentiality and (2) the foreseeable uses of the information generated through their psychological activities. (See also Standard 3.10, Informed Consent.)

(b) Unless it is not feasible or is contraindicated, the discussion of confidentiality occurs at the outset of the relationship and thereafter as new circumstances may warrant.

(c) Psychologists who offer services, products, or information via electronic transmission inform clients/patients of the risks to privacy and limits of confidentiality.

4.03 Recording Before recording the voices or images of individuals to whom they provide services, psychologists obtain permission from all such persons or their legal representatives. (See also Standards 8.03, Informed Consent for Recording Voices and Images in Research; 8.05, Dispensing With Informed Consent for Research; and 8.07, Deception in Research.)

4.04 Minimizing Intrusions on Privacy

(a) Psychologists include in written and oral reports and consultations, only information germane to the purpose for which the communication is made.

(b) Psychologists discuss confidential information obtained in their work only for appropriate scientific or professional purposes and only with persons clearly concerned with such matters.

4.05 Disclosures

(a) Psychologists may disclose confidential information with the appropriate consent of the organizational client, the individual client/patient, or another legally authorized person on behalf of the client/patient unless prohibited by law.

(b) Psychologists disclose confidential information without the consent of the individual only as mandated by law, or where permitted by law for a valid purpose such as to (1) provide needed professional services; (2) obtain appropriate professional consultations; (3) protect the client/patient, psychologist, or others from harm; or (4) obtain payment for services from a client/patient, in which instance disclosure is limited to the minimum that is necessary to achieve the purpose. (See also Standard 6.04e, Fees and Financial Arrangements.)

4.06 Consultations When consulting with colleagues, (1) psychologists do not disclose confidential information that reasonably could lead to the identification of a client/patient, research participant, or other person or organization with whom they have a confidential relationship unless they have obtained the prior consent of the person or organization or the disclosure cannot be avoided, and (2) they disclose information only to the extent necessary to achieve the purposes of the consultation. (See also Standard 4.01, Maintaining Confidentiality.)

4.07 Use of Confidential Information for Didactic or Other Purposes Psychologists do not disclose in their writings, lectures, or other public media, confidential, personally identifiable information concerning their clients/patients, students, research participants, organizational clients, or other recipients of their services that they obtained during the course of their work, unless (1) they take reasonable steps to disguise the person or organization, (2) the person or organization has consented in writing, or (3) there is legal authorization for doing so.

5. Advertising and Other Public Statements

5.01 Avoidance of False or Deceptive Statements

(a) Public statements include but are not limited to paid or unpaid advertising, product endorsements, grant applications, licensing applications, other credentialing applications, brochures, printed matter, directory listings, personal resumes or curricula vitae, or comments for use in media such as print or electronic transmission, statements in legal proceedings, lectures and public oral presentations, and published materials. Psychologists do not knowingly make public statements that are false, deceptive, or fraudulent concerning their research, practice, or other work activities or those of persons or organizations with which they are affiliated.

(b) Psychologists do not make false, deceptive, or fraudulent statements concerning (1) their training, experience, or competence; (2) their academic degrees; (3) their credentials; (4) their institutional or association affiliations; (5) their services; (6) the scientific or clinical basis for, or results or degree of success of, their services; (7) their fees; or (8) their publications or research findings.

(c) Psychologists claim degrees as credentials for their health services only if those degrees (1) were earned from a regionally accredited educational institution or (2) were the basis for psychology licensure by the state in which they practice.

5.02 **Statements by Others**

(a) Psychologists who engage others to create or place public statements that promote their professional practice, products, or activities retain professional responsibility for such statements.

(b) Psychologists do not compensate employees of press, radio, television, or other communication media in return for publicity in a news item. (See also Standard 1.01, Misuse of Psychologists' Work.)

(c) A paid advertisement relating to psychologists' activities must be identified or clearly recognizable as such.

5.03 **Descriptions of Workshops and Non-Degree-Granting Educational Programs** To the degree to which they exercise control, psychologists responsible for announcements, catalogs, brochures, or advertisements describing workshops, seminars, or other non-degree-granting educational programs ensure that they accurately describe the audience for which the program is intended, the educational objectives, the presenters, and the fees involved.

5.04 **Media Presentations** When psychologists provide public advice or comment via print, internet, or other electronic transmission, they take precautions to ensure that statements (1) are based on their professional knowledge, training, or experience in accord with appropriate psychological literature and practice; (2) are otherwise consistent with this Ethics Code; and (3) do not indicate that a professional relationship has been established with the recipient. (See also Standard 2.04, Bases for Scientific and Professional Judgments.)

5.05 **Testimonials** Psychologists do not solicit testimonials from current therapy clients/patients or other persons who because of their particular circumstances are vulnerable to undue influence.

5.06 **In-Person Solicitation** Psychologists do not engage, directly or through agents, in uninvited in-person solicitation of business from actual or potential therapy clients/patients or other persons who because of their particular circumstances are vulnerable to undue influence. However, this prohibition does not preclude (1) attempting to implement appropriate collateral contacts for the purpose of benefiting an already engaged therapy client/patient or (2) providing disaster or community outreach services.

6. **Record Keeping and Fees**

6.01 **Documentation of Professional and Scientific Work and Maintenance of Records** Psychologists create, and to the extent the records are under their control, maintain, disseminate, store, retain, and dispose of records and data relating to their professional and scientific work in order to (1) facilitate provision of services later by them or by other professionals, (2) allow for replication of research design and analyses, (3) meet institutional requirements, (4) ensure accuracy of billing and payments, and (5) ensure compliance with law. (See also Standard 4.01, Maintaining Confidentiality.)

6.02 **Maintenance, Dissemination, and Disposal of Confidential Records of Professional and Scientific Work**

(a) Psychologists maintain confidentiality in creating, storing, accessing, transferring, and disposing of records under their control, whether these are written, automated, or in any other medium. (See also Standards 4.01, Maintaining Confidentiality, and 6.01, Documentation of Professional and Scientific Work and Maintenance of Records.)

(b) If confidential information concerning recipients of psychological services is entered into databases or systems of records available to persons whose access has not been consented to by the recipient, psychologists use coding or other techniques to avoid the inclusion of personal identifiers.

(c) Psychologists make plans in advance to facilitate the appropriate transfer and to protect the confidentiality of records and data in the event of psychologists' withdrawal from positions or practice. (See also Standards 3.12, Interruption of Psychological Services, and 10.09, Interruption of Therapy.)

6.03 **Withholding Records for Nonpayment** Psychologists may not withhold records under their control that are requested and needed for a client's/patient's emergency treatment solely because payment has not been received.

6.04 **Fees and Financial Arrangements**

(a) As early as is feasible in a professional or scientific relationship, psychologists and recipients of psychological services reach an agreement specifying compensation and billing arrangements.

(b) Psychologists' fee practices are consistent with law.

(c) Psychologists do not misrepresent their fees.

(d) If limitations to services can be anticipated because of limitations in financing, this is discussed with the recipient of services as early as is feasible. (See also Standards 10.09, Interruption of Therapy, and 10.10, Terminating Therapy.)

(e) If the recipient of services does not pay for services as agreed, and if psychologists intend to use collection agencies or legal measures to collect the fees, psychologists first inform the person that such measures will be taken and provide that person an opportunity to make prompt payment. (See also Standards 4.05, Disclosures; 6.03, Withholding Records for Nonpayment; and 10.01, Informed Consent to Therapy.)

6.05 **Barter With Clients/Patients** Barter is the acceptance of goods, services, or other nonmonetary remuneration from clients/patients in return for psychological services. Psychologists may barter only if (1) it is not clinically contraindicated, and (2) the resulting arrangement is not exploitative. (See also Standards 3.05, Multiple Relationships, and 6.04, Fees and Financial Arrangements.)

6.06 **Accuracy in Reports to Payors and Funding Sources** In their reports to payors for services or sources of research funding, psychologists take reasonable steps to ensure the accurate reporting of the nature of the service provided or research conducted, the fees, charges, or payments, and where applicable, the identity of the provider, the findings, and the diagnosis. (See also Standards 4.01, Maintaining Confidentiality; 4.04, Minimizing Intrusions on Privacy; and 4.05, Disclosures.)

6.07 **Referrals and Fees** When psychologists pay, receive payment from, or divide fees with another professional, other than in an employer-employee relationship, the payment to each is based on the services provided (clinical, consultative, administrative, or other) and is not based on the referral itself. (See also Standard 3.09, Cooperation With Other Professionals.)

7. Education and Training

7.01 **Design of Education and Training Programs** Psychologists responsible for education and training programs take reasonable steps to ensure that the programs are designed to provide the appropriate knowledge and proper experiences, and to meet the requirements for licensure, certification, or other goals for which claims are made by the program. (See also Standard 5.03, Descriptions of Workshops and Non-Degree-Granting Educational Programs.)

7.02 **Descriptions of Education and Training Programs** Psychologists responsible for education and training programs take reasonable steps to ensure that there is a current and accurate description of the program content (including participation in required course- or program-related counseling, psychotherapy, experiential groups, consulting projects, or community service), training goals and objectives, stipends and benefits, and requirements that must be met for satisfactory completion of the program. This information must be made readily available to all interested parties.

7.03 **Accuracy in Teaching**
(a) Psychologists take reasonable steps to ensure that course syllabi are accurate regarding the subject matter to be covered, bases for evaluating progress, and the nature of course experiences. This standard does not preclude an instructor from modifying course content or requirements when the instructor considers it pedagogically necessary or desirable, so long as students are made aware of these modifications in a manner that enables them to fulfill course requirements. (See also Standard 5.01, Avoidance of False or Deceptive Statements.)
(b) When engaged in teaching or training, psychologists present psychological information accurately. (See also Standard 2.03, Maintaining Competence.)

7.04 **Student Disclosure of Personal Information** Psychologists do not require students or supervisees to disclose personal information in course- or program-related activities, either orally or in writing, regarding sexual history, history of abuse and neglect, psychological treatment, and relationships with parents, peers, and spouses or significant others except if (1) the program or training facility has clearly identified this requirement in its admissions and program materials or (2) the information is necessary to evaluate or obtain assistance for students whose personal problems could reasonably be judged to be preventing them from performing their training- or professionally related activities in a competent manner or posing a threat to the students or others.

7.05 **Mandatory Individual or Group Therapy**
(a) When individual or group therapy is a program or course requirement, psychologists responsible for that program allow students in undergraduate and graduate programs the option of selecting such therapy from practitioners unaffiliated with the program. (See also Standard 7.02, Descriptions of Education and Training Programs.)
(b) Faculty who are or are likely to be responsible for evaluating students' academic performance do not themselves provide that therapy. (See also Standard 3.05, Multiple Relationships.)

7.06 **Assessing Student and Supervisee Performance**
(a) In academic and supervisory relationships, psychologists establish a

timely and specific process for providing feedback to students and supervisees. Information regarding the process is provided to the student at the beginning of supervision.

(b) Psychologists evaluate students and supervisees on the basis of their actual performance on relevant and established program requirements.

7.07 **Sexual Relationships With Students and Supervisees** Psychologists do not engage in sexual relationships with students or supervisees who are in their department, agency, or training center or over whom psychologists have or are likely to have evaluative authority. (See also Standard 3.05, Multiple Relationships.)

8. **Research and Publication**

8.01 **Institutional Approval** When institutional approval is required, psychologists provide accurate information about their research proposals and obtain approval prior to conducting the research. They conduct the research in accordance with the approved research protocol.

8.02 **Informed Consent to Research**

(a) When obtaining informed consent as required in Standard 3.10, Informed Consent, psychologists inform participants about (1) the purpose of the research, expected duration, and procedures; (2) their right to decline to participate and to withdraw from the research once participation has begun; (3) the foreseeable consequences of declining or withdrawing; (4) reasonably foreseeable factors that may be expected to influence their willingness to participate such as potential risks, discomfort, or adverse effects; (5) any prospective research benefits; (6) limits of confidentiality; (7) incentives for participation; and (8) whom to contact for questions about the research and research participants' rights. They provide opportunity for the prospective participants to ask questions and

receive answers. (See also Standards 8.03, Informed Consent for Recording Voices and Images in Research; 8.05, Dispensing With Informed Consent for Research; and 8.07, Deception in Research.)

(b) Psychologists conducting intervention research involving the use of experimental treatments clarify to participants at the outset of the research (1) the experimental nature of the treatment; (2) the services that will or will not be available to the control group(s) if appropriate; (3) the means by which assignment to treatment and control groups will be made; (4) available treatment alternatives if an individual does not wish to participate in the research or wishes to withdraw once a study has begun; and (5) compensation for or monetary costs of participating including, if appropriate, whether reimbursement from the participant or a third-party payor will be sought. (See also Standard 8.02a, Informed Consent to Research.)

8.03 **Informed Consent for Recording Voices and Images in Research** Psychologists obtain informed consent from research participants prior to recording their voices or images for data collection unless (1) the research consists solely of naturalistic observations in public places, and it is not anticipated that the recording will be used in a manner that could cause personal identification or harm, or (2) the research design includes deception, and consent for the use of the recording is obtained during debriefing. (See also Standard 8.07, Deception in Research.)

8.04 **Client/Patient, Student, and Subordinate Research Participants**

(a) When psychologists conduct research with clients/patients, students, or subordinates as participants, psychologists take steps to protect the prospective participants from adverse consequences of declining or withdrawing from participation.

(b) When research participation is a course requirement or an opportunity for extra credit, the prospective participant is given the choice of equitable alternative activities.

8.05 **Dispensing With Informed Consent for Research** Psychologists may dispense with informed consent only (1) where research would not reasonably be assumed to create distress or harm and involves (a) the study of normal educational practices, curricula, or classroom management methods conducted in educational settings; (b) only anonymous questionnaires, naturalistic observations, or archival research for which disclosure of responses would not place participants at risk of criminal or civil liability or damage their financial standing, employability, or reputation, and confidentiality is protected; or (c) the study of factors related to job or organization effectiveness conducted in organizational settings for which there is no risk to participants' employability, and confidentiality is protected or (2) where otherwise permitted by law or federal or institutional regulations.

8.06 **Offering Inducements for Research Participation**

(a) Psychologists make reasonable efforts to avoid offering excessive or inappropriate financial or other inducements for research participation when such inducements are likely to coerce participation.

(b) When offering professional services as an inducement for research participation, psychologists clarify the nature of the services, as well as the risks, obligations, and limitations. (See also Standard 6.05, Barter With Clients/Patients.)

8.07 **Deception in Research**

(a) Psychologists do not conduct a study involving deception unless they have determined that the use of deceptive techniques is justified by the study's significant prospective scientific, educational, or applied value and that

effective nondeceptive alternative procedures are not feasible.

(b) Psychologists do not deceive prospective participants about research that is reasonably expected to cause physical pain or severe emotional distress.

(c) Psychologists explain any deception that is an integral feature of the design and conduct of an experiment to participants as early as is feasible, preferably at the conclusion of their participation, but no later than at the conclusion of the data collection, and permit participants to withdraw their data. (See also Standard 8.08, Debriefing.)

8.08 **Debriefing**

(a) Psychologists provide a prompt opportunity for participants to obtain appropriate information about the nature, results, and conclusions of the research, and they take reasonable steps to correct any misconceptions that participants may have of which the psychologists are aware.

(b) If scientific or humane values justify delaying or withholding this information, psychologists take reasonable measures to reduce the risk of harm.

(c) When psychologists become aware that research procedures have harmed a participant, they take reasonable steps to minimize the harm.

8.09 **Humane Care and Use of Animals in Research**

(a) Psychologists acquire, care for, use, and dispose of animals in compliance with current federal, state, and local laws and regulations, and with professional standards.

(b) Psychologists trained in research methods and experienced in the care of laboratory animals supervise all procedures involving animals and are responsible for ensuring appropriate consideration of their comfort, health, and humane treatment.

(c) Psychologists ensure that all individuals under their supervision who are using animals have received instruction in research methods and in the care, maintenance, and handling of the species being used, to the extent appropriate to their role. (See also Standard 2.05, Delegation of Work to Others.)

(d) Psychologists make reasonable efforts to minimize the discomfort, infection, illness, and pain of animal subjects.

(e) Psychologists use a procedure subjecting animals to pain, stress, or privation only when an alternative procedure is unavailable and the goal is justified by its prospective scientific, educational, or applied value.

(f) Psychologists perform surgical procedures under appropriate anesthesia and follow techniques to avoid infection and minimize pain during and after surgery.

(g) When it is appropriate that an animal's life be terminated, psychologists proceed rapidly, with an effort to minimize pain and in accordance with accepted procedures.

8.10 **Reporting Research Results**

(a) Psychologists do not fabricate data. (See also Standard 5.01a, Avoidance of False or Deceptive Statements.)

(b) If psychologists discover significant errors in their published data, they take reasonable steps to correct such errors in a correction, retraction, erratum, or other appropriate publication means.

8.11 **Plaglarism** Psychologists do not present portions of another's work or data as their own, even if the other work or data source is cited occasionally.

8.12 **Publication Credit**

(a) Psychologists take responsibility and credit, including authorship credit, only for work they have actually performed or to which they have substantially contributed. (See also Standard 8.12b, Publication Credit.)

(b) Principal authorship and other publication credits accurately reflect the relative scientific or professional contributions of the individuals involved, regardless of their relative status. Mere possession of an institutional position, such as department chair, does not justify authorship credit. Minor contributions to the research or to the writing for publications are acknowledged appropriately, such as in footnotes or in an introductory statement.

(c) Except under exceptional circumstances, a student is listed as principal author on any multiple-authored article that is substantially based on the student's doctoral dissertation. Faculty advisors discuss publication credit with students as early as feasible and throughout the research and publication process as appropriate. (See also Standard 8.12b, Publication Credit.)

8.13 **Duplicate Publication of Data** Psychologists do not publish, as original data, data that have been previously published. This does not preclude republishing data when they are accompanied by proper acknowledgment.

8.14 **Sharing Research Data for Verification**

(a) After research results are published, psychologists do not withhold the data on which their conclusions are based from other competent professionals who seek to verify the substantive claims through reanalysis and who intend to use such data only for that purpose, provided that the confidentiality of the participants can be protected and unless legal rights concerning proprietary data preclude their release. This does not preclude psychologists from requiring that such individuals or groups be responsible for costs associated with the provision of such information.

(b) Psychologists who request data from other psychologists to verify the substantive claims through reanalysis may use shared data only for the declared purpose. Requesting psychologists obtain prior written agreement for all other uses of the data.

8.15 **Reviewers** Psychologists who review material submitted for presentation, publication, grant, or research proposal review respect the confidentiality of and the proprietary rights in such information of those who submitted it.

9. Assessment

9.01 **Bases for Assessments**

(a) Psychologists base the opinions contained in their recommendations, reports, and diagnostic or evaluative statements, including forensic testimony, on information and techniques sufficient to substantiate their findings. (See also Standard 2.04, Bases for Scientific and Professional Judgments.)

(b) Except as noted in 9.01c, psychologists provide opinions of the psychological characteristics of individuals only after they have conducted an examination of the individuals adequate to support their statements or conclusions. When, despite reasonable efforts, such an examination is not practical, psychologists document the efforts they made and the result of those efforts, clarify the probable impact of their limited information on the reliability and validity of their opinions, and appropriately limit the nature and extent of their conclusions or recommendations. (See also Standards 2.01, Boundaries of Competence, and 9.06, Interpreting Assessment Results.)

(c) When psychologists conduct a record review or provide consultation or supervision and an individual examination is not warranted or necessary for the opinion, psychologists explain this and the sources of information on which they based their conclusions and recommendations.

9.02 **Use of Assessments**

(a) Psychologists administer, adapt, score, interpret, or use assessment techniques, interviews, tests, or instruments in a manner and for purposes that are appropriate in light of the research on or evidence of the usefulness and proper application of the techniques.

(b) Psychologists use assessment instruments whose validity and reliability have been established for use with members of the population tested. When such validity or reliability has not been established, psychologists describe the strengths and limitations of test results and interpretation.

(c) Psychologists use assessment methods that are appropriate to an individual's language preference and competence, unless the use of an alternative language is relevant to the assessment issues.

9.03 **Informed Consent in Assessments**

(a) Psychologists obtain informed consent for assessments, evaluations, or diagnostic services, as described in Standard 3.10, Informed Consent, except when (1) testing is mandated by law or governmental regulations; (2) informed consent is implied because testing is conducted as a routine educational, institutional, or organizational activity (e.g., when participants voluntarily agree to assessment when applying for a job); or (3) one purpose of the testing is to evaluate decisional capacity. Informed consent includes an explanation of the nature and purpose of the assessment, fees, involvement of third parties, and limits of confidentiality and sufficient opportunity for the client/patient to ask questions and receive answers.

(b) Psychologists inform persons with questionable capacity to consent or for whom testing is mandated by law or governmental regulations about the nature and purpose of the proposed assessment services, using language that is reasonably understandable to the person being assessed.

(c) Psychologists using the services of an interpreter obtain informed consent from the client/patient to use that interpreter, ensure that confidentiality of test results and test security are maintained, and include in their recommendations, reports, and diagnostic or evaluative statements, including forensic testimony, discussion of any limitations on the data obtained. (See also Standards 2.05, Delegation of Work to Others; 4.01, Maintaining Confidentiality; 9.01, Bases for Assessments; 9.06, Interpreting Assessment Results; and 9.07, Assessment by Unqualified Persons.)

9.04 **Release of Test Data**

(a) The term *test data* refers to raw and scaled scores, client/patient responses to test questions or stimuli, and psychologists' notes and recordings concerning client/patient statements and behavior during an examination. Those portions of test materials that include client/patient responses are included in the definition of *test data*. Pursuant to a client/patient release, psychologists provide test data to the client/patient or other persons identified in the release. Psychologists may refrain from releasing test data to protect a client/patient or others from substantial harm or misuse or misrepresentation of the data or the test, recognizing that in many instances release of confidential information under these circumstances is regulated by law. (See also Standard 9.11, Maintaining Test Security.)

(b) In the absence of a client/patient release, psychologists provide test data only as required by law or court order.

9.05 **Test Construction** Psychologists who develop tests and other assessment techniques use appropriate psychometric procedures and current scientific or professional knowledge for test design, standardization, validation, reduction or elimination of bias, and recommendations for use.

9.06 **Interpreting Assessment Results** When interpreting assessment results, including automated interpretations, psychologists take into account the purpose of the assessment as well as the various test factors, test-taking abilities, and other characteristics of the person being assessed, such as situational, personal, linguistic, and cultural differences, that might affect psychologists' judgments or reduce the accuracy of their interpretations. They indicate any significant limitations of their interpretations. (See also Standards 2.01b and c, Boundaries of Competence, and 3.01, Unfair Discrimination.)

9.07 **Assessment by Unqualified Persons** Psychologists do not promote the use of psychological assessment techniques by unqualified persons, except when such use is conducted for training purposes with appropriate supervision. (See also Standard 2.05, Delegation of Work to Others.)

9.08 **Obsolete Tests and Outdated Test Results**

(a) Psychologists do not base their assessment or intervention decisions or recommendations on data or test results that are outdated for the current purpose.

(b) Psychologists do not base such decisions or recommendations on tests and measures that are obsolete and not useful for the current purpose.

9.09 **Test Scoring and Interpretation Services**

(a) Psychologists who offer assessment or scoring services to other professionals accurately describe the purpose, norms, validity, reliability, and applications of the procedures and any special qualifications applicable to their use.

(b) Psychologists select scoring and interpretation services (including automated services) on the basis of evidence of the validity of the program and procedures as well as on other appropriate considerations. (See also Standard 2.01b and c, Boundaries of Competence.)

(c) Psychologists retain responsibility for the appropriate application, interpretation, and use of assessment instruments, whether they score and interpret such tests themselves or use automated or other services.

9.10 **Explaining Assessment Results** Regardless of whether the scoring and interpretation are done by psychologists, by employees or assistants, or by automated or other outside services, psychologists take reasonable steps to ensure that explanations of results are given to the individual or designated representative unless the nature of the relationship precludes provision of an explanation of results (such as in some organizational consulting, preemployment or security screenings, and forensic evaluations), and this fact has been clearly explained to the person being assessed in advance.

9.11 **Maintaining Test Security** The term *test materials* refers to manuals, instruments, protocols, and test questions or stimuli and does not include *test data* as defined in Standard 9.04, Release of Test Data. Psychologists make reasonable efforts to maintain the integrity and security of test materials and other assessment techniques consistent with law and contractual obligations, and in a manner that permits adherence to this Ethics Code.

10. Therapy

10.01 **Informed Consent to Therapy**

(a) When obtaining informed consent to therapy as required in Standard 3.10, Informed Consent, psychologists inform clients/patients as early as is feasible in the therapeutic relationship about the nature and anticipated course of therapy, fees, involvement of third parties, and limits of confidentiality and provide sufficient opportunity for the client/patient to ask questions and receive answers. (See also Standards 4.02, Discussing the Limits of Confidentiality, and 6.04, Fees and Financial Arrangements.)

(b) When obtaining informed consent for treatment for which generally recognized techniques and procedures have not been established, psychologists inform their clients/patients of the developing nature of the treatment, the potential risks involved, alternative treatments that may be available, and the voluntary nature of their participation. (See also Standards 2.01e, Boundaries of Competence, and 3.10, Informed Consent.)

(c) When the therapist is a trainee and the legal responsibility for the treatment provided resides with the supervisor, the client/patient, as part of the informed consent procedure, is informed that the therapist is in training and is being supervised and is given the name of the supervisor.

10.02 **Therapy Involving Couples or Families**

(a) When psychologists agree to provide services to several persons who have a relationship (such as spouses, significant others, or parents and children), they take reasonable steps to clarify at the outset (1) which of the individuals are clients/patients and (2) the relationship the psychologist will have with each person. This clarification includes the psychologist's role and the probable uses of the services provided or the information obtained. (See also Standard 4.02, Discussing the Limits of Confidentiality.)

(b) If it becomes apparent that psychologists may be called on to perform potentially conflicting roles (such as family therapist and then witness for one party in divorce proceedings), psychologists take reasonable steps to clarify and modify, or withdraw from, roles appropriately. (See also Standard 3.05c, Multiple Relationships.)

10.03 **Group Therapy** When psychologists provide services to several persons in a group setting, they describe at the outset the roles and responsibilities of all parties and the limits of confidentiality.

10.04 **Providing Therapy to Those Served by Others** In deciding whether to offer or provide services to those already receiving mental health services elsewhere, psychologists carefully consider the treatment issues and the potential client's/patient's welfare. Psychologists discuss these issues with the client/patient or another legally authorized person on behalf of the client/patient in order to minimize the risk of confusion and conflict, consult with the other service providers when appropriate, and proceed with caution and sensitivity to the therapeutic issues.

10.05 **Sexual Intimacies With Current Therapy Clients/Patients** Psychologists do not engage in sexual intimacies with current therapy clients/patients.

10.06 **Sexual Intimacies With Relatives or Significant Others of Current Therapy Clients/Patients** Psychologists do not engage in sexual intimacies with individuals they know to be close relatives, guardians, or significant others of current clients/patients. Psychologists do not terminate therapy to circumvent this standard.

10.07 **Therapy With Former Sexual Partners** Psychologists do not accept as therapy clients/patients persons with whom they have engaged in sexual intimacies.

10.08 **Sexual Intimacies With Former Therapy Clients/Patients**
   (a) Psychologists do not engage in sexual intimacies with former clients/patients for at least two years after cessation or termination of therapy.

(b) Psychologists do not engage in sexual intimacies with former clients/patients even after a two-year interval except in the most unusual circumstances. Psychologists who engage in such activity after the two years following cessation or termination of therapy and of having no sexual contact with the former client/patient bear the burden of demonstrating that there has been no exploitation, in light of all relevant factors, including (1) the amount of time that has passed since therapy terminated; (2) the nature, duration, and intensity of the therapy; (3) the circumstances of termination; (4) the client's/patient's personal history; (5) the client's/patient's current mental status; (6) the likelihood of adverse impact on the client/patient; and (7) any statements or actions made by the therapist during the course of therapy suggesting or inviting the possibility of a posttermination sexual or romantic relationship with the client/patient. (See also Standard 3.05, Multiple Relationships.)

10.09 **Interruption of Therapy** When entering into employment or contractual relationships, psychologists make reasonable efforts to provide for orderly and appropriate resolution of responsibility for client/patient care in the event that the employment or contractual relationship ends, with paramount consideration given to the welfare of the client/patient. (See also Standard 3.12, Interruption of Psychological Services.)

10.10 **Terminating Therapy**
   (a) Psychologists terminate therapy when it becomes reasonably clear that the client/patient no longer needs the service, is not likely to benefit, or is being harmed by continued service.
   (b) Psychologists may terminate therapy when threatened or otherwise endangered by the client/patient or another person with whom the client/patient has a relationship.

(c) Except where precluded by the actions of clients/patients or third-party payors, prior to termination psychologists provide pretermination counseling and suggest alternative service providers as appropriate.

HISTORY AND EFFECTIVE DATE FOOTNOTE

This version of the APA Ethics Code was adopted by the American Psychological Association's Council of Representatives during its meeting, August 21, 2002, and is effective beginning June 1, 2003. Inquiries concerning the substance or interpretation of the APA Ethics Code should be addressed to the Director, Office of Ethics, American Psychological Association, 750 First Street, NE, Washington, DC 20002-4242. The Ethics Code and information regarding the Code can be found on the APA web site, http://www.apa.org/ethics. The standards in this Ethics Code will be used to adjudicate complaints brought concerning alleged conduct occurring on or after the effective date. Complaints regarding conduct occurring prior to the effective date will be adjudicated on the basis of the version of the Ethics Code that was in effect at the time the conduct occurred.

The APA has previously published its Ethics Code as follows:

American Psychological Association. (1953). Ethical standards of psychologists. Washington, DC: Author.

American Psychological Association. (1959). Ethical standards of psychologists. American Psychologist, 14, 279-282.

American Psychological Association. (1963). Ethical standards of psychologists. American Psychologist, 18, 56-60.

American Psychological Association. (1968). Ethical standards of psychologists. American Psychologist, 23, 357-361.

American Psychological Association. (1977, March). Ethical standards of psychologists. APA Monitor, 22-23.

American Psychological Association. (1979). Ethical standards of psychologists. Washington, DC: Author.

American Psychological Association. (1981). Ethical principles of psychologists. American Psychologist, 36, 633-638.

American Psychological Association. (1990). Ethical principles of psychologists (Amended June 2, 1989). American Psychologist, 45, 390-395.

American Psychological Association. (1992). Ethical principles of psychologists and code of conduct. American Psychologist, 47, 1597-1611.

Request copies of the APA's Ethical Principles of Psychologists and Code of Conduct from the APA Order Department, 750 First Street, NE, Washington, DC 20002-4242, or phone (202) 336-5510.

REFERENCES

Agar, M. (1994). *Language shock: Understanding the culture of conversation*. New York: Morrow.

Albrecht, A. C., & Jones, D. G. (2004). Planning for cyberlearning: A framework for counselor educators. In J. W. Bloom & G. R. Walz (Eds.), *Cybercounseling & cyberlearning: An encore* (pp. 57–80). Greensboro, NC: CAPS Press and Alexandria, VA: American Counseling Association.

Americans with Disabilities Act Handbook. (1991). Washington, DC: U. S. Government Printing Office.

American Psychological Association. (2003). Multicultural guidelines for education and training, research, practice, and organizational development for psychologists. *American Psychologist, 58*, 377–402.

Anastasi, A., & Urbina, S. (1997). *Psychological testing* (7th ed.). Upper Saddle River, NJ: Prentice Hall.

Anderson, W. T. (2001). *All connected now: Life in the first global civilization*. Boulder, CO: Westview Press.

Arredondo, P., Toporek, R., Brown, S., Jones, J., Locke, D., Sanchez, J., et al. (1996). Operationalization of multicultural counseling competencies, *Journal of Multicultural Counseling and Development, 24*, 42–78.

Association of Counselor Education and Supervision (1999). Technical competencies for counselor education students: Recommended guidelines for program development. In J. W. Bloom & G. R. Walz (Eds.), *Cybercounseling and cyberlearning: Strategies and resources for the millennium* (pp. 429–430). Alexandria, VA: American Counseling Association and Greensboro, NC: CAPS, Inc. (ERIC Counseling and Student services Clearinghouse).

Auerbach, J. E. (2001). *Personal and executive coaching: The complete guide for mental health professionals*. Ventura, CA: Executive College Press.

Baker, S. B., & Gerler, E. R., Jr. (2004). *School counseling for the 21st century*. Upper Saddle River, NJ: Merrill/Prentice Hall.

Bandura, A. (1997). *Social learning theory*. Upper Saddle River, NJ: Prentice Hall.

Bloom, J. W., & Walz, G. R. (Eds.). (2000). *Cybercounseling and cyberlearning: Strategies and resources for the millennium*. Alexandria, VA: American Counseling Association and Greensboro, NC: CAPS, Inc. (ERIC Counseling and Student Services Clearinghouse).

Bordin, E. S. (1984). Psychodynamic model of career choice and satisfaction. In D. Brown & L. Brooks & Associates, *Career choice and development* (pp. 94–136). San Francisco: Jossey-Bass.

Borgen, F. H. (1991). Megatrends and milestones in vocational behavior: A 20-year counseling psychology retrospective. *Journal of Vocational Behavior, 39*(3), 263–290.

Bowlsbey, J. H., Dikel, M. R., & Sampson, J. P., Jr. (1998). *A tool for career planning*. Columbus, OH: National Career Development Association.

Brandt, J. E., & Hood, A. B. (1968). Effect of personality adjustment on the predictive validity of the Strong Vocational Interest Blank. *Journal of Counseling Psychology, 15*, 547–551.

Brown, D. (1996). A holistic, values-based model of career and life role choice and satisfaction. In D. Brown & L. Brooks & Associates. *Career choice and development*. (3rd ed.) San Francisco: Jossey-Bass.

Brown, D. (2002). The role of work and cultural values in occupational choice, satisfaction, and success: A theoretical statement. *Journal of Counseling & Development, 80*(1), 48–56.

Brown, D. (2003). *Career information, career counseling, and career development*. (8th ed.). Boston: Allyn and Bacon

Brown, D., & Brooks, L., & Associates. (1990). *Career choice and development: Applying contemporary theories to practice*. (2nd. ed.). San Francisco: Jossey-Bass.

Brown, D., & Lent, R. W. (Eds.) (1992). *Handbook of counseling psychology*. New York: Wiley.

Cattell, R. B., Eber, H. W., & Tatsuoka, M. M. (1970). *Handbook for the sixteen personality actor questionnaire*. Champaign, IL: Institute for Personality and Ability Testing.

Cauchon, D. *USA Today*. (May 19, 2003, p. 3A).

Chartrand, J. M. (1991). The evolution of trait-and-factor career counseling: The person X environment fit approach. *Journal of Counseling and Development, 69*, 518–524.

Clawson, T. J., & Jordan, J. H. (2001). Globalization of professions: A U.S. perspective with the cyberworld in mind. *Eric/Cass Digest*, September. (EDO-CG-01-02).

Code of Fair Testing Practices in Education. (2002). Washington, DC: Joint Committee on Testing Practices. American Psychological Association.

College Entrance Examination Board. (1986, October). *Keeping the options open: Recommendations.* Final report of the Commission on Precollege Guidance and Counseling. New York: Author.

Daalder, I. H., & Lindsay, J. M. (2003, Winter). The globalization of politics. *Brookings Review, 21*(1), 12–17.

Davis, R., & Lofquist, L. H. (1984). *A psychological theory of work adjustment.* Minneapolis: University of Minnesota Press.

Denton, N. A., & Tolnay, S. E. (Eds.). (2002). *American diversity: A demographic challenge for the twenty-first century.* Albany, NY: State University of New York Press.

Dolliver, R. H. (1982). Review of card sorts. In J. T. Kapes & M. M. Mastie (Eds.), *A counselor's guide to vocational guidance instruments* (pp. 147–160). Falls Church, VA: National Vocational Guidance Association.

Drasgow, J., & Carkhuff, R. R. (1964). Kuder neuropsychiatric keys before and after psychotherapy. *Journal of Counseling Psychology, 11,* 67–69.

Elias, M. (2001, May 22). Online therapy clicks, *USA Today*, p. 19.

Erchak, G. (1992). *The anthropology of self and mind.* New Brunswick, NJ: Rutgers University Press.

Future of Technology. [Special section]. *Business Week* (August 18–25, 2003), 64–160.

Gallwey, T. W. (1997). *The inner game of tennis.* New York: Random House.

Gati, I., & Saka, N. (2001). High school students' career-related decision-making difficulties. *Journal of Counseling & Development, 79*(3), 333.

Geertz, C. (1983). *Local knowledge.* New York: Basic Books.

Gelatt, H. B. (1989). Positive uncertainty: A new decision-making framework for counseling. *Journal of Counseling Psychology, 36* (2), 252–256.

Gibson, R. L., Mitchell, M. H., & Basile, S. K. (1993). *Counseling in the elementary schools: A comprehensive approach.* Needham Heights, MA: Allyn and Bacon.

Gibson, R. L., & Mitchell, M. H. (2003). *Introduction to counseling and guidance.* (6th ed.). Upper Saddle River, NJ: Merrill/Prentice Hall.

Ginzberg, E. (1972). Restatement of the theory of occupational choice. *Vocational Guidance Quarterly, 20*(3), 169–176.

Ginzberg, E. (1984). Career development. In D. Brown & L. Brooks (Eds.), *Career choice and development.* San Francisco: Jossey-Bass.

Ginzberg, E., Ginsburg, S. W., Axelrad, S., & Herma, J. L. (1951). *Occupational choice: An approach to general theory.* New York: Columbia University Press.

Goldman, L. (1990). Qualitative assessment. *The Counseling Psychologist, 18*(2), 205–213.

Goodenough, W. H. (1981). *Culture, language and society.* Reading, MA: Benjamin Cummings.

Gottfredson, L. S. (1996). A theory of circumscription and compromise: A revision. (1996). In D. Brown & L. Brooks & Associates. *Career choice and development* (3rd. ed.). pp. 179–232. San Francisco: Jossey-Bass.

Hall, C. S., & Lindzey, G. (1957). *Theories of personality.* New York: Wiley.

Harmon, L. W. (1996). A moving target: The widening gap between theory and practice. In M. L. Savickas & W. B. Walsh (Eds.), *Handbook of career counseling: Theory and practice,* pp. 37–44. Washington, DC: American Psychological Association.

Havighurst, R. J. (1953). *Human development and education.* New York: Longmans, Green.

Havighurst, R. J. (1964). *Youth in exploration and man emergent.* Alexandria, VA: American Counseling Association.

Herr, E. L. (1996). Toward the convergence of career theory and practice. In M. L. Savickas & W. B. Walsh (Eds.), *Handbook of career counseling theory and practice* (pp. 13–35). Palo Alto, CA: Davies-Black Publishing.

Herr, E. L., & Cramer, S. H. (1992). *Career guidance and counseling through the lifespan: Systematic approaches.* New York: HarperCollins.

Holland, J. L. (1973). *Making vocational choices: A theory of careers.* Upper Saddle River, NJ: Prentice Hall.

Holland, J. L. (1984). *A theory of careers: Some new developments and revisions.* Paper presented at the American Psychological Association Convention, Toronto, Canada.

Holland, J. L. (1985) *Making vocational choices: A theory of vocational personalities and work environments.* (2nd ed.). Upper Saddle River, NJ: Prentice Hall.

Hood, A. B., & Johnson, R. W. (1997). *Assessment in counseling: A guide to the use of psychological assessment procedures.* Alexandria, VA: American Counseling Association.

International Labor Office. (1998). *The world employment report, 1998–1999.* Geneva, Switzerland: Author.

Isaacson, L. E., & Brown, D. (1993). *Career information, career counseling & career development.* (2nd ed.). Boston: Allyn and Bacon.

Isaacson, L. E., & Brown, D. (2000). *Career information, career counseling, and career development* (7th ed.). Needham Heights, MA: Allyn and Bacon.

Ishisaka, H. A., Nguyen, Q. T., & Okimoto, J. T. (1985). The role in the mental health treatment of Indochinese refugees. In T. C. Owan (Ed.), *Southeast Asian mental health treatment, prevention services, training and research.* Washington, DC: National Institute of Mental Health.

Jencius, M., & Paez, S. (2004). Converting counselor Luddites: Winning over technology-resistant counselors. In J. W. Bloom & G. R. Walz (Eds.), *Cybercounseling & cyberlearning: An encore* (pp. 81–114). Greensboro, NC: CAPS Press and Alexandria, VA: American Counseling Association.

Johansson, C. B., & Campbell, D. P. (1971). Stability of the Strong Vocational Interest Blank for men. *Journal of Applied Psychology, 55,* 34–36.

Judy, R. W., & D'Amico, C. D. (1997). *Workforce 2020: Work and workers in the 21st century.* Indianapolis, IN: Hudson Institute.

Kennedy, A. (2004, January). Career counselors can benefit from earning global credential. *Counseling Today,* 27.

Kososki, C. (1994, October). Legislative Update. *American Vocational Association Guidance Division Newsletter, 21*(4).

Krumboltz, J. D. (1979). A social learning theory of career decision-making. In A. M. Mitchell, G. B. Jones, & J. D. Krumboltz (Eds.), *Social learning and career decision making* (pp.19–49). (1979). Cranston, RI: Carroll Press.

Krumboltz, J. D., & Levin, A. S. (2004). *Luck is no accident.* Atascadero, CA: Impact.

Krumboltz, J. D., & Nichols, C. (1990). Integrating the social learning theory of career decision making. In W. B. Walsh & S. H. Osipow (Eds.), *Career counseling: Contemporary topics in vocational psychology* (pp. 159–192). Hillsdale, NJ: Erlbaum.

Lorenzo, M. K., & Adler, D. A. (1984). Mental health services for Chinese in a community health center. *Social Casework, 65,* 600–610.

Lunneborg, P. W. (1984). Practical applications of Roe's theory of career development. In D. Brown & L. Brooks & Associates. (Eds.) *Career choice and development: Applying contemporary theories to practice* (pp. 54–60). San Francisco: Jossey-Bass.

Malone, J. F., Miller, K. S., & Miller, R. M. (2002). The evolution of a distance career counseling model: Implications for training, practice and supervision of cybercounselors. In J. W. Bloom & G. R. Walz (Eds.) *Cybercounseling and cyberlearning: An encore* (pp. 151–282). Greensboro, NC: CAPS Press and Alexandria, VA: American Counseling Association.

Manzanares, M. G., O'Halloran, T. M., McCartney, T. J., Filer, R. D., Varhely, S. C., & Calhoun, K. (2004). CD-ROM technology for education and support of site supervisors. *Counselor Education and Supervision, 43*(3), 220–231.

Maslow, A. (1954). *Motivation and personality.* New York: Harper & Row.

McFadden, J. (Ed.) (1993). *Transcultural counseling: Bilateral and international perspectives.* Alexandria, VA: American Counseling Association.

Mitchell, D. L., & Murphy, L. J. (2004). E-mail rules! Organization and individuals creating ethical excellence in telemental health. In J. W. Bloom & G. R. Walz (Eds.), *Cybercounseling & cyberlearning: An encore* (pp. 203–217). Greensboro, NC: CAPS Press and Alexandria, VA: American Counseling Association.

Murray, H., Barrett, W. G., & Honburger, E. (1938). *Exploration in personality: A clinical and experimental study of fifty men of college age.* New York: Oxford University Press.

National Center for Juvenile Justice, Pittsburgh, PA: Juvenile Court Statistics, annual, p. 1998. (2001). *Statistical Abstract of the United States: 2001.* U.S. Census Bureau: Washington, DC: Government Printing Office.

Nidorf, J. F. (1985). Mental health and refugee youths: A model for diagnostic training. In T. C. Owan (Ed.), *Southeast Asian mental health treatment, prevention services, training, and research*. Washington, DC: National Institute of Mental Health.

Ohmae, Kenichi. (1995). *The end of the nation state: The rise of regional economies*. New York: The Free Press.

Okun, B. F., Fried, J., & Okun, M. L. (1999). *Understanding diversity: A learning-as-practice primer*. Pacific Grove, CA: Brooks/Cole.

Osipow, S. H. (1983). *Theories of career development* (3rd. ed.). New York: Appleton-Century-Crofts.

Osipow, S. H. (1990). Convergence in theories of career choice and development: Review and prospect. *Journal of Vocational Behavior, 36*, 122–131.

Parsons, F. (1909). *Choosing a vocation*. Boston: Houghton Mifflin.

Pascarel, E. T., & Terenzi, P. T. (1991). *How college affects students: Findings and insights from twenty years of research*. San Francisco: Jossey-Bass.

Pope, M. (2000). A brief history of career counseling in the United States. *The Career Development Quarterly, 48*(3), 194–211.

Quinn, J. R. (1993). Evaluation and assessment for transcultural counseling. In J. McFadden (Ed.), *Transcultural counseling: Bilateral and international perspectives* (pp. 287–302). Alexandria, VA: American Counseling Association.

Remley, T. P., Jr., & Herlihy, B. (2001). *Ethical, legal, and professional issues in counseling*. Upper Saddle River, NJ: Merrill/Prentice Hall.

Responsibilities of Users of Standardized Tests (RUST). (3rd ed.) (2003). Alexandria, VA: Association for Assessment in Counseling.

Ridley, C. R. (1995). *Overcoming unintentional racism in counseling and therapy: A practitioner's guide to intervention*. Thousand Oaks, CA: Sage.

Rifkin, J. (1995). *The end of work: The decline of the global labor force and the dawn of the post-market era*. New York: Tarcher/Putnam.

Roe, A. (1956). *The psychology of occupations*. New York: Wiley.

Roe, A. (1984). Personality development and career choice. In D. Brown & L. Brooks & Associates (Eds.). *Career choice and development* (pp. 31–54). San Francisco: Jossey-Bass.

Rounds, J. B., & Tracey, T. J. (1990). From trait-and-factor to person-environment fit counseling: Theory and process. In W. B. Walsh & S. H. Osipow (Eds.). *Career counseling: Contemporary topics in vocational psychology* (pp. 1–44). Hillsdale, NJ: Erlbaum.

Sabella, R. A. (2003) *SchoolCounselor.com: A friendly and practical guide to the World Wide Web* (2nd ed.). Minneapolis, MN: Educational Media Corporation.

Sampson, J. P., Jr., Carr, D. L., Panke, J., Arkin, S., Vernick, S. H., & Minvielle, M. (2004). Implementing Internet Web sites in counseling services. In J. W. Bloom & G. R. Walz (Eds.), *Cybercounseling & cyberlearning: An encore* (pp. 247–258). Greensboro, NC: CAPS Press and Alexandria, VA: American Counseling Association.

Sapir, E. (1958). *Culture, language and personality*. Berkeley, CA: University of California Press.

Savickas, M. L., & Lent, R. W. (Eds.). (1994). *Convergence in career development theories: Implications for science and practice*. Palo Alto, CA: Consulting Psychologists Press.

Savickas, M. L., & Walsh, W. B. (Eds.). (1996). *Handbook of career counseling theory and practice*. Palo Alto, CA: Davies-Black.

Schwebel, M. (1984). From past to present: Counseling pscyhology's socially prescribed role. In J. M. Whiteley, N. Kagan, L. W. Harmon, B. R. Fretz, & F. Tanney (Eds.), *The coming decade in counseling psychology* (pp. 25–49). Schenectady, NY: Character Research.

Sexton, T. L. (1999). *Evidence-based counseling: Implications for counseling practice, preparation, and professionalism*. Greensboro, NC: ERIC Counseling and Student Services Clearinghouse. (ERIC Document Reproduction Service No. ED 435948)

Sharf, R. S. (1992). *Applying career development theory to counseling*. Pacific Grove, CA: Brooks/Cole.

Slaney, R. B., Moran, W. J., & Wade, J. C. (1994). Vocational card sorts. In J. T. Kapes, M. M. Mastie, & E. A. Whitfield (Eds.), *A counselor's guide to career assessment instruments* (3rd ed., pp. 236–240). Alexandria, VA: National Career Development Association.

Standards for Multicultural Assessment. (2003). Alexandria, VA: Association for Assessment in Counseling.

Stigler, J. W., & Hiebert, J. (1999). *The teaching gap: Best ideas from the world's teachers for improving education in the classroom.* New York: The Free Press.

Streeten, P. *Globalization: Threat or opportunity?* Handelshojskolens Forlag: Copenhagen Business School Press.

Sue, D. W., Arredondo, P. A., & McDavis, R. J. (1992). Multicultural competencies/standards: A call to the profession. *Journal of Counseling and Development, 70,* 477–486.

Sue, D. W., & Sue, D. (2003). *Counseling the culturally diverse: Theory and practice.* (4th ed.). New York: Wiley.

Sue, D. W., & Sue, D. M. (1990). *Counseling the culturally different: Theory and practice* (2nd ed.). New York: Wiley.

Super, D. E. (1942). *The dynamics of vocational adjustment.* New York: Harper & Brothers.

Super, D. E. (1957). *The psychology of careers.* New York: Harper & Row.

Super, D. E. (1990). A life-span, life-space approach to career development. In D. Brown & L. Brooks, *Career choice development: Applying contemporary theories to practice* (pp. 197–261). San Francisco: Jossey-Bass.

Super, D. E., Savickas, M. L., & Super, C. M. (1996). The life-span, life-space approach to careers. In D. Brown, L. Brooks & Associates. *Career choice and development* (pp. 121–178). San Francisco: Jossey-Bass.

Swanson, J. L. (1994). The theory *is* the practice: Trait-and-factor/person-environment fit counseling. In M. L. Savickas & R. W. Lent. (Eds.). *Convergence in career development theories: Implications for science and practice* (pp. 93–108). Palo Alto, CA: Consulting Psychologists Press.

Technology and School Counseling. (2004). [Special section]. *ASCA School Counselor, 41*(4), 10–35.

Tung, T. M. (1985). Psychiatric care for South Asians: How different is different? In T. C. Owan (Ed.), *Southeast Asian mental health, treatment, prevention services, training and research.* Washington, DC: National Institute of Mental Health.

Tyler, J. M., & Sabella, R. A. (2004). *Using technology to improve counseling practice: A primer for the 21st century.* Alexandria, VA: American Counseling Association.

U.S. Bureau of the Census. (1996). *Statistical Abstracts of the United States:* 1996 (1116th ed.). Washington, D.C.: Author.

U.S. Bureau of Justice Statistics. (2001). Correctional Populations in the United States, annual, p. 202. *Statistical Abstract of the United States: 2001.* U.S. Census Bureau: Washington, DC: Government Printing Office.

Useem, J. (2001, November 26). Globalization. *Fortune, 144*(11), 76–84.

Wall, J. E. (2000). Technology-delivered assessment: Power, problems, and promise. In J. W. Bloom & G. R. Walz (Eds.), *Cybercounseling and cyberlearning: Strategies and resources for the millennium.* Alexandria, VA: American Counseling Association and Greensboro, NC: CAPS, Inc., in association with the ERIC Counseling and Student Services Clearinghouse.

Wheaton, J. E., & Granello, P. F. (2004). Designing Web pages that are usable and accessible to all. In J. W. Bloom & G. R. Walz (Eds.), *Cybercounseling and cyberlearning: An encore* (pp. 3–17). Greensboro, NC: CAPS Press and Alexandria, VA: American Counseling Association.

Whiston, S. C., & Brecheisen, B. K. (2002). Practice and research in career counseling and development—2001. *Career Development Quarterly, 51*(2), 98–154.

Williamson, E. G. (1939). *How to counsel students.* New York: McGraw-Hill.

Williamson, E. G. (1965). *Vocational counseling: Some historical, philosophical, and theoretical perspectives.* New York: McGraw-Hill.

Winfield, S. (Ed.) (2001). The great online job hunt. *Beginner's Guide to the World Wide Web, 1*(2).

Yost, E. B., & Corbishley, M. A. (1987). *Career counseling: A psychological approach.* San Francisco, CA: Jossey-Bass.

Yuen, M. (2003). Exploring Hong Kong Chinese guidance teachers' positive beliefs: A focus group study. *International Journal for the Advancement of Counseling, 24,* 169–182.

Zunker, V. G. (1998). *Career counseling: Applied concepts of life planning.* (5th ed.). Pacific Grove, CA: Brooks/Cole.

Zytowski, D. G. (1972). Four hundred years before Parsons. *Personnel and Guidance Journal, 50,* 443–450.

AUTHOR INDEX

Page numbers followed by f indicate figure; those followed by t indicate table.

A

Abdel-Jaber, A-R, 34
Abu-Jaber, M., 34
Agar, M., 176
Albrecht, A. C., 55
Alexander, C. M., 118
Alfeld, C., 157
Allport, G. W., 104
Amundson, N. E., 117, 173
Anastasi, A., 95
Anderson, K. T., 51–53
Anderson, W. T., 19–20, 23
Arkin, S., 55
Arora, A. G., 189
Ashton, L., 203
Auerbach, J. E., 123, 124
Austin, B. D., 203
Axelrad, S., 70, 71t

B

Baker, S. B., 121–122
Bandura, A., 76
Basile, S. K., 128t, 135f,
   138, 200
Beale, A. V., 88, 157
Bingham, R. P., 189
Bloom, J. W., 38, 39, 55, 117,
   118, 203
Bordin, E. S., 78, 82
Borgen, F. H., 59
Borgen, W. M., 173
Bowlsbey, J. H., 45
Boyles, D., 155
Brandt, J. E., 98
Brecheisen, B. K., 24
Brown, D., 57, 62, 64, 72f,
   79–82, 88, 153t, 168f

C

Calhoun, K., 55
Campbell, C. A., 134t, 147t
Campbell, D. P., 98
Cancelli, A. A., 189
Capuzzi, D., 189
Carkhuff, R. R., 98
Carr, D. L., 55
Carter, R. T., 15

Cattell, A. K., 103
Cattell, H. E. P., 103
Cattell, R. B., 103
Chartrand, J. M., 62
Chipazi, L., 28
Choudhuni, E., 173
Clawson, T. J., 38
Clements, C. B., 189
Corbishley, M. A., 65t
Cottone, R. R., 203
Cramer, S. H., 59
Creed, P. A., 173
Curcio, C. C., 157

D

Daalder, I. H., 38
Dahir, C. A., 134t, 147t
D'Amico, C. D., 20, 38
Davis, R., 77, 82
DeMato, D. S., 157
Denton, N. A., 177
Dickson, J., 24–25
DiGiuseppe, R., 89
Dikel, M. R., 45
Donahue, P., 151, 156
Drasgow, J., 98
Dussich, M., 50–51

E

Egisdottir, S., 189
Elias, M., 45
Ellis, A., 89
Erchak, G., 176
Erickson, E., 68, 69t, 129–130
Erlebach, A. C., 173

F

Feit, S. S., 119
Filer, R. D., 55
Flores, L. Y., 88
Freeman, B., 157
Fried, J., 176
Frigault, C., 29–31

G

Gallwey, T. W., 124
Garrett, M. T., 189

Gati, I., 146, 148f
Gayle, A. U., 203
Geertz, C., 176
Gelatt, H. B., 60
Gerber, S., 89
Gerler, E. R., Jr., 122
Gerstein, L. H., 189
Gesell, A., 67
Gibson, R. L., 6–7, 46, 84,
   92–93, 107–108, 107f, 126,
   128t, 129, 135f, 138,
   143–144, 163, 200
Ginter, E. J., 15
Ginsburg, S. W., 70, 71t
Ginzberg, E., 70–71, 71t
Goldman, L., 110–111
Goodenough, W. H., 176
Gottfredson, L. S., 80, 82
Graham-Migel, J., 31–32
Granello, P. F., 55, 189
Gross, D. R., 189
Guth, L. J., 55
Gysbers, N. C., 89

H

Hablitzel, C., 154–155
Hakin-Larson, J., 189
Hall, C. S., 58
Hall, G. Stanley, 65, 67
Hanna, F. J., 189
Harmon, L. W., 60
Harper, M. C., 173
Havighurst, R. J., 68–69, 70f,
   128–130
Heinlen, K. T., 55
Helwig, A. A., 157
Herlihy, B., 196f, 203
Herma, J. L., 70, 71t
Herr, E. L., 59, 159
Hiebert, J., 39
Holland, J. L., 63–65, 65t,
   66t, 67t, 82, 99–100,
   102, 170
Holmes, B., 34–36
Hood, A. B., 98
Hoyt, K. B., 1, 7, 15, 157
Hunt, B., 189

SUBJECT INDEX

Page numbers followed by f indicate figure; those followed by t indicate table.